The Frozen Food Cookbook
and
Guide to Home Freezing

other AVI books on food preparation and cooking

THE FROZEN FOOD
COOKBOOK

and Guide to Home Freezing

by JEAN I. SIMPSON, PH.D.

Professor of Foods
College of Home Economics, Syracuse University
Formerly, Chief of Research Kitchens, Frozen Food
Foundation, Inc.; Associate Professor and
Associate Chief in Experiment Station,
University of Illinois; Assistant
Professor of Household Science,
University of Toronto

COMPLETELY REVISED AND AUGMENTED EDITION

Westport, Connecticut

THE AVI PUBLISHING COMPANY, INC.

1962

Contents

v

SECTION IV

HOW TO USE FROZEN FOODS

Preface

The first edition of this book was a contribution from the Frozen Food Foundation, Inc., of Syracuse, New York, and was published in 1948 by Simon and Schuster, Inc. The entire staff of that organization cooperated in the preparation of the manuscript, and Mr. Gerald A. Fitzgerald, Director of the organization, took a major interest in it. Miss Demetria M. Taylor served as special editor and co-author.

Much of the work in the preparation of the first edition was pioneering, since home freezing was comparatively new at that time. Also, commercially frozen foods were limited, as was space for home storage of frozen foods.

The book has been completely revised and brought up-to-date. The frozen food industry has expanded greatly during recent years. More families have home freezers, or larger ones, and home freezing is far more extensive than it was a decade ago. Many families enjoy freezer food plans or similar services. More is known concerning the nutritive value of frozen foods, and concerning questions of safety in using them. This revision of the book is in keeping with these developments.

The author is grateful for the use of many federal government publications concerning frozen foods, particularly publications from the United States Departments of Agriculture, of Interior, and of Health, Education and Welfare; also, publications from the Association of Food and Drug Officials of the United States. The author is also thankful for the use of many Experiment Station Bulletins concerned with food freezing and the use of frozen foods.

Particular appreciation is expressed to the following specialists for reviewing portions of the book:

To Dr. Faith Clark, Director of Consumer and Food Economics Research Division, United States Department of Agriculture; Dr. Faith Fenton, Professor Emeritus of Food and Nutrition, Cornell University; and Dr. Ruth Leverton, Assistant Administrator, Agricultural Research Service. These three specialists reviewed portions of the manuscript concerned with frozen foods and our nutrition.

To Mr. H. P. Smith, Research Director of the National Association of Frozen Food Packers, for reviewing the portions of the book entitled "Storage Temperature and Frozen Food Quality," and "How Safe to Eat Are Frozen Foods?"

To Mr. Daniel C. McCoy, Consultant and formerly of Frigidaire Division of General Motors Corporation, and to Mr. W. R. Ruston of the General Electric Company, for reviewing the chapter entitled *Home Freezers*.

To Mr. Robert L. Madeira, Executive Director of the National Institute of Locker and Freezer Provisioners, for reviewing the chapter entitled *Locker Plant Services and Freezer Food Plans*.

The recipes throughout the book have been laboratory- or kitchen-tested under the author's supervision. She is indebted to Mrs. Joan Sanderson Vogt of Syracuse, for her assistance in bringing the recipes and menus up-to-date in the present edition.

Appreciation is expressed to Mrs. Dorothy Farrell of Syracuse, for typing the entire manuscript, and to Mrs. Dorothy Watson Burtt, and Miss Margaret Woods, both of Syracuse, for their assistance in proofreading.

Many offices and individuals have been contacted for various kinds of information, and the response in every case has been appreciated. These include the following:

Miss Ria Aubrey and Mr. Joseph B. Smith, Westinghouse Electric Corp., Columbus, Ohio

Mr. Walter Bennett, General Electric Co., Louisville, Ky.

Mrs. Carol Best, National Association of Frozen Food Packers, Washington, D.C.

Mrs. Clesta M. Brown, Sunkist Growers, Los Angeles, Calif.

Mr. Garth J. Brown, Amana Refrigeration, Inc., Amana, Iowa

Mr. Harvey H. Bundy, Jr., National Fisheries Institute, Washington, D.C.

Mr. Frank A. Buttler, Kelvinator Division of American Motors Corp., Detroit, Mich.

Miss Nancy Carter and Miss Alice M. Cooley, National Dairy Council, Chicago, Ill.

Miss Jessie Cartright, Norge Sales Corp., Chicago, Ill.

Mr. Dick Circle, Marshburn Farms, Norwalk, Calif.

Miss Lorane Cooley, Dole Corp., San Jose, Calif.

Mrs. Rita K. DiNoia, General Foods Kitchens, White Plains, N.Y.

Mr. J. Richard Duntley, Pacific Hawaiian Products Co., Fullerton, Calif.

Miss Jean Eggert, Hotpoint Home Economics Institute, Chicago, Ill.

Ekco Products Co., Chicago, Ill.

Miss Dolores L. Elliott, The Dow Chemical Co., Midland, Mich.

Miss Beverly J. Evans, Wear-Ever Aluminum, Inc., New Kensington, Pa.

Mr. Robert J. Fast, Marathon, a Division of American Can Co., Menasha, Wis.

Mrs. Adelaide Fellows, Philco Corp., Philadelphia, Pa.

Mr. George A. Glenn, *Supermarket Grocery Editions, Chain Store Age,* New York, N.Y.

Miss Cleo Grush, Town and Country Food Co., Inc., Fort Wayne, Ind.

Mrs. Ivy Hall and Mr. Albert Todoroff, *Freezer Provisioning,* St. Louis, Mo.

Miss Helen C. Hamilton, Corn Products Co., New York, N.Y.

Mr. Held and Miss Shirley Potter, Frozen Prepared Foods Division, Stouffer Foods Corp., Cleveland, Ohio

Mrs. Bertie Hodes, KVP Sutherland Paper Co., Kalamazoo, Mich.

Mrs. Berta C. Horrock and Mr. Sam Martin, *Quick Frozen Foods,* New York, N.Y.

Mrs. Joan M. Huber, Southland Frozen Foods, Inc., New York, N.Y.

Mrs. Helena M. Hunt, American Institute of Baking, Chicago, Ill.

Miss Alice Hutchinson, The R. T. French Co., Rochester, N.Y.

Dr. Wallace F. Janssen, Department of Health, Education and Welfare, Food and Drug Administration, Washington, D.C.

Mrs. Myrna Johnson and Mrs. Karla Tillotson, *Better Homes and Gardens,* Meredith Press, Des Moines, Iowa

Mr. R. Kaffenberger and Mr. Robert A. Purinton, E. I. du Pont de Nemours and Co., Wilmington, Del.

Miss Jane Kelly, *Good Housekeeping,* New York, N.Y.

Mrs. Rose Kerr, Fish and Wildlife Service, Department of Interior, College Park, Md.

Miss Gladys Kimbrough, Ball Brothers Co., Muncie, Ind.

Mr. J. F. Lakey, Association of Food and Drug Officials of the United States, Austin, Texas

Mr. Mario Lelmini, Patterson Frozen Foods, Inc., Patterson, Calif.

Mr. Paul J. Lembeck, The Great Atlantic and Pacific Tea Co., New York, N.Y.

Miss Floris Lipsett, Dixie Cup Division of American Can Co., Easton, Pa.

Miss Eleanor Lynch, Reynolds Metals Co., New York, N.Y.

Mr. A. Gordon Lyon, Your Home Food Service, Dewitt, N.Y.

Miss Lucy Maltby, Corning Glass Works, Corning, N.Y.

Mr. A. Marsh, Washington Fruit and Produce Co., Inc., Yakima, Wash.

Dr. C. Earl McCracken, Housing and Equipment Laboratory, United States Department of Agriculture, Washington, D.C.

Mr. J. R. McLaughlin, Packaging Films Department, Goodyear Tire and Rubber Co., Akron, Ohio

Miss Joan Miller, Campbell Soup Co., Camden, N.J.

Miss Nancy Morton, Food Information Service, Swift and Co., Chicago, Ill.

Mr. Thomas Mottin, *Food Merchandising*, St. Louis, Mo.

Mrs. Kathryn B. Niles and Miss Bernice Stilwell, Poultry and Egg National Board, Chicago, Ill.

Mr. Thomas Niles, American Viscose Corp., Philadelphia, Pa.

Miss Dolores Palmer, Consumer Service Department, Armour and Co., Chicago, Ill.

Mr. E. B. Peterson, Marquette Corp., Minneapolis, Minn.

Miss Hildegarde Popper, Sumner Rider and Associates, New York, N.Y.

Miss Ruth Power, Cryovac Division of W. R. Grace Co., Cambridge, Mass.

Mr. Juel M. Ranum, Whirlpool Corp., Benton Harbor, Mich.

Mr. C. E. Rondomanski, Sealright Co., Inc., Fulton, N.Y.

Mr. Robert J. Sax, Kordite Corp., Macedon, N.Y.

Mr. Harry K. Schauffler, National Frozen Food Association, New York, N.Y.

Mr. Martin Sheridan, Admiral Corp., Chicago, Ill.

Mr. Rex Smith, Frigidaire Division of General Motors Corp., Dayton, Ohio

Mr. Wm. C. Smith, Frozen Foods Division, Milprint, Inc., Milwaukee, Wis.

Miss Reba Staggs, National Live Stock and Meat Board, Chicago, Ill.

Mr. Earl H. Steimle, Sodus Fruit Exchange, Inc., Sodus, Mich.

Miss Barbara Stock, Aluminum Company of America, Pittsburgh, Pa.

Mr. F. E. Sunden, National Fruit Canning, Seattle, Wash.

Mrs. Janet Taylor, Ocean Spray Cranberries, Inc., Hanson, Mass.

Miss Cheryll Walters, J. Walter Thompson Co., New York, N.Y.

Mr. William J. Wilson, Fruit Growers Coorperative, Sturgeon Bay, Wis.

The author wishes to express her special appreciation to Dr. Donald K. Tressler, national authority in food freezing and frozen foods, and President and Editor of the Avi Publishing Company, for his invitation to prepare this edition of the book. Special appreciation is also expressed to Syracuse University and its College of Home Economics, for granting leave of absence for an academic year which made possible the preparation of the manuscript.

JEAN I. SIMPSON

July 1962

Advantages of Frozen Foods

CHAPTER 1

This Age of Frozen Foods

INTRODUCTION

We may well consider that we are living in the age of frozen foods. Only a few decades ago, any thought of having so many delicious fruits and vegetables available all year long would have seemed fantastic. In addition to these, we have frozen meats, fish, shellfish and poultry of practically every kind, and prepared and cooked foods in abundance.

In the early 1920's, Clarence Birdseye, a biologist and fur trapper, noticed while in Labrador, that fish which had been caught and immediately frozen in the extreme cold of winter were far superior to those frozen any other time. In fact, he thought that such fish were remarkably similar to those used the same day they were caught. Following his observation, he devoted himself to the development of methods of freezing which led to the freezing of a large variety of products in consumer-size packages. This is an outstanding instance of a keen scientist, intrigued by a dream and with the ambition and ability to make it come true.

Then it was in the late twenties and early thirties that the retail frozen food industry had its beginning, first in the freezing of fish and then a few fruits and vegetables. Freezing meats, fish and poultry soon became more or less common practice, and in the early forties prepared and cooked frozen foods made their debut on the market. During these few decades, progress has been astounding.

TODAY'S FROZEN FOOD MARKETS

The total production of commercially frozen foods has increased tenfold during the last decade. And every day, more than 20 million pounds of frozen foods are currently rolling off the processors' production lines, to be on their way to warehouses, then to retail stores and finally to various institutions and American homes. This is providing about 50 pounds of frozen foods per person, annually, but

3

since only about half of our population so far is using commercially frozen foods regularly, many persons are using far more than this.

The following figures give us a comprehension of today's retail market for frozen foods. Note that in the figures for both pounds and dollar-values, three zeros have been omitted. These figures prove beyond doubt that the frozen food retail business is indeed "big business." This is in addition to frozen foods being used by hotels, restaurants and other institutions.

Estimated Retail Sales and Production of Frozen Foods, 1960

Product	Pounds[1]	Value[1]
Poultry	1,714,652	$ 581,932
Vegetables	963,900	323,700
Prepared specialties	790,000	492,600
Juices and drinks	1,292,000	430,194
Seafoods	192,145	141,130
Meat	147,000	116,000
Fruit	124,417	56,575
	5,224,114	$2,142,131

[1] Last three zeros omitted.
Source: *Quick Frozen Foods Magazine.*

Fruits and Vegetables

From a day-by-day standpoint, probably the greatest advantage of commercially frozen foods to most families is the all-year-long supply of so many kinds of fruits and vegetables. For many people nowadays, the time when asparagus, peas, corn on the cob, berries, peaches and so many other items were available for only a few weeks is almost forgotten.

Of the frozen fruits, strawberries were the first to meet with all-out success at the dining-room table. Annual sales tell us they are still by far the most popular of the frozen fruits. Red raspberries are next on the list for popularity rating. The first few years that frozen peaches were available, they posed a serious problem because they darkened soon after thawing. Then it was discovered that the addition of ascorbic acid helped to keep their color, and this has been a major improvement. So peaches are third on the list of popular frozen fruits. Blueberries, boysenberries, red sour pitted cherries, blackberries and others are popular, too.

By far the most spectacular development in frozen fruits and fruit juices is that of frozen orange juice concentrate which was introduced to the retail market in the early 1940's. The production of frozen orange juice concentrate has grown steadily since that time. In fact, for several recent years, consumer purchases of frozen orange juice concentrate has exceeded the combined purchases of fresh oranges, chilled fresh orange juice and canned orange juice.

Frozen vegetables had their beginnings with peas, lima beans and spinach, and nowadays practically every kind of vegetable, except tomatoes and crisp salad vegetables, is frozen for the retail market. It may be surprising that far more frozen potatoes in one form or another are sold than any other kind of vegetable. In fact, during 1960, frozen potatoes accounted for about one-fifth of the total weight of frozen vegetables which were sold at retail. Most of these were French fried, which is an indication of how much these are enjoyed by many families, and when purchased ready for a brief reheating, there is no need for a frying kettle in the kitchen. A recent survey in a large city, too, showed that in more than half of the restaurants, French fried potatoes were frozen ones.

Next to potatoes in popularity (as shown by weights sold) are green peas. A close third is broccoli, then spinach, lima beans and green beans.

Meats

The total pounds of meat sold at retail, according to the above table, seem small in comparison with some of the other foods. This is probably due in part, at least, to the tremendous amount of frozen meat delivered directly to homes by the freezer food plan or other similar organizations. Many of these families buy their meats in wholesale or near-wholesale quantities, and the actual weights sold are difficult to estimate.

One of the opportunities to which families have responded is the specialty type of meat sold as thin steaks (sandwich type), for quick cooking. One processor reports it is selling 75,000 of these daily.

Poultry

Not long ago, chicken was chiefly a Sunday treat in many families, and turkey was for Thanksgiving and Christmas dinner. Not so, nowadays! Frozen chickens for broiling, frying, roasting and fricassée are available and used extensively all year. So are frozen capons, and the large proportion of meat to bone on these birds has made them especially popular. Large, broad-breasted frozen turkeys, weighing up to 24 pounds are the favorite for large dinner parties, and these may be purchased unstuffed or already stuffed. Smaller turkeys for broiling, frying and roasting are welcome for smaller dinner parties, and these birds are mostly the Beltsville breed. Turkey halves or quarters, or turkey parts (legs, wings and so on) are fine for the family wanting turkey but not wanting much at one time. Frozen Rock Cornish hens, ducklings, geese and squabs are proving popular, too. Cut-up poultry has added to the convenience in purchasing and cooking birds. Since frozen poultry is practically always sold ready-to-cook, it requires little, if any, additional cleaning after it reaches the home. The retail sale of frozen poultry has increased nearly ten times during the last decade.

Fish and Shellfish

Fresh fish are so perishable that when we depended on them for our supply, good quality fish were not available in parts of the United States which are distant from fishing areas. Today, by contrast, everyone may enjoy good fish in some form, since frozen fish fillets, steaks or sticks are found even in small villages in remote places.

Our total consumption of frozen fish and shellfish has about doubled since 1940. And we are using almost five times as much frozen shellfish as we did in 1940, with special increase in frozen shrimp. Fish sticks and other fish portions were introduced in about 1953 and have become the largest-selling fish item. These are pieces cut from large blocks of frozen fillets, into portions of uniform dimensions, then breaded. In popularity, fillets and steaks are next, then breaded shrimp and other shrimp and fish portions.

Specialty Foods

It is difficult to comprehend fully the extent to which frozen specialty foods are finding their way into American homes. The following figures, giving retail sales of such foods for 1960, present an interesting picture.

These figures, it will be seen, are for the total pounds and dollar values for each kind of specialty sold, with three zeros omitted. It is interesting, too, to know how these foods compare when they are considered as to the number of units of each that was sold. For instance, there was a larger number of packages of French fried potatoes sold than any other single food, next in line were pot pies,

Estimated Retail Sales and Poundage of Specialty Frozen Foods, 1960

Products	Pounds[1]	Value[1]
Platters	137,000	$128,000
Meat pies	160,000	82,000
Nationality foods	85,000	76,000
Fruit pies	182,000	68,000
Bakery products	59,000	44,000
Entrées (includes pouches)	86,000	42,000
Soups	30,000	14,000
Seafood specialties	13,000	12,000
Cream pies	16,000	9,600
Breaded precooked poultry	7,000	5,000
Prepared vegetables	5,000	4,000
Miscellaneous	10,000	8,000
	790,000	$492,600

Source: *Quick Frozen Foods Magazine.*
[1] Last three zeros omitted.

then dinner platters, then the various nationality foods, fruit pies, fish sticks, baked goods, soups and entrées.

Since there are at least a thousand different specialty items on the market nowadays, it is impossible to enumerate them here. The following list merely gives a bird's-eye view of the types most commonly found, in addition to dinner platters of many kinds. Not all of these are apt, of course, to be found in any one store or locality.

Some of these foods need only to be thawed in preparation for serving them. Others need to be reheated, and some need cooking or baking after they are purchased. In practically all cases, instructions are given on the package for the consumer to follow in preparing the food for the table. These instructions should be followed, for best results.

Cooked Vegtables.—Almost all kinds of prepared or cooked potatoes, including French fried and crinkle cut, mashed, hashed, baked, au gratin, puffs, pancakes, rissole and soufflés are sold at retail.

Many other cooked vegetables such as squash and pumpkin, vegetables in sauces, creamed, fritters, soufflés, candied sweet potatoes and yams, and French fried onion rings are available.

Canapés and Hors D'oeuvres.—Cocktail franks, tiny sandwiches, chopped and seasoned chicken livers, liver puffs, small pizzas and other "dainties" are sold in many retail stores.

Soups.—Many cream soups, oyster stews, seafood soups and chowders, egg drop soup, minestrone, vegetable, bean, lentil and pea soups, snapper, vichyssoise and others are frozen and sold at retail.

Entrées.—A great variety of poultry entrées, including pot pies, à la king dishes, fricassées, chop sueys, chow meins, fried, creamed and roasted poultry, cutlets, stews, croquettes and poultry with giblet gravy are offered.

An almost endless line of meat entrées such as barbecued meats, stews, goulashes, beef Stroganoff, meat balls, cuts with sauce, Swiss steak, meat sticks and hashes are frozen by many packers.

Fish and seafood entrées are prepared and frozen from many kinds of fish and shellfish. These entrées include breaded, au gratin, creole and deviled dishes, also Newburgs, thermidors, patties, pies, sticks and croquettes.

Meatless entrées include rarebits, macaroni and cheese, Spanish rice and egg foo young.

Entrée Sauces.—Sauces for meat, fish, poultry and spaghetti include cranberry, cranberry-orange relish, cheese, horseradish, barbecue, mushroom sauces and others.

Baked Goods.—Muffins, dinner rolls, sweet rolls and coffee cakes, baking powder biscuits, doughnuts, waffles, cakes, cookies, brownies, patty shells, garlic and other breads are baked and frozen by many bakers.

Desserts.—Desserts include custard, cream and chiffon pies, un-baked mince and fruit pies, turnovers, cobblers, shortcakes, strudels, upside down cakes, many kinds of ice cream pies and ice cream rolls.

PACKAGING DEVELOPMENTS

The array of frozen foods in retail storage cabinets makes evident the diversity of packages and containers in use nowadays, and the assortment continues to increase.

The most important feature of the package is that it should help to retain the quality of the food in it. This is most important for meats, fish, shellfish and poultry. If the package is not a good one, moisture will be lost and so the product will be dry. Also, with a poor package, air will enter and encourage the development of off-flavors. On the whole, these products are far better packaged now than they were a few years ago. This is particularly true of fish, for during the first few years that frozen fish were on the retail market extensively, wrapping materials too often were poor, so frozen fish lost moisture and gained the reputation for being dry. This seldom

The "heat-in" bag is convenient to use and retains flavor and nutrients. To reheat the vegetable or entrée, the unopened bag is immersed into boiling water. Then the bag is opened and the food is poured directly onto the serving plate.

happens today. Frozen poultry is also much better wrapped now-adays.

Another essential is the convenience of the package—ease in opening it and ease in preparing the food for the table. An extensive survey of consumer opinion not long ago showed that not all the containers are considered easy to open, and these problems are likely to be overcome in the near future. Containers of different types make it possible to put the food in its container in the oven for reheating. A fairly recent innovation is the "cook-in" bag or "cook-in" pouch. These bags or pouches may contain a vegetable with a sauce, or an entrée such as a stew. The unopened bag is immersed into boiling water to cook or reheat the food. This is not only convenient, but also helps to retain the flavor and nutritive value of the food.

Another convenient arrangement is the bag from which some of the food may be "poured"—sometimes called the "pour-and-store" bag. After taking as much food from the bag as needed at one time, the bag is reclosed and put back into the freezer.

There is a far greater assortment of sizes of packages for many foods, so one may conveniently purchase in one package, more nearly the amount needed.

Lastly, every processor, of course, wants the package in which his product is presented to the public to be an attractive one. The general styling of many frozen food packages is appealing, often with a design to give an idea of just what it contains. And many packages are transparent, or have a transparent "window" so the buyer sees what she is getting.

FROZEN FOODS OUTSIDE THE HOME

Quite some time before frozen foods found their way into American homes, they were widely used in restaurants, hotels and other institutions, because of the saving in kitchen labor. And a number of chain restaurants freeze their specialty dishes in a main plant and distribute them to their member restaurants.

Airlines have long been accustomed to taking full advantage of frozen foods for serving meals during their flights. In some areas, frozen foods are available in vending machines for motorists on highways. The food is quickly reheated by microwave so the motorist is promptly served and on his way again. In some large cafeterias, frozen foods are available with a "cook it yourself" arrangement, in a Radarrange. Such cafeterias need no kitchens of their own.

Some of us may have heard of freeze-dried foods and dehydrofrozen ones. For freeze-drying, the food is first frozen, then dehydrated. Such a product is rather sponge-like but intact. Since most of the moisture is removed, the freeze-dried foods can be kept for long periods without refrigeration if they are kept dry. Some freeze-dried foods are used in manufacturing dehydrated soups. And some are available for use by campers, hunters and outdoor sportsmen.

In dehydrofreezing, about 70 per cent of the moisture is first removed from the food, then the food is frozen. These foods need to be stored in the freezer, since they contain considerable moisture. A number of these dehydrofrozen foods are in rather general use in institutions, and some are used as ingredients by food manufacturers. For instance, the pimento in the pimento cheese which you buy was probably dehydrofrozen.

Except for the few instances mentioned above, the expected use for both freeze-dried and dehydrofrozen foods for the immediate future seems to be for military purposes and in institutions.

CHAPTER 2

Frozen Foods and Our Health

INTRODUCTION

The American people seem to have gained a reputation for liking good steaks, apple pie and coffee. This makes us appear to be a nation liking the good things of life, and in many respects this is no doubt true. But along with this, we must have a lot of good sense, for we are recognized as one of the best nourished countries in the world.

FROZEN FOODS AND OUR NUTRITION

Nutritionists nowadays know of about half a hundred different substances which are essential to life and well-being. These include water, minerals, vitamins, amino acids and fatty acids. Here are a few of these specific substances, the reasons why we need them and the chief sources of each in our diets.

Some of the Nutrients and Their Sources

Protein is required to build and repair all tissues, to help form antibodies to fight infections and to supply food energy. The chief sources are: meats, fish, poultry, eggs, milk, cheese, legumes, cereals and nuts.

Fat is needed to supply a large amount of food energy in a small amount of food and to supply essential fatty acids. The chief sources are: all fats and oils, cream, ice cream, cheese made from whole milk, bacon, pork and fatty meats, peanut butter and nuts.

Carbohydrates supply food energy and help the body use other nutrients. The chief sources are: cereals and cereal products, potatoes, sweet potatoes, dried fruits, bananas, sugars and syrups, jams and jellies and candies.

Calcium is required to help build bones and teeth, to help blood to clot and to help muscles and nerves react normally. The chief sources are: milk, cheese, ice cream, beets and leafy vegetables.

Iron combines with protein to make hemoglobin, the red substance in the blood that carries oxygen to the cells. The chief

This is the Meat Group, one of the four main food groups of A Daily Food Guide.
For the daily requirements, see p. 15

sources are: meats (liver, kidney and heart are especially good sources), shellfish, poultry, eggs, legumes, whole grain and enriched cereals, dark green and leafy vegetables, prunes and raisins.

Ascorbic Acid (vitamin C) is needed to help cement body cells together and to strengthen the walls of the blood vessels, to help resist infection and to help in healing. The chief sources are: fruits and vegetables, especially citrus fruits, tomatoes, cabbage, strawberries, cantaloup, broccoli, dark green and leafy vegetables, potatoes and sweet potatoes.

Vitamin A is required to help keep the skin and mucous membranes healthy and resistant to infection, and to protect against night blindness. The chief sources are: deep-yellow fruits and vegetables, dark green and leafy vegetables, eggs, cream, liver, butter and fortified margarine.

Thiamin is required for normal appetite and digestion, for a healthy nervous system and to help change substances in food into energy for work and heat. The chief sources are: meats (especially pork), fish, poultry, eggs, milk, whole grain and enriched cereals and legumes.

Riboflavin is needed to help the cells use oxygen, to help keep vision clear and for smooth skin without scaling around the mouth or cracking at the corners of the mouth. The chief sources are: milk, cheese, ice cream, eggs, meats (especially liver), fish, poultry, whole grain or enriched cereals, dark green and leafy vegetables.

Vitamin D is essential to help the body absorb calcium and to help build strong bones. The chief sources are: milk fortified with vitamin D, butter or fortified margarine, eggs, fish liver oil, and sardines, salmon and tuna.

SELECTING FOODS FOR GOOD NUTRITION

The next question is, how are we to have a guide for selecting foods for our menus, which will give us reasonable assurance that we are getting enough of each of these and other essentials? The Basic Seven is a plan which nutritionists worked out some years ago to help do this. In this plan foods are divided into seven groups and the recommended amounts of foods in each group are listed. If you are accustomed to using this and like it, there is no reason for changing it. But more recently, a plan called A Daily Food Guide has been devised which divides the foods into four main groups. This plan is considered somewhat easier to use. Here it is.

A Daily Food Guide

Each homemaker should serve her family daily the number of servings indicated of each of the four main groups of foods listed below.

Meat Group.—Serve two or more servings of one or more of the following: beef, veal, pork, lamb, poultry, fish, eggs; as alternates give them occasionally dry beans, dry peas and nuts.

Milk Group.—Provide some milk for everyone: children, three to four cups; teen-agers, four or more cups; adults, two or more cups. Cheese and ice cream may replace part of the milk.

Vegetable and Fruit Group.—Give four or more servings of fruits or vegetables. Include each of the following: a citrus fruit or other fruit or vegetable important for ascorbic acid; a dark green or deep-yellow vegetable for vitamin A at least every other day; and other vegetables and fruits including potatoes.

Bread and Cereal Group.—Give four or more servings of whole grain, enriched or restored bread or other cereal foods.

Plus.—Other foods should be provided as needed to complete meals and to furnish energy and other food values.

SOME RECENT FOOD TRENDS

Foods for Optimum Health

It would be interesting to take a brief look at ourselves to see some of the trends in our food habits in recent decades, and to see how these have affected our health. Some years ago, nutritionists needed to concern themselves with diets which were so poor in one or more nutrients that they caused disease. Pellagra was such a disease until it was discovered that insufficient niacin (the pellagra-preventing factor) was the cause of it. By 1945, pellagra as a widespread disease was a thing of the past in our country. More recently, emphasis has been on encouraging diets which provide not only freedom from disease but optimum health. It is well-recognized that good nutrition is the best guarantee of an able, energetic, long-lived population.

Some manufacturers are nowadays regularly adding certain nutrients to their foods before putting them on the market. Millers usually add to their refined cereals iron, thiamin, riboflavin and niacin, the nutrients known to have been partially removed from the whole grain when it was refined. Milk is usually fortified with vitamin D, and margarines are usually fortified with vitamin A (making them nutritionally similar to butter) and sometimes with vitamin D. We probably take these additions for granted as we do our day by day shopping, but they have made substantial additions to our diets. Also, the addition of iodine to table salt (iodized salt) has helped prevent goiter in regions where the water, the soil and food grown in it are low in iodine.

Some National Trends

From time to time, the United States Department of Agriculture and other government agencies make extensive studies to estimate the total amounts of different kinds of foods being produced. From these estimates, they figure the average amounts being used per person or per family. Of course, some individuals and some families will use far more than the average, some far less, but the figures give us a picture of national trends in food consumption and so are very interesting.

Since 1930, we have used more meats, especially beef, and since 1940 our use of poultry has doubled. These have given us proteins which are more valuable nutritionally than proteins from plant sources such as cereals and legumes.

Our total consumption of frozen fish has doubled since 1939. Those using frozen fish extensively are having the benefits of good quality protein (as in meats and poultry), and of a good source of minerals and of the B vitamins. Fish also contain certain unsaturated fatty acids which are of special interest because they reduce the amount of cholesterol in the blood. Some researchers believe there is a connection between the presence of cholesterol in the blood and the occurrence of atherosclerosis, a common form of heart disease. However, the total consumption of fish in all forms has not shown any appreciable increase to date. There is every reason to expect it will increase in the next few years, and this will be very definitely to our advantage.

The two nutrients most often found to be below the recommended allowance in our diets in recent years are calcium and ascorbic acid. The amount of calcium tends to be high or low, according to the

This is the Milk Group, one of the four main food groups of A Daily Food Guide.
For the daily requirements, see p. 15

amount of milk (and milk products such as cheese and ice cream) that are used. While our consumption of milk has increased, it has not brought the calcium in our diets to the desired amount. In 1955, the diets of 3 out of 10 households were low in calcium.

Also in 1955, 1 out of 4 households was not getting enough ascorbic acid. During the first decade of this century, potatoes and sweet potatoes were used extensively. A serving of potatoes does not provide as much ascorbic acid as many other vegetables or as much as most fruits. But when they are used extensively throughout the year, they contribute substantially to our ascorbic acid. Since 1910, our use of potatoes and sweet potatoes has steadily declined. The use of green and yellow vegetables, citrus fruits and tomatoes increased, thus bringing an increase in ascorbic acid, which offset the lower use of potatoes. Our intake of ascorbic acid reached a peak in 1945. Since then, our use of fresh fruits and vegetables has decreased, and our use of processed fruits and vegetables (frozen, canned and dried combined) has increased. However, the increase in processed products is not yet sufficient to offset the decrease in fresh ones. So we are not yet as well placed so far as ascorbic acid goes, as we were in 1945. Citrus fruits (and their juices) and tomatoes in all forms provide the largest proportion of our ascorbic acid nowadays.

Differences Among Families

If we could visit typical families throughout all parts of the United States, we would find a tremendous variety of recipes and menus, and this is a good feature of our American way of life. But we would find far less difference nowadays than in recent decades, as to the essentials we are getting, nutritionally, from family to family. Food habits in this respect are not so different between families in the south and those in the north, as they were a generation ago. Neither is there so much difference between the food habits of those living in cities and those on farms. There is less difference according to family income, too. In fact, the greatest improvement in diets has been in those of low income families, due largely to the efforts of public health nutritionists. A high income does not by any means insure an adequate diet, though more often than not, families without any special limits in their food budgets select enough of the essentials. They tend to use more of the luxury type foods such as expensive meats (which are no better, nutritionally, than inexpensive ones), more of the convenience foods and more fruits and vegetables, especially citrus fruits.

THE NUTRITIVE VALUE OF FROZEN FOODS

With the tremendous increase in our use of frozen foods, we are rightly very much interested in their nutritive value.   One important fact can be stated briefly.   No evidence has been obtained to show any decrease in any nutrient due to freezing itself.   That is, from the time the food is first put into the freezer until it is hard-frozen, the nutritional value is not changed.

So any losses which occur are the result of allowing the fresh product to stand at room temperature, or of steps in preparing the food for freezing, or they happen during freezer storage or in preparing the frozen foods for the table.   Let's consider, then, the various nutrients and what may happen to them at these stages.

How Losses Can Occur

There are only two ways in which the amount of any nutrient in any food can be decreased.   Firstly, almost all the minerals in our foods, and many vitamins, can be dissolved in water.   Such minerals or vitamins may be found in the water, juice or syrup in which the foods have been allowed to stand.   The more soluble the nutrient, the longer the time of standing, the hotter the liquid, and the larger the proportion of liquid to food, the more of the nutrient will be dissolved.   Then, too, nutrients leach more quickly from thin vegetables like spinach than from thick ones like large asparagus spears, and from fruits like strawberries or cut-up fruits and vegetables than from vegetables like peas or corn with their protective coatings.

Secondly, vitamins (though not minerals) can be actually destroyed, some more easily than others.   This is the result of a chemical change in the vitamin, making it no longer effective for nutritional purposes. When a substance reacts chemically with oxygen, it is oxidized.   Ascorbic acid and vitamin A are rather easily destroyed by oxidation. This can happen when the food is left exposed to air (which has oxygen as a component), especially if the food is crushed so that oxygen reaches the inside of the tissue more readily.   Oxidation is hastened by heat, so occurs rapidly during cooking in the presence of air, but occurs only slowly at room temperature, still more slowly in the refrigerator and far more slowly in the freezer.

Most foods contain enzymes which are present in small amounts and which can cause changes in some of the food constituents. While some of these changes are beneficial, others cause deterioration. Certain enzymes can accelerate the oxidation of ascorbic acid and vitamin A. Light hastens oxidation, so do some heavy metals, including copper. Oxidation occurs more slowly in acid foods such as rhubarb and fruits (particularly those which are distinctly acid such as citrus fruits and tomatoes) than in low-acid foods like most vegetables.

Proteins

These are not appreciably dissolved in water, and as a rule they are not affected by freezer storage. So the protein content of frozen foods when they reach the table is as good as that of fresh foods. There is one possible exception to this. If some fish or shellfish are held in freezer storage for long periods, the protein becomes somewhat less digestible than in the fresh or freshly frozen product.

Fats

If the fat of meat, fish or poultry or other foods high in fat does not initially have high quality, or if these products have not been properly packaged, or have been held in the freezer too long, or at too high temperature, the fat may become rancid. Such fats are oxidized, and the vitamin A dissolved in them may also be oxidized and so loses its nutritional value. Otherwise, there is no change in fat, nutritionally, during freezing or freezer storage.

Carbohydrates

The starch in foods which have been frozen is the same, nutritionally, as the starch in fresh foods. During rather extensive freezer storage, sucrose, which is the form in which sugar occurs in fruits (and is the same substance as granulated sugar) changes gradually to simpler sugars, dextrose and levulose. This is exactly what happens to sucrose when we digest it, so this is of no concern to us.

Minerals

While minerals cannot be destroyed, occasionally one may occur in a food in a form in which the body cannot use it and it is then not "available" to the body. Sometimes this is a problem with iron, sometimes with calcium. However, the iron in a number of vegetables has been shown to be at least as available (occasionally more

This is the Vegetable and Fruit Group, one of the four main food groups of A Daily Food Guide. For the requirements, see p. 15

so) in frozen foods than in similar fresh ones. So the chief problem with minerals is the possibility of their being lost by solution. If meats, fish or poultry are allowed to thaw excessively, they may "leak" or "drip" (lose some of their juices). In such juices there will be some minerals.

The chief loss of minerals is by solution during the blanching and subsequent chilling in preparing vegetables for freezing, and in cooking the frozen vegetables. Some work has shown the extent of losses in blanching, and subsequent chilling, but little has been reported to tell us how much is lost in cooking frozen vegetables. Losses during preparation for freezing are apt to be offset by fewer losses in cooking frozen vegetables than in cooking fresh ones. So servings from frozen vegetables should be as high in minerals as those from fresh ones. For a discussion of this question, see pp. 23 to 28 in connection with losses of ascorbic acid which is also soluble in water.

Vitamin A and Carotene

These are not appreciably soluble in water but are soluble in fat, so when they occur in a food they are usually dissolved in the fat. Note comments, p. 20, concerning the destruction of vitamin A in rancid fats. The fresher the "fresh" fruits or vegetables, used for freezing, the higher their carotene (the precursor of vitamin A) content, and so the higher the frozen fruits or vegetables will be in this nutrient. It is rather readily oxidized, and losses from 0 to 20 per cent have been reported during blanching in preparing vegetables for freezing. During a year in the freezer at 0°F. little if any loss occurs in blanched vegetables. Unblanched vegetables, on the other hand, may lose a substantial amount at this temperature.

Thiamin and Riboflavin

These are members of the B complex vitamins and are the only ones which have been studied to any extent in frozen foods. These and all the other B vitamins are soluble in water. Riboflavin is not destroyed by heat, but under some conditions heat can destroy thiamin. The few studies which have been concerned with other B vitamins indicate that the procedures which help to retain thiamin and riboflavin also help to retain the other vitamins in this group.

Since thiamin is soluble in water and may also be destroyed by heat, some loss is inevitable in preparing vegetables for freezing. On an average, of the vegetables studied, about 25 per cent has been found to be lost during blanching (including subsequent chilling) and another 25 per cent dissolved in the cooking of frozen vegetables. No loss of thiamin has been reported from blanched vegetables during six months of storage at 0°F., and little loss within a year. Unblanched vegetables, however, lose a large proportion of this vitamin when stored at this temperature.

The studies concerning riboflavin in vegetables have shown that from 0 to 20 per cent may be lost during blanching and subsequent chilling in preparing them for freezing. Little is lost during freezer storage of blanched vegetables at 0°F., but loss may be substantial from unblanched ones.

Meats, fish and poultry are important sources of thiamin and are also good sources of riboflavin. There is no indication of loss of either of these vitamins from these foods during freezing or freezer storage. This is to be expected, since preparation for freezing does not involve standing in water or heating. So the only way in which loss of these vitamins can occur, it seems, is by dissolving small amounts of them (or of other B vitamins) into the juices which "drip" during excessive thawing. This should not happen at all, when the products are cooked from the frozen state or are correctly thawed. If drip does occur, the juice can be added to the meat during cooking.

Ascorbic Acid (Vitamin C)

By far the greatest amount of work carried out to determine the nutritive value of frozen foods has been in connection with the ascorbic acid in frozen fruits and vegetables. The reason for this is because fruits and vegetables are almost our only source of this nutrient, so their ascorbic acid content when frozen is important. Ascorbic acid dissolves in water more readily than any of the other vitamins, so may be lost this way. Also, it is readily destroyed by oxidation. Certain enzymes, if present, and heavy metals can hasten its oxidation.

So of all the vitamins, ascorbic acid is the one most readily lost or destroyed. We may therefore be fairly confident that if the ascorbic acid retention of a fruit or vegetable is good, other nutrients will also have been retained. Furthermore, it has been noticed repeatedly that when the ascorbic acid retention of a fruit or vegetable is high, its flavor, texture and color are also good. This is not a hard and fast rule, but it is so generally true that the ascorbic acid retention of a fruit or vegetable is often considered an indication of its general quality.

In Fresh Fruits and Vegetables.—The quality of frozen fruits and vegetables depends on the quality of the fresh products used in freezing, and this includes their ascorbic acid content. The fresh produce itself may vary widely in its ascorbic acid. In fact, one lot of a certain kind of fruit or vegetable may easily have half again or even twice as much as another lot of the same kind of produce, due to a number of influences. The stage of maturity of the produce when harvested is important, and the ascorbic acid is often at or near its peak at the "just ripe" stage. How much time has elapsed between harvesting and freezing is particularly important, especially if the product has not been refrigerated. Holding vegetables a day or so at room temperature may easily cause loss of half of its ascorbic acid. Vegetables grown in your own garden and frozen 2 or 3 hours after they are picked should be high in ascorbic acid as well as in other qualities. While vegetables purchased on the market are, in general, far better nowadays than some years ago (thanks to refrigerated transportation), they are not likely to be as fine for freezing as those which have stood only an hour or two before freezing.

Since fruits and rhubarb are acid, this effect of standing after harvesting is not quite so important as for most vegetables, but the sooner they are frozen the better. Commercial freezing plants usually have their fields of growing crops close to their freezing operations, so the fruits and vegetables are in the freezers soon after harvesting.

In Frozen Fruits.—Frozen strawberries (with their juice or syrup) are also an excellent source of ascorbic acid, more so than many people realize. Rather conflicting figures have been reported, but it seems safe to say that when losses in preparation for freezing, in freezer storage and in normal thawing are considered, we can count on their having about 80 per cent of the ascorbic acid in the fresh strawberries. Frozen raspberries, too, should have about this portion of the original ascorbic acid when served.

The two other best sources of ascorbic acid among frozen fruits are peaches and apricots to which ascorbic acid has been added in prepa-

This is the Bread and Cereal Group, one of the four main food groups of A Daily Food Guide. For the daily requirements, see p. 15

ration for freezing, primarily to preserve the light color in these fruits.

Frozen fruits should be served when they are barely thawed and still "frosty," since their flavor, aroma and texture are best then. More information is needed as to the effect of holding thawed fruits for longer periods. The few studies which have been made tell us that strawberries frozen without sugar or syrup (for diabetics, for instance) and those which are sliced lose their ascorbic acid rather more quickly than those frozen whole, with sugar or syrup.

In Frozen Fruit Juices.—Because of the very large amounts of frozen orange juice being used, and the fact that we count on it as a very important source of ascorbic acid, information about it is of special interest. Several extensive studies have been made to learn the difference in ascorbic acid content among different brands of frozen orange juice and on different markets, from both Florida and California oranges. Upon reconstitution, the ascorbic acid contents of a large proportion of these were very similar to those of freshly squeezed orange juices. In other studies, after a year of freezer storage at 0°F., the juices had retained almost all their original ascorbic acid. Frozen orange, grapefruit and tangerine juices, when reconstituted and held in covered containers in the refrigerator two days, had not lost more than ten per cent of this vitamin. This high retention is no doubt due to the acidity of these juices which protects them against ascorbic acid destruction.

In Frozen Vegetables.—Effect of blanching and chilling: Blanching is essential to destroy vegetable enzymes which would cause off-flavors during freezer storage. This amounts to a short, partial cooking in boiling water or steam. Inevitably, this causes some loss of ascorbic acid, due in part to oxidation of the vitamin and in part to dissolving some of it in the hot water or condensed steam. The longer the blanching period, the greater the loss is apt to be, but the time must be long enough to have the interior of the vegetable reach the temperature necessary to destroy the enzymes. It does not take as long for the inside of a leaf of spinach to reach this temperature as the inside of a thick stalk of asparagus. This is the reason for the different times recommended for different vegetables, and in spite of the loss of nutrients which results, these times must be followed.

There is another reason for blanching, too. If the vegetables were not blanched and chilled correctly, the enzymes left in them would cause the destruction of ascorbic acid during freezer storage. Unblanched vegetables have been shown to lose ascorbic acid rather readily in freezer storage, along with the development of off-flavors.

Immediately after blanching, it is important that the vegetables be cooled quickly to stop the cooking effect, and for this purpose they are transferred from the blanching kettle to very cold water for a short, recommended time. This causes further solution of nutrients, though they do not dissolve in cold water as quickly as in hot water or steam.

On an average, most vegetables may be expected to lose a total of about 15 to 30 per cent of their original ascorbic acid during blanching and subsequent chilling in cold water. This assumes that recommended procedures have been followed. Greens lose more than this, and corn, which is blanched on the cob and has a rather tough, protective coating, loses little.

Effect of freezer storage: When vegetables have been properly blanched, chilled and packaged, few of them lose appreciable amounts of ascorbic acid when stored for a year at 0°F. But when the freezer temperature is 10°F., losses increase, and at 20°F. even in one month loss can be considerable. This is one reason why it is so important to have your freezer at least as low as 0°F. and it is one of the reasons the frozen food industry is making an effort to maintain a low storage temperature from the time the food has been frozen until it is purchased by the consumer. Unblanched vegetables lose ascorbic acid readily, even when stored at 0°F. for a short time.

Effect of thawing: Vegetables are usually cooked from the hard-frozen state, and this is good procedure. However, if the vegetables were correctly blanched so as to destroy the enzymes, then chilled and packaged correctly, there is no reason to expect any substantial losses if the vegetables are kept in their original, unopened container and held a day or two in the refrigerator. Frozen peas held this way have shown negligible losses in ascorbic acid.

Effect of cooking: The blanching, preliminary to freezing, amounts to a partial cooking of the vegetables, and the process of freezing, itself, softens the vegetables somewhat, too. So the time for cooking vegetables, after boiling is resumed, is substantially less than the time for similar, fresh vegetables. Recommended boiling times for frozen vegetables are usually about half the time for the same vegetable when fresh.

Blanching also destroys enzymes in the fresh vegetables, and this is a benefit when it comes to cooking the frozen vegetables. If the enzymes were present in the frozen vegetables in the early stages of cooking, they would hasten the destruction of ascorbic acid. Since few if any such enzymes are present, little destruction of ascorbic acid occurs.

So the chief decrease in ascorbic acid in cooking frozen vegetables is due to its solution in the cooking water. Many research workers have shown that nutrients dissolve to a greater extent when vegetables are cooked in large amounts of water. The small amount of water recommended for cooking frozen vegetables reduces the loss of ascorbic acid to a minimum. If the small amount of cooking water left can be used in sauces, gravies or soups, so much the better.

Because of the combined effects of shorter time of cooking and the use of smaller amounts of water, losses of ascorbic acid from cooking frozen vegetables are less than from cooking similar fresh ones. Since these effects are particularly evident in pressure saucepans, losses of ascorbic acid by this method of cooking vegetables are especially low. However, it is all the more important to use the exact recommended time, since an extra minute at the high temperature in the pressure saucepan would cause more loss than in boiling water.

The net result of all this is that the loss of ascorbic acid in blanching and chilling vegetables in preparation for freezing is offset by smaller losses during cooking of frozen vegetables. So the nutritive value of cooked frozen vegetables can be every bit as high as that of cooked, fresh vegetables.

It is important, however, when comparing the nutritive value of fresh, cooked vegetables with frozen, cooked ones, to remember that there are many ways in which the quality of both kinds can be affected. Those cooked from high-quality fresh ones will be better than those from low-quality frozen ones, and vice versa. But when both the fresh and frozen vegetables are of good quality and correctly cooked, their nutritive value when they reach the table should be similar.

ALL THIS IN A NUTSHELL—AND OUR FUTURE

There is no doubt but what the food habits of the American people as a whole have improved greatly in recent decades. We have great diversity of recipes and menus from family to family, but a far greater proportion of us are getting what nutritionists believe to be the essentials of a good diet. Malnutrition as a cause of widespread disease in the United States is in the past, and emphasis nowadays is on foods which will not only prevent disease but will keep us in the very best of health.

By the time frozen foods reach the table, they should be just as nutritious as the corresponding fresh ones. This is true of meats, fish, poultry and many other frozen foods. It is particularly fortunate that it is also true of frozen fruits and vegetables, since they are our only important source of ascorbic acid.

The readers of this book will probably be surprised to know that at present (1962) only about half of the families in the United States use frozen foods regularly. While the increase in the use of frozen fruits and vegetables has been spectacular during the last decade, and they have added substantially to the ascorbic acid in our diets, we are still not getting quite as much of this vitamin as we did when the amount was at its peak in 1945. As our use of frozen fruits and vegetables increases, as inevitably it will, we will get more ascorbic acid. And since many fruits and vegetables are also high in vitamin A, this increase will also give us more of this vitamin.

Surveys show that in families where the shopping is done by young homemakers, especially those with considerable formal education, more frozen fruits and vegetables are purchased. Families with liberal incomes purchase more, too. Probably some families have an impression that these foods are more expensive than they really are, so this indicates the need for education concerning the comparative costs of the frozen products with those which are fresh or preserved by other methods.

With still further use of frozen foods in general, the homemaker's hours in the kitchen will be fewer and easier, the family hours at the dining-room table will be more enjoyable and families will be better nourished.

HOW SAFE TO EAT ARE FROZEN FOODS?

What Can Make a Food Unsafe to Eat?

Everyone is concerned as to whether any food is "fit to eat" in the sense of not making us ill, and all are interested in knowing what can happen to make food dangerous to eat.

The presence of large numbers of certain micro-organisms in foods can cause illness. These are living creatures of microscopic size, and they include bacteria, yeasts and molds. Fortunately, only a few of these are harmful. Yeast is used to make bread and rolls. Yeasts can grow rather readily in fruits, causing the fruits to ferment, but fermented fruits do not make us ill. Molds can grow on almost any kind of food but if there are only a few specks and these are removed, the rest of the food can be eaten safely. And we depend on certain kinds of bacteria and molds to make some kinds of cheese.

It is with certain bacteria that we are concerned when considering the possibility of food being dangerous to eat. Some of these, or the toxins (poisons) which they produce can cause infection or illness. These bacteria are called pathogenic ones. If large numbers of them are found in a food, the food may make us ill.

The kind of food in which bacteria find themselves makes a lot of difference to them. In fruits, particularly distinctly acid ones like orange, grapefruit and tomatoes, they do not thrive at all well, so these foods are not so easily made dangerous to eat. On the other hand, in less acid foods like milk, meat, fish, poultry, eggs and most vegetables, they thrive better, so it is with these foods we need to be more careful. This is particularly true of some high-protein foods (meat, fish, poultry and eggs) because in these putrefaction can occur, giving the food a foul odor and taste, and such food may make us ill.

An important respect in which types of bacteria differ from one another is the temperature at which they grow and multiply. Very few of them grow at all below 20°F., and practically none below 10°F. Some kinds grow best just below 45°F. and these find the refrigerator a good environment. Many, however, require lukewarm or slightly higher temperatures to grow and multiply. The temperature (and time held at that temperature) necessary to kill them differs, too.

Some Questions About Frozen Foods

Very few, if any foods or containers are actually sterile (free from all micro-organisms) when they are put into the freezer. During freezing and freezer storage, on an average, about half of the micro-organisms present are killed and the rest remain dormant, or sleeping, as it were, not growing or multiplying. So in a freezer at or near 0°F. none of them grows or multiplies.

But when the foods are taken from the freezer and allowed to thaw, their temperature gradually rises, and as the temperature suitable for bacteria to grow is reached, they will grow and multiply. So one might expect that this would be a source of serious danger in precooked dinners or pot pies or other foods of the type in which bacteria grow well and which are not boiled before serving. This is the reason that such foods have sometimes been considered to be a possible source of trouble and therefore a public health hazard.

And yet, it is a fact that from all the forty billion pounds of frozen foods which have been sold since the frozen food industry had its beginning, there have been few cases where these foods have been considered the probable cause of illness, and there has not been a single outbreak of food poisoning which has been legally shown to have been caused by them. This is a very remarkable record, and an explanation based on the way different bacteria behave is especially interesting.

When a frozen product like a precooked dinner or pot pie is taken from the freezer and allowed to thaw at room temperature, the first bacteria to grow are those which thrive well in cold food—the same type which thrive well in the refrigerator. But the fact is that none of these bacteria which grow at this temperature is pathogenic, so their presence does not make us ill. Foods with large numbers of such bacteria will gradually acquire sour odors and taste and become generally unpalatable, so we would not want to taste them. Even if we did, they would not give us an infection or a disease.

Since none of the pathogenic bacteria grows below 45°F., it is not until the food reaches temperatures somewhat higher than this that there is any danger of poison from it. Furthermore, it takes at least some hours at higher temperatures for such poisonous effects to develop. In the meantime, the bacteria which had been growing at the lower (thawing) temperature would probably have made the food so unpalatable we would not want to taste it.

This gives us considerable assurance that such frozen foods as precooked dinners are not the public health hazard which off-hand they might be considered. Gross mishandling, such as keeping the fully thawed food for a number of hours at 50°F. to 100°F., might make the food dangerous. Whether it would be dangerous then would depend largely on the kind of food, whether it was thoroughly cleaned before freezing, and frozen promptly (thereby preventing large numbers of pathogenic bacteria from being in the food when it was put in the freezer).

What Are The Precautions For Safety?

The fact that frozen foods are not to be looked upon as the serious public health hazard which might be expected does not mean for a moment that precautions are not necessary to be sure they are safe when they reach the table.   When meats, fish, poultry, milk, eggs and vegetables go into the freezer there should be as few pathogenic bacteria in them as possible.   This is somewhat less important for raw vegetables, because in cooking these the bacteria are killed.   But fresh foods should be clean, and to avoid having them contaminated, everything with which they come in contact should be clean.   In commercial freezing plants, efforts are being made for good sanitation, and the majority of them have high standards.   This is in part voluntary by the companies, and in part due to inspection by government officials.   In the home kitchen, cleanliness is just as important.   When preparing precooked foods for freezing, in the commercial plant and in the home kitchen, they should be chilled rapidly and frozen promptly, since it is at lukewarm temperatures that pathogenic bacteria grow well.

Good measures are necessary in the home, too, in reheating precooked foods for serving.   As a rule, these are heated without preliminary thawing and the instructions on the packages of such foods have been shown by tests to be usually satisfactory for killing any pathogenic bacteria which may be present.   But if the homemaker does not follow these instructions exactly, she should be on the safe side and use slightly higher temperatures or longer times, rather than lower temperatures or shorter times.

What About Refreezing?

Many packages of frozen foods have Do Not Refreeze in rather conspicuous lettering.   This has given people an impression that any frozen food which has been refrozen is dangerous.   It is true that refreezing will affect texture and other qualities, and we should be cautious as to what may be refrozen and what may not.   But it is not at all true that all refrozen foods are harmful.   This is discussed in connection with the care of foods which have been partially thawed when your freezer stops running (see p. 67).

Trouble From Botulism or Trichinosis?

Some freezer owners may be aware of the serious problem which non-acid vegetables sometimes present in home canning, because of the possibility of botulinus bacteria developing their toxin during storage of improperly home-canned vegetables. They will be relieved to know that this dangerous botulinus toxin has not been known to develop below 40°F. so there is no chance of its developing during freezer storage. No case of botulism has been traced to frozen foods.

Also, many of us are aware of the worm-like parasite which is occasionally found in pork, causing trichinosis, and may wonder whether this can give trouble in pork from the freezer. Freezing is known to destroy this parasite at all stages of its growth, so we cannot get trichinosis from frozen pork.

CHAPTER 3

Economy and Quality of Frozen Foods

ECONOMY OF FROZEN FOODS

Frozen foods are all ready for the saucepan, the oven or the table. With the exception of the bone in some cuts of meat and in certain fish, you eat all that you buy. On the other hand, when you buy three pounds of fresh lima beans, you pay for two pounds of pods. If you were to buy fresh, whole fish, as much as 75 per cent of the purchase might go into the garbage can. And if you were to buy fresh poultry (killed, bled and feathers removed), from one-fourth to one-third of the bird would be waste.

And at how much per hour do you value your time? What is the value of the time spent in trimming and paring vegetables, washing sandy spinach and doing all the multitudinous tasks that are no longer yours when you buy frozen foods?

How much better to drop frozen spinach into a little boiling water and serve it, minutes later, with a fine green color, tender and with no suspicion of sand or grit? Or is it not advantageous for you to place a package of frozen strawberries on the refrigerator shelf and find them at dinner time, ready to serve, colorful and delicious?

Waste Eliminated, and Cost

The tables which follow show the percentage of waste in a number of foods which are commonly frozen. These figures can be used to compare the cost of the fresh and frozen products. For instance, when you buy fresh, green peas, you get a large bag, so it seems a lot for the money, whereas a package of frozen peas is so small. However, a realistic comparison of costs may be surprising. Right in season, a reasonable price for fresh peas is 15 cents per pound. But according to the table for the percentage of waste, 63 per cent of this as-purchased weight is waste. So for 15 cents you are only getting 37 per cent of 16 ounces, or about 6 ounces of edible portion of peas. At this rate, 10 ounces of edible portion cost 25 cents. When you

35

buy a 10-ounce package of frozen peas (all of which is edible) you pay 22 cents.   So at these prices, frozen peas cost even less than fresh ones.

A reasonable price for fresh broccoli in the winter is 40 cents for a 1½-pound bunch.   So 24 ounces of this as-purchased weight costs 40 cents.   But 45 per cent of this is waste, so you are paying 40 cents for about 13 ounces of edible portion.   At this rate, 10 ounces of edible-portion of fresh broccoli cost 30 cents.   A 10-ounce package of frozen broccoli usually costs 29 cents.   So at these prices, the same weight of edible portion of the fresh costs about the same as the frozen.

Waste Eliminated in Frozen Vegetables and Fruits
(All equivalent figures given below are approximate averages)

	Size package	Equivalent before packing	Per cent waste eliminated
Vegetables			
Asparagus tips	12 oz.	1 lb. 10 oz.	54
Asparagus cuts	12 oz.	1 lb. 10 oz.	54
Beans, green and wax	10 oz.	14 oz.	30
Broccoli	13 oz.	1 lb. 7 oz.	45
Brussels sprouts	13 oz.	1 qt.	50
Cauliflower	13 oz.	1 med. head	70
Corn on the cob	2 ears	2 ears	40
Cut corn	10 oz.	5 ears	80
Lima beans	12 oz.	2 lbs.	63
Peas	12 oz.	2 lbs.	63
Peas and carrots	12 oz.	2 lbs.	63
Spinach	14 oz.	½ peck	48
Squash	16 oz.	1 lb. 6 oz.	27
Succotash	12 oz.	2 lbs.	62.5
Fruits			
Blueberries	12 oz.	1¼ pts.	9
Boysenberries	12 oz.	1¼ pts.	6
Cherries, sour	16 oz.	3¾ cups	16
Peaches	16 oz.	4½ medium	35
Raspberries	12 oz.	1⅓ pts.	6
Rhubarb	16 oz.	2½ lbs.	35
Strawberries	16 oz.	1 pt.	10

Source: Tressler, D. K., and Evers, C. F., *The Freezing Preservation of Foods*, Vol. I (3rd ed.; Avi Publishing Co., 1957).

In view of the extensive use of frozen orange juice concentrate, the cost of this in comparison with freshly squeezed juice is of special interest.   A reasonable price for fresh, juice-oranges in season is 45 cents per dozen.   The dozen oranges yield from 24 to 40 ounces of juice, so the price per ounce is 1.1 to 1.8 cents.   The highest price you are apt to pay at present (1962), for a 6-ounce can of frozen orange-

Waste Eliminated in Frozen Meats, Poultry, Seafoods and Shellfish

(All equivalent figures given below are approximate averages)

	Size package	*Equivalent before packing*	*Per cent waste eliminated*
Beef			
Sirloin steak	Av. 1 lb.	2 lbs.	50
Rib roast	Av. 4 lbs.	7 lbs. 4 oz.	45
Pot roast	Av. 3 lbs.	3 lbs. 12 oz.	20
Beef for stew	8 oz.	10 oz.	20
Chuck roast	Av. 4 lbs.	6 lbs. 10 oz.	40
Back of rump	Av. 3 lbs. 6 oz.	4 lbs. 13 oz.	30
Lamb			
Chops, loin (two)	Av. 4 oz. each	4¾ oz.	15
Chops, rib (two)	Av. 4 oz. each	5 oz.	20
Legs, whole or half	Av. 5 lbs.	6 lbs. 10 oz.	25
Lamb for stew	Av. 8 oz.	14 oz.	43
Pork			
Chops, center (two)	Av. 4 oz. each	4½ oz.	12
Chops, end (two)	Av. 5 oz. each	5¾ oz.	12
Pork loin roast	Av. 4 lbs.	4 lbs. 11 oz.	15
Poultry			
Broilers	Av. 1 lb.	1 lb. 8 oz.	33
Fryers	Av. 2 lbs.	3 lbs.	33
Roasters	Av. 3 lbs.	4 lbs.	25
Fowl for fricassee	Av. 2 lbs. 8 oz.	3 lbs. 12 oz.	33
Turkey	Av. 9 lbs.	12 lbs.	25
Ducks	Av. 4 lbs.	5 lbs. 12 oz.	30
Seafoods			
Cod fillets	1 lb.	3 lbs.	66
Mackerel fillets	1 lb.	1 lb. 12 oz.	44
Sole fillets	1 lb.	4 lbs.	75
Swordfish steaks	1 lb.	1 lb. 4 oz.	25
Shellfish			
Shrimp	12 oz.	12 oz.	None
Oysters	12 oz.	1 pt.	None
Scallops	12 oz.	1 pt.	None
Lobster meat	10 oz.	3 lbs.	80

Source: Tressler, D. K., and Evers, C. F., *The Freezing Preservation of Foods*, Vol. I (3rd ed.; Avi Publishing Co. 1957).

juice concentrate is 25 cents, and when reconstituted this gives 24 ounces. So the cost per ounce of reconstituted orange juice is one cent, and this is the lowest of the price range for the freshly squeezed juice. Incidentally, orange and grapefruit juices and raw cabbage give us more ascorbic acid for the money we spend than do any other foods.

Furthermore, if you buy these or other frozen foods in bulk lots of 6 or 12 packages or cans at lower prices, then the cost of the frozen food is still less.

Using the per cent waste for your calculations, you can make similar comparisons for the cost of any fresh and frozen fruits and vegetables. It surprises a lot of people to learn that many frozen fruits and vegetables are not nearly as expensive as they are often assumed to be.

It is more difficult to compare the cost of frozen prepared and cooked foods with those prepared at home, for many reasons, especially because of the number of ingredients included in some of them. Also, the difference between the cost of these foods when prepared at home and when purchased frozen is greater for some than for others. But servings of even the most deluxe, frozen main-course dishes and desserts do not cost any more, if as much, as we would pay for similar servings in a good restaurant. And there are many times when we prefer to have a nice meal right in our own home rather than at even the best restaurant.

QUALITY OF FROZEN FOODS

There is no question but what freezing captures the color, flavor, texture and nutritive value of fresh foods better than any other method of preservation. And the quality of frozen foods on the market, in general, has shown marked improvement in recent years. This is true of staples—fruits, vegetables, meats, fish and poultry. In any business, keen competition between manufacturers helps to keep standards of products high, and this is true, too, among companies freezing foods. The quality of frozen foods is due to the combined efforts of food technologists, refrigeration and packaging experts, engineers and others in related fields. While some processors have higher standards of quality than others, those putting low-quality foods on the market soon find that their products do not gain consumer acceptance.

Especially evident is the improvement in the quality of many frozen prepared and cooked foods. While the convenience features of these products will often induce a consumer to try them once, if the quality is not satisfactory, repeat sales do not occur. Realizing this, most processors make an effort to meet the consumer demand for good quality. For some of the products, the problem is chiefly just to use good ingredients and to package the product so it will keep its quality. But for others, problems in securing high quality are far more complicated.

Control in the Processing Plant

Much of the good quality of frozen foods is due to voluntary efforts on the part of companies freezing foods. Most large food manufacturers and freezing plants have their quality control departments which have the responsibility for establishing standards of quality, and for constant vigilance of all details of their operations which affect quality. In addition, some freezing plants have government officials on hand at all times the plant is in operation, continuously checking all features which affect quality. These companies are permitted to state on their package labels that the products are packed under the continuous inspection of the United States Department of Agriculture (or Interior).

Each packer has its own standards of quality, and these differ somewhat from one packer to another. In addition, the Federal Government has established grades of some frozen foods. These include some frozen fruits and vegetables, and most of the products on the retail market comply with the requirements for the best grade which is Grade "A" or Fancy, though packages are not often so labelled. Grades for frozen poultry have been established, and these are similar to those for fresh poultry. Further, grades for some frozen fish have been established.

Distribution of Frozen Foods

After the food leaves the freezing plant, it must travel by refrigerated transportation to a wholesale warehouse, as a rule, then to the retail store and finally to the home where it will be used. It is a recognized fact that American food processors have developed the most extensive and efficient marketing system in the world. It is fair to say that the frozen food industry is faced with as complicated a problem as any in the whole food industry, in distributing its products. The aim of the industry is to have the products kept at a temperature as near 0°F. as possible at all times during refrigerated transportation, during loading and unloading, and during storage in warehouses and in retail stores.

Storage Temperature and Frozen Food Quality

Food cannot become unsafe to eat as a result of being held any length of time while it remains frozen, regardless of the storage temperature (see pp. 29 to 33). So the question is, why are we so concerned that we maintain a constant temperature of 0°F. as recommended for the home freezer? This is because at temperatures above 0°F. some of the vitamins will gradually be lost (see pp. 19 to 28) and there will also be a gradual loss of quality—flavor, color, and texture.

In a good home freezer, there is a fairly constant temperature of 0°F. But the frozen food industry is very differently situated in placing its products on the market. As already mentioned, after the food is frozen in the freezing plant, it is usually taken to a wholesale warehouse for storage, then to a retail store for storage, with loading and unloading during these trips. It is a good deal to expect that at no time would the food be in an environment above 0°F. So very extensive studies have been made to learn how long it takes different foods to begin to deteriorate at different temperatures. Poultry has been found not to deteriorate as rapidly as fruits and vegetables, when held above 0°F. Fruits and vegetables, however, lose quality rather rapidly above 0°F. and the higher the temperature the more rapid the loss of quality. Following are the periods during which some fruits and vegetables have shown as much loss of quality as in one year when stored at 0°F.: in 6 weeks to 3 months when stored at 10°F.; in 1 to 3 weeks when stored at 20°F.; and in 1 to 5 days when stored at 30°F. Very frequent ups and downs of temperature for shorter periods will eventually cause deterioration, too. Incidentally, this gives us a good reason for the recommendation for keeping our own freezers at 0°F. And the various branches of the industry are making an effort to see that the food is kept at a temperature as near 0°F. as possible, at all times of storage and during all phases of transportation.

One interesting question is how to know whether a package has at any time reached an undesirably high temperature, and devices for this purpose, called indicators, are being manufactured. For instance, in a "window" in the package, there may be a chemical which changes color when a certain temperature is reached. So if the chemical is a certain color, this tells us that a certain temperature was reached. Better yet is an indicator which tells us not only what temperature was reached, but for how long the food remained at that temperature. A recently devised indicator does not show primarily the highest temperature to which the food has been subjected, but rather the total amount of time the food has been held at temperatures above 0°F., and the color on this indicator changes far faster near thawing than at temperatures just above 0°F. At such temperatures as these, the palatability of the food is impaired but it should be remembered that unless the food has been held at rather high temperatures for some hours after being fully thawed, it is not dangerous to eat (see pp. 29 to 33).

The buyer has an important part in this, too. Many stores are nowadays providing separate bags for frozen foods, some of them insulated. This is good practice, and the buyer can encourage it by asking for one. She should make her frozen food purchases just before going home, and put the packages into her freezer at once.

Home Freezers, Locker Plants and Freezer Food Plans

CHAPTER 4

Your Home Freezer

HOW TO SELECT IT, TAKE CARE OF IT, USE IT

DO YOU NEED A HOME FREEZER?

In 1935, home freezers were practically unknown, and it has been estimated that by 1961, there were more than twelve million freezers in American homes. So while home freezing and home storage of frozen foods is a rather recent innovation, it is one which has taken strong hold.

Long before the manufacture of home freezers, zero storage rooms for holding supplies of frozen foods were very popular among better hotels, hospitals and other institutions serving food. Institution managers recognized the fact that frozen foods resembled fresh ones more nearly than those preserved by any other method, and they realized the value of frozen foods in saving the labor of kitchen personnel, in sorting, trimming, cleaning, cutting, paring or other preparation needed for fresh produce to be used in cooking.

Homes have been the last of the "institutions" to make regular and substantial use of frozen foods. During recent years, refrigerating engineers have designed units for home freezing and home storage of frozen foods to meet the needs of practically every type of family, from the apartment dweller with limited kitchen space, to the farm family freezing a large part of its annual food supply. As a result, the whole pattern of life has changed in many families, so far as food shopping, kitchen work, menu planning and year-round quality of family meals are concerned.

For Convenience and Quality

In many families, home freezers are valued chiefly because of their convenience and the high quality of food which they make readily available. Frozen fruits and vegetables are so much like fresh ones

45

that many families have come to insist on using them the year 'round, except for the short period that each is at its peak fresh. As frozen meats, fish and poultry have come to the retail market in increasing amounts, and the consumer has learned how to use them, they too, have become a "must" in many homes. The wide variety of pre-pared foods and specialities now available adds greatly to the assort-ment of food which can be on hand in the freezer. So the freezer has come to be looked upon as "the supermarket in the kitchen"— with not only a wide selection of food at all times, but food very largely of high quality. The laborious work of home canning has been largely replaced by the far easier task of home freezing. And the tedious, day-by-day job of preparing fruits and vegetables for cooking has been dispensed with to a large extent.

The freezer is a major help in countless ways. Left-overs can go into the freezer to avoid waste, or to avoid using them so soon after they are first served they are not relished to their full extent. Or one can deliberately prepare at one time more than will be needed for one meal, freezing the "planned left-over" for future use.

The need for planning day-to-day meals long in advance, and the need for making extensive shopping lists several times weekly is no longer necessary when one owns a freezer. In planning festive oc-casions, many party dishes can go into the freezer well ahead of the time they will be needed, so that the day of the party is unhurried. Entertaining becomes a real joy, and with a hostess who is happy and who provides an atmosphere of pride and pleasure, guests are happy, too.

Those who own freezers for these reasons are not especially con-cerned with financial savings from them. Just as they look upon their automobile as a source of convenience and pleasure, they look upon their freezer as a means of "more time for better living." There are many families today who enjoy these advantages of owning a home freezer.

For Financial Savings

There are other families—many of them, too—who appreciate these advantages in owning a home freezer, but who are chiefly interested in it because of the financial savings which they can realize from it.

Families counting on financial savings are usually those in rural areas, who freeze large portions of their home-grown fruits, vegetables and meats. It is a well-established fact that families so situated are able not only to make the freezer pay for itself, but before long they have the benefit of real savings in their annual budget.

To do this, good planning is necessary. The farm family that practically "lives out of the freezer" is the one to experience best financial returns from it. A good freezer-owner plans to *use* foods from the freezer, *not* to hoard them for long periods. Especially is this true if the freezer is looked upon as an investment for financial savings. For the freezer to be a money-saver, a good turnover of food in it is essential, and this seems to be the fact that freezer-owners find hardest to believe. The tendency, rather too often, is to look upon the freezer as a place of storage, rather than as the chief source of the family food supply, and this defeats the purpose of economy. The more pounds of home-grown fruits and vegetables and other products that go into the freezer and come out of it during the year, the less is the cost per pound for freezing and storing the food, and so the greater the amount of money saved. For an explanation of this fact, see pp. 68–69.

There are many other ways, too, in which farm families may use their freezers for financial purposes. Those raising poultry and other items for sale may freeze some of them and sell them later when better prices may be obtained. Many women have a reputation for making specialty items like mince or other pies, cakes or chicken à la king, which they can prepare in quantity when convenient and sell later for various occasions. The fine feature of this is that work can be done any time that "business" is slack. Then, too, to avoid the expense of extra help in the kitchen at harvesting or other especially busy seasons, many foods can be prepared ahead and frozen, and they only need to be reheated for serving. Cooking and baking in large amounts at one time, and freezing most of it, saves fuel, too.

Farm families who are accustomed to slaughtering their own beef or other meat, often have to postpone slaughtering until the supply of meat on hand is used, and in the meantime, the animals must be fed. With a freezer, the animals can be slaughtered when it is advantageous to do so, and there are financial savings from the feed not used. Of course, for this to be feasible, facilities must be available for aging the beef after slaughtering and before freezing. In some instances, reliance for this is placed on the weather. But the services of a locker plant may be available for aging the carcass.

The city dweller who wishes to experience financial savings from a home freezer will do so largely by buying frozen foods in large quantities (at reduced prices) or buying marked-down items frequently. Most retail stores have "bargain prices" on numerous frozen foods frequently, and wise purchasing of these will help considerably. Only occasionally are these "seconds" for one reason or another. If a retailer has marked down the price of an item because it did not sell well, it may have been stored too long to be first-class, but it may be entirely satisfactory for some purposes. When a new product is being introduced to the market, it is often sold at a low price to attract the customer. This is the time to stock a good supply of it. Substantial savings are also available by buying meats in large enough quantities to obtain reduced prices. In doing this, it is important to consider the kind and cuts of meat acceptable to the family. No one food should be purchased in such large amounts that it will need to be stored too long before it is used.

In the course of a year, buying ice cream in gallon rather than in pint containers can be a real help to the pocketbook. This is especially true in families with children who want plenty of ice cream in the summer. Many city families buy certain fresh fruits and vegetables in quantity when the price is low at the peak of the season, and freeze them. These sometimes cost less than those purchased frozen.

The suburban dweller is between the farm dweller and the city dweller, so far as financial savings from the freezer go. If considerable produce from the home garden is frozen, savings will be realized from them. Also, the suburban dweller is apt to have special opportunities to purchase good meat at wholesale prices, and such meats in the freezer represent financial savings.

WHAT SIZE FREEZER DO YOU NEED?

Not very many years ago, smaller freezers with 3 to 4 cubic feet capacity, or refrigerators with freezer compartments were the selection of many families. Home freezing and home storage of frozen foods were looked upon as a novelty, and so these small units looked just right. Since then, however, many of these families have come to look upon the freezer not at all as a novelty for occasional use, but as a daily necessity. As the "frozen food habit" has grown in many families, the small units have become entirely inadequate and have been replaced by larger ones whenever space is available.

There are many circumstances which help to determine the size of home freezer which a family should have, and some suggestions in making the choice follow. Too small a freezer is an annoyance, so price alone should not be the determining factor. On the other hand, the investment in a size larger than necessary is an extravagance.

For Farm Families

Since the owner of a freezer on a farm usually depends upon the freezer far more than the city dweller does, the size of the freezer is especially important. It will pay every prospective buyer to spend time *before* making the purchase, in estimating the family needs as accurately as possible, so that the size will be the one to give best service. This is not always an easy task, but it is much better than buying on impulse and being sorry for years afterwards.

On an average, one cubic foot of space in the freezer will store about 35 pounds of food. If much of the food is heavy and compact, like meat, the weight stored per cubic foot will be larger, and on the other hand, if much of the food is baked goods and whole meals, the figure will be smaller. Also, items which take more space are those with irregular shapes like whole poultry. In a freezer filled with considerable variety of foods such as these, the number of pounds per cubic foot may not be more than 30, or even 25. Meat from a whole, baby beef (400 pounds, dressed weight) takes 10–12 cubic feet of storage space (after cutting and packaging).

If at all possible, the prospective buyer should try to figure out how many pounds of fruits, vegetables, meat, prepared foods and commercially frozen foods are apt to be in the freezer at one time. Of course, the full year's supply will not all be in the freezer at one time, but the maximum amount to be taken care of at one time should be estimated.

In making such an estimate, consider the years ahead, during which the freezer will be used. If there are small children in the family now, their food needs will be greatly increased when they are adolescents.

Estimating the amount of food the family uses in the course of a year brings a big surprise to most of us. For instance, think of vegetables alone. It seems reasonable that for good menu planning, each person may be expected to have an average of at least seven servings weekly of the various kinds of vegetables that are apt to come from the freezer. This means at least 350 servings per person in the course of the year, and for a family of five, this will require at least, 1,750 servings. Assuming that a pound package provides three good servings, this will need almost 600 packages. Are you convinced that feeding the family is really "big business?" It certainly is. Next, you will need to consider what portion of the 600 packages will be in the freezer at one time, and this is a matter for each freezer-owner to estimate for herself, according to how many of the vegetables will be frozen during the spring, summer or fall, and how many will be purchased frozen.

Continue like this for other foods to come from the freezer, to estimate your total needs. You are almost bound to be surprised to find out how much food the family uses and so how much freezer space you should have. It is well worth a day's time to consider just what you want in freezer space. The United States Department of Agriculture has made suggestions to help in selecting the size of the freezer, though these may or may not apply to any individual family. They suggest that six cubic feet of freezer space per person will meet the general needs of most families. If freezing is to supplement other methods of preservation, or if a locker plant is to serve as the main source of storage, three cubic feet per person will usually be ample allowance for the home freezer. When most of the food for the year is stored in the home freezer, and there is much overlapping of storage times for the various foods, ten cubic feet per person may not be excessive. If your own estimates seem incredibly high, maybe these average figures will encourage you in making a good choice of size.

Some families wanting a substantial amount of freezer space find that two freezers make a convenient arrangement. One of these can be used chiefly (not exclusively) for freezing, and the other for storage. Both will be needed at high load peak, and maybe sometimes one can be shut off. The two can be placed advantageously for the sake of convenience, with at least one in or near the kitchen and perhaps the other in the basement. This is more expensive than one large freezer, but it is a good plan if you can afford it.

There are occasional families whose needs are far greater than these. Some farm operations require actual rooms for holding food at temperatures similar to those in refrigerators, and also rooms for freezing and storing frozen foods. These are called "walk-in" types and they are often a combination of a zero-room and a cold-storage room. If the user is skillful with tools and is familiar with the proper application of insulation and refrigeration equipment, he may be able himself, to construct a unit of this kind. For instructions for home building of walk-in freezers and cold storage rooms, write to the Agricultural Extension Office of the Experiment Station in your state, many of which have helpful information. But unless the builder is thoroughly competent to undertake this, it is better to purchase a commercially built unit or have one constructed by a reliable contractor or commercial refrigeration dealer.

For City and Suburban Families

Increasing numbers of city families are "living out of the freezer." When they do, they depend chiefly upon commercially frozen foods, and the supply can be replenished when needed. So that as a rule, a somewhat smaller freezer is satisfactory for these families. However, some of the preceding suggestions for the farm dweller will be helpful, too, for city and suburban families.

These families differ widely as to amount of entertaining they do, as to how often they wish to go shopping, and in other respects which determine the size of freezer which best fits their needs.

More often than not, the space available for the freezer will decide the size to be purchased. In many modern homes, especially apartment houses, it is impossible to accommodate the freezer of the first-choice size and so the owner can only do her best with the space she has, planning the frozen food supply accordingly. If there is a choice in the matter, however, don't make the mistake of choosing too small a unit. The difference between the cost of too small a unit and a suitable one readily pays for itself in convenience. A freezer of from 3 to 5 cubic feet capacity per person is recommended for a city or suburban family. If there is space for a unit with 12 to 16 cubic feet, it is seldom wise to choose a smaller one. For some families, having two freezers is a good solution (see p. 50).

This is especially true of suburban dwellers, and they are less apt to be hampered by lack of space. With produce to freeze from the home garden, they may need more space in the freezer, and if not located near a shopping center they may want to count on being able to keep a larger supply of commercially frozen foods on hand. They often keep wholesale purchases of meat in the freezer, too.

WHAT TYPE OF FREEZER SHOULD YOU SELECT?

Basic Features of a Good Freezer

Provides a Satisfactory Temperature.—The most important feature of any freezer is that it should maintain an average temperature of 0°F. or below, even when the surrounding air temperature is as high as 100°F. It is sometimes assumed that this is because otherwise the food will be spoiled in the sense of making us ill, but this is not true. For a discussion of this question, see *How safe to eat are frozen foods?* p. 29. Instead, the low temperature is to prevent loss of quality (palatability) and decrease in vitamin content. For a discussion of this, see *Storage temperature and frozen food quality,* p. 38. The low temperature prevents enzyme activities which would hasten undesirable chemical changes in the food. The enzymes would cause unpleasant flavors, change in color and in some instances decrease in vitamin content. At temperatures of 10°F. or higher, these changes occur more rapidly. Most freezers do maintain the recommended temperature of 0°F. and some provide temperatures of —5°F. or —10°F. These lower temperatures are fine for all foods in the freezer, and are especially advantageous for some foods like pork and precooked foods.

It is important, too, that the temperature should not fluctuate appreciably. Accepted, commercial standards allow the temperature to go two degrees above or below its expected temperature. In a freezer claiming a temperature of 0°F. the temperature near the top of the freezer when it is unloaded should remain between —2°F. and +2°F. and when loaded it should remain between 0°F. and 4°F. If the fluctuation is much greater than this, the ice crystals in the food stored in the freezer will grow and the food may be desiccated (dried out). The temperature in the lower part of the freezer will be somewhat lower than in the top part. But, circulation within the freezer should be such that the temperature throughout is as uniform as possible. The air next to a freezing plate or shelf will be colder than elsewhere.

Good Insulation.—To maintain the low temperature without excessive frost, good insulation around the unit is essential, since it serves to reduce the flow of heat through the cabinet. As a rule, from 3 to 6 inches are recommended around all sides of the unit and almost this much on the lid or door. In a chest type freezer, with the compressor at the bottom, at least this much insulation must be provided at the bottom, between the compressor and the food storage compartment. Good insulation also helps to keep the food cold at any time the power is off. It adds considerably to the size of the freezer, and if good insulating materials requiring less space are manufactured in the future, the exterior size of the freezers will be reduced per given cubic foot of capacity.

A Satisfactory Compressor.—The compressor is the part of the freezing mechanism which keeps the refrigerant in circulation. Most current models have sealed-in compressors. These are rather compact, they need no oiling and they operate quietly and as a rule, exceedingly well. But if one of these goes out of order, it must be replaced. Some freezers may have an open compressor. This type is larger than the sealed in, and is somewhat noisier, but when out of order, it may be repaired by replacing the motor or the belt or valves or other parts.

The size of the compressor is important in determining the efficiency of the freezer and also in determining its life expectancy. The compressor should be large enough so that it runs only about half the time in a room at 90°F. when food is not being frozen. During freezing, it may run continuously until the food reaches the "zone of crystallization." If it is too small and yet maintains the correct temperature in the unit, it will run too much of the time, and provide insufficient reserve for food freezing. Some manufacturers provide larger-than-usual compressors for freezers to be used in freezing large amounts of food. This may be an advantage or it may be an extravagance, depending on the usage. If the owner finds that the compressor seems to be running more than half the time when food is not being frozen, or notices it gets too warm, or if it gets noisy, the service man should be called.

Good Finish and Hardware.—Both the exterior and interior finish of the freezer should be such that the material is durable and easily taken care of. The exterior of most units is metal, coated with baked-on enamel or porcelain, and it should be treated so that it will not rust if it is chipped. A few are stainless steel. The interior is often a similar finish, or it may be aluminum or aluminum alloy.

All the hardware for a freezer needs to be very sturdy and rust-resistant. Most owners want a lock on the freezer, especially if there is any chance it might be located on a porch or in a garage. If the freezer is not equipped with one, it can be purchased.

Good Seals on Lids or Doors.—When frost collects in the freezer, it does so because the difference in the temperature within the freezer and that of the surrounding air drives water vapor into the freezer and there it condenses as frost or ice. The more nearly airtight the freezer is, and the less frequently it is opened, the less frost will collect. Frost on the walls and shelves of the freezer does not interfere with the efficiency of the freezer as much as often assumed, but when it becomes excessive it makes the freezer inconvenient, and it reduces the amount of storage space.

Good seals on all freezer lids or doors (especially on upright models) are extremely important in preventing excessive frost. They are usually a flexible rubber or plastic gasket. Manufacturers have designed numerous devices for good sealing and this explains the differences in construction around the doors and lids of different units. If you find excessive frost collecting around the door or lid of your unit, call your service man.

Features of Frost-Free Freezers.—In some current upright freezers, complete defrosting is entirely automatic every 24 hours. An electric timer automatically starts and stops defrosting, daily. The defrost water drips into a trough and through a drain into a drain pan. Ordinarily, the defrost water is evaporated by heat from the refrigeration system, but during periods of high or prolonged humidity, the pan should be checked weekly, to see if it needs emptying. In these frost-free freezers, the zero temperature is maintained by constant circulation of freezing air, carrying moisture away from the shelves and food packages.

In at least some of the frost-free models, frost does not collect at all in the food compartments. Manufacturers tell us that while the temperature of the air in the frost-free freezers may vary considerably during the defrosting cycle, in those with fan-blown-air circulation, the temperature of the food remains relatively constant. This is an important feature, for if the temperature of the food fluctuates, desiccation and loss of quality occur. If this happens in your freezer, the food will not remain in good condition for the periods ordinarily recommended for storage. So if you are thinking of purchasing a frost-free model, find out whether the manufacturer gives assurance of a relatively constant food temperature during the defrosting cycle.

In these frost-free freezers with fan-blown-air circulation, good packaging materials and good methods for sealing them are important, since there is a tendency otherwise for desiccation to occur during storage.

There are other freezers which are self-defrosting, but not automatic. When you turn a switch, the freezer defrosts itself quickly.

Control of Temperature and Warning Signals.—In practically all freezers nowadays, the temperature is well controlled. In some units, a control is provided for the owner to use in securing a choice of temperatures, none of which are too high for good usage. Such a control usually provides the possibility of having an especially low temperature to use when food is being frozen.

It is important that there be some way for the owner to know whether her freezer is operating properly, and maintaining the necessary temperature. Manufacturers have devised several ways of doing this. The most usual is to have the freezer equipped with a signal light on the outside of the unit, which continues to burn as long as the freezer temperature is normal. The light usually stops burning when the freezer temperature goes up to $+15°F$.

If this signal light is not burning, you will want to find out at once what the trouble is. Assuming that the electric power in your neighborhood is not off, here are ways to find out the cause of the trouble:

(1) Find out if the signal light bulb has merely burned out (try another one in its place).

(2) If the unit is provided with an interior light, see if it is burning; if it is, the freezer is connected with the electric current.

(3) See if the temperature control for the freezer has accidentally been turned to the "off" position, if the control has this position.

(4) See if the freezer plug has accidentally been pulled out of the wall outlet, or if a house fuse has blown.

If none of these explains why the signal light is not burning, call your service man at once, for the trouble is probably with the motor in your freezer.

Some freezers are equipped with an alarm which gives a signal when the temperature gets too high. The battery for this needs to be kept in good condition. An alarm is especially appropriate if the freezer is to be in the basement or where a signal light might not be noticed. It is a splendid idea to have a thermometer and be able to check the temperature yourself, from time to time. You can purchase one, but be sure to get one with a temperature range low enough to use in the freezer.

Chest or Horizontal Freezers

These are freezers of low, horizontal design, with the lid opening upward. The lid opens with a feather-touch, and has a device for holding the door open while food is being put in or taken out. With the opening of the door, a light floods the interior. This type of freezer requires more floor space than an upright one of the same capacity, but the top provides work space for the kitchen or other room where it is placed.

Most of the units nowadays have only one door, but have a compartment for freezing, separate from the storage space. In such a freezing compartment, a lower temperature is provided. However, at least one manufacturer is making a freezer without such a freezing compartment, but instead, all the walls of the freezer are lined with a metal which gives rapid freezing in all parts of the freezer.

The chief problem encountered in using this chest or horizontal type of freezer is the difficulty of reaching to the bottom of the freezer (usually about 30 inches). The result is that there may be a tendency to let products remain in remote corners of the freezer too long, perhaps until the food is all rearranged as in defrosting. This is poor practice, since the quality of the food is impaired by too long storage. Naturally, manufacturers are trying to find ways of overcoming this problem. Most units have toe space at the front of the freezer, and this helps in reaching into the freezer. And one manufacturer has provided sloping sides, making the freezer narrower at the bottom than the top.

Many devices are available to help in an orderly storage of food in these freezers, and in making the packages more accessible. Some units have adjustable dividers or partitions which separate the storage part of the freezer into compartments for holding different kinds of food. Baskets and racks of different sizes are often provided for holding packages, including special racks for pies and cakes. Some baskets are arranged so as to slide to and fro, and this makes it easy to reach packages under them. If the baskets do not slide, they should not be too large, for then they would be very heavy to lift when filled. All these, and other devices are helpful, and the ingenious freezer-owner will find additional ways of organizing her freezer contents. One suggestion is to place together in one container, all packages of the same kind of food. For instance, all packages of strawberries could be placed in one bag, and labelled so that the contents are evident at a glance. This is a good way to give oneself a warning to replenish the supply when necessary, too. Large, plastic bags may be used for this purpose, and even large, sturdy paper bags from the grocery store. Mesh bags from sports stores are useful, too.

Upright Freezers

These are tall in design, with the door opening outward, and from the outside they look much like refrigerators. The door opens easily (in some units, even from the inside) and on being opened, the interior is flooded with light. In some units, immediately after placing warm foods in the freezer, or after having the door open more than usual, the door may not open easily. This is caused by a temporary vacuum inside the freezer, due to the effective door seal. Just wait a few minutes, and the door will open easily.

These freezers occupy less floor space than horizontal ones of the same capacity, but remember that room space is needed to allow for opening the door. As already mentioned, the chief problem in using the horizontal type of freezer is that of reaching down to the bottom of the freezer (about 30 inches). The problem in the upright type of freezer is that of reaching to the back of the freezer, but this is only about 18 inches. An advantage of the horizontal type in this connection is that while moving packages around, you can always place them temporarily on top of others in the freezer. Such space for temporary holding is not always available in upright freezers. But in some, there are tilt-down grilles in front of the shelves. These are to use as temporary shelves or trays, while rearranging packages in the freezer.

All the upright freezers have several shelves, similar in appearance to the shelves of a refrigerator. Most of these are freezing plates, but some units have adjustable shelves for storage only, which slide in and out to facilitate getting the food. Toward the bottom of the freezer they usually have sliding baskets for the same purpose. Also, some have drawers which slide in and out, much like the drawers of a filing cabinet. All these sliding devices are helpful, if frost does not collect in such a way as to make them difficult to move.

One good idea is that the food for storage be arranged so that most of any one kind of food will be found on one shelf. With this in mind, some manufacturers suggest the most advantageous arrangement for the food to be stored in their units. Most freezers have a bookshelf type of storage on the inside of the door, and a dispenser for a good supply of fruit juices.

A number of upright freezers also have a special arrangement for ice cubes. This is an ice-cube ejector with trays, which zips out cubes at the touch of a lever, and stores them without having them stick together.

Refrigerator-Food-Freezers

These are a combination of refrigerator and freezer, and they are popular in homes where space does not permit a separate unit for frozen food. To qualify as a freezer, however, the freezer compartment must maintain a temperature of approximately 0°F. If the temperature, instead, is +15°F. or +20°F. it is a conventional ice-cube compartment (see below).

Ice-Cube Compartments

These usually maintain an air temperature of +15°F. or +20°F., and they are not to be confused with freezers, since the temperature is substantially higher than that of freezers. Also, there is usually greater fluctuation in temperature in these compartments, and this affects food adversely. Since they are recommended sometimes for storing frozen foods for short periods, and even in some instances for freezing, they are occasionally spoken of as "freezers." It is a mistake to assume that because the package of food remains hard (does not thaw) the quality of the food is unchanged. To be sure, few, if any, micro-organisms (bacteria, yeast and molds) will grow at this temperature, so the food will not spoil in the usual sense of spoilage.

But other changes can take place which makes the food inferior from the standpoints of taste, color, odor and nutritive value. Some foods will begin to deteriorate after a day or two at these temperatures, others may be satisfactory for a couple of weeks, if they have been well packaged. But they should not be stored in the ice-cube compartment for longer than this.

These compartments cannot be used to any great extent for freezing. With the refrigerator turned to its coldest temperature, two or three packages of food may be frozen at a time, if each package is placed directly on the metal plate. The plate must be dry, for otherwise the package will be frozen to it.

WHERE WILL YOU PLACE YOUR FREEZER?

So far as the operation of the freezer is concerned, there are only a few things which are imperative regarding its location. It must not be placed where it is excessively damp, since any metal parts may be damaged. If the floor under it is damp, place a long block of wood underneath each side, raising the freezer an inch or two. In a very damp place, furthermore, moisture may condense on the outer walls of the freezer and even drip to form pools on the floor. Also, the freezer should be placed in a well-ventilated room. Most manufacturers strongly recommend that a few inches be left free around all sides of the freezer, to allow warm air to escape from the condenser, though there are a few units for which this is not a requirement. It must not be placed in direct sunlight. It costs somewhat more to operate the freezer if the room temperature is very high, but if the freezer is well insulated this difference is not great. Neither should the freezer be placed where the temperature is below 40°F., unless the particular unit has been specifically designed to operate at low temperatures. So a room of moderate temperature is best.

It would be easy to forget that freezers are very heavy, and when filled with food they are still heavier, and that the floor where the unit is to be placed must be able to carry the load. The dealer from whom you buy your freezer can tell you the weight of the freezer when it is filled with food, and you need to be sure the floor will carry the weight. Upright freezers put more weight per square foot on the floor, than horizontal ones of the same cubic capacity. Be sure that the freezer rests solidly on the floor and is level.

Assuming that these basic requirements concerning the place for the freezer have been taken care of, then convenience should be the consideration. In most families, the freezer is opened numerous times daily, and so the most convenient arrangement, by far, is to have it in or near the kitchen. A utility room or hallway adjoining the kitchen is often a good location. It may be placed in a garage attached to the house, if the temperature there is not too cold in the winter (see above).

If you are thinking of placing the freezer in the basement, several things need to be taken into account. Be sure the freezer can be taken through the necessary doorways and down the stairway. For safety of those carrying food up and down stairs, be sure the stairway is well lighted and well constructed. This is nevertheless not convenient for the owner, unless perhaps she can bring the day's supply up from the basement at one time, and store it in the ice-cube compartment of the refrigerator. If there is to be a second freezer, used chiefly for freezing, the basement may be a good place for it, provided, as mentioned above, that questions of dampness do not pose a problem.

WHERE WILL YOU BUY YOUR FREEZER AND WHICH BRAND?

A very important consideration in deciding where the freezer will be purchased is that you are able to arrange for prompt and reliable servicing. Even in the best makes of freezers, as in the best makes of automobiles, there are apt to be occasional electrical or mechanical failures. If an emergency arises, you will want to be able to rely upon the people who have the responsibility for servicing it. So you should find out before you buy it, whether needed parts and competent service personnel will be available and whether you can count upon good servicing when you need it. Having started out with such assurance, all the better if you never need to call for help.

No matter how good your faith in your dealer may be, it is better for his sake and yours, to have a written warranty concerning the freezer. All of the better freezer manufacturers nowadays provide a warranty as standard practice. The manufacturer usually guarantees the entire freezer for one year, and guarantees the refrigerating system for five years. In addition, most manufacturers insure the owner against food spoilage due to mechanical or structural failure, or if the freezer fails to maintain an appropriate temperature for a specified number of hours following power interruption.

Choosing between different makes or brands is not easy. Remember, however, that manufacturers operate on a highly competitive basis and this is especially true of nationally advertised brands which are all well known. From a strictly selfish standpoint, each wants to be able to claim and prove superiority. Each one realizes that its good reputation depends on good customer relations, and if this had not been well established, the manufacturer would not have remained in business. Since the buyer has no way of checking the manufacturer's claims as to what the unit will do, she is dependent upon his word. A manufacturer stakes his reputation on the promises he makes to you, and good companies cannot afford to make false promises.

You may well say in response to this, that if all buyers choose well-known brands, new or less-well-known manufacturers are not given an opportunity to make the good reputation they may well deserve. This is very true. Whether to give one of the new, or less-well-known manufacturers a chance to prove its worth is the decision of the individual buyer. But if perchance, the company manufacturing your unit were to go out of business while you are still using it, you might not be able to replace parts when necessary, and this would be disconcerting, to say the least.

HOW BEST TO USE YOUR FREEZER

Some questions concerning the use of your freezer have been discussed in the preceding pages. Here are some other suggestions:

For Freezing

If your freezer is equipped with a set of controls for providing different temperatures, you may need to set the control for the freezing temperature. See the manufacturer's instructions for this.

When the food has been properly prepared for freezing, and well packaged, you are ready to freeze it. The manufacturer tells you where the food should be placed in the freezer for freezing. In some (not all) units, there are special shelves or compartments for freezing, and it is important to follow the manufacturer's instructions. Here are a couple of *Don'ts,* in this connection:

Don't: place a package of food to be frozen in contact with one already frozen, for the temperature of the frozen food will rise and this will impair its quality.

Don't: stack packages to be frozen, since this slows down freezing (especially of the packages in the center of the stack). Leave about an inch between packages for good circulation of air.

The amount of food which should be frozen at one time in any freezer is limited. Freezing more than this would result in prolonging the freezing process, and may also increase the temperature of the freezer. The freezer manufacturer usually tells you how much may be frozen at one time in your freezer, and these instructions should be followed carefully. The United States Department of Agriculture recommends that the freezing load be limited to one-fifteenth, or at most one-tenth of the total capacity of the freezer, since this is usually the maximum quantity of food that can be frozen and reduced to storage temperature in 24 hours.

How long it will be before the foods are frozen will depend on a number of things. For instance, fruits frozen with considerable sugar will take longer than vegetables, and a large package of solid food like meat will take longer than a small package. Assuming that you have followed the manufacturer's instructions as to the amount to freeze in your unit at one time, 24 hours is a safe time to allow for the food to be frozen. After this time, arrange the frozen packages for storage. If you turned the control down for a freezing temperature, you are now ready to turn it back to storage temperature.

For Storage

For a description of storage facilities in freezers, see the preceding descriptions of chest and upright freezers. A good librarian looks upon her library as a place where books are easily obtained and used freely, rather than a place for hoarding them in remote shelves. In a similar fashion, a good freezer-owner looks upon her freezer as a place where good food is available at a moment's notice, rather than a place where frozen foods are stored for long periods.

There are a number of very important reasons why food should not be stored too long. Recommended storage periods for specific foods are given in connection with detailed instructions for freezing. Prolonged storage increases the storage cost of food, too. The cost of electricity for operating the freezer is practically the same, whether 300 or 600 pounds of frozen foods pass through the same unit in the course of the year. So the larger the amount of food passing through the unit, the less the storage cost per pound. Storing foods for long periods makes a good turnover impossible. For an explanation of these statements, see pp. 68–69.

From a practical standpoint, the problems known to every freezer-owner are arranging the food so that it is easily accessible, and keeping track of the contents so they will be used and replenished in good time. Freezers nowadays have many devices which help in an orderly arrangement, and to aid the owner to keep track of the contents of their units, numerous excellent plans for keeping inventory have been suggested. Sheets for keeping such records are available, listing the date each product was frozen and when products are taken out, so that at a glance one has a picture of just what is in the freezer. This sounds like the easy, natural and best answer to the problem, and so it may seem surprising that, according to surveys, few women keep such an inventory. Maybe as time goes on, we shall take more happily to the task of keeping written records.

WHAT CARE DOES YOUR FREEZER NEED?

Some of the ways in which your freezer needs care and watching have been mentioned in the preceding pages. Others will be discussed now.

When You First Buy Your Freezer

When you have decided to buy a freezer, you will need to arrange for electric current for it. The best plan is to have a separate line for the freezer outlet to the house distribution box, with nothing except the freezer installed on this line.

The new freezer may need an initial cleaning before you connect it with the electric current. To do this, wash the interior with a warm solution of baking soda (1–3 tbsp. per quart of water), rinse it with clear water and dry it. Then close the lid or door and connect it with the electric current. Do not use an outlet which is controlled by a wall switch or pull cord, since someone might accidentally turn off the current. The unit will run continuously for several hours after connecting it.

About four hours after turning on the current, you can safely load the freezer with frozen foods. Do not use the equipment for freezing for 12 or preferably 24 hours. After this, the freezer should take care of itself. However, note the suggestions on the preceding pages for special attention it may need. Try to plan your needs so as to open the door (or lid) no more than necessary, and never keep it open for long.

For the exterior surface, as a rule, just wiping with a warm, mild soap solution is sufficient. For stubborn stains, special cleaners are available, but never use gritty soaps or hard abrasive cleaners. Wax occasionally, if you wish, with special waxes available for use on the kind of surface which your freezer has.

Defrosting

The only real work in taking care of a freezer is the very occasional defrosting which is necessary in most models. Even for a large, farm family, this need not be done more than once or twice a year as a rule, unless the air is very humid. Choose a time when the stock is lowest (often late winter or early spring, before you begin freezing your own fruits and vegetables), so there will be the least amount of food to be handled. It is important that the freezer be defrosted before there is more than ¼ to ½ inch of frost over much of the surface, since excessive frost decreases the storage capacity and makes the freezer inconvenient to use.

If no great amount of frost has collected, and you do not feel the freezer needs a thorough cleaning, the defrosting can be a rather simple matter, particularly if there is not very much food in the freezer. In this case, maybe you can merely move the packages from one place to another in the unit, scraping frost from the surface as you do this. Use a plastic scraper, and if possible, one which is cup-shaped to collect the frost as it falls. *Never use a tool which might scratch the surface,* for this might damage the refrigerating tubes or coils just beneath the surface.

Collect the frost as it falls, on a tray, Turkish towel, or papers, and get it into the sink before it melts. When all the frost has been removed, arrange the food in the freezer and close the lid or door.

However, if you have not only frost but glazed frost or ice, or if the freezer needs a thorough cleaning, then you have a bigger operation. Disconnect the freezer from the electric current, and remove all packages of food. If there is room in your refrigerator, some of it may be held there. Place the remainder in cartons or on trays or heavy layers of newspaper. Stack the packages tightly together, so they will help keep each other cold, and cover tightly with a number of layers of newspaper or with a heavy blanket or other insulating material. Have all these ready before you disconnect the freezer. If possible, keep these packages in a cool place during the defrosting.

At once, scrape off as much frost as possible, before it melts, since it is easier to dispose of frost than of water. Then, to speed up the melting of the ice, place pans of hot water on the shelves or on the bottom of the freezer. *Do not pour hot water over any refrigerating surface,* since this would damage the refrigerating system. It further speeds up defrosting to place a portable fan so that it throws warm air into the freezer, and cold air out of it. Remove layers of frost or ice as soon as they can be loosened from the surfaces, and before much of the ice has been melted. As defrosting continues, wipe up any water with cloths or a sponge, and clean non-refrigerating shelves and removable parts.

Some units have a drain at the bottom for draining off water. See the manufacturer's instructions for using this.

Wash the interior with a warm (*not hot*) solution of baking soda (1–3 tbsp. per quart of water), then rinse with clear water and dry the surface.

Very seldom will you have any unpleasant odor in your freezer, due to food spoilage, but if this appears, the above cleaning will probably remove it. If it persists, however, try washing the surface with vinegar (1 cup to a gallon of water), or with a solution of warm water and baking soda (1 tsp. of soda to each quart of water). An electric heater placed inside the freezer, or a toaster, may drive out the odor, or a wick-type air freshener may help. After using any of these which might themselves have an odor, leave the door or lid open for a while and drive out the odor with an electric fan.

Then you are ready to connect the freezer with the electricity. Let it run half an hour or so before putting food back into it. This defrosting should not take more than a couple of hours, unless you have trouble with stubborn odors, and this very seldom happens. At the time of reloading, you have a splendid opportunity to make a note of just what you have on hand, and to start an inventory if you have not had one before. Certainly, notice any foods which have been stored for a considerable time, and earmark them to be used soon.

Cleaning the Frost-Free Freezer

Freezers which are self-defrosting need to be kept clean. For this purpose, a thorough cleaning every 6 to12 months is recommended. This is done just as for defrosting the freezer which had frost collected in it, but of course there is no frost to be removed. Have arrangements ready for temporary storage of the food, disconnect the freezer from the electric current, and pack foods compactly in well-insulated arrangements, as in defrosting. Clean and dry the interior and finally replace the food in the freezer, exactly as suggested above, for the unit from which frost was removed.

When the Freezer Stops Running

No matter how good your automobile is, it may stall once in a while, and experience tells us it does not always do this at the most convenient time. So with a home freezer. At the time of purchasing it, secure complete instructions as to what to do if this should happen, especially if it should happen during a week-end when most offices are closed. A large, well-stocked freezer represents a substantial investment in food, and advance arrangements for taking care of it in an emergency are rewarded. Remember, however, that most manufacturers provide a warranty against food spoilage due to mechanical fault of the freezer, or due to interruption of electrical power.

For deciding what the trouble is, when the motor is not running, see suggestions on p. 55.

The first question the owner wants answered, when she finds the freezer is not running, is how long before the food will spoil if it is left right in the freezer. The larger the freezer, the more nearly fully loaded it is, the better insulated it is, and the colder the surrounding air, the longer before the food will be damaged. In a 4 to 6 cubic foot freezer, with the lid or door kept closed, food is not apt to begin to spoil in less than 3 or 4 days. In a freezer of 12 to 35 cubic foot capacity, this time is more apt to be five days. As a rule, the freezer will be back in working order within these periods.

As soon as you realize the freezer is not operating properly, let your service man know, and he should attend to it promptly. Get an estimate from him as to when it will be back in working order, then make your plans accordingly. If it is not apt to be running within 24 hours, you may want to get a supply of Dry Ice which is usually available at an ice cream dealer or cold storage warehouse. From 25 to 35 pounds will protect the freezer for this long if the temperature is moderate, but in hot weather, 50 pounds is better. Replenish this supply every 24 to 36 hours until power is resumed. Have the Dry Ice sawed into thick pieces, and place them near the top of the unit if it is a horizontal one (so the cold air will flow down through the freezer), or place some on top of the food on each shelf of an upright unit, with a board or several layers of heavy cardboard between the packages and the Dry Ice.   When handling Dry Ice, wear gloves— *never handle it with your bare hands,* for it will freeze your fingers. As soon as the freezer is running again, remove the Dry Ice.

Do not open the freezer at all, while it is not operating, except to add Dry Ice, or to remove food for an emergency.   And do not open it for several hours after it has been put back into operation.

If you do not have assurance that the freezer will be running within the time you can keep the food in good condition (this happens very seldom), arrange to move the food to the nearest locker plant or other zero storage.   Before opening the freezer, have all the containers ready for transferring the food, much like the containers for temporary storage during defrosting (see p. 64).   Get the food into well-insulated containers as quickly as possible, and make the trip to the storage room at once.

If Frozen Food is Partially Thawed

What to do about foods which have partially thawed is one of the questions most frequently asked by freezer-owners.   If all the packages in the freezer are still hard, you can refreeze them without serious damage to any of them.   If the contents are rather soft, you are less fortunate.   In this case, follow the suggestions given below for different kinds of foods.   The suggestions apply, too, if you allow packages of frozen food which you purchased at the store, to thaw before you get them in your freezer.

Fruits.—Of the various foods in the freezer, these are probably the least damaged by partial thawing.   Fruits which have thawed even to the extent of beginning to ferment can be tasted, without danger, to test them.   Open a few packages, and smell and taste them.   If they seem satisfactory, you can refreeze them.   They will not be so palatable when you serve them, but they are perfectly safe to eat.   If you prefer not to have so much second-rate frozen fruit on hand, use some of it right away for cooking, or use some of it in making jellies, jams or preserves.

Vegetables.—On opening a package of vegetables, if you find some ice crystals, the vegetables can be refrozen.   As mentioned above for fruits, the vegetables will not be so palatable, but there is no danger in eating them. But if the vegetables seem to be completely thawed, do not refreeze them. However, if the vegetables are still quite cold and seem to be in good condition (appearance and color), it is probably safe to cook them thoroughly at once, and serve them. But if they seem at all questionable, do not taste them but dispose of them. Spoiled vegetables can be dangerous to eat.

Shellfish and Cooked Foods (such as stews and creamed dishes).— Make your decision as to what to do about these, in the same way as for vegetables. When spoiled, these foods can be a health hazard.

Meat, Fish and Poultry.—These become unsafe to eat when they start to spoil, so you need to examine each package before you decide what to do with it. If the product still contains some ice crystals, it may be refrozen, though it will be somewhat drier. If it is completely thawed but still cold, cook it thoroughly at once, then you can eat it or refreeze the cooked product. *If the odor or appearance of the product makes you question it, by all means dispose of it without tasting it.*

Refreezing of thawed food should be done as quickly as possible. If your freezer is largely filled with partially thawed food (at the stage where refreezing can be done), the best plan may be to get it to a locker plant or other zero storage room and have it refrozen where adequate facilities are available. For the trip to the zero storage location, wrap the foods as suggested on p. 64, for defrosting the freezer.

THE COST OF OPERATING YOUR FREEZER

You will be interested in knowing the various costs which should be taken into account in operating your freezer. The figures below are taken from the United States Department of Agriculture *Home and Garden Bulletin,* No. 48, revised in 1961. They are used to compute a year's cost for home freezing exclusive of the cost of the food itself. The example is based on the use of a $300, 12-cubic-foot freezer (360 pound capacity) with three conditions—no turnover of frozen food, a turnover of 50 per cent and one of 150 per cent. Since all costs except those for packaging and freezing food remain the same, regardless of the quantity of food in the freezer, the higher the rate of turnover, the lower the cost per pound of food, as the figures show.

**Cost Per Pound of Freezing and Storing Food in a Home Freezer
with Three Rates of Turnover**

Expenditure item	360 lbs. of food	540 lbs. of food	900 lbs. of food
Net depreciation (15 years' expected life, 3 per cent interest, compounded annually)	$16.39	$16.39	$16.39
Return on investment foregone (3 per cent interest, compounded semi-annually)	11.26	11.26	11.26
Repairs (2 per cent of purchase price)	6.00	6.00	6.00
Electricity for			
Freezing food (0.1 kw.-hr. per lb. at 2½ cents per kw.-hr.)	0.90	1.35	2.25
Maintaining 0°F. (0.25 kw.-hr. per cu. ft. per 24 hr. at 2½ cents per kw.-hr.)	27.38	27.38	27.38
Packaging (2 cents per lb.)	7.20	10.80	18.00
Total cost	$69.13	$73.18	$81.28
Cost per pound of food	$ 0.19	$ 0.135	$ 0.09

Courtesy of United States Department of Agriculture, from *Home and Garden Bulletin, No. 48.*

So the difference in the cost per pound of food, according to the turnover, shows very clearly the financial advantages of a good turnover of food throughout the year. This explains the suggestion on p. 47 that a farm family interested in the freezer as a money-saver should freeze as much as possible for the annual food supply. The chief costs are those of owning the freezer and maintaining the temperature of 0°F. The operating costs are just the same, whether the freezer is only half full or filled to capacity. It costs somewhat more to operate in very hot weather, but the difference is not great if the unit is well insulated. The life expectancy of the freezer is conservatively estimated at 15 years, but many freezers will be in good condition for longer than this.

AN IMPORTANT WARNING ABOUT YOUR DISCARDED FREEZER

Children are often very curious about the inside of a refrigerator or freezer. Don't let this curiosity cost the life of a child in your freezer. Since it is airtight, human life will not survive in it for long, and children have lost their lives in them. When you have finished with yours, remove the latches or lids (or doors), or take some precaution that will make it harmless.

CHAPTER 5

Locker Plant Services and Freezer Food Plans

INTRODUCTION

Modern locker plant services and freezer food plans are the result of several decades of development in these branches of the industry. These services are of interest to families with limited freezer space, and also to those with ample facilities for freezing food at home and storing it. The growth of some of these services indicates clearly that many families are taking advantage of the opportunities they offer. Many other families, on the other hand, are not as aware of them as they might be. Following is a description of these services.

LOCKER PLANT SERVICES

Locker plants really pioneered in providing facilities for preparing foods for freezing, for freezing and storing frozen foods, long before home freezers were plentiful. As the number and sizes of home freezers have increased, there has been less need for storage space in lockers, and so the number of locker plants has decreased. However, in 1961, there were nine thousand plants throughout the United States, and they provide valuable services to many families.

If your own freezer is ever out of order and you do not have assurance that it will be running again within the time the food in it will remain in good condition, you will be glad to make arrangements to have a locker plant store your frozen foods temporarily (see p. 67).

Rental of locker space is a service which all locker plants offer. The lockers usually range in size from 3 to 8 cubic feet. The most popular size is six cubic feet, storing from 150 to 250 pounds of frozen foods. Some of the lockers are drawer-type which pull out, others are cupboard-type with doors which open. The choice is just a matter of personal preference. The lockers are exceedingly useful for families without their own freezers, and for those with limited freezer space. Then too, even families with rather large freezers are apt to find from time to time that they need additional space for freezing food or storing it, and the combination of a locker and a freezer has real advantages from the standpoints of both convenience and economy. Just as in a home freezer, the locker should maintain a constant temperature of at least as low as 0°F. And as for a home freezer, to make good use of a locker, financially, it pays to have a good "turnover" of the foods in it (see pp. 68–69).

Courtesy of Freezer Provisioning

In a meat processing room like this, meat is cut and wrapped for freezing. These processing plants supply frozen meats in large quantities to home freezer owners and locker users

The kinds of service available, in addition to locker rental, vary greatly from plant to plant. Many plants will slaughter farm animals, chill, age and cut the carcass (see p. 136), and they will wrap and freeze the meat. If the plant itself does not do the slaughtering, they will often arrange to have this done for you. Before arranging to have the meat handled at a locker plant, however, it is a good idea to become acquainted with its facilities.   Everything should be scrupulously clean, since meat is readily contaminated by unclean knives, meat block and aprons.   Most modern locker plants do have high standards of sanitation.   Discuss with the locker plant manager just how you want your meat cut (size of roasts and steaks, and how much of the meat should be ground) so it will fit your family needs.   Be sure, too, that the plant uses wrapping material which is suitable for meats (see p. 141).   Find out what the charges for these and other services are.   If you can adjust the time of slaughtering, plan it so the locker plant will not be too busy, then you can expect the best of service.   Some plants will buy portions of the carcass which you do not want.   And many of them will cure and smoke meats, will render lard and make sausage.   In addition to providing processing services, many locker plants sell meat.   Quite a few have meat departments in which fresh meat is sold at retail; the great majority also sell meat in wholesale quantities—sides, quarters and primal cuts.

Some locker plants will prepare fruits and vegetables for freezing, wrap and freeze them for you.   If you plan to have them do this, be sure the produce will be frozen without delay to avoid loss of quality.

Locker plant services are also very useful when you want to freeze so much at one time that doing it all in your own freezer would overload the freezer (see p. 62).   If you want to prepare your own fruits vegetables, meats, poultry or other foods, and wrap them, be sure to take them promptly to the locker plant and have them frozen promptly.

If there is a locker plant near your hunting or fishing camp, the operator will usually be glad to give your game or fish prompt attention.   Then you can take it home, frozen, in an insulated container with Dry Ice.   This is a good way to avoid loss of quality through delay in freezing it.

The locker plant often carries a good assortment of packaging and other supplies, and may sell commercially frozen foods.   And experts are usually on hand, who will gladly help you with any of your problems in food freezing or in using frozen foods.   So when you make a trip to the plant, be prepared with the questions you would like to ask.   Most plants are pleased to be of service.

FREEZER FOOD PLANS

Freezer food plans had their beginning in the early 1950's, and like many enterprises in their early stages, the selling practices of some of the firms going into this business were far from sound. Unfair profits were realized from the sale of freezers. Prospective customers were given to understand they would make large financial savings by buying meat in large quantities, but some families buying a side of beef, for instance, found that a considerable portion of such meat did not suit their family needs at all. Many of these firms remained in business for only a short time when people found that they had grossly exaggerated the savings claims.

It did not take long for such unethical companies to go out of business. Unfortunately, because of these activities, freezer food plans gained a poor reputation, and the public became skeptical of them. But many of the firms which were primarily engaged in the selling of food on a food plan basis continued to conduct their business legitimately and many other firms have launched successful operations.

In a freezer food plan, the customer buys the freezer and a supply of frozen foods for it on an installment plan. It is usually expected that the food will be paid for by the time it is all used (usually four months), and the freezer is usually paid for in two years. After the first food order is consumed (and paid for), the firm continues to supply bulk meat and frozen food orders on a financed basis, each order being delivered to the home and placed right in the freezer. Firms doing this kind of business call themselves by various names— freezer provisioners, frozen food centers, home food service firms and food plans. Some of them also rent locker space to customers wanting it. By the early part of 1961, there were almost 1,500 home freezer plans throughout the United States, supplying frozen foods to three million families. And a substantial proportion of home freezers which are sold nowadays, are sold through these plans.

For Convenience and Service

For many families, purchasing the freezer and a supply of frozen food with it on an installment plan is a help in planning a budget. Practically all of the firms have trained food counselors who call at the home when the customer begins the freezer plan, to help make the food selection one which is suited to the family needs. It is this long range planning of food procurement and use which led to the name "food plan." The counselor is available after that, for advice in the selection and use of frozen foods. Future frozen food orders are placed at 4 to 6 month intervals, and may be made by telephone, by mail or by a personal call at the firm's office. The need for shopping

Courtesy of Freezer Provisioning

Freezer food plans and similar organizations arrange to have a trained food counselor call on the homemaker to give helpful information in getting the most from her freezer and in using her frozen foods to best advantage

expeditions for frozen foods is entirely dispensed with. The customer is expected to order only the food she wants, and the supply she needs becomes evident with a little experience and the help of the counselor. The firms carry a complete line of frozen foods, so their customers can depend on them entirely for their supply.

In all cases, the firm delivers the frozen foods to the home, packing the food in the home freezer under the supervision of the homemaker. Food plan services may also be available to families not buying a freezer from the firm. Some establishments, which sell freezers with their food plan, make their food services available to families already owning a freezer if they will obtain "membership" in their organization. Firms which do not sell freezers but which offer their meat and frozen foods on a food plan basis usually sell to anyone, without requiring purchase of a "membership."

The freezers are always accompanied by factory warranties for the freezers themselves, and also warranties in case of food spoilage due to mechanical trouble in the freezer or due to power failure.

For Quality

A distinctive feature of all the better freezer provisioning or food plan firms is their insistence on high quality in their frozen foods. They sell only United States Inspected and Graded meats, and many of them do not carry any grade below Choice. They also use only Grade A or Fancy fruits and vegetables. Some of them give a guarantee of satisfaction with every food order that is sold. They also guarantee that the frozen foods are held continuously at 0°F. or lower during storage and delivery, thereby assuring no loss of quality due to high temperature.

For Economy

Meats are sold to consumers in wholesale or near-wholesale amounts, and in a selection of only the kinds the family wants. In doing this, the meat bill for a year is often from 10 to 20 per cent less than the same purchases would cost retail. Fruits and vegetables are purchased in lots of 6 to 12 packages, again providing savings through bulk prices. Other foods may be purchased in bulk, too.

However, the effect of the food plan on the family budget depends entirely on the customer's planning. With the opportunity so easily available of selecting luxury-type foods delivered right to the freezer and readily prepared in the kitchen, the dining room table can achieve a new kind of enjoyment—but the food budget can reach an all-time high. Families that can afford this are delighted with it.

On the other hand, financial savings can be realized if plans to do this are carefully made, and the help of the food counselor is available for this purpose. Anyone who is experienced in food buying knows that careful planning is essential, to keep within a food budget. Customers buying their frozen foods on a food plan are no exception.

Some freezer provisioning firms claim that savings derived from the plan will make the freezer pay for itself in a year or two. While this is no doubt possible, others take the more realistic view that, with good planning, the freezer can provide better eating for the entire family at little or no increase in cost.

Precautions

Just how can you tell whether the firm with which you are considering signing a contract is a reliable one? There are several ways. Read and understand the contract before you sign it, as in signing an arrangement for any business transaction. Learn just what you will pay for the freezer. Compare this with the price you would pay for a freezer of the same size, made by a reputable manufacturer, purchased from another source. And note the charge for financing it. Be sure there are satisfactory warranties for the freezer and for food spoilage.

Be wary of firms which are selling freezers but which only pretend to be in the frozen food business. And be wary of firms promising fabulous financial savings. The more reliable ones promote their business on the basis of convenience, service and quality, with financial savings as an additional possibility. Be sure you are at liberty to buy only the frozen foods you want—that you are not obligated to buy a side or quarter of beef, for instance, if you do not want it.

In 1955, locker plant and freezer provisioning members of the National Institute of Locker and Freezer Provisioners adopted a code of ethics covering freezer food plan selling practices. This group has done a good deal to keep the industry on a sound basis. It works with Chambers of Commerce and Better Business Bureaus throughout the nation. The Bureau in your locality may be able to tell you whether the firm with which you are considering dealing is a reliable one.

For the Future

This branch of the frozen food industry is well established, and there is every reason to expect it to continue to grow. Convenience, service and quality are considered the main reasons for its success, with financial savings a fourth possibility. Particularly for married women working outside the home, freedom from frozen-food shopping is a great asset. According to the Bureau of Census, about one-third of married women were employed in 1961, and they predict that by 1970, 30 million women will be in the work force. These families will find this kind of service especially helpful.

SECTION III

Home Freezing of Foods

CHAPTER 6

Hows and Whys of Packaging

WHY DOES PACKAGING MATTER?

The air in your freezer is very dry and will draw moisture from the food in it, unless you prevent it from doing this. Loss of moisture means loss of quality in any food, and is more serious in some than others. It is particularly serious if the storage period for some foods is long. Meats, fish and poultry suffer most in quality by moisture loss, and they show this effect as "freezerburn"—light gray specks or speckled areas. A small amount of such moisture loss will not affect the quality seriously, but if extensive, the meat itself will be dry and even tough and the fat may be rancid. This is one of the reasons why these foods when frozen, occasionally get themselves the reputation of being dry and tough, whereas this change in freezer storage is not at all necessary.

In frost-free freezers, it is especially important that packaging materials and methods of sealing be the very best. This is because in these freezers, the circulating fan-blown air tends to draw moisture from a package which is not well protected against such loss (see p. 55).

If air can get to the food, the oxygen in it will cause changes in flavor. This, too, is more important for some foods which show decided tendencies to develop rancidity during freezer storage. Some meats (particularly pork) develop off-flavors rather readily, and eventually become rancid. But the flavor of different foods is affected in different ways, so good protection from air is essential for all foods going into the freezer for any length of time.

There is a tendency, too, for foods like cured meats and fish to impart some of their "strong" flavors and odors to other foods which have a delicate flavor. To protect against this exchange of flavors and odors, the foods need to be well packaged.

It is for these reasons that good packaging is important. All your trouble in selecting good food for freezing, and in preparing it correctly for freezing will be in vain unless the food is packaged to prevent any of these misfortunes.

81

WHAT MAKES A GOOD PACKAGING MATERIAL?

Materials for packaging foods to be frozen must be not only water-proof but moisture-vapor-proof (often abbreviated as M.V.P.). Some materials will prevent the passage of water (are waterproof), but will permit the passage of moisture vapor (are not moisture-vapor-proof), and will permit the passage of odors and exchange of flavors.

They also need to be good "oxygen barriers." This means they will not permit oxygen to pass through them, and since oxygen is a component of air, they must therefore be airtight. This is important in retaining the best flavor for foods which are to be freezer-stored for long.

They should not themselves absorb fat or oil, water or blood. And they should not impart flavors or odors of their own to the food. They need to be scrupulously clean.

They should be convenient to use in packaging the food, and in removing the food afterwards, often without complete thawing. They should be sturdy and not too easily punctured. If they are to be used for wrapping around the food, they need to be pliable.

In choosing between materials as to cost, many things need to be considered, since some which seem to be inexpensive can be costly in the long run. If a double thickness of an inexpensive wrapper is needed to give good protection, maybe it would cost less to use one requiring only a single thickness. If a wrapper or container can be used only once, it may be extravagant in comparison with one which can be used many times. Think of the effect on the food, too. If you invest a good price in high-quality meat, for instance, but use a poor package for it, your original investment is largely wasted. If you pay a dollar or two for a good steak, it will pay to invest a few cents more for the kind of package which will keep it good. Further-more, meat may lose as much as ten per cent of its weight (moisture loss) during a year's storage in the freezer, if it is not well packaged. So the selection of poor packaging which may seem to save expense is false economy.

The trouble is, we are inclined to think of packaging as paper, and so many kinds of paper are rather cheap. But few of us hesitate to have a good raincoat to protect our good dresses from the weather. We surely should have good packages to protect good food in "freezer weather."

SOME GENERAL SUGGESTIONS

Whatever kind of wrapper or container you may be using, see that there is as little air as possible left in the package when you close it. And close it so it will be airtight, since air gets in through tiny crevices. Water expands about one-tenth of its volume during freezing, so in packaging watery foods, leave room for expansion, otherwise the pressure during freezing may force the container open. Containers with watery foods like fruits, syrups, sauces and soups, should be filled only about nine-tenths full.

If you will want to separate pieces of moist foods before they are thawed, pack them in layers with *two* thicknesses of moisture-proof wrapper between the layers. Several hamburg patties, chops or steaks in one package, for instance, should be separated this way, otherwise they would be frozen together and you could not separate them until they were thawed. If you keep small odds and ends of packaging materials, they will come in handy for this purpose.

As a rule, to avoid left-overs put into one package only as much food as will be used at one meal. There are exceptions to this, of course, such as whole poultry, roasts, loaves of bread and perhaps cakes. But many foods like cooked dishes, ground meat patties, chops and rolls may well be packaged in one-meal portions.

A food which is a soft mass may be difficult to handle, but if it is frozen first, the solid block is easily packaged. These can usually be packaged a few hours after they are put into the freezer—not later than a day afterwards. For additional suggestions for packaging individual foods, see directions for freezing them.

LABEL EVERYTHING CLEARLY

Every package going into the freezer should be clearly labelled to show what is in it and the date it was frozen. It is also well to indicate how much is in the package too; for instance, how many chops or patties, or how many eggs or the weight of a roast. It is a mistake to put anything into the freezer and assume that several months later you will know what is in the package.

For use on different wrappers, different kinds of marking pencils or crayons are necessary, and special pens with their own ink are available. Write in *large* letters on all labels. Labels or tags may be attached to the package by freezer tape, or you can write on the tape itself before you attach it to the package.   To label cellophane with crayon, run a warm iron over the cellophane just before marking (the warm cellophane melts the crayon to make it mark more easily); you can do this, of course, only if the food underneath permits.   Different colored crayons, overwraps, strings for attaching tags or paper for labels will help in identifying different foods.

If you are doing some experimenting to try out your own ideas (and there is still plenty to learn), keep a notebook for recording what you do each time, so you can benefit from your experience.

WRAPPING (SHEET) MATERIALS

These materials are especially appropriate for irregularly shaped, solid foods which do not fit readily into any container, or for baked products for which a container of just the right size is not available. Sheets of 18-inch width are the most popular and are satisfactory for most foods.   Occasionally, 12-inch width may be used, and for large poultry and roasts the 24-inch width will be needed.   These materials are usually sold in long rolls in containers from which the desired length may be torn readily.

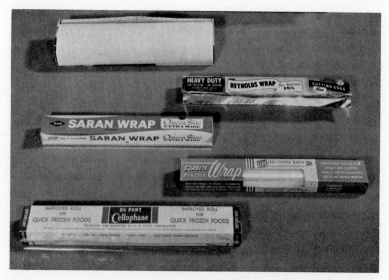

Courtesy of Frigidaire Division, General Motors Corp.

Wrapping (sheet) materials for freezing must be moisture-vapor-proof and pliable.   A few of those available for home freezing are shown above

There are many such wrapping materials for frozen foods on the market nowadays, and the number is increasing. It is important that one be chosen which is thoroughly satisfactory for frozen foods, and this is not always easy to do. The fact that occasionally some materials not really suited for this purpose are marked "locker papers" or "for frozen foods" does not help the beginner in making her selection. Ordinary waxed paper, and many other kinds of material entirely satisfactory for many kitchen uses are not at all satisfactory for freezing, since they are by no means moisture-vapor-proof; neither is the wrapper in which your butcher sells fresh meat.

WRAPPING METHODS

It is equally important that the food be wrapped so that air is excluded from the package as it is sealed, and so that it is impossible for moisture to escape from the package or for air to enter it during freezer storage. Following are the two methods of wrapping. For further suggestions concerning any special precautions for a particular type of wrapping, see the comments concerning these materials which follow. Also, for help in wrapping any particular type of food, see the instructions for freezing the food.

The Drug Store or Freezer Method

This is much the best method of wrapping for insuring good quality of frozen foods, since it is the best way to make tight folds and a snug wrap. It also requires less packaging material than the butcher method described below. Place the product on the center of the wrapper, with the long way of the food the long way of the wrapper. Bring the opposite, long sides of the wrapper together, up and over the product. Starting at the center, fold these two layers of material together about an inch from the edge, creasing the two sheets together to make a tight seam all the way across the wrapper. Then make at least one more similar fold, creasing tightly again. Experience will help you to select the amount of wrapping material to use. Two good folds are essential, but too many will make the package awkward and are wasteful of material. Seal the last seam tightly against the product (except with aluminum foil, which holds itself in place). Force as much air as possible out of the package by squeezing the wrapper tightly against the product at all its crevices. Then turn the product over. Fold the end corners toward each other

THE DRUG STORE WRAP

Place the product on the center of the wrapper, with the long way of the product the long way of the wrapper

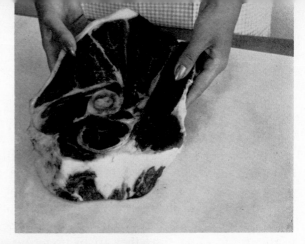

Bring the opposite, long sides of the wrapper over the product and fold to make a tight crease across the entire length of the wrapper

Make at least one more such tight fold and bring the wrapper tightly down on the product

Turn the product over, fold the ends toward each other, then make two tight folds over the top of the package. Seal

Courtesy of KVP Sutherland Paper Co.

and make two tight folds of the wrapper, just as for the folds over the top of the package. Bring the folded ends tightly up over the product, squeezing the wrapper tightly against it. Then seal (except for aluminum foil).

The Butcher Method

There may be occasional, very irregularly shaped foods which are difficult to wrap by the drug store method, and somewhat easier to wrap this way. But when there is a choice, use the drug store method since it gives a better package. To make the butcher wrap, place the product on the wrapper, near one corner of it. Pull the corner up over the product, then roll the product toward the opposite corner, pulling tightly. When slightly more than half the wrapper has been used, fold one side of it tightly over, against the product. Roll a little farther, and fold the other side against it. Finally, roll up the remainder, squeezing the wrapper closely to the product, and fasten with freezer tape or twine.

Freezer Tape

Tape to be used in sealing packages for freezing should be one especially marked for freezer use. It is made so it will stick to the package at freezer temperatures, whereas others may not.

Heat Sealing

This is an efficient way of sealing products wrapped in numerous kinds of sheet materials. For suggestions as to which of the wrapping materials may be heat-sealed, see the comments concerning each material which follow. First, be sure the sides of the wrapper to be sealed together are perfectly dry. Place the edges flatly together, avoiding wrinkles. Use an iron which is warm, *not hot*. If the iron is not warm enough, the seal will not be perfect, and if it is hot some materials will stick to the iron. The tip of an electric hand iron may be used, and it should be regulated to be no warmer than for wool. It is a convenience in some cases, to have a smooth, flat piece of wood or cardboard on which to make the seal. Or a curling iron may be used. Also, there are special, heat-sealing irons made for this purpose. For some film materials, if a heat-sealing iron coated with Teflon is not used, a piece of paper toweling or similar material must be placed between the iron and the wrapper to be sealed.

Courtesy of Donald K. Tressler and Associates

For heat-sealing packages, the tip of an electric hand iron may be used, regulated to be no warmer than for wool.   There are also special, heat-sealing irons, see p. 87 for instructions

TYPES OF WRAPPING (SHEET) MATERIALS

Aluminum Foil

It has been shown repeatedly, that no frozen food wrapping material has better moisture-vapor-proofness than aluminum foil which has been manufactured especially for food freezing.   However, ordinary household foils which have many other uses are not suited at all to food freezing, since they are too light in weight and puncture too easily. So select one which is marked for freezing.   In wrapping by the drug store method, do not draw the foil too tightly as you make the folds; instead, allow a little surplus to use in pressing and molding the foil tightly into the crevices of the food.   No tape is needed for holding the foil in place, when wrapped by this method. But since the foil may be punctured in the freezer as it is handled, it should be overwrapped.   Since it is difficult to write on foil, label the package.   If the overwrap is transparent, place a label between the foil and the overwrap. Or write the information on freezer tape and attach the tape to the foil.

Salt tends to corrode aluminum, causing tiny holes in it. So foods containing much salt should not be wrapped in it.

The edges of aluminum foil are very sharp, so take care not to cut yourself on them.

An advantage of freezing in foil is that the package can be placed in the oven for reheating cooked foods, and since metal is a good conductor of heat, the food heats quickly.

Foil can be used a second time only if it can be thoroughly cleaned after using it, and if there were no holes in it.

Transparent Materials

There are many of these available, and only the most common types can be mentioned. These can be used a second time only if they can be thoroughly cleaned after using them, and if there are no holes. Since most of them become punctured rather readily, they should usually be overwrapped. If not overwrapped, the label can be placed between the food and the wrapper.

Cellophane.—Of the many kinds of cellophane, only those which are made expressly for food freezing and are so marked, should be selected. These are good, moisture-vapor-proof wrappers. You can heat-seal the package by applying the warm iron directly to the cellophane. Or seal with freezer tape. Since cellophane becomes brittle in the freezer, it is important that these packages be overwrapped.

Cellophane also tends to become brittle on standing any appreciable length of time at room temperature in a dry place. It is best to keep it in a damp place like the basement. If you find when you come to use it that it is brittle, placing it in a damp place like the basement a day or two, or placing it between damp (not wet) towels for several hours may help. You are not apt to be able to use it after many months of storage, so it is best not to purchase at one time more than can be used within a few months.

Polyethylene.—This is a pliable, plastic film and is entirely moisture-vapor-proof. Unfortunately, it permits oxygen to pass through it to some extent, so meats and other foods which have a good deal of fat (and so would become rancid readily) should not be stored in it for longer than 4 to 6 months, unless the food or the polyethylene have been treated with an antioxidant, and this is unusual. These packages can be heat-sealed, but unless a Teflon coated, heat-sealing iron is used, the iron must not be in direct contact with the polyethylene, since the film would stick to the iron. So unless such an iron is used, place paper toweling or similar material between the iron and the film. Or the package may be sealed with freezer tape.

Pliofilm.—This is a rubber composition material which is moisture-vapor-proof, strong and pliable, and makes a good frozen food wrapper. It may be heat-sealed, but as for polyethylene, paper toweling or other material must be placed between the film and the iron, unless a Teflon coated, heat-sealing iron is used. Or the package may be sealed with freezer tape.

Saran Film.—This is a good, moisture-vapor-proof material and gives good protection to foods in the freezer. It clings closely to the product, so makes a snug wrap. It can be sealed with a Teflon coated, heat-sealing iron. But without such an iron, heat-sealing cannot be done by home methods, so sealing should be done by freezer tape.

Laminated Wrappings

Many types of these layered wrappings are available, and they combine the desirable qualities of two or more materials. Polyethylene, glassine or pliofilm are materials sometimes laminated to kraft paper which is itself very sturdy. Aluminum foil may also be laminated to paper. Many of these are unusually good for food freezing. For polyethylene laminated to paper, there is the same question mentioned above for polyethylene alone, as to oxygen passing through it. Follow the manufacturer's instructions for laminated materials, as to which side should be placed next to the food, in wrapping, and also as to whether the material can be heat-sealed. Label by writing on the wrapper with marking pencil. None of these laminated materials should be used a second time.

Wax Coated Papers

Ordinary waxed locker papers are not recommended for food to be held in the freezer for more than 60 days at most, especially if the food contains much fat. Some are better than others, but as a rule they are not sufficiently moisture-vapor-proof to give satisfaction, even when a double thickness of wrapper is used.

Overwraps

These are used for protecting moisture-vapor-proof wrappers from being punctured or from coming loose as the package is handled in the freezer. If you plan to do a good deal of overwrapping, you will find stockinette very useful. This is a roll of close-meshed cotton, scarcely three inches wide. As you pull it over a thick package, it can stretch to be 15 inches wide (30 inches around) and it fits the

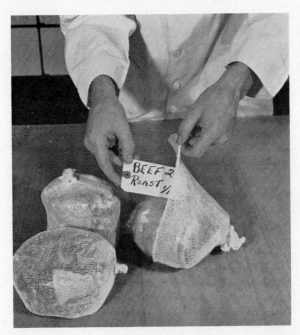

Courtesy of Donald K. Tressler and Associates

Stockinette makes a fine overwrap for packages which puncture readily. The stockinette fits the package closely and the label may be placed between the wrapper and the stockinette

package closely. When you cut off the stockinette for a package, remember that as it stretches to fit a package, it will be shorter—just like your stocking—so give yourself plenty of length in the beginning. Tie a knot at one end, pull the stockinette over the package, slipping the label between the package and the stockinette, if you wish. Then tie a knot at the other end. It can be washed and used again.

Any inexpensive, strong paper can be used as an overwrap. If you keep wax coated paper on hand for short storage, this can well be used, so can ordinary butcher paper. Large bags make good overwraps. As already suggested, a number of packages of one kind of food in one bag has many advantages.

BAGS AND BAGS IN BOXES

Many of the sheet materials described above are also sold as bags, and those which are good for freezing as sheet material are also good when made into bags. The general care of the bags is the same as the care of the corresponding sheet materials, as described above. Some of the bags are provided with folding boxes in which they are stored in the freezer. Some of the boxes open at the end, others at the top.

When filling the bags with wet food, fill them scarcely nine-tenths full to allow for expansion, and also allow enough of the bag at the top for making a good closure. If the bags come with boxes, it is a good idea to place the bag in the box before filling it. To keep end-opening bags in place while you are filling them, rectangular funnels or wire holders are available. For an "assembly line," when a number of such bags are to be filled, line up all the bags in their boxes first, and stacking them close together in a deep, straight-sided pan or box will keep them from tipping over when you fill them. If you get liquid on a surface to be heat-sealed, dry it thoroughly before sealing it.

To know whether the bag may be heat-sealed, follow the instructions given above for sealing the same kind of material when used as a sheet. For some of the laminated bags, the top may be folded over several times as for the drug store wrap, then held securely in place. Some of these are provided with a metal strip attached to the top of the bag, for making a tight fold.

If the bag is heat-sealed, the top of the bag will need to be cut off when the food is to be used, so the remaining bag will be smaller for future use. With some film-type bags, the manufacturer provides rubber bands or other devices for making a tight closure. Twist the top of the bag tightly, fold the end down over the twist, and tie it firmly in place with a rubber band or other device. Pipe cleaners or "Twist-ems" (which are available at florist shops) serve this purpose well.

RIGID CONTAINERS

In addition to being made of moisture-vapor-proof material, these need to be designed so they can be filled and closed easily, and so that frozen food can be removed without complete thawing. They also need to be watertight so they can be inverted without leaking, when used for wet food. Many of these have miscellaneous kitchen uses when they are not in the freezer.

Courtesy of Frigidaire Division, General Motors Corp.

There is a great variety of containers for home freezing. They need to be moisture-vapor-proof and have a closure which can be tightly sealed. Some of those available are shown above

Aluminum Containers

These come in a number of styles and sizes, with tightly fitting lids. When the lids are fitted tightly in place, they are good, moisture-vapor-proof containers. Some aluminum foil boxes are sealed by pressing the lids on with a tool which comes with the box.

These containers can be transferred directly from the freezer to the oven for quickly reheating cooked foods. Many of them can be used repeatedly.

Home Canning Equipment

Plain tin or R-enamel cans be may used for freezing many foods, but some foods are better packed in cans with special linings. C-enamel is best for foods containing sulfur (corn, lima beans and carrots), and R-enamel for highly colored foods (berries, beets, red cherries, fruit juices, plums, squash and sweet potatoes). Cans which require a sealer must be reflanged with a special attachment to the sealer before they are reused. Any lid or can which is dented should not be reused if it cannot be sealed.

Coffee, Potato Chip and Shortening Cans

These are splendid for freezing. Clean them thoroughly, and air coffee cans so there will be no coffee odor left. Seal the rim with freezer tape. These can be used for any type of food. Other cans should be used only for freezing dry foods, since the inside of the can is not treated to prevent rust.

Glass Jars

Glass jars made expressly for freezing are available in pint and quart sizes. These are wide-mouthed, in contrast to the conventional canning jar which is rather narrow at the top. The jar is designed this way so the food can be removed without complete thawing. They have slightly tapering sides, and stippled ribs to prevent slipping during handling. With reasonable care, these do not break readily, and they are very satisfactory.

The conventional canning jars may be used for freezing, but because of the narrower mouth, the food must be almost completely thawed before removing it.

Paperboard Cartons

These differ widely in their moisture-vapor-proofness and therefore in their suitability for freezing.

Paperboard cartons which have not been treated, or have only been lightly waxed are not suitable for many products, except for very short periods of freezer storage. Paper drinking cups, and paperboard cartons in which ice cream and cottage cheese are sold belong in this category. Some are better than the ice cream and cottage cheese containers but are not sufficiently waxed or otherwise treated to be satisfactory for storing food in the freezer longer than a couple of weeks, or a month at most.

There is, however, a wide variety of paperboard containers which are heavily waxed or treated with plastic material to make them moisture-vapor-proof. They come in sizes from one-half pint to one-half gallon. They have round, square or rectangular sides, some straight, others tapering, and accordingly they may or may not be space-savers. They may have cap or snap-on or insert-style lids, and the lids and containers can sometimes be purchased separately. Containers with small openings are not good, because they are hard to fill and the food cannot be removed from them until it is completely thawed.

In filling waxed cartons, the food must not be hot, for it would melt the wax and the wax would lose its effectiveness.

These cartons cannot be washed in hot water, so reuse of them is questionable from a standpoint of sanitation. If they have been used for dry-pack food and can be easily cleaned, you may be able to use them again. Dry and air them thoroughly and store them where they will keep clean.

Plastic Containers

There are many of these, made from different plastic materials, with different shapes and different sizes. These materials are all moisture-vapor-proof, so when the lid is closed tightly, they make splendid containers. They are good for any type of food, and especially for moist ones. Most of these can be labelled with a marking pencil. As a rule, they cannot be placed in the oven for reheating cooked foods. Those with flared sides will stack, one inside another, for saving space when they are not in use.

Containers to Save Freezer Space

Rectangular shaped containers stack well in the freezer, and in this way they make far better use of space in the freezer than do those which are cylindrical. Each cubic foot of freezer space will hold 40 pints of rectangular containers, 27 to 30 pints of cylindrical cartons and 25 pints of glass freezer jars. So by using rectangular shaped containers, you can get a good many more in the same amount of freezer space, than when cylindrical ones are used.   Since freezer space is usually very precious, this is an important consideration when selecting containers.

Pie Plates

Frozen pies are often prepared to be put directly into the oven from the freezer, and for this purpose the pie plate needs to be one which can be used this way.   Picnic paper plates are not at all suitable.   There are, however, pie plates made of paper which has been treated to stand baking, and also supplied with a metal rim around the edge so they are easy to handle.   These are available in various widths and depths.   They can be used only once.

There are also aluminum pie plates, heavy enough to be handled without "flopping."   They come in various sizes.

Your oven-glass pie plates can be used successfully, too, since they can be transferred directly from the freezer to the oven, without danger of breaking.

Wrapping is often easier if the pie is frozen first.   When you are ready to wrap it, invert over the top of the pie another pie plate of the same size (any pie plate, such as a picnic paper plate is satisfactory).   Then wrap in moisture-vapor-proof material and seal.   Or if preferred, place the pie in a waxed carton of the right size, overwrap the carton with moisture-vapor-proof material and seal well.

Oven-Glass Casseroles

Your oven-glass casseroles can be used for freezing foods which are to be heated in the oven.   If you can spare the casserole until you have used the food in it, seal the cover to the casserole with freezer tape.   When ready to use the food, remove the freezer tape and the casserole can be transferred directly from the freezer to the oven to reheat for serving.

On the other hand, if you need the casserole while the food is in the freezer, the solution is simple.   Freeze the food in the casserole, covering it only lightly.   When the food is hard-frozen, place the casserole in a pan of water (not hot) barely long enough to thaw the food around the edges.   Quickly remove the hard block of food from the casserole, wrap it in sheet wrapping material by the drug store method, and get it back into the freezer at once.   When you are ready to use the food, unwrap it and place it in the casserole in which it was frozen and put into the oven to reheat.

FOR SHORT STORAGE PERIODS

For storing foods in the freezer two weeks or less, it is not necessary to use moisture-vapor-proof materials. Bread may be stored in the waxed paper in which it was purchased. Ordinary household aluminum foil can be used for short storage periods. Several thicknesses of heavy waxed paper which you have in the kitchen can be used for some foods. Don't use this for moist foods, however, because it will absorb water and will stick to the food. Cooked dishes (stews and creamed dishes) for such short periods can be held in refrigerator dishes with their own covers, or with oiled silk covers, or covered with aluminum foil.

For storage periods of about two months, some of the waxed "locker papers" can be used—those not sufficiently moisture-vapor-proof to be good for longer periods. And for periods of 2 to 4 weeks, paperboard ice cream and cottage cheese containers may be used.

TAKING CARE OF PACKAGING MATERIALS

Packaging materials and containers all need to be stored where they will not get dusty, and away from any possibility of insects getting to them. And note the special care necessary for storing cellophane, in the instructions given on p. 89 for using this wrapper.

WHERE CAN THESE SUPPLIES BE PURCHASED?

It would be splendid if you could be assured that all these packaging supplies could be purchased just where it is most convenient for you to get them. Unfortunately, this is not always true. Locker plants are often one of the best sources; supermarkets, department stores and hardware stores also usually have a good assortment. Your freezer dealer is apt to know where the best supply is available, and a wholesale paper merchant in your locality should be able to help you. It is better in the beginning not to get too large a supply of any one kind of wrapping material or container, until you are sure it is the kind you like best.

CHAPTER 7

Freezing Fruits and Vegetables

SELECTING FRUITS AND VEGETABLES

Freezing captures the quality of fresh fruits and vegetables far better than any other method of preservation. But even freezing cannot improve the quality of the original product. So it is essential that fruits and vegetables for freezing should be of the best quality and at the right stage of maturity. In fact, the quality of the original fruit and vegetable is the most important single factor in determining its quality when it is served.

Variety Is Important

The variety of fruit or vegetable selected for freezing is very important. Some varieties are best for eating raw, others are best for canning, and still others may be best for freezing. The right variety will give you an excellent product when it reaches the table, but the wrong one may give you a product which is poor in flavor, texture, color or in all three of these qualities.

For many fruits and vegetables, different varieties are grown in different parts of the United States. The varieties recommended for freezing in one region may not be grown in another region. So it is not practical in this book to give a list of recommended varieties for freezer-owners throughout the United States.

If you plan to grow some of your own fruits and vegetables for freezing, secure information about the recommended varieties which may be grown in your locality. The Experiment Station in the state where you live will gladly provide you with this information. You can address a card to the Agricultural Extension Service Office in your state. Or if you happen to know someone in your County Extension Service, she will get this information for you.

Stage of Maturity

As a rule, the best stage of maturity for freezing is reached when fruits and vegetables are at their best for eating. If they are immature, they lack their full, characteristic flavor, they may be too firm and fibrous, and on thawing, they may taste bitter.   Overripe ones, on the other hand, lose their shape on thawing and are generally less attractive.   Some products pass very quickly from the just-ripe to the overripe stage and it is for these that the time of harvesting is especially important.   Such products include peas, corn, snap beans, lima beans, soybeans and asparagus.   Starchy vegetables like corn, peas and lima beans are at their best just *before* they are fully mature, for at that time they are at their peak of sweetness and tenderness. Even a day or two beyond the ideal harvesting time may mean less-than-the-best quality, since they become starchy and less sweet. Other vegetables do not require quite so close timing as this.   Fruits which are ripened on the tree or vine are best for freezing.   Fruits should be at the just-right stage for eating raw.

If fruits were not harvested at the appropriate time and have become too soft, they can be sorted carefully and those not spoiled can be made into purée and then frozen.   When thawed, purées can be used for making ice cream, jams or jellies.   Overripe vegetables, too, can be frozen and used in some recipes where the quality of the vegetables is not so important.

Promptness in Handling

Having taken the trouble to harvest produce when best for freezing, the next step is to plan to get it from the garden to the freezer as quickly as possible.   Ideally, the produce should be in the freezer two or three hours after it is harvested.   Delays will cause loss of ascorbic acid and other vitamins, as already discussed in Chapter 2. Even after harvesting, the sugar in peas and corn changes rather rapidly to starch.   The flavor and texture of all kinds of berries, of peaches, and cherries are best if they are frozen very soon after they are picked.

It is a good idea to have all your freezing equipment ready, and all your plans made for freezing, before you harvest the fruits or vegetables.   In warm weather, it is best to harvest the produce in the early morning, while they are still cool and succulent.   And to be able to proceed with immediate freezing, have everything in the kitchen ready the night before.

Don't pick so many at one time that it will be impossible to get them all into the freezer within a few hours.

However, if an unavoidable delay occurs, the most important

precaution is to see that the produce is kept as cold as possible while it is being held between harvesting and freezing. This is because fruits and vegetables are living materials for a while after they are harvested, and continue to respire. During respiration, they use up oxygen and liberate heat and carbon dioxide. So if they are piled rather deep (as in a hamper) the products in the center will get warm, and this can cause considerable loss of vitamin content and palatability.

Prompt cooling in ice water of many freshly picked vegetables like asparagus and unshelled peas, followed by storage in the refrigerator will help retain flavor and will greatly reduce vitamin loss if they must be held before freezing. Or sometimes they may be spread out loosely in a well-ventilated, cool room, or packed loosely in the refrigerator. If they must be stored for several hours, pack them in crushed ice.

Peas or beans should not be shelled, vegetables should not be cut nor corn husked until you are ready to proceed at once with freezing.

PACKING FRUITS AND VEGETABLES INTO CONTAINERS

When the fruit or vegetable is ready to be frozen, pack it cold into cold containers. To reduce the amount of air in the package, pack foods as tightly as possible without injuring those which are readily injured. When packing in bags, press air out of unfilled parts of bag.

With only a few exceptions, allowance must be made for headspace (space between the packed food and the top of the container). This is because water and watery foods expand during freezing, and if space is not allowed, the expansion causes the lid to be pushed up or the container to burst. A guide to the amount of headspace for vegetables and fruits, according to the kind of pack, follows. A few

Headspace to Allow Between Packed Food and Closure[1]

Type of Pack	Container with Wide Top Opening[2]		Container with Narrow Top Opening[3]	
	Pint	Quart	Pint	Quart
Liquid pack (fruit packed in juice, sugar, syrup, or water; crushed or purée; juice)	½ in.	1 in.	¾ in.	1½ in.
Dry pack[4] (fruit or vegetable packed without added sugar or liquid)	½ in.	½ in.	½ in.	½ in.

[1] From *Home and Garden Bulletin No. 10*, U. S. Dept. Agr.
[2] This is headspace for tall containers—either straight or slightly flared.
[3] Glass canning jars may be used for freezing most fruits and vegetables except those packed in water.
[4] Vegetables that pack loosely, such as broccoli and asparagus, require no headspace.

vegetables which are frozen in large pieces have enough air in the package to make headspace unnecessary. Seal containers carefully in all cases.

PREPARING VEGETABLES FOR FREEZING

Which Ones Can be Frozen?

Most vegetables give entirely satisfactory products when frozen. However, those which are usually eaten raw, with crispness an important characteristic, should not be frozen for use in salads. This includes salad greens, radishes, cucumbers, cabbage, Chinese cabbage and celery. Cabbage, Chinese cabbage and celery are satisfactory frozen, if they are to be used as a cooked vegetable. Whole tomatoes are not good for freezing, since they collapse too quickly on thawing.

Irish potatoes can only be frozen raw if they are new potatoes, or if they are frozen as strips or cubes for French frying.

Cleaning and Trimming

Freezing does not by any means kill all the microorganisms in any food. It kills some, but merely stops the growth of others while they are in the freezer. So it is important to have the food and all the equipment as clean as possible. Most vegetables need to be thoroughly washed in cold water. Exceptions are corn, lima beans, soybeans, green peas and any other vegetables that are protected by pods. All greens need to be washed in several waters, lifting them from the water as sand or grit settles to the bottom of the pan.

Examine vegetables carefully, and remove overmature, off-color or bruised parts. It is often necessary to sort them as to size, because larger pieces need longer blanching than small ones, and so must be blanched separately.

Vegetables are usually prepared for freezing just as they would be prepared if they were to be cooked immediately. Devices are available for cutting or slicing, and if substantial amounts are to be prepared this way, it pays to have these on hand. They save a good deal of time, and make it easier to have the products uniform in appearance.

Blanching

With a few exceptions, if vegetables are frozen without further treatment, they will develop off-flavors, will have poor texture and low ascorbic acid content after only a few weeks in the freezer. These changes are caused by certain enzymes in the vegetables which have been discussed in Chapter 2 in connection with the vitamin content of fruits and vegetables. It is essential that these enzymes be destroyed before the vegetables are frozen, and a short scalding (blanching) achieves this. It is important that the time of blanching be exactly long enough to destroy the enzymes, and to do this, the inside of the vegetable must reach a certain temperature. This will take longer for large, thick pieces than for small thin ones, and this is the reason for different times for blanching different vegetables. It is essential that the recommended times be followed. For timing to be accurate enough, your clock or watch needs a second hand.

If vegetables are under-blanched, not all the enzymes will be destroyed. On the other hand, if they are over-blanched, the vegetables will be "cooked" and when served they will be somewhat like leftovers—poor in color, flavor and texture, and low in vitamin content.

Fortunately, blanching actually improves the color of some vegetables, particularly green ones, and then freezing "sets" this attractive color. Hence, well-prepared frozen green vegetables are particularly attractive in color.

Blanching is also important for "greens" because it makes them pack readily into a small space. It also helps to reduce the characteristic "bitterness"" of some greens, by dissolving some of the substances responsible for these flavors into the blanching water.

For a discussion of the effect of blanching on the mineral and vitamin content of vegetables, see Chapter 2.

Blanching in Boiling Water.—For home freezing, this is the most common method, since the necessary equipment for it is usually available. For most products, this method is entirely satisfactory. It requires a 1- or 2-gallon kettle of aluminum, enamelware or stainless steel, or a deep-well cooker is good. Since copper destroys ascorbic acid, foods should not be in contact with this metal. And metallic off-flavors may result from the use of iron kettles.

The moment the blanching time has elapsed, it is essential that all the vegetables be removed from the boiling water at once. To facilitate doing this, they are placed in a rack or loosely tied bag, so that the basket or bag containing the vegetables can be removed from the water. For this purpose, blanching kettles with their own baskets are available, and these are a good investment if you plan to do much boiling-water blanching. A wire basket which fits into a large kettle and which permits having the kettle very tightly covered is satisfactory. Or several thicknesses of cheesecloth made into a *loose* bag (to permit movement of the vegetables in the bag and insure even heating) can be used for holding the vegetables.

Courtesy of Frigidaire Division, General Motors Corp.

A kettle holding a large amount of water and with a tightly fitting lid is essential for blanching vegetables in boiling water. The deep-well cooker on your range is splendid, and special blanching kettles are available

The proportion of 1 gallon of water to each pound of vegetable is the usual recommendation. This large proportion of water to vegetable is used so that the water will resume boiling quickly after the vegetables have been added.

First, have the water boiling very vigorously. Put the vegetables in the basket or bag and lower them into the boiling water. See that *all* the vegetables are submerged in water. Cover the kettle tightly, and keep the heat turned as high as possible. The water should resume boiling within 60 seconds, or 75 seconds at most. If you cannot get intense enough heat to do this, then you will need to use a still larger proportion of boiling water to vegetable.

The time for blanching is sometimes counted from the moment the vegetables have been added to the boiling water, and sometimes it is counted from the moment the water resumes boiling after the vegetables have been added. In using the directions for boiling-water blanching in the following pages, count the time from the moment the water resumes boiling after adding the vegetables. This necessitates raising the lid slightly, to know exactly when this happens. After that, keep the kettle covered tightly.

The same blanching water can be used for three or four successive batches of vegetables, as a rule. But before adding each new batch, add enough boiling water to keep it to the required level in the kettle. For some vegetables with a very distinct taste, the water may acquire a flavor which is not desirable. Vegetables such as asparagus, spinach, cauliflower and broccoli may give this problem. After blanching these vegetables, taste the water before adding a new lot, and if the taste is too distinct, discard it.

Blanching in Steam.—This is a very good method for blanching many kinds of vegetables, but it requires a very efficient steamer. This means one with a tightly fitting lid which will hold in the steam and keep the vegetables well surrounded with an abundance of live steam. If the vegetables are not well surrounded with live steam, they will not be properly heated, so the enzymes will not be destroyed. This method is particularly recommended for pumpkin and squash, because the flavor does not leach out into the steam as much as into boiling water. On the other hand, the boiling-water method is preferred by some for broccoli and other strong-juiced vegetables, since this gives them a milder flavor. But some people feel it is easier to avoid breaking broccoli flowerets in the steamer than in boiling water, so this is a matter of personal preference. Steam-blanching is *not* recommended for spinach and other greens, since these "mat" in the steamer and so do not heat uniformly.

Put several inches of water in the kettle, bring it to a vigorous boil, then put in the container with the vegetables. The container must be one which allows free circulation of steam all around the vegetables. And so the steam will reach all the pieces, the vegetables should be in a *thin* layer, only one layer if the pieces are very thick. Start timing from the moment the kettle is covered after the vegetables have been added. A pressure saucepan can be used, but do not close the petcock. Steam will escape during blanching, so use plenty of water to prevent the saucepan from going dry.

Chilling

The moment blanching is completed, it is important to chill the vegetables rapidly. To do this, remove the bag or basket containing the vegetables and plunge it into a large pan of cold water to quickly

Courtesy of Frigidaire Division, General Motors Corp.

As soon as blanching is completed, vegetables must be chilled rapidly by immersing them into a large amount of ice-cold water

stop the "cooking" effect. If the tap water is very cold, use this but keep it running continuously into the pan during chilling. Otherwise, add ice to the cold water, using about one pound of ice per pound of vegetable. Times for chilling are usually at least as long as for blanching, often a little longer. In addition, it is a good idea to taste a couple of pieces to be sure they are cool to the center.

Then remove the vegetables from the cold water and drain them thoroughly. They should be packed immediately. If they are to be taken to a locker plant for freezing, get them there as quickly as possible, and arrange to have them frozen promptly.

Types of Vegetable Packs

Solid Pack.—This type of pack gives a solid block of frozen vegetables when you come to use it. In preparing this pack, merely put all the vegetable pieces in the container immediately after draining them, leave headspace, seal and put the packages in the freezer.

Loose Pack.—If there is a chance that you might like to use only a portion of the vegetables from one package at a time, you will be glad to be able to "pour" out some of the frozen vegetables from the package. You have probably purchased some vegetables this way, and you can prepare them at home, too. After draining the vegetables, spread them out in a single layer on trays or pie plates, and put them in the freezer. When they are hard-frozen, pack into containers leaving no headspace.

Containers for Freezing Vegetables

Select a container which will hold a meal-size portion for your family, to avoid having left-overs. As a rule, a pint container provides three servings, four at most. However, if vegetables are frozen by the loose pack method, this is not necessary, since the desired portion may be taken from the bag and the remainder returned to the freezer for future use.

So far as retaining the quality of the vegetables during freezer storage is concerned, the only essential is that the containers be moisture-vapor-proof. Apart from that, the selection is a matter of convenience and your perference.

Following are the types of containers most convenient for freezing vegetables:

Bags in Boxes.—These are moisture-vapor-proof bags, provided with boxes of the proper size. Follow directions for using these, as given on p. 92. Even if you do not wish to leave the box in the freezer, it is a good idea to have the bag in its rectangular box until the vegetable is frozen, for this will give you a rectangular-shaped frozen package which will stack advantageously in your freezer.

Rigid Containers.—These include plastic, aluminum or other metal containers or cans, glass jars and paperboard containers. Follow directions for using these, as given on pp. 93–95.

For broccoli or asparagus spears, or any vegetable for which arrangement in the package is important, top-opening containers are best. These may be paperboard containers, or flat, aluminum containers with slip-on lids.

For wrapping corn on the cob, see directions for freezing this product.

Selection and Preparation of Each Vegetable

When a range of time is given for blanching or chilling, select the time according to the size of piece, the larger the piece the longer the time. Count time for blanching accurately, from the moment the water has resumed boiling after vegetables have been added. If you live at an altitude of 2,500–5,000 feet, blanch in steam or boiling water half again as long as in the following recommendations; if at an altitude of more than 5000 feet, blanch twice as long.

Immediately after packing into containers, seal, leaving headspace according to directions on p. 100.

Artichokes, Globe.—Select small, tender artichokes or artichoke hearts. Pull off and discard outer leaves until thin, inner light ones are reached. Cut off tops of buds and trim butts to a cone. Submerge in cold water and wash.

Blanch in boiling water: small hearts, 4 min.; mature hearts, 5 min.; small, whole artichokes 10 min. To prevent darkening, for blanching 1 lb. artichokes use 1 tbsp. citric acid crystals or ½ c. lemon juice in 2 qt. water.

Chill in cold water 5–15 min., depending on size, or until inside is cool. Drain.

Pack in containers, leaving no headspace.

Asparagus.—Select young, tender stalks with compact tips. Wash and trim as for table use and sort according to size and thickness of stalk. For spears, cut length to fit carton. Boxes with slits for cutting desired length are useful. For cut-up asparagus, cut into 2-inch lengths, using only tender parts.

Blanch in boiling water: small spears (⅜–¾ inch diameter, butt-end) or cut-up, 3 min.; larger spears (¾–1 inch diameter), 4 min.; or in steam: small spears, or cut-up, 3½ min.; larger spears, 4½ min.

Chill in cold water 3–5 min. Drain.

Pack in containers, leaving no headspace. When packing spears, alternate tips and stem ends, or if using tapering containers, pack with tips at narrow end.

Beans, Green Shell.—Select pods that are plump, not dry or wrinkled. Shell the beans but do not wash them afterwards.

Blanch in boiling water: 60 sec.; or in steam: 100 sec.

Chill in cold water about 3 min. Drain.

Pack into containers, leaving ½-inch headspace.

Beans, Green Snap, or Wax.—Select young, tender, stringless beans which snap when broken. Wash thoroughly, then snip off ends. Cut in about 1½-inch pieces or slice lengthwise for Frenched (julienne-style) by hand or with French slicing utensil. Small beans (3–4 inches long) may be left whole.

Blanch in boiling water: Frenched, 2 min.; cut-up, 2½ min.; whole, 3 min., or in steam: Frenched, 2½ min.; cut-up, 3 min.; whole, 3½ min.

Chill in cold water 3–5 min. Drain.

Pack in containers, leaving ½-inch headspace.

Beans, Lima.—Select well filled pods while green and somewhat immature (not starchy or mealy). Shell and sort according to size. If diffcult to open pods, cut off tough edge with kitchen shears.

Blanch in boiling water: small, 1½ min.; medium, 2 min.; large, 2½ min.; or in steam: small, 2 min.; medium, 2½ min.; large, 3 min.

Chill in cold water about 5 min. Drain.

Pack in containers, leaving ½-inch headspace.

Beans, Soybeans, Green.—Select firm, well filled, bright green pods. Wash, scald beans in boiling water 4–5 min., and chill in running cold water 5 min. Squeeze beans out of pods. No further heating is necessary.

Pack in containers, leaving ½-inch headspace.

Beets.—Select tender beets, either young or mature, but not more than 3 inches in diameter. Wash thoroughly, trim off tops, leaving ½-inch of stem. Sort acording to size and cook in boiling water or steam until tender. Chill in cold water until cool to the center, and remove skins. Leave tiny beets (less than 2 inches diameter) whole, and slice or cube others.

Pack into containers, leaving ½-inch headspace.

Beet Greens.—*See Greens.*

Broccoli.—Select compact, dark green heads with tender stalks, removing any off-colored heads which have begun to blossom, tough leaves and woody ends. If necessary to remove insects, soak stalks (flowerets down) for ½ hr. in brine (2 tbsp. salt per gallon cold water), then rinse thoroughly in fresh water. Cut lengths to fit container and cut through entire stalks lengthwise so the heads (flowerets) are not more than 1½ inch in diameter.

Blanch in boiling water: small flowerets, 3 min.; medium, 4 min.; large, 5 min. Blanching in water gives more delicate flavor, since "strong" substances dissolve into water, but it difficult to blanch in cloth bag without breaking flowerets; or in steam: small flowerets, 4 min.; medium, 5 min.; large, 6 min.

Chill in cold water 4–5 min. Drain.

Pack in containers, leaving no headspace.

Brussels Sprouts.—Select firm, compact heads with good green color, not wilted. Cut sprouts from main stem, trim off outer, coarse leaves and wash thoroughly in cold water. Discard insect-infested sprouts. Sort into small, medium and large sprouts. For delicate flavor, blanch in boiling water, for the same reason as in blanching broccoli.

Blanch in boiling water: small heads, 3 min.; medium, 4.; large, 5 min.; or in steam: 5–6 min., depending on size.

Chill in cold water 6–8 min. Drain.

Pack in containers, leaving no headspace.

Cabbage and Chinese Cabbage.—Select very fresh, compact heads with some green leaves. The frozen product can only be used in cooked dishes. Remove outer, coarse leaves, cut into medium or coarse shreds or thin wedges, or separate into leaves.

Blanch in boiling water: medium shreds, 1½ min., coarse shreds, wedges or leaves, 2–3 min.; or in steam: medium shreds, 2½ min.; coarse shreds, wedges or leaves, 3–4 min.

Chill in cold water: shredded, 2 min.; leaves or wedges 3 min. Drain.

Pack into containers, leaving ½-inch headspace.

Cantaloup.—*Listed with Fruits.*

Carrots.—Select tender, mild-flavored carrots, remove tops, scrape young carrots or pare older ones. Leave tiny carrots whole, cut others into ¼-inch slices or dice, or French them (lengthwise strips) by hand or with French slicing utensil.

Blanch in boiling water: Frenched, 2 min.; sliced or diced, 3 min.; whole (tiny), 4½ min.; or in steam: Frenched, 3 min.; sliced or diced, 4 min.; whole (tiny), 5½ min.

Chill in cold water about 5 min.   Drain.

Pack in containers, leaving ½-inch headspace.

Cauliflower.—Select firm, tender, snow-white heads.   Break or cut into pieces with flowerets about 1-inch in diameter.   Wash thoroughly.   If necessary to remove insects, soak (flowerets down) for ½ hr. in brine (2 tbsp. salt per gallon cold water), then rinse thoroughly in fresh water.   Sort into medium and small pieces.

Blanch in boiling water: small pieces, 3 min.; medium, 4 min.; or in steam: small pieces, 4 min.; medium, 5 min.

Chill in cold water, 4–5 min.   Drain.

Pack in containers, leaving no headspace.

Celery.—Select crisp, tender stalks, not stringy or pithy.   Green varieties are best for flavor.   Like cabbage, frozen celery can only be used in cooked dishes.   Wash and cut into 1-inch lengths.   Cook in small amount of water or steam until tender, about 3 min.

Chill in cold water, or preferably let pan with drained celery stand in another pan of cold water, stirring occasionally until cool.

Pack in containers, leaving ½-inch headspace.

Chard.—*See Greens.*

Collards.—*See Greens.*

Corn, Sweet.—Select ears with plump, tender kernels and thin, sweet milk.   If milk is thick and starchy, freeze the corn cream-style. Husk ears, and remove silk.   Corn is best if blanched while still on the ears.

Blanch in boiling water: small ears (1¼-inch or less in diameter), 6 min.; medium (1¼–1½-inch in diameter), 8 min.; large (over 1½-inch in diameter), 10 min.; or in steam: (without piling ears on top of one another) small ears, 6½ min.; medium, 8½ min.; large, 10½ min.

Chill in cold water at least 10–15 min.   Drain.

For cut corn (whole kernel):   cut kernels from blanched cob deep enough to get whole kernels.

For cream-style corn: cut from blanched cob at about center of kernels, then scrape with back of knife to remove juice and heart of kernel.

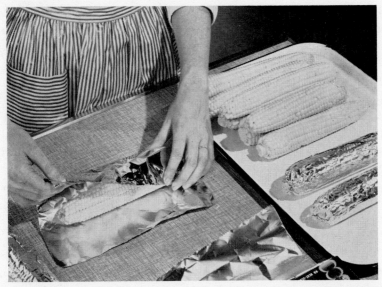

When individual ears of corn are wrapped in aluminum foil, they can be boiled or baked in the foil. In wrapping, seal all edges with a tight, double fold of foil

Pack corn on the cob individually in moisture-vapor-proof material and seal; or wrap individually, then pack in large, rectangular carton and seal. Pack cut or cream-style corn in containers, leaving ½-inch headspace.

Dandelion Greens.—*See Greens.*

Eggplant.—Select heavy, firm eggplant with uniform dark color. Pick before too mature, when seeds are tender. Wash, pare and cut into $^1/_3$-inch slices or $^1/_3$-inch cubes.

Blanch in boiling water 4 min.; or in steam 5 min.

Then to prevent darkening, at once dip slices for about 5 sec. in a solution of ½ tsp. ascorbic acid or 1 tbsp. citric acid or ½ c. lemon juice in 2½ pt. cold water.

Chill in cold water 4 min. Drain.

Pack in container, leaving ½-inch headspace. If cut in slices, place two thicknesses of moisture-vapor-proof wrapping material between slices.

Greens (Beet Greens, Collards, Dandelion Greens, Kale, Mustard Greens, New Zealand Spinach, Spinach, Swiss Chard and Turnip Greens).—Select young, tender leaves. Wash thoroughly in several waters. Remove tough stems and imperfect leaves. Cut leaves of chard into pieces, as desired.

Blanch in boiling water 2 min., except: collards and stem portions of Swiss chard, 3–4 min., and small tender spinach leaves, 1½ min.

Steam blanching not recommended because leaves "mat;" also, blanching in water dissolves some of the "bitter" flavor, making the greens more delicate in flavor.

Chill in cold water about 5 min., less for very tender spinach leaves. Drain.

Pack into container, leaving ½-inch headspace.

Kale.—*See Greens.*

Kohlrabi.—Select young, tender, mild-flavored kohlrabi, small to medium in size. Cut off tops and roots. Wash, peel and cut into ½-inch cubes.

Blanch in boiling water 1 min.; or in steam 100 sec.

Chill in cold water about 5 min. Drain.

Pack in containers, leaving ½-inch headspace.

Mixed Vegetables.—Prepare each vegetable separately, blanching and chilling each for the recommended time. Then combine in the desired proportion. For succotash, use half corn and half lima beans, soybeans or green beans. Half carrots and half peas are a good combination. If some vegetables to be used are already frozen, a loose pack (see p. 106) is desirable for them. If frozen as solid pack, thaw barely enough to combine with the freshly prepared vegetables.

Pack in containers, leaving ½-inch headspace if all vegetables were freshly prepared. If half were frozen, no headspace is necessary.

Mushrooms.—Select mushrooms which are free from spots and decay, with white, tight caps, and edible varieties only. During pulling and trimming, do not bruise, since bruised parts discolor readily. Freeze the same day they are picked. Wash thoroughly in cold water to remove soil. Trim off ends of stems. Small mushrooms (not more than 1-inch diameter) may be frozen whole. Cut larger ones into slices or quarters. Sort according to size.

Blanch in boiling water: slices, 2 min.; quarters, 3 min.; whole, 3–4 min.; or in steam: slices, 3 min.; quarters, 3½ min.; whole, 4 min.

Chill in cold water about 2 min. Drain. Then to prevent darkening, let stand 2 min. in a solution of ½ tsp. ascorbic acid or 1 tbsp. citric acid or ½ c. lemon juice in 2½ pt. cold water. Chill again in running cold water 2 min., and drain thoroughly.

Alternative treatment: Sauté small quantities of mushrooms at a time in hot table fat, until almost done. Cool in air, or set pan in which mushrooms were cooked in cold water. These need no further treatment.

Pack in containers, leaving ½-inch headspace.

Muskmelons.—*Listed with Fruits.*

Mustard Greens.—*See Greens.*

New Zealand Spinach.—*See Greens.*

Okra.—Select young, tender, green pods. Wash thoroughly and cut off stems without cutting seeds open. Sort into small and large pods.

Blanch in boiling water: small pods, 2–3 min.; large, 3–4 min.; or in steam: small pods, 3–4 min.; large 4–5 min.

Chill in cold water 3–5 min. Drain. If desired, they may then be sliced crosswise.

Pack in containers, leaving ½-inch headspace.

Parsley.—Select tender, crisp sprays. Clean thoroughly in cold water and cut off tough stems. Frozen parsley is suited only for use in cooking. It need not be blanched. But if preferred, heat in boiling water 15 sec. and chill in cold water 2 min.

Pack in small containers from which meal-portions can be readily removed. If chopped parsely is desired, chop while still frozen.

Parsnips.—Select small to medium parsnips, tender and free from woodiness. Cut off tops, wash, pare and cut into ½-inch cubes or cut into lengthwise slices ¾-inch thick.

Blanch in boiling water: cubes, 60 sec.; slices, 2 min.; or in steam: cubes, 100 sec.; slices, 3 min.

Chill in cold water 5 min. Drain.

Pack in containers, leaving ½-inch headspace.

Peas, Black-Eyed (Field).—Select well-filled, flexible pods with tender peas. Shell. Do not wash the shelled peas, but discard any that are hard.

Blanch in boiling water 2 min., or in steam 3 min.

Chill in cold water about 5 min. Drain.

Pack in containers, leaving ½-inch headspace.

Peas, Green.—Select bright green, plump, firm pods with peas that are sweet and tender, not overmature.   Shell peas, discarding any that are starchy.   Do not wash the shelled peas.

Blanch in boiling water: small peas, 45 sec.; large, 60 sec.; or in steam: small peas, 90 sec.; large, 2 min.

Chill in cold water about 3 min.   Drain.

Pack in containers, leaving ½-inch headspace.

Peppers (Green).—Select deep-green, crisp, thick-walled peppers. Wash, cut off stems, cut in halves and remove all seeds.   If desired, cut into ½-inch slices or into rings.   For use in uncooked foods, these are best unblanched (pack into containers, leaving no head-space).   When thawed, these are not as crisp as fresh peppers but can be used raw.   But blanched peppers are easier to pack and are good for use in cooking.

Blanch in boiling water: rings or slices, 2 min.; halves, 3 min.; or in steam: rings or slices, 3 min.; halves, 4 min.

Chill in cold water 3–4 min.   Drain.

Pack in containers, leaving ½-inch headspace if blanched.

Peppers, Red (Hot).—Select peppers with glossy skins, thick flesh, tender and crisp.   Prepare exactly as for Green Peppers, blanching or not, as preferred.

Pimientos.—Select firm, dark red, thick-walled pimientos, slightly shrivelled.   Roast in oven at 400°F., 3–4 min., then remove charred skins under running, cold water.   Drain.   Remove stem end and halve, slice or dice.

Pack in containers, leaving ½-inch headspace.

Potatoes, Irish.—Irish potatoes can only be frozen raw as new potatoes, or as strips (ready to French-fry), or as cubes.

Select mature potatoes which have been stored as least a month, for freezing as sticks or cubes.   Wash, pare and cut into $^1/_3$-inch sticks or cubes.   For freezing whole, select immature potatoes about the size of walnuts.   Wash these, scrub thoroughly to remove some of the skins.   Scrape, if desired, but do not pare.

Blanch in boiling water: sticks or cubes, 2 min.; walnut-size whole, 4 min.; or in steam: sticks or cubes, 3 min.; walnut-size whole, 5 min.

Chill in cold water: sticks or cubes, 3 min.; walnut-size whole, 5 min.   Drain.

Pack in containers, leaving ½-inch headspace.

Potatoes, Sweet.—Select medium to large sweet potatoes, with firm roots and bright appearance, that have been cured. Wash thoroughly and sort according to size. Cook by any preferred method, until about three-fourths done except for those to be mashed, and cook these until done. Let stand at room temperature until cool. Peel, then cut in halves or slices, or mash.

If desired, to prevent darkening, dip whole or sliced sweet potatoes for 5 sec. in a solution of ½ tsp. ascorbic acid or 1 tbsp. citric acid or ½ c. lemon juice in 2½ pt. cold water. Or to keep mashed sweet potatoes from darkening, mix 2 tbsp. orange or lemon juice with each quart of mashed sweet potatoes. For candied sweet potatoes, roll in granulated sugar before packing.

Pack in containers, leaving ½-inch headspace.

Pumpkin.—Select full-colored, mature pumpkin with fine texture, and not stringy. Wash, cut into chunks and remove seeds, Cool until tender, preferably by steam. Then remove pulp from rind and mash or press it through a sieve. Cool by placing pan with pumpkin in another pan of cold water.

If desired, pumpkin may be made into pumpkin pie mixture before freezing, adding all ingredients except clove (omit this since it may become strong during freezer storage).

Pack in containers, leaving ½-inch headspace.

Purées, Vegetable.—Select well-matured vegetables, free from molds or decay. Cook the vegetable by any preferred method until tender, then mash until very smooth, avoiding whipping air into the purée. For mashing, the vegetable may be put through a sieve, food chopper, ricer or equipment for making purées. Then chill quickly.

Pack in containers, leaving ½-inch headspace.

Rhubarb.—*Listed with Fruits.*

Rutabagas (Yellow Turnips).—Select young, tender, medium-sized turnips without tough fibers. Cut off tops, wash and peel, then cut into ½-inch cubes.

Blanch in boiling water 2–2½ min.; or in steam 3–4 min.

Chill in cold water 3–4 min. Drain.

Pack in containers, leaving ½-inch headspace.

If preferred, prepare and pack as rutabaga purée, following directions above for vegetable purées.

Soybeans.—*See Beans, Soybeans.*

Spinach.—*See Greens.*

Squash, Summer (Including Crookneck and Zuccini).—Select young squash with small seeds and tender rind. Wash and cut into ½-inch slices.

Blanch in boiling water 3½ min.; or in steam 4½ min.

Chill in cold water about 5 min. Drain.

Pack in containers, leaving ½-inch headspace.

Squash, Winter (Including Hubbard and Butternut).—Select firm, mature squash. Wash, cut into pieces and remove seeds. Then prepare exactly as for pumpkin, above.

Succotash.—*See Mixed Vegetables.*

Swiss Chard.—*See Greens.*

Sweet Potatoes.—*See Potatoes, Sweet.*

Tomatoes.—Whole tomatoes are not recommended for freezing, since they collapse immediately after thawing and so are difficult to serve. Stewed tomatoes may be frozen statisfactorily, though they are no better than canned tomatoes, and if freezer space is limited, there are better uses for it.

Select uniformly red, fully ripe tomatoes, wash, remove stems, scald and peel. Simmer 5–10 min. Cool by placing pan containing tomatoes in another pan of cold water. If desired, add ½ tsp. salt per pint of tomatoes.

Pack in containers, leaving headspace.

For tomato juice, press simmered tomatoes through sieve while hot, and finish as for stewed tomatoes, adding salt if desired.

Turnip Greens.—*See Greens.*

Turnips.—Select small to medium, firm, tender turnips with mild flavor. Wash, pare and cut into ½-inch cubes. Blanching in boiling water is recommended since it gives a milder flavor, as for blanching broccoli.

Blanch in boiling water 2–2½ min. Drain.

Chill in cold water 4–5 min. Drain.

Pack in containers, leaving ½-inch headspace.

Recommended Storage Period for Vegetables at 0°F.

All vegetables will keep satisfactorily for at least 9–12 months when stored at 0°F. or lower. So if you freeze your home-grown vegetables, you can count on having a supply of them in your freezer from one season to the next.

Approximate Yield of Frozen Vegetables from Fresh

Vegetable	Fresh, as purchased or picked	Frozen, pt.
Asparagus	1 crate (12 2-lb. bunches)	15 to 22
	1 to 1½ lbs.	1
Beans, lima (in pods)	1 bu. (32 lbs.)	12 to 16
	2 to 2½ lbs.	1
Beans, snap, green and wax	1 bu. (30 lbs.)	30 to 45
	⅔ to 1 lb.	1
Beet greens	15 lbs.	10 to 15
	1 to 1½ lbs.	1
Beets (without tops)	1 bu. (52 lbs.)	35 to 42
	1¼ to 1½ lbs.	1
Broccoli	1 crate (25 lbs.)	24
	1 lb.	1
Brussels sprouts	4 quart boxes	6
	1 lb.	1
Carrots (without tops)	1 bu. (50 lbs.)	32 to 40
	1¼ to 1½ lbs.	1
Cauliflower	2 medium heads	3
	1⅓ lbs.	1
Chard	1 bu. (12 lbs.)	8 to 12
	1 to 1½ lbs.	1
Collards	1 bu. (12 lbs.)	8 to 12
	1 to 1½ lbs.	1
Corn, sweet (in husks)	1 bu. (35 lbs.)	14 to 17
	2 to 2½ lbs.	1
Eggplant	1 lb.	1
Kale	1 bu. (18 lbs.)	12 to 18
	1 to 1½ lbs.	1
Mustard greens	1 bu. (12 lbs.)	8 to 12
	1 to 1½ lbs.	1
Peas	1 bu. (30 lbs.)	12 to 15
	2 to 2½ lbs.	1
Peppers, green	⅔ lb. (3 peppers)	1
Pumpkin	3 lbs.	2
Spinach	1 bu. (18 lbs.)	12 to 18
	1 to 1½ lbs.	1
Squash, summer	1 bu. (40 lbs.)	32 to 40
	1 to 1¼ lbs.	1
Squash, winter	3 lbs.	2
Sweet potatoes	⅔ lb.	1

Courtesy of United States Department of Agriculture, from *Home and Garden Bulletin No. 10.*

PREPARING FRUITS FOR FREEZING

Which Ones Can be Frozen?

Most fruits give very satisfactory products when frozen, but there are a few exceptions. Bananas are only satisfactory in a mixture like ice cream. Avocados need to be frozen mashed, for use in spreads or desserts. Pears and grapes are not very satisfactory, but they can be frozen for combining with other fruits in fruit cups and other recipes. Freezing affects the texture of these fruits more than most others, but this is not noticeable when used in such combinations.

Special Points in Selection

Only fruits which are of the best quality in flavor, color and texture should be used. Freeze them at the stage when they are best for eating raw. Freezing softens the texture to some extent, so those which are over-soft when fresh will be mushy when frozen. Such fruits may be satisfactory when frozen as purées, but do not include any that have developed off-flavors or are bruised or moldy.

The variety of some fruits is particularly important, and this includes strawberries, peaches and apples. In general, fruits which are of deep color and rather firm texture when fully ripe are best for freezing.

Promptness in Handling

The importance of prompt handling after picking has already been mentioned for fruits and vegetables in general. This is essential for fruits which have a delicate flavor as a distinctive quality, including all berries, particularly raspberries. Do not begin actual preparation of the fruit until everything is ready. And plan to freeze at one time only as much as can be handled without delay.

Kinds of Packs

Most fruits are better if they are protected from air during freezer storage. For this reason, they are usually covered with liquid. The liquid may be a syrup, or juice drawn from the fruit by sugar, making its own syrup. For special diets with restricted sugar, some fruits are covered with water, but these do not keep their quality as long, in the freezer. A few fruits may be frozen without any addition. In general, sugar not only gives a desirable, sweet flavor, but also helps to retain the natural flavor and texture of the fruit.

Syrup Packs.—Fruits which are rather firm, like apricots, cherries, peaches and plums are usually packed in syrup to cover them. The syrup may be light, medium or heavy, according to the family preference and according to the tartness of the fruit. The sweetness of a heavy pack may mask the flavor of the fruit, though adding a small amount of lemon juice offsets the sweetness. On the other hand, with a light syrup, the fruit should be served while still frosty, for otherwise it softens readily on thawing. To prevent masking the flavor of delicately flavored fruits like melons and pineapple, these are often packed in light syrup. But sour fruits like sour cherries may need a heavy syrup. And if your family feels that fruits in general are "richer" when frozen in heavy syrup, there is no reason why you should not freeze other fruits in heavy syrup, too.

Sugar syrups: In the following table are the proportions of water and sugar to use, to secure the type of solutions you wish to use. The table also tells you how much solution you will obtain from these amounts. Allow about one-half to two-thirds cup of syrup for each pint package of fruit.

Preparation of Sugar Syrups

Approximate per cent of sugar in syrup	Amount of water (c.)	Amount of sugar (c.)	Yield of syrup (c.)
30	4	2	5
35	4	2½	5⅓
40	4	3	5½
50	4	4¾	6½
60	4	7	7¾
65	4	8¾	8⅔
70	4	11	9⅓

To prepare the syrup, add the sugar to the cold water, and see that it is entirely dissolved before using the syrup. For heavy syrups, it may be necessary to heat the solution to dissolve the sugar, and in that case it must be thoroughly *cold* before using it. The syrup may well be prepared the day before, and held in the refrigerator.

Use of corn syrup.—Light corn syrup may be used to replace some of the sugar in preparing the solutions. Dark corn syrup should not be used, since its flavor is too pronounced. Up to one-fourth of the sugar in the above solutions may be replaced by light corn syrup.

Or if you prefer, the following are the proportions of sugar and corn syrup to use for preparing medium and heavy syrups. There is some evidence that using part corn syrup helps to retain the quality of the fruit, especially its natural flavor.

Preparation of Sugar and Corn Syrup Solutions

Ingredients	For two pints of fruit		For twelve pints of fruit	
	medium syrup	heavy syrup	medium syrup	heavy syrup
Cold water	1 c.	1 c.	5 c.	4 c.
Sugar	½ c.	⅔ c.	2 c.	3 c.
Light corn syrup	⅓ c.	⅔ c.	2 c.	2 c.

Use of honey.—Honey can be used in place of corn syrup, but it imparts a slight flavor of its own, so should only be used where its flavor will be acceptable. It blends well with melons.

Packing in containers.—In most cases, put the fruit in the container, then add enough syrup to cover the fruit. Fruits have a tendency to float at the top of the syrup, leaving pieces at the top exposed to the air. If the fruit is light in color, this may cause darkening during freezer storage. To prevent this, place a crumpled piece of water-resistant material at the top of the container, so when the container is closed the fruit will be submerged in the syrup. For this purpose, parchment paper, locker paper, heavy waxed paper or any moisture-vapor-proof material may be used. Keeping fruits submerged in liquid also helps to retain flavor, so this measure may well be used for darker fruits as well as light-colored ones.

Sugar Packs.—For softer, juicier fruits, a sugar pack is often used. This includes berries from which the sugar will extract enough juice from the fruit to provide liquid to cover it. As a rule, place the fruit in a shallow pan or bowl avoiding so many layers that the weight of fruit on top would crush the fruit underneath. Sprinkle sugar over the fruit, mixing it very lightly so as to cover the fruit without injuring it. During a short time of standing, the sugar draws juices from the fruit and so the fruit becomes covered with liquid.

Then pack the fruit with its juice in containers, sometimes placing crumpled water-resistant material at the top, as for syrup-packed fruits.

Unsweetened Packs.—A few fruits, including blueberries, gooseberries, cranberries and currants, can be packed without any addition, but most fruits are better if they are packed with some sugar or syrup. However, for use in special diets where sugar is restricted, many fruits can be frozen unsweetened. Most of them will deteriorate more rapidly in freezer storage, and the time for which they will remain acceptable will depend on the fruit and its quality. It is recommended that packages of such fruits be used rather frequently in the early stages of freezer storage, and when they show signs of becoming inferior, the rest of the supply should be used without delay.

These unsweetened fruits for use in special diets will remain in good condition longer in the freezer, if they are covered with liquid. Unsweetened juice from the same fruit is splendid for this purpose, when it is available. Light-colored fruits like peaches and apricots must be covered with water or they will darken very quickly. Ascorbic acid, citric acid or lemon juice added to the water help greatly in retaining both color and flavor (see below).

Measures to Retain Light Color

Unless measures are taken to prevent it, light-colored fruits like apples, peaches and apricots will darken during freezer storage and very quickly on thawing. Following are the recommended ways of preventing such darkening. Some of these measures also help to retain the flavor and so are recommended, too, for some fruits which are not light in color.

Ascorbic Acid.—Powdered (crystalline) ascorbic acid is available in most drug stores, and directions for using it, as given in the following pages, are in measurements by teaspoons. It is rather expensive, but a little goes a long way, so it does not increase the freezing costs substantially. It is also available in the tablet form, used to supplement ascorbic acid in the diet. When you buy the tablets, the bottle will tell you how many milligrams of ascorbic acid are in each tablet. The following gives the equivalent amounts of ascorbic acid in powdered form and in tablet form.

Equivalent Amounts of Powdered (Crystalline) Ascorbic Acid, and Tablets of Ascorbic Acid

Powdered (crystalline), tsp.	Tablets, milligrams
1/8	375
1/4	750
1/2	1,500
3/4	2,250
1	3,000

Before using, the ascorbic acid should be dissolved in a little cold water. The tablets will dissolve more easily if they are crushed. The addition of ascorbic acid increases the nutritive value of the fruit.

When ascorbic acid is to be used in syrup packs, dissolve it in a little cold water and add it to the syrup a short time before using it. As you add the ascorbic acid to the syrup, stir only gently so as to avoid getting air into the syrup. Keep the syrup cold until it is used. Add ascorbic acid this way, also, to water or juice in which fruit is to be frozen.

To use it with dry sugar packs, dissolve it in a little cold water and sprinkle this solution over the fruit, as evenly as you can. Add it this way, also, to fruits frozen without any sugar or liquid.

Ascorbic Acid Mixtures.—Various ascorbic acid mixtures can be purchased, having different trade names, some containing sugar, citric acid and other ingredients. These are very satisfactory, and in using them follow the manufacturer's instructions.

Citric Acid and Lemon Juice.—These may be used in place of ascorbic acid, but they are somewhat less effective. Lemon juice contains both citric acid and ascorbic acid, but it cannot be used in large enough amounts because of its flavor. Citric acid is available at most drug stores and should be dissolved in water or syrup (as for ascorbic acid), but in different amounts. It is sometimes used in addition to ascorbic acid.

Sulfite Treatment.—Sliced apples may be treated with sodium sulfite or sodium bisulfite, to prevent darkening. For details, see directions for preparing apple slices for freezing.

Steam Treatment.—Some fruits are steamed for a short period, thereby preventing darkening during freezer storage.

Containers for Freezing Fruits

Containers for freezing fruits should be selected on the same basis as for freezing vegetables, see p. 106. The top opening containers are splendid, but are not so essential for freezing any fruits as they are for freezing some vegetables for which arrangement in the package is important.

Selection and Preparation of Each Fruit

For fruits to be treated with ascorbic acid, the amount given in the following instructions is in teaspoons of powdered (crystalline) ascorbic acid. For instructions to use ascorbic acid in tablet form or ascorbic acid mixtures, see p. 121. And for instructions as to head-space required, see p. 100.

Apples, Sliced.—Select firm-ripe, fully mature apples that are crisp and not mealy. Skins should be bright and free from dark spots. To avoid having pared apples stand exposed to the air, do not start preparing them until equipment and solutions are ready for immediate handling. Also, do not prepare so many at one time that they cannot be handled promptly. Wash, pare and core apples. Slice them into twelfths or sixteenths, according to size, directly into a brine solution (2 tbsp. salt to 1 gallon cold water), except when packing them in syrup with ascorbic acid. Keep them in this solution until enough slices are prepared to proceed with treatment, but not more than 15–20 min.

If apple slices are to be used in a pie to be baked *before* freezing, there is no tendency for them to darken. But otherwise, treatment to prevent darkening is essential. Any one of the following three treatments is recommended:

Blanching Treatment.—Slice apples into brine solution, as described above, then blanch, as for vegetables. Blanch in steam (preferred to boiling water), with slices not more than ½-inch deep, for 90 sec.; or in boiling water for 60 sec. Chill in cold water. Drain. Pack into containers with no addition, or with 40 per cent syrup. Or sprinkle ½ c. sugar evenly over each quart (1½ lbs.) of apples, stir carefully, let stand until sugar is dissolved into fruit juice, and pack in containers, leaving headspace.

Sulfite Treatment.—Slice apples into brine, as described above. Have ready a solution made by dissolving 1½ tsp. sodium sulfite or sodium bisulfite (either U.S.P. or C.P. grade, available at drug stores) per gallon of water, in a glass, earthenware, stainless steel or unchipped porcelain container. Do not make this solution stronger than recommended, since this would cause toughening of the apples and give them an off-taste.

When slices from 15 to 20 apples are ready, transfer them from the brine to the sulfite solution for 5 min. A deep wire basket or loose cheesecloth bag is convenient for moving the apples to and from the solutions. Drain slices well and place them in an earthenware, china or glass bowl in the refrigerator for 1–5 hr. before freezing, to allow sulfite solution to penetrate the slices.

Following this treatment, apple slices may be packed without any addition. Or they may be packed in sugar, using 1 lb. sugar to 5–7 lbs. apples (1 c. sugar to 10–12 c. apples). Sprinkle the sugar evenly over the slices, allow them to stand until the sugar is dissolved in juice, then stir carefully until each slice is coated with sugar solution. Pack in containers, leaving headspace.

Syrup Pack with Ascorbic Acid.—Prepare 40 per cent syrup and add ½ tsp. ascorbic acid to each quart of syrup. Pour ½ c. syrup into each pint container and slice apples directly into syrup, then cover apples with syrup. Place crumpled water-resistant material on top of slices, and leave headspace.

Applesauce.—Select full-flavored apples. Wash, pare if desired, core and slice apples. To each quart of apple slices, add about $^1/_3$ c. water and cook until tender. Strain if desired. Sweeten to taste, usually ½–¾ c. sugar for each quart (2 lbs.) of sauce. Add lemon juice or cinnamon if desired. Pack into containers, leaving headspace.

Apricots.—Select well-ripened fruits of uniformly golden-yellow color. They may be frozen peeled or unpeeled. To peel, cover them with boiling water for 15–30 sec., then chill in cold water 1–2 min. and rub off skins. If not to be peeled, heat apricots in boiling water ½ min. to keep skins from toughening during freezer storage, then chill in cold water. Cut in halves or quarters, removing pits.

In Syrup.—Use 40–60 per cent syrup, adding ¾ tsp. ascorbic acid per quart of syrup. Put ½ c. syrup in each pint container, and cut apricots directly into syrup. Add syrup to cover, and put crumpled water-resistant material on top, leaving headspace.

In Sugar.—This is good for use in pies and other cooked desserts. Dissolve ¼ tsp. ascorbic acid in ¼ c. cold water and sprinkle over each quart of apricots. Add ½ c. sugar per quart of apricots, stirring until sugar is dissolved. Pack in containers, leaving headspace

Crushed.—Select fully ripe fruit, peel, pit and crush coarsely. Pack as for halves or quarters, but using 1 c. sugar per quart of crushed apricots. For a better product, dissolve ¼ tsp. ascorbic acid in ¼ c. water and add to each quart of crushed fruit just before adding sugar.

Avocados.—These cannot be frozen satisfactorily as whole or sliced avocados, but must be mashed. Select soft-ripe fruit (neither hard nor mushy), with bright-green rind, free from blemishes. Peel, cut in half and remove pit, then mash the pulp. The pulp may be frozen as sweetened or unsweetened pack.

Sweetened Pack.—For use in ice creams or other desserts. Add 1 c. sugar to each quart of pureé, and mix. Pack in container, leaving headspace.

Unsweetened Pack.—For use in salads, sandwiches, dips. Add ¼ tsp. ascorbic acid or 3 tbsp. lemon juice to each quart of purée, combining well. Pack in containers, leaving headspace.

Blackberries, Boysenberries, Dewberries, Loganberries, Nectarberries, Youngberries.—Select firm, plump, full-ripe berries with glossy skins. Sort, discarding any green berries. Remove leaves and stems, wash quickly in very cold water and drain at once.

In Syrup.—This is preferred for berries to be served without cooking. Pack berries in containers and cover with 40–60 per cent syrup, depending on sweetness and preference. Leave headspace.

In Sugar.—This is satisfactory for berries to be used in cooked products such as pie or other recipes. Place berries in shallow pan or bowl, and add ¾ c. sugar per quart of berries. Turn berries over and over carefully until most of the sugar is dissolved. Pack in containers, leaving headspace.

Unsweetened.—The berries can be packed into containers, leaving no headspace. But a better product is obtained if they are frozen as a loose pack. For this, spread berries in a single layer on a tray or pan, place in freezer until they are frozen, then pack in containers, leaving headspace.

Crushed or Purée.—Prepare berries as for packing whole, then crush berries or press through sieve for purée. Add 1 c. sugar to each quart of berries and stir until sugar is dissolved. Pack in containers, leaving headspace.

Blueberries, Elderberries, Huckleberries.—Select full-flavored, ripe berries with tender skins. Sort, wash quickly in very cold water and drain. To make wild berries more tender-skinned and better flavored, blanch in steam for 1 min. (preferred), or in boiling water 20-30 sec. Chill quickly by placing them in a pan immersed in very cold water. Large, cultivated berries should not be blanched.

In syrup.—This is preferred for berries to be served without cooking. Pack berries into containers and cover with 40 per cent syrup, leaving headspace.

In sugar.—Mix prepared berries with dry sugar in the proportion of ½ c. sugar to 1 quart of berries, stirring gently to draw out juice and dissolve sugar. Pack in containers, leaving headspace.

Unsweetened.- These are satisfactory for use in cooking. Pack into containers, leaving headspace.

Crushed or Purée.—Select fully ripe berries, prepare as for packing whole. Crush or press through sieve. To each quart of berries, add 1-1⅛ c. sugar, stir until sugar is dissolved and pack into containers, leaving headspace.

Boysenberries.—*See Blackberries.*

Cherries, Red Sour.—Select tree-ripened, bright red cherries. Sort, wash quickly in cold water, drain and remove pits.

In Sugar.—Sour cherries are usually used in cooking, and for this they are best packed in sugar. To each quart of cherries, add ¾–1 c. sugar, and mix until sugar is dissolved. Pack in containers, leaving headspace.

In Syrup.—These are for use in uncooked desserts. Place prepared cherries in containers and cover with 50–70 per cent syrup. Leave headspace.

Crushed.—Crush prepared cherries coarsely and to each quart of cherries add 1–1½ c. sugar. Mix until sugar is dissolved. Pack in containers, leaving headspace.

Cherries, Sweet.—Select tree-ripened, large, well colored fruit with sweet, rich flavor. Sort, wash quickly in cold water and drain. It is recommended that pits be removed, since they may impart an almond flavor. Pack in containers and cover with 40 or 50 per cent syrup to which ½ tsp. ascorbic acid has been added per quart of syrup. Place crumpled, water-resistant material on top and leave headspace.

Sweet and sour cherries may be combined in equal amounts, and packed in 50 per cent syrup. Ascorbic acid may be added, as for sweet cherries, but it is not so essential as for sweet cherries alone.

Coconut.—Select fully ripe, moist coconut and grate or grind it rather finely. Pack tightly as dry coconut, or add ½ c. sugar to each 2 lbs. (about 6 c.) grated coconut. Leave headspace.

Cranberries.—Select firm, deep-red cranberries with glossy skins. Stem and sort, discarding any imperfect ones. Wash in cold water and drain.

Unsweetened.—This is one of the few fruits which can be frozen satisfactorily without any addition. Pack into containers, leaving headspace.

In syrup.—If preferred, pack berries into containers and cover with 50 per cent syrup. Leave headspace.

Sauce or Purée.—Prepare cranberry sauce according to your favorite recipe, or make a purée (strain cooked cranberries), sweetening according to taste. Pack in containers, leaving headspace.

Cranberry and Orange Relish.—This relish stands freezer-storage very well. Use the fruits in the proportion of 1 large orange to 2 c. cranberries. Put cranberries, orange rind and orange pulp all through a food chopper, using the medium-fine grind. Add ¾ c. sugar to each 2 c. pulp, and combine thoroughly. Pack in containers, leaving headspace.

Currants.—Select plump, fully ripe, bright-red currants. Wash quickly in cold water, drain at once, and remove stems.

Unsweetened.—These can be packed without any addition, leaving headspace.

In sugar.—Add ¾ c. sugar to each quart of currants, stirring until sugar is dissolved, or crushing slightly. Pack in containers, leaving headspace.

Dates.—Select fresh dates with good flavor, tender and free from blemishes. Wash and slit, then remove pits. Pack in containers, without any addition, and leave headspace.

Dewberries.—*See Blackberries.*

Elderberries.—*See Blueberries.*

Figs.—Select tree-ripened, soft-ripe fruit with tender flesh and skins, and rich flavor. Make sure that figs have not become sour in the center. Sort, discarding immature fruit. Wash and cut off stems and peel if desired. Leave whole, cut in halves or slice.

In syrup.—Pack in containers and cover with 40–60 per cent syrup to which ¾ tsp. ascorbic acid has been added per quart of syrup. One-half cup lemon juice per quart of syrup may be used in place of ascorbic acid. Leave headspace.

Unsweetened.—Pack into containers, leaving headspace. Water may be added to cover, if desired. If water is used, add ¾ tsp. ascorbic acid per quart of water. Use these within three months after freezing.

Fruit Cocktails, Fruit Cups or Fruit Salads.—See Mixed Fruits.

Gooseberries.—Select fully ripe fruit for use in pies, but for making jelly or preserves, select slightly underripe fruit. Sort, remove stems and blossom ends and wash.

Unsweetened.—These are preferred for use in pie or preserves. Pack in containers, without any addition, leaving headspace.

In Sugar.—Crush berries slightly, and add ⅔ c. sugar for each quart of berries, stirring gently until juice is drawn from berries to dissolve most of the sugar. Pack in containers, leaving headspace.

Grapefruit and Oranges.—Select firm fruit, heavy for its size, free from soft spots and tree-ripened if possible. Using a stainless steel knife, peel the fruit, cutting just deep enough to remove all white membrane under the skin. Then section the fruit (or slice oranges, if preferred), removing all section membranes and seeds.

In syrup.—Prepare 40–70 per cent syrup, using excess fruit juice as part of liquid and only as much water as necessary to give the required amount of liquid. Add ½ tsp. ascorbic acid to each quart of syrup. Pack in containers, cover with syrup and leave headspace. Use within 3–4 months.

Grapefruit and Orange Juice.—Select fruit as above and ream *very lightly* so as to avoid pressing any oil from the rind (juice remaining in the fruit after light reaming may be served immediately but should not be frozen). To each quart of juice, add ¼ tsp. ascorbic acid, and if desired, 2 tbsp. sugar. Avoid getting air into juice during reaming or filling containers. Pour into container, leaving headspace. For best flavor, use plastic containers, glass jars or citrus-enamel tin cans.

Grapes.—These are not generally recommended for freezing, since when completely thawed they are quite soft. But they may be used in combining with other fruits. And they are very satisfactory as purée or juice. Select firm-ripe grapes with tender skins, full color and flavor. Wash quickly and remove stems. Seedless grapes may be frozen whole. Cut others in half and remove seeds.

In Syrup.—For serving as dessert, this is preferred. Pack in containers, and cover with 40 per cent syrup, leaving headspace.

Unsweetened.—They may be frozen without any addition, for use in making jelly or preserves. Pack in containers, leaving headspace.

Purée.—Wash, stem and crush grapes, then heat barely to boiling. Drain off free juice and freeze it separately (see below). Cool the grapes and press through a sieve. To each quart (2 lbs.) of purée, add ½ c. sugar and pack in containers, leaving headspace. The purée may develop a gritty texture due to tartrate crystals but these are harmless and will disappear when the purée is heated.

Juice.—For use as a beverage, select grapes as for greezing whole or halved; for use in making jelly, select according to your jelly recipe which may require slightly underripe fruit. Prepare as for purée, but heat only to 150°F. (not quite simmering). Pour into jelly bag to drain. Then let juice stand in refrigerator or other cool place, while sediment sinks to bottom. Pour off clear juice for freezing. Pour into containers, leaving headspace. If tartrate crystals form, they may be removed by straining the thawed juice.

Huckleberries.—*See Blueberries.*

Loganberries.—*See Blackberries.*

Melons (Cantaloup or Muskmelons, Crenshaw, Honeydew, Persian and Watermelon).—These are not strongly recommended for freezing, but are satisfactory for use in combination with other fruits. They should be served when barely thawed. Select firm-fleshed, well-colored, ripe melons. Cut in half, remove seeds and peel. Cut into balls, slices, cubes or wedges.

In Sugar.—Use melons cut into ½–¾-inch cubes or balls. Sprinkle 1 lb. (2 c.) sugar over each 5 lbs. (about 3 quarts) melon, stir until sugar is mostly dissolved. Pack in containers, leaving headspace.

In Syrup.—Pack melon in containers and cover with 30 or 40 per cent syrup. Leave headspace.

Mixed Fruits.—Almost any fruits may be chosen, for combining to provide a variety in color and flavor. Prepare each fruit as for freezing by itself. Pack the combined fruits in containers, cover with 50–70 per cent syrup and leave headspace.

If some of the fruits were frozen at an earlier season, thaw these barely enough to separate pieces, and combine with freshly prepared fruits.

Nectarberries.—*See Blackberries.*

Peaches.—Select firm, ripe peaches with no green color in the skins. Immerse in boiling water about 1 min., then dip in cold water and skins can easily be removed. Cut in halves and remove pits, then slice if desired. But do not peel or cut peaches until containers are ready and syrup is in them.

In Pectin Syrup.—This is the best pack for peaches, since it preserves their texture and color best. Syrup may be prepared from either powdered or liquid pectin, as follows:

Liquid Pectin Syrup

2¾ c. water   1½ c. sugar
½ bottle (about ⅓ c.) liquid fruit pectin

Mix water and sugar in saucepan, and place over low heat, stirring constantly until sugar is dissolved. Remove from heat and stir in pectin. Cover, and chill thoroughly. Just before using, add ½ tsp. ascorbic acid. Makes 1 quart of syrup.

Powdered Pectin Syrup

3⅓ c. water   1¼ c. sugar
1 pkg. powdered fruit pectin

Mix water and pectin in saucepan, bring to boil and boil hard 1 min., stirring constantly. Remove from heat and add sugar, stirring until sugar is dissolved. Cover and chill thoroughly. Just before using, add ½ tsp. ascorbic acid. Makes 1 quart of syrup.

Pour ½ c. syrup into each container, and then peel peaches and cut them directly into syrup. Cover with syrup, and place crumpled water-resistant material on top. Leave headspace.

Courtesy of Frigidaire Division, General Motors Corp.

Slice peaches directly into cold syrup. Then place crumpled, water-resistant material over the peaches to keep them submerged in syrup during storage. These measures help to retain their color

In syrup.—Prepare 40–70 per cent syrup, according to preference, adding ½ tsp. ascorbic acid to each quart. Place ½ c. syrup in each container, then peel peaches and cut them directly into syrup. Add syrup to cover peaches, and place crumpled, water-resistant material on top. Leave headspace.

Unsweetened.—These are only suited for use in diets with restricted sugar. To each quart of water, add 1 tsp. ascorbic acid, and place ½ c. of this in each container. Then peel peaches and cut them directly into water. Cover with water and place crumpled water-resistant material on top. Leave headspace.

Crushed or Purée.—Peaches suited to freezing as halves or slices may be frozen crushed or puréed. Also, those which are somewhat riper may be crushed or puréed. The riper the fruit, the shorter time for scalding to peel them. Crush the peeled and pitted fruit coarsely, or sieve them to make purée. To each quart of crushed or puréed fruit, add ¼ tsp. ascorbic acid and 1 pkg. powdered pectin, combine well and let stand 15 min., stirring occasionally. Add 1 c. sugar and stir to dissolve sugar. Pack in containers, leaving headspace.

Pears.—These do not give a very satisfactory product frozen, but may be useful in combining with other fruits. Select pears that are well-ripened, firm but not hard. Wash in cold water, peel and cut in halves or quarters, removing core. At once place pears in boiling 40 per cent syrup for 1 to 2 min., depending on size. Drain and cool. Then pack in containers with cold 40–60 per cent syrup to which ¾ tsp. ascorbic acid has been added to each quart of syrup. Place crumpled water-resistant material at top and leave headspace.

Persimmons.—It is best to freeze these as purée for use in ice cream, or as an ice cream topping. Select orange-colored, soft-ripe fruit. Sort, wash, peel and cut into sections, then press through sieve. To each quart of purée, add ⅛ tsp. ascorbic acid and combine thoroughly. If desired, 1 c. sugar may also be added. Pack in containers, leaving headspace.

Pineapple.—Select firm, ripe pineapple with full flavor and aroma. Pare and remove core and eyes. Slice, dice or cut pineapple into wedges, or put through food chopper, using medium grind. Prepare 40–70 per cent syrup, according to preference, using pineapple juice if available. Pack fruit tightly into containers, and cover with syrup, leaving headspace.

Pineapple sometimes acquires an off-flavor during freezer storage, so it should be used in a relatively short time.

Plums and Prunes.—Select firm, tree-ripened fruit with deep color. Sort and wash. Leave whole or cut in quarters or halves, removing pit.

In Syrup.—This is suitable for plums or prunes to be used as sauce or in uncooked desserts. Pack in containers and cover with 40–70 per cent syrup to which ½ tsp. ascorbic acid has been added per quart. Leave headspace.

Raspberries, Black, Purple and Red.—Select fully ripe, juicy berries. Sort carefully, and wash *very quickly* in ice water, lifting berries out of water.

In Sugar.—Spread berries in shallow pan or bowl and sprinkle with sugar, using ¾ c. sugar per quart of berries. Mix very lightly to avoid crushing berries, and let stand until sugar is partly dissolved in berry juice. Pack in containers, leaving headspace.

In Syrup.—Pack berries in container and cover with 40–65 per cent syrup, leaving headspace. This is the preferred pack for black raspberries for dessert use.

Unsweetened Pack.—Pack whole berries in containers, leaving headspace. This is good for black raspberries to be used in jam, but berries are usually better if packed in sugar or syrup.

A better product is obtained with unsweetened berries if they are frozen as a loose pack. For this, spead them in a single layer on a tray or pan and place them in the freezer until they are frozen. Pack the frozen berries in containers, leaving no headspace.

Rhubarb.—Select firm, tender, well-colored stalks with good flavor and few fibers. Wash, trim and cut into 1- or 2-inch stalks. To help retain flavor and color, immerse in boiling water for 1 min., chill in cold water and drain.

Unsweetened.—Pack raw or preheated rhubarb tightly into containers, without any addition. Leave headspace.

In Syrup.—Pack raw or preheated rhubarb tightly into containers and cover with 40–60 per cent syrup. Leave headspace.

In Sugar.—Combine raw rhubarb with sugar, using 1 c. sugar to 1 quart rhubarb. Pack in containers, leaving headspace. This is suitable for making pie and no further sugar need be added.

Strawberries.—Select firm, ripe, red berries, preferably with a slightly tart flavor. Sort berries, wash quickly in very cold water, and hull. Berries may be packed whole, crushed, or cut in ½-inch slices. Large berries should be sliced or crushed.

In Syrup.—This is recommended for whole berries. Pack in containers and cover with 40 or 50 per cent syrup. Leave headspace.

In Sugar.—Place sliced or crushed berries in shallow pan or bowl, sprinkle with sugar, using ¾–1 c. to each quart of berries. Mix carefully and let stand until sugar is mostly dissolved. Pack in containers, leaving headspace.

Unsweetened.—Pack sliced or crushed berries in containers, leaving headspace. To help retain better flavor and color, cover with water

Courtesy of Frigidaire Division, General Motors Corp.

To pack in sugar, place sliced or crushed strawberries in a shallow pan or bowl, sprinkle them with sugar, mix carefully and let them stand until the sugar is dissolved. The sugar draws juice from the berries, providing a syrup

(or preferably with strawberry juice) to which 1 tsp. ascorbic acid has been added per quart of water. These are only suited for special diets with restricted sugar.

Youngberries.—*See Blackberries.*

Recommended Storage Period for Fruits at 0°F.

Most fruits will keep satisfactorily for 9–12 months when stored at 0°F. or lower. For a few exceptions, see instructions above, for preparing each fruit. Fruits packed without sugar or syrup for use in diets with restricted sugar keep their good flavor for much shorter periods.

Approximate Yield of Frozen Fruits from Fresh

Fruit	Fresh, as purchased or picked	Frozen, pt.
Apples	1 bu. (48 lbs.) 1 box (44 lbs.) 1¼ to 1½ lbs.	32 to 40 29 to 35 1
Apricots	1 bu. (48 lbs.) 1 crate (22 lbs.) ⅔ to ⅘ lb.	60 to 72 28 to 33 1
Berries[1]	1 crate (24 qt.) 1⅓ to 1½ pt.	32 to 36 1
Cantaloups	1 dozen (28 lbs.) 1 to 1¼ lbs.	22 1
Cherries, sweet or sour	1 bu. (56 lbs.) 1¼ to 1½ lbs.	36 to 44 1
Cranberries	1 box (25 lbs.) 1 peck (8 lbs.) ½ lb.	50 16 1
Currants	2 qts. (3 lbs.) ¾ lb.	4 1
Peaches	1 bu. (48 lbs.) 1 lug box (20 lbs.) 1 to 1½ lbs.	32 to 48 13 to 20 1
Pears	1 bu. (50 lbs.) 1 western box (46 lbs.) 1 to 1¼ lbs.	40 to 50 37 to 46 1
Pineapple	5 lbs.	4
Plums and prunes	1 bu. (56 lbs.) 1 crate (20 lbs.) 1 to 1½ lbs.	38 to 56 13 to 20 1
Raspberries	1 crate (24 pts.) 1 pt.	24 1
Rhubarb	15 lbs. ⅔ to 1 lb.	15 to 22 1
Strawberries	1 crate (24 qts.) ⅔ qt.	38 1

[1] Includes blackberries, blueberries, boysenberries, dewberries, elderberries, gooseberries, huckleberries, loganberries and youngberries.
Courtesy of United States Department of Agriculture, from *Home and Garden Bulletin No 10.*

CHAPTER 8

Freezing Meats, Fish, Poultry, Game and Dairy Products

PREPARING MEATS, FISH, POULTRY AND GAME FOR FREEZING

What Quality Can You Expect?

The quality of the fresh product is more important for meats, fish and poultry than for any other foods. If the product in the beginning is fine in quality, if it is packaged by recommended methods, stored for the recommended time at 0°F. and correctly prepared for the table, it will be of excellent quality when served. Since tenderness, juiciness and flavor are the qualities of special interest in meat, fish and poultry, a discussion of ways in which these can be affected follows.

Tenderness.—Research has shown that freezing may make meat somewhat more tender, but this effect is probably so slight it is scarcely noticeable from a practical standpoint. But this fact does give us assurance that meat which was tender before freezing can certainly give us a frozen product which is at least as tender as the fresh. There is a very occasional exception to this. If some fish or shellfish are held in the freezer for extended periods, they may be rather tough. And if meat, fish or poultry are allowed to lose much of their moisture, they seem tough.

Juiciness.—There are occasional rumors that frozen meats, fish and poultry are dry. But when these products are dry, it is not because freezing has made them so. They will only dry out (become desiccated) when they lose moisture, and this can only happen in two ways. Over an extensive storage period, the dry air in the freezer draws moisture from the product if it is not well packaged in moisture-vapor-proof material. This is especially true in some frost-free freezers (see p. 54). This is one of the reasons why good packaging is essential.

Much fluctuation in freezer temperature above 0°F. during storage will cause desiccation, too. Evidence of this is found in packages which have much frost accumulated inside the package.

The effect of drying out on the surface is called freezerburn. This causes light-colored specks on the surface at first, and eventually the whole surface becomes light in color, and spongy. Such a product will have an off-flavor and be generally unpalatable, but it is safe to eat.

Then, too, if juices escape (leak) from the product during thawing, the product will be dry, for once the juices have escaped it is impossible to get them back into the food.

If loss of moisture during freezer storage, and leakage during thawing are prevented, frozen meats, fish and poultry will be just as juicy as these products when fresh.

Flavor.—When flavor changes occur during freezer storage of meat, fish or poultry, they are due largely to the oxidation of fat. These oxidative changes first give off-flavors and eventually cause rancidity. The tendency for these changes varies greatly with the kind of meat, fish or poultry. Pork becomes rancid more quickly than beef, veal, lamb or poultry; fatty fish more quickly than lean fish; salted products more quickly than unsalted; and variety meats (liver, heart and sweetbreads) more quickly than muscle meats. This explains the different storage periods recommended for these products.

Protecting these foods from the air in the freezer helps to slow down the tendency to become rancid. This is the second reason why good packaging is important. And the lower the storage temperature, the longer the time before off-flavors develop. So if your freezer is one in which the temperature differs from one place to another, store any meat, fish or poultry products which develop off-flavors readily in the coldest part of it.

Selection and Preparation of Meats for Freezing

For meat to be frozen, animals should have the same high quality as for meat to be used fresh. Only healthy, young animals with good "finish" will provide meat which is suitable for freezing. Animals which have been fattened recently and are gaining weight at the time of slaughtering give the best meat.

Slaughtering the Animals.—Slaughtering should be undertaken at the farm only if adequate facilities are available, and it must be skillfully performed by an experienced worker. For many farm families it is best to have it done at a locker plant, or by arrangements with a plant.

Chilling the Meat.—Immediately after slaughtering, hang the meat to chill rapidly to at least as low at 40°F., but do not allow the meat to freeze.

The best temperature for chilling is 32–36°F., and the carcass should reach a temperature of 40°F. within 24–48 hr. Improper or delayed chilling can cause meat spoilage, for example, souring around the bones in heavy animals. Also, rapid chilling has the advantage of retarding bacterial growth and enzyme activity. If outdoor temperature at the time of slaughter is not above 40°F., or if there is a walk-in chilling room, the chilling can be done on the farm. Otherwise, take the carcass to a locker plant or arrange to have it chilled at a meat market.

Immediately after chilling, pork and veal should be frozen, and some authorities include lamb. They should be frozen after at least 24 hr. but not more than 48 hr. of chilling. Pork which is chilled to 40°F. and frozen within 48 hr. after slaughter should keep well in the freezer for one year at 0°F. If it is held for 8–10 days before freezing, it may turn rancid in a few months at this temperature.

Variety meats, including liver, heart, sweetbreads, tongue and kidneys should be frozen immediately after chilling.

Aging the Meat.—Beef is improved in tenderness and in flavor by aging (ripening). Aging should be done under very sanitary conditions, and the best temperature is 34–38°F. Separate rooms for chilling and aging are desirable, so that incoming, warm carcasses are separated from cool ones. The humidity in the aging room should be between 85 and 90 per cent. If it is too low, the meat will dry out, and if too high the meat may get slimy on the cut surfaces.

Most beef should be aged for 8–10 days, depending largely on the amount of fat in it. Prime or choice beef may be aged 14 days and even longer for the most tender product, but beef with poor fat covering should be aged only 5–6 days. Too long aging may impart a strong flavor which some people find objectionable, and it also reduces the time for which it may be held in the freezer.

Mutton to be frozen is improved by aging for 5–7 days. Some authorities recommend that lamb be aged for the same period, but others believe that this has little if any benefit.

Cutting the Carcass.—First, cut the carcass into large, wholesale cuts, then cut these into smaller pieces suited to the family needs. Separate steaks from roasts, pot roasts from stew meat and from meat that should be ground. Cut into portions which are suitable for cooking at one time. To save freezer space, remove all protruding bones and excess fat. Rolled rib roasts take less space than standing rib roasts. Thick steaks dry out less than thin ones. Keep all trimmings and combine these with less tender meat such as from the shank and flank, using these as stew meat, or for grinding for patties or meat loaves.

Bones removed from the carcass, and meat with them, may well be used for making soup stock. It may be frozen as stock, or made into your favorite soup recipe and frozen as soup (see p. 165).

Salt added to ground meat of any kind will increase its tendency to acquire off-flavors during freezer storage, so should be omitted.

If you are inexperienced in cutting a carcass into suitable pieces for freezing, an illustrated, government bulletin is available, giving instructions for doing this. Write to the Superintendent of Documents, Government Printing Office, Washington 25, D. C. (enclosing five cents) and ask for *Home and Garden Bulletin No. 15,* of the United States Department of Agriculture, which is entitled *Freezing Meat and Poultry Products for Home Use.*

In the tables on p. 139, from a Cornell Extension Bulletin, are the approximate weights of cuts obtainable from beef and pig carcasses. In the same bulletin are the following statements concerning these yields:

"A 1000 pound steer will yield about 580 pounds in the carcass (hindquarters—278 pounds, forequarters—302 pounds). This carcass in turn will yield about 435 pounds of retail cuts. The 145 pounds difference (25 per cent) between the carcass and the retail cuts is due to fat, bone and cutting shrinkage. This may vary considerably depending on the amount of fat and bone removed during the processing of the retail cuts. A live pig weighing 220 pounds will yield a carcass weighing about 155 pounds."

Sausage Meat.—The most important precaution in freezing sausage is that salt should not be added before freezing, since this makes it become rancid more quickly in freezer storage. Spices, on the other hand, retard the development of rancidity, so may well be added before freezing. At some locker plants, a prepared seasoning is avail-

Approximate Weights of the Cuts Obtainable from the Hindquarter of a Beef Carcass

	Weight of cut, less cutting and trimming losses	
One hindquarter = 139 lbs.	*25 per cent loss,*[1] *lbs.*	*20 per cent loss,*[1] *lbs.*
Short loin, porterhouse, T-bone and club steaks	19.5	21.0
Sirloin, steaks or roasts	17.5	18.5
Round, steaks or roasts	31.0	34.0
Rump, roasts	6.5	7.0
Flank	2.0	2.0
Ground or stew beef	27.5	28.5
Total weight of cuts	104.0	111.0
Fat, bone, and cutting loss	35.0	28.0
Total	139.0	139.0

[1] Per cent loss will depend upon amount of trimming in cutting the carcass.
Courtesy of New York State College of Home Economics, from *Cornell Extension Bulletin 1038.*

Approximate Weights of the Cuts Obtainable from the Forequarter of a Beef Carcass

	Weight of cut, less cutting and trimming losses	
One forequarter = 151 lbs.	*25 per cent loss,*[1] *lbs.*	*20 per cent loss,*[1] *lbs.*
Rib roasts	16.0	17.5
Short ribs	4.0	4.0
Chuck, steaks or roasts	42.0	45.5
Brisket	14.5	15.5
Plate	15.0	16.0
Ground or stew beef	21.5	22.5
Total weight of cuts	113.0	121.0
Fat, bone, and cutting loss	38.0	30.0
Total	151.0	151.0

[1] Per cent loss will depend upon amount of trimming in cutting the carcass.
Courtesy of New York State College of Home Economics, from *Cornell Extension Bulletin 1038.*

Approximate Weights of the Cuts Obtainable from a Pig Carcass Weighing About 155 Lbs.

Cuts	*Per cent of carcass*	*Pounds*
Hams	18.0–20.0	28.0–31.0
Loins	14.0–16.0	22.0–25.0
Picnics	6.0– 8.0	9.0–12.0
Boston butts	6.0– 8.0	9.0–12.0
Bacon or belly	12.0–14.0	19.0–22.0
Fat	17.0–20.0	26.0–31.0
Lean trimmings	4.0– 5.0	6.0– 8.0
Spareribs and neck bones	4.0– 5.0	6.0– 8.0
Jowl	2.0– 3.0	3.0– 5.0

Courtesy of New York State College of Home Economics, from *Cornell Extension Bulletin 1038.*

able for use in sausage meat, which does not contain salt but does contain an antioxidant to help postpone the development of rancidity. Smoked sausage meat can be held in the freezer somewhat longer than unsmoked.

Ham, Bacon and Other Cured Meats.—These do not keep well in the freezer, the precise time depending on the degree of freshness, curing and smoking. Bacon, especially, does not keep well in the freezer, particularly if it is sliced. Bacon purchased at the store should not be frozen unless it has been freshly cured, and this can seldom be assured. If pork cuts are to be cured, it is best to freeze them fresh and cure them after thawing.

Variety Meats.—Livers, sweetbreads, kidneys, hearts and tongue may be kept very well in the freezer for short periods, but they develop off-flavors if held for long. This is especially true of pork livers.

Lard.—The fat trimmed from hog carcasses should be rendered into lard as quickly as possible, and may be packed into grease-proof containers for storing in the freezer. The time for which the flavor will remain good can be prolonged by adding an antioxidant which is usually available at a locker plant. Or it helps to add a 3-lb. can of hydrogenated vegetable shortening to each 50 lbs. of lard while the lard is cooling.

Purchasing Meat to Be Frozen.—Questions in purchasing meat to be frozen are the same as for meat to be used fresh, except it is better to select only the better grades for freezing. The United States government grades suitable for freezing are Prime (not often available on the retail market), Choice and Good. Meat packers have their own grades, corresponding to government ones. The lower grades are just as nutritious, but not tender or juicy or flavorsome enough to be suitable for freezing.

It is a good idea to make a survey of market prices and compare the price you would pay for purchasing meats retail and wholesale. Very definite savings can be made by wholesale purchases. If you do not have enough space in your freezer for all the meat to be purchased wholesale, this is a good use for space in a locker in a locker plant. But before purchasing a quarter or side of beef, or any other wholesale quantity, try to estimate the amount your family will enjoy of the various cuts to be included in your purchase. You will not want to buy more of any one kind of meat than your family will enjoy within the time it is in good condition in your freezer or locker.   The information concerning cuts available from quarters of beef and from a pig carcass, in the tables on p. 139 will help you in making such an estimate.

Packaging Meats.—Put into one package only as much meat as will be cooked at one time.   This is especially important for variety meats, since these should be cooked soon after removal from the freezer.

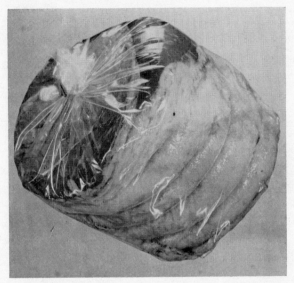

Courtesy of Kordite Corp.

Roasts of any kind need to be snugly wrapped in moisture-vapor-proof material.   This one is wrapped in a plastic bag, and tightly sealed.   Whole poultry may also be wrapped in this way

Most meats are wrapped in sheet wrapping materials (see p. 184), and only those which are moisture-vapor-proof should be used.   The drug store method of wrapping is strongly recommended as giving the best protection.   Wrap packages snugly and seal well, to exclude air and keep in moisture.   Cut off sharp, protruding bones, since these are apt to tear the wrapping material.   Use an overwrap if the wrapping material punctures easily.

Ground meat patties, chops or steaks should be packed with *two* thicknesses of wrapping material between them, so the pieces can be separated without thawing in case this is desirable. These are usually wrapped by the drug store method, but if bags or containers of suitable size and shape are available, these may be used. They are not good, however, unless air can be well excluded from them.

Label each package to show the date and exact contents. This should include the number of meat patties, the number and kind of chops or steaks, for instance.

Meat patties, steaks or chops need to be separated with two thicknesses of wrapping material between them, before freezing. Otherwise, on taking them from the freezer they cannot be separated until they are thawed

Freezing Meats.—When the meat is packaged, you are ready to freeze it. Follow the manufacturer's instructions as to whether the meat should be frozen in any particular place in your freezer. And see p. 62 or follow the manufacturer's instructions as to how much can be frozen at one time. If you are freezing more than this, take it to a locker plant for freezing.

Storage Periods for Meats.—It is impossible to give definite periods for which meats may be stored, for this depends on many factors, including the quality of the meat when it is frozen, how well it is wrapped and whether your freezer maintains a constant temperature of approximately 0°F. Following are recommendations which serve as a guide.

Recommended Storage Periods for Meats, at 0°F.

Storage period, in months	Kind of meat
9–12	Beef, lamb and veal, not ground
4–6	Fresh pork, not ground; all ground meats, except pork
3–4	All variety meats, except pork livers
2–3	Smoked ham or pork; bacon slab; unsalted, ground pork; smoked and seasoned sausage; wieners with skins
1–2	Pork livers; pork links; sausage, seasoned and salted but not smoked; sliced bacon (not recommended)

Selection and Preparation of Fish and Shellfish for Freezing

Fish.—The freshness of "fresh" fish is extremely important, since they deteriorate rapidly after they are caught. They should be frozen the day they are caught, if possible, or be well surrounded by ice or refrigerated. Any kind of fish, correctly prepared and wrapped for freezing can be held in the freezer, though the time of storage differs according to the kind of fish.

Fish should be prepared for freezing exactly as for cooking. Scale it, eviscerate it and wash it thoroughly, especially the eviscerated cavity. Remove the head and cut off fins. Small fish may be frozen whole but large ones should be cut into steaks, chunks or fillets.

Whole Fish.—Small fish may be frozen whole. The size needs to be such that the whole fish will be used at one meal.

Fish Steaks.—Large fish may be cut into steaks. Cut the fish crosswise, retaining one vertebra in each steak, or else making steaks ⅝-inch thick, each steak the size for one serving. Toward the narrow, tail end, steaks should be cut thicker, to give pieces of about the same weight.

Fish Chunks.—These are cut from large fish as for steaks, but thicker. They may be 4–6 inches thick, each one providing several servings, perhaps enough for the family. They are especially useful for fish to be baked.

Fish Fillets.—Cut a fillet from each side of a large fish. Run the knife along the backbone of one side, removing a fillet, then turn the fish over and cut a similar fillet from the other side of the backbone.

If the fillet is very long, it may be cut in half, crosswise. Any bones remaining should be pulled or cut out.

Treatment of Prepared Fish.—In brine solution. Whole fish should not be given this treatment, but all lean (not fatty), cut fish should be held a short time in this solution. For a list of some lean fish, see p. 254. This treatment is chiefly to reduce the amount of leakage (drip) during thawing, and it also helps to retain the flavor and firmness of the flesh.

Dissolve ¼ c. salt in each quart of cold water and immerse the fish in it for 20–30 sec.

Fatty fish should not be treated this way, since it tends to make them acquire off-flavors more quickly in the freezer.

In ascorbic acid solution. All fatty fish which have been cut into steaks, chunks or fillets should be treated in an ascorbic acid solution. This is chiefly to prevent off-flavors during freezer storage, and it also helps to prevent "rusting" (yellowing of the surface) of the fish. For a list of some fatty fish, see p. 254.

Dissolve from 1 tsp. to 1 tbsp. powdered (crystalline) ascorbic acid in each quart of cold water and immerse the fish in this solution for 20 sec.

Packaging Fish:—In moisture-vapor-proof materials or containers. Fish may be wrapped in moisture-vapor-proof wrapping materials and sealed, as for meats (see p. 141). Or they may be packaged in moisture-vapor-proof containers or bags, if sizes and shapes are available so that air can be excluded from them. If the pieces fit well into glass jars, these are especially good. In all containers or bags, leave ½-inch headspace.

Pieces of fish should be separated by *two* thicknesses of wrapping material, so they can be separated before thawing, if this is desirable.

In ice glaze. Place whole fish in the freezer, unwrapped fish into covered, until it is frozen hard. Then dip the unwrapped fish into a pan of water which is at near-freezing temperature, and at once put the fish back into the freezer. The water freezes, forming a thin film of ice (glaze) over the surface of the fish. Repeat this three or four times, or until the fish is uniformly glazed with a coating of ⅛-inch of ice.

Wrap the glazed fish in moisture-vapor-proof material. This not only prevents evaporation of ice but also prevents it from being chipped or cracked.

In ice. Place the fish in a pan of suitable size, cover it with cold water and place in freezer until the ice is a solid block. Then place the pan in water just long enough to remove the frozen block containing the fish. Wrap and return to the freezer. This provides splendid protection, and is especially good for small fish like smelts.

Labelling packages. Label each package with the date and exactly what is in it—the kind and number of steaks, or fillets, or the number of servings in fish chunks.

Courtesy of Reynolds Metals

Small, whole fish, or fish fillets may be wrapped in aluminum foil. Seal all the edges together by making a tight, double fold of foil

Shellfish.—*Clams, Oysters and Scallops.*—Chill thoroughly and freeze the same day they are removed from water or beds, if possible; or keep on ice or refrigerated. Wash thoroughly, to remove shell fragments, sand and foreign matter on the outside of the shell.

Shuck, or open, and remove the whole clam, oyster or scallop. Collect meats in strainer and let drain, reserving liquor. Wash thoroughly in brine, using 1 tbsp. salt per quart of water, and leaving in this solution not more than 3–4 min.

Pack into water-tight containers and cover with liquid, using drained liquor and brine made as above.   Place crumpled, water-resistant wrapping material on top, and leave headspace.

Crabs and Lobsters.   Use only *live* crabs or lobsters, and prepare for freezing immediately after taking from the water.   Steam or boil for 15–20 min., to preserve color and flavor.   Cool (for easier handling), and pick meat from shells.   For crabs, pack meat from legs separate from meat from body.   Pack in any container recommended for fruits or vegetables.   For dry pack, pack meat tightly to prevent formation of large crystals which make meat tough.   If the meat is to be held for more than 4 months, cover with brine made from ¾ c. salt per quart of water, place crumpled water-resistant wrapping material on top, and leave headspace.

Shrimp.   Cooked shrimp become tough rapidly in freezer storage, so they should be frozen raw.   Remove and discard heads, wash in brine (using 1 tsp. salt to 1 quart water), drain and pack in containers or bags without removing shells.   Any containers or bags recommended for fruits and vegetables are satisfactory.   Leave ¼-inch headspace.

If definite plans are made to use shrimp within a few weeks, it may be a convenience to cook them before freezing, but they should not be held longer than this.   Remove heads from shrimp, cook as for serving fresh, remove shells and veins.   Pack closely in moisture-vapor-proof containers, leaving ½-inch headspace.

Freezing Fish and Shellfish.—For freezing these products, follow the instructions for freezing meats, p. 142.

Recommended Storage Periods for Fish and Shellfish at 0 °F.

Storage period	Kind of fish or shellfish
4–6 months	Lean fish
3–4 months	Fatty fish, clams, oysters, scallops, raw shrimp
2–3 months	Cooked crab and lobster meat
1–2 months	Cooked shrimp

Selection and Preparation of Poultry for Freezing

Chickens, ducks, geese and turkeys can be frozen successfully.   If well selected and handled, and if correctly packed and stored for only the recommended time, they are as good as fresh birds.   Occasionally, there may be a brownish color around the joints of young birds, but this is not in the least harmful, nor does it give any off-flavor.

Selecting, Killing and Cleaning Birds.—Birds, which are healthy, plump and of good "finish" should be selected for freezing. They should be starved for 24 hr. prior to freezing, but should be given plenty of water. They may be killed by disjointing the neck, by "sticking" or by cutting off the head. Immediately after killing, hang by the feet for about 1 min. to bleed thoroughly. Feathers on the tail and wings can then be removed.

Then semiscald the bird by holding it in water at 125°–135°F. for 20–30 sec. Hang the bird by the feet for easy removal of the feathers. A good way to singe for removing hairs is to light 2–3 tbsp. rubbing alcohol in a tin can, since this gives no discoloration or smoke. During these operations, avoid tearing or bruising the skin. Remove the head and cut off the neck close to the body, then wash the bird in cold water. Cut off the oil sac and remove the feet and any sharp, protruding wing projections. Eviscerate the bird, reserving the heart, liver and gizzards from which the lining and contents have been removed, and wash these thoroughly. Wash and rinse the visceral cavity very thoroughly and drain. If the bird is to be stored in the freezer for long, it is well to freeze separately the fat which was around the entrails before they were removed, since this fat becomes rancid more quickly than the fat which is under the skin.

To insure maximum tenderness, leave the cleaned bird in the refrigerator for 12–24 hr. before freezing it.

Giblets.—Giblets, especially livers, will only remain in good condition in the freezer for about 3 months, whereas the birds will be good for 6–12 months, depending on the kind. If the birds are sure to be used within 3 months, giblets may be wrapped and placed in the cavity of whole birds, or in the package with others. Otherwise, pack the giblets by themselves in suitable sized moisture-vapor-proof containers or bags, leaving headspace.

Kinds of Poultry and Methods of Packing.—*Chickens.*—*Broilers.* Young, tender birds, 1–2½ lbs. Usually broiled as halves, or if large as quarters, and packed for freezing in these pieces. If large, may be roasted whole for a small family, freezing them whole.

Fryers. Young, tender birds, 2½–3½ lbs. Usually fried in serving pieces and packed for freezing in these pieces. May be broiled in quarters and packed for freezing accordingly.

Capons. Young castrated male birds over 4 lbs., with the most popular market size 5–7 lbs. Roasted and packed whole for freezing.

Roasters.   Young tender birds, over 3½ lbs.   Usually roasted whole and packed whole for freezing.   May be fried, and for this are packed cut-up for freezing.

Pullets.   Young tender birds, 3½–5½ lbs.   May be cooked as preferred and packed accordingly.

Fowl.   Older females, 2½ lbs. and over, usually more than 3½ lbs. when purchased.   Less tender birds to be used for fricasseeing, stewing or braising.   Packed cut-up for freezing.

Turkeys.—For birds from 8–15 lbs. hen turkeys are best, but for larger ones select tom turkeys.   May be packed in parts, quarters, halves or whole for freezing, according to intended use.

Ducks.—Young birds, 4–6 lbs., usually packed whole for freezing.

Geese.—Tender birds, usually 8–12 lbs., packed whole for freezing.

Preparing Whole Birds.—Any birds may be frozen whole, for roasting.   If these are to be roasted without complete thawing, it is important that the visceral cavity be well cleaned, since this cannot be done on removal from the freezer until the bird is thawed.

Truss the bird to make it as compact as possible.   Use heavy twine to hold the wings and legs close to the body, but not so tightly as to tear the skin.   Sharp, protruding pieces of bone which cannot be removed should be padded well with wrapping material to prevent puncturing the wrapper during storage.

Stuffing birds for home freezing is *not* recommended, because spoilage is apt to occur as a result of bacterial growth at lukewarm temperatures.   Commercially stuffed poultry is prepared under special conditions and with extreme speed not available in the home.

Using moisture-vapor-proof material, wrap the bird snugly by the drug store method and seal, as for meats (see p. 141).   Or the birds may be wrapped in large plastic bags, excluding as much air as possible.   If polyethylene bags are used, lower the bag containing the bird three-fourths of the way down into a deep pan or tub of hot (not boiling) water, not allowing water to get into the bag.   The hot water collapses the bag firmly around the bird, expelling air.   Make the proper closure on the bag.

Whole birds are best if overwrapped (see p. 91) to prevent the wrapping material from being punctured during storage.

Preparing Half and Quarter Birds.—Broiling chickens are usually cut in halves (large ones in quarters) and other chickens may be frozen in halves, if desired.

To cut a turkey in half, lay the bird on its side and remove the neck-and-back strip by cutting from neck to tail along both sides of the inside of the breastbone. It may then be cut crosswise to make quarters. If this is difficult for you to do, your butcher may do it for you.

Place the pieces together, as a whole bird, or package the pieces separately. If several pieces are in the same package, place *two* thicknesses of wrapping material between them, to facilitate separating them without complete thawing. Wrap snugly, by the drug store method, and seal well.

Preparing Cut-Up Birds.—Chicken or turkey to be fried, fricasseed, stewed or braised takes less space in the freezer and is more convenient to use if it is cut-up before freezing.

Disjoint into serving pieces, leaving the leg whole or separating the thigh, as preferred. Disjoint turkey the same way, or leave the wing attached to the breast. Be sure each piece is clean and well drained. Bony pieces (back, neck and wings) are not usually frozen since there are better uses for freezer space.

For wrapping, place the pieces compactly in a freezer bag, or wrap snugly in wrapping material by the drug store method, and seal. If cartons of the right size and shape are available so that air can be excluded, these can be used.

To speed thawing, and to be able to separate pieces before complete thawing, each piece may be wrapped in wrapping material before packing.

Fresh, Purchased Poultry.—As a rule, if you buy market poultry, it is better to buy it already frozen, rather than buy it fresh and freeze it yourself. However, if you buy a fresh bird and find you do not want to use it soon, it can be frozen. *Do not* freeze it in the wrapper in which you buy it.

Be sure the bird is clean; remove any remaining lung tissue inside the cavity, and remove pinfeathers. For wrapping, follow the instructions above, according to whether the bird is whole or cut-up.

Labelling.—Label all packages clearly with the date and the exact contents.

Freezing Poultry.—For freezing poultry, follow the instructions for freezing meats, p. 142. As evident from the following storage periods, turkeys, ducks, or geese cannot be held in the freezer as long as chickens, since they become rancid more quickly.   Poultry giblets should be stored a still shorter time.

Recommended Storage Periods for Poultry, at 0°F.

Storage period in months	Kind of poultry
12	Chickens
6	Ducks, geese and turkeys
3	Poultry giblets

Preparation of Wild Game for Freezing

There are laws in most states that govern the amount of game any one person may put into storage, and how long it may be kept there. These laws differ from state to state, and it is necessary to be familiar with them.   Your State Game Warden is the man who has this information, probably also your locker plant operator.   They will also be able to tell you how the game must be "tagged" for storage.

The care of game after killing should be much the same as of domestic animals of a similar type.   Promptness and sanitary conditions in handling are important, since spoilage starts soon in the area of the wound.   Never heap small game together (as in the trunk of a car) but keep them as cool as possible and with good air circulation. If there is a locker plant in the vicinity, it is a good plan to have the plant handle the game and freeze it, then you can take it home packed in Dry Ice to keep it frozen until you get it into your freezer.

Large Game.—Deer, moose, antelope and other large game must be handled much like beef.   If the carcass is in very good condition and can be quickly chilled, it may be ripened for 5-6 days, otherwise it is better to freeze the meat without aging it.

Small Game.—Small four-footed animals like rabbits and squirrels should be bled, skinned, cleaned and washed thoroughly.   Most people freeze only the meaty back and hind quarters, using the ribs, neck and forelegs fresh in stews.

Game Birds.—Pheasants and other game birds are handled much as poultry is handled.   Prompt care is essential, to prevent tainting of meat from undigested food in the intestine.

Fish.—Follow directions for preparing fish for freezing, remembering especially that keeping fish surrounded by ice or in the refrigerator until time of freezing is especially important.

Packaging and Labelling Game.—Package and label game in the same way as for corresponding domestic animals.

Freezing and Freezer Storage of Game.—Freeze according to the instructions for corresponding domestic animals. The time for which game may be held in the freezer is similar to the time for similar, domestic animals, if the game is well handled. Venison, rabbits and all game birds may be stored at 0°F. for one year. For storage periods for fish, see p. 146. However, if delays occur or if conditions are not entirely satisfactory, the storage periods will be shorter.

SELECTION AND PREPARATION OF DAIRY PRODUCTS FOR FREEZING

A number of dairy products which are usually stored in the refrigerator for short periods can be stored for much longer in the freezer. Instructions for freezing these products follow.

Butter and Margarines

Butter made from unpasteurized, sweet or sour cream turns rancid rapidly, and for best results, butter for freezing should be made from pasteurized sweet cream. If you make your own butter, pasteurize the cream by holding it at 145°F. for 30 min., then cool rapidly. Salted butter does not keep so long, so if it is to be held in the freezer for long, do not add salt or salt only lightly. Wrap in moisture-vapor-proof material.

If you purchase butter, try to get it freshly made. Margarines may be frozen, too, and will keep somewhat longer than butter.

Cream

Sweet cream which has been pasteurized and has at least 40 per cent butter fat (heavy cream) may be frozen for use in making ice cream or in cooking. Pour into moisture-vapor-proof containers, leaving headspace. Or add 3–4 tbsp. sugar per pint of cream and whip. Drop the whipped cream by tablespoon portions on a pan and freeze, then package into containers, placing *two* thicknesses of wrapping material between layers. On removing from the freezer, these mounds of whipped cream are ready to serve within minutes.

Ice Cream

For making your own ice cream, use a generous proportion of pasteurized cream, and pack into moisture-vapor-proof containers, leav-

ing headspace. Ice cream which you purchase and leave in the original paperboard containers will become coarse and grainy after 2 or
3 weeks, so to keep it longer, tranfer it to moisture-vapor-proof containers.

Eggs

Fresh eggs may well be frozen when they are plentiful, for use
when they are scarce or high-priced. They should be strictly fresh,
with thoroughly cleaned shells to avoid getting foreign material into

Courtesy of Ball Brothers Corp.

*Egg whites may be frozen "as is," with no addition, taking
care to include no egg yolk if they are to be whipped on thawing. For directions for freezing egg yolks and whole eggs, see p. 153*

the contents to be frozen. They should not be frozen in the shell,
since the contents expand during freezing, and may crack the shell.
Also, the yolks in such eggs would be gummy and thick.

Package eggs in small, moisture-vapor-proof containers, with only
the amount to be used at one time. Label each package to indicate
how many whole eggs, yolks or whites, or the measure in cups.

Eggs may be frozen as whole eggs, egg whites or egg yolks. Break each egg into a saucer first before combining with other eggs, so that if it is not in good condition it can be discarded and not contaminate the rest of the eggs.

Egg Whites.—In separating the whites from the yolks, be sure that no specks of yolk get into the whites, if they are to be used for whipping. After freezer storage, these can be used exactly as fresh whites are used, including whipping for angel food cakes. Nothing needs to be added. Pour into containers, leaving headspace.

Whole Eggs.—Measures are essential to prevent the yolks from becoming gummy or thick during freezer storage. For eggs to be used in making cakes or other baking, or for desserts, add 1 tbsp. corn syrup or sugar to each cup of eggs. For those to be used in non-sweet foods like mayonnaise or scrambled eggs, add 1 tsp. salt per cup of eggs. Break the yolks with a fork and combine yolks and whites well, but do not incorporate air. Pour into containers, leaving headspace.

Egg Yolks.—These need an addition, for the same reason as for whole eggs. For each cup of egg yolks, add 2 tbsp. corn syrup or sugar, or 1 tsp. salt, according to intended use. Break yolks with a fork and combine well but do not incorporate air. Pour into containers, leaving headspace.

Equivalents.—The following equivalents are useful in using frozen eggs:

> 1 tbsp. egg yolk equals 1 egg yolk
> 1½ tbsp. egg white equals 1 egg white
> 2½ tbsp. whole egg equals 1 whole egg

Cheeses

Many kinds of cheese may be held in the freezer far longer than in the refrigerator. Except for cottage cheese, they are best if wrapped in aluminum foil.

Hard cheeses like Cheddar, or semihard brick cheese should be frozen in packages of not more than ½ lb. These may be drier after freezer storage, but otherwise are like the fresh.

Blue-mold cheeses, including bleu cheese, Roquefort and Gorgonzola keep well in the freezer. On thawing, they may be more crumbly than when fresh, but this is fine for use in salads or salad dressings. For use in spreads, work in enough cream to secure the desired consistency.

Soft cheeses like Camembert and Liederkranz are very satisfactory when frozen, since in freezer storage, they do not ripen further. For best flavor, they should be at room temperature when served. Removing them from the freezer and holding them in the refrigerator a day or two before serving, further improves their flavor.

Cottage cheese, especially when uncreamed and made from pasteurized cream, can be frozen satisfactorily. It is best if frozen rapidly, so freeze in half-pint, moisture-vapor-proof containers, leaving headspace.

Recommended Storage Periods for Dairy Products at 0 °F.

Storage period in months	Kind of dairy product
12	Margarines
6–9	Unsalted, or lightly salted butter, and cheeses except cottage cheese
3–4	Heavy cream, cottage cheese
2–3	Ice cream

CHAPTER 9

Freezing Prepared and Cooked Main Course Foods and Soups

MAIN-COURSE FOODS

Many meat, fish and poultry preparations and main-course dishes, and some cooked vegetables can be frozen satisfactorily. In many instances, it is a splendid idea to prepare 2 or 3 times the usual recipe, and freeze the portion not used at once. Often, it requires very little extra work to prepare the large amount at one time, and this also saves cooking fuel. And it is a great convenience to have these in the freezer for parties or emergencies, or day-to-day use. These are sometimes called "planned left-overs," or "planned-overs."

Then, too, if you find you have prepared more than you need for the present, the left-over portion of these dishes can be frozen. Many times, the family will enjoy it more if it is served at a later date, rather than the day following its first appearance at the table.

Cleanliness

Freezing does not by any means kill all the micro-organisms in foods, and since many of these products are high-protein ones in which harmful bacteria thrive well, every effort should be made to have as few as possible of these in the food when it is put into the freezer. The "fresh" food should be as fresh as possible, high quality and clean. And all utensils with which the food comes in contact should be clean, to avoid contamination.

Speed in Freezing

There are two very important reasons why these foods should be frozen promptly after they are prepared. It is at lukewarm temperatures that harmful bacteria grow best, so if the food is allowed to cool slowly and remain at room temperature for some time before freezing, there may be larger numbers of these bacteria in the food when frozen. For a discussion of problems in this connection, see p. 29.

While cooked foods are cooling, the flavoring materials gradually

155

escape, partly with the steam, and this is the chief reason why warmed-over foods seldom taste as delicious as freshly prepared ones. Any of these meat, fish or poultry preparations, or main-course dishes which were left from a meal will have stood some time before freezing, and will not have as good flavor when served as those which are planned for freezing and are cooled and frozen immediately.

So any of these products which have been cooked should be cooled promptly. When possible, submerge the pan containing the hot food in another pan of ice water. Keep the food covered, to hold in the steam, stirring occasionally to cool the food uniformly. If the pan is a very heavy one, the food will cool more quickly if it is transferred to a light-weight pan. As soon as thoroughly cooled, pack into containers and freeze at once.

Selection of Containers

The containers must be moisture-vapor-proof and in many cases must be suitable for moist foods. The size should be such that in one container there will be only enough food for preparing to serve at one time, except for a few foods like roasts. Cooked foods must not be put into waxed paperboard containers until thoroughly cooled, otherwise the wax will melt. If the food is to be reheated in the oven, packing in aluminum containers or oven-glass casseroles makes it possible to put them directly into the oven from the freezer. For the use of oven-glass casseroles, see p. 96. Leave headspace for all moist foods. For products like stews it is a good idea to place crumpled, water-resistant wrapping material at the top before closing the container, since this will keep the pieces submerged in the liquid, and so will preserve their flavor and color.

Many of these foods may be frozen in wrapping (sheet) material, using the drug store method of wrapping (see p. 86).

Meat, Fish and Poultry Preparations

Preparation for Freezing.—As a rule, meat or poultry to be roasted is better if frozen raw and cooked after freezing. However, when more has been prepared than can be used at once, the left-over portion can be frozen. It is well to roast beef to the rare or medium stage if it is to be reheated for serving, for then it need not be overdone in preparation for the table. Pork, however, must always be roasted to the well done stage. Baked or boiled ham can be frozen, too.

The fact that meat (or other food) has been frozen before it was cooked does not mean it cannot be frozen again after it is cooked.

Stuffings should be removed from the birds and frozen separately.

When meat is sliced, more surface is exposed to the air in the container and this causes surface drying and may give off-flavors. So it is better left unsliced. Or if sliced and to be reheated for serving, place some gravy or sauce in the container, add the sliced meat and cover with gravy or sauce.

Courtesy of Swift and Co.

Left-over turkey or other poultry or meat may be wrapped in meal-sized portions for freezing. Stuffing should be removed from the poultry and wrapped separately

Roast poultry takes less space in the freezer if the bones (at least the large ones) are removed. Then the meat can be packed compactly in the container, or wrapped in wrapping (sheet) material.

Swiss steaks and other braised meats and poultry, and cooked meat balls may be frozen. These keep better if covered with gravy or sauce. Raw hash or scrapple may be packed snugly into containers. Stew meats and fricassee poultry or veal can be cooked and frozen in their gravy or sauce.   Or if preferred, some of the vegetables may be added to this before freezing (see pp. 160 and 161–162).

Meat, fish and poultry loaves can be frozen before or after baking. But it takes about as long to reheat a frozen, baked loaf as to bake one which is frozen raw, so there is no advantage in baking it before freezing.   If it is to be served as cold slices, then it is convenient to bake it before freezing.

Courtesy of Aluminum Company of America

Meat, fish or poultry loaves come in handy, in your freezer.   Prepare several at a time, and freeze those not needed right away

Fried foods can be frozen, but these are not as crisp as when served fresh.   It is especially important that these be thoroughly cooled before packing into containers, otherwise they will be soggy.

For directions for freezing cooked shrimp, crabs and lobster meat, see p. 146.

Preparation for Serving.—Roasts may be reheated in the oven for serving, thawed first or not, as you wish.   If not thawed first, use a very slow oven so the inside will be heated before the outside is too crusty.

Many cooked meats and poultry are splendid when served sliced on a cold luncheon or dinner plate, or in sandwiches. Thaw these in the unopened container and serve as soon as completely thawed. Those which are frozen in sauce or gravy may be reheated in the top of the double boiler, in a heavy skillet over very low heat until completely thawed, or in a covered casserole or steamer. To insure uniform heating, it may be necessary to stir occasionally, but do not break up pieces or mash them.

Before stuffing is completely thawed, place it in a greased casserole, cover and heat in oven at 350°F., uncovering for the last few minutes of heating.

Stewed or braised meats, fricassees or similar products may be reheated in their gravy or sauce, over direct heat, keeping the heat low until thawed. Or some of these may be reheated in the top of the double boiler. Hash may be baked or fried without preliminary thawing, if a low temperature is used until thawed. Scrapple, too, may be fried without preliminary thawing. To remove these from their freezing containers, place the container in water until the frozen block will slip out.

Foods to be baked or reheated in the oven for serving can be transferred directly from the freezer to the oven, if the freezing container is suitable for this. This includes meat, fish and poultry loaves, and from 1 to 1½ hr. should be allowed in an oven at 350°F. depending on the size of loaf. Baked loaves may be reheated or thawed and sliced cold.

To reheat fried foods, place them, hard-frozen, in a single layer on a pan in the oven at 400°F., and heat to serving temperature. This will usually take 15 min., or longer, depending on the size of piece.

Once any of these products has been completely thawed it should not be refrozen.

Gravies and Main-Course Sauces

Many gravies and a great variety of main-course sauces freeze well. Sauces include tomato, creole, curry, barbecue and many others. If these are "left-overs" and have stood any length of time since being prepared, it is well to bring them to a vigorous boil (to kill harmful bacteria), chill quickly and freeze at once. These are usually reheated in the top of the double boiler, but direct heat may be used if heat is kept low and if the sauce is one which does not burn readily.

These products are apt to appear "curdled" during thawing, but on stirring they may regain their smoothness. This tendency to curdling of cream sauce is reduced if the flour and fat are thoroughly combined when the sauce is being prepared. These gravies and sauces may be somewhat thicker than when freshly prepared, but suitable liquid can be added to give the desired consistency.

Cooked Vegetables

Except in combination with other foods, most vegetables should not be cooked before freezing, since they will taste like warmed-over ones when served. However, pumpkin, winter squash and sweet potatoes are usually cooked before freezing, and directions for these are given in connection with freezing these vegetables. Harvard beets freeze well, and may be reheated for serving in the top of the double boiler.

French-fried onion rings may be frozen, using a high-quality fat for frying, and following the general directions for deep-fat frying potatoes, given below, but without scalding.

Potatoes may be prepared in several ways for freezing, as follows:

French-Fried or Shoe-String Potatoes.—Cut the potatoes rather thinly, and scald them. Scalding gives a lighter colored fried potato, so select the time of scalding which gives the desired color. Use a high-quality fat for frying, otherwise an off-flavor will develop during freezer storage. Fry as usual, drain, and when cooled to room temperature, pack in containers. To reheat, place in a single layer on pan in oven at 400°F. for 10–20 min., turning frequently. If preferred, these may be reheated in a small amount of hot fat in a skillet over low heat, turning them frequently. Potato chips may also be frozen.

Baked Stuffed Potatoes.—Prepare as for serving fresh, cool and pack in containers. To reheat, remove the wrapper and place in oven at 350°F. for 30–50 min., depending on size.

Mashed Potatoes.—Prepare mashed potatoes as for serving fresh, cool and pack in containers, leaving headspace. Reheat in top of double boiler, whipping occasionally to regain their lightness. The time for reheating these is so long, however, there is not much advantage in freezing them, but they may be a convenience. If pre-

ferred, make the freshly prepared, mashed potatoes into potato patties, and freeze the patties with *two* thicknesses of wrapping material
between them; then these can be fried on removal from the freezer.

Scalloped Potatoes.—Your favorite recipe for scalloped potatoes
will freeze well. Stop cooking before the potatoes are quite done.
These take longer to reheat from the frozen state than to bake when
fresh, the time depending on the size of casserole.

Combination Main-Course Dishes

There is an almost endless number of main-course dishes which are
very satisfactory when frozen, and are a great convenience to have
on hand. For the best quality when served, there are some essentials
in preparing them for freezing, and these follow. And for suggestions
for freezing fried foods, see pp. 158, 159, 160 and 163.

Some Flavor Problems.—The chief problem with some of these
dishes is that of having less-than-the-best flavor when they are served.
The flavor of black pepper, clove, onion and garlic becomes stronger
during freezer storage, so these should be added when the dish is
being prepared for serving.

The flavor of meat and poultry pies is better if they are baked after
freezing.

For a good many of these dishes, adding a small amount of monosodium glutamate helps to retain the best flavor. This is sold under
various trade names and directions for using it should be followed.
As a rule, about ¼ tsp. is a suitable amount to add to a family-size
portion.

Also, for good flavor in these products, note the suggestions for
speed in freezing, pp. 155–156.

Some Ingredient Problems.—There are a few ingredients which
become too soft or mushy during freezer storage. This happens to
regular or quick-cooking rice, and "converted" rice is preferred in
dishes to be frozen. Spaghetti, macaroni and noodles become somewhat softer, so it is a good idea not to cook them completely.
These products take space in the freezer, so often it is better to freeze
only the sauce or ingredients with which these are to be combined.
While you reheat the sauce for serving, you can cook the cereal, then
combine them.

Boiled or steamed potatoes (except small, new ones) are changed in
texture when frozen. So it is better to add potatoes to dishes like

stews at the time of serving. Other vegetables soften a little during freezer storage, too, so that the best plan is to slightly undercook them, or at least be sure not to overcook them before freezing.

Cooked egg whites become tough and rubbery in freezer storage, so these should not be included.

Pork to be used in any precooked dishes should be very fresh, otherwise it does not keep well in the freezer.

Many main-course, combination dishes (such as Lasagna, above) may be frozen and need only to be reheated for serving. Or meal-size portions of Lasagna sauce may be frozen, then the rest of the preparation at meal time is easy

Some Typical Dishes for Freezing.—The following are some types of main course dishes which can be frozen satisfactorily. Except for the above suggestions, prepare them as for serving fresh. It is far better to plan ahead to freeze these, so you may proceed as suggested on p. 155, with prompt chilling and freezing. If they are left from a meal and have stood any appreciable length of time at room temperature, they will not have as fine flavor and they will not keep as long in the freezer.

Chop Sueys
Chow Meins
Creole Dishes
Spaghetti, Macaroni or
    Noodle or Rice Dishes,
    with Meat, Fish or
    Poultry
Beef, Lamb or Veal Stew
Chicken or Turkey à la King
Meat, Fish and Poultry
    Creamed Dishes
Casserole Dishes, including
    Seafood

Oven-Baked Beans
Stuffed Green Peppers
Newburgs and Thermidors
Meat, Fish and Poultry
    Croquettes
Fish or Poultry Sticks
Codfish Cakes
Chili Con Carne
Meat and Poultry Pies
Ravioli
Macaroni and Cheese

Reheating for Serving.—If dishes to be reheated in the oven were frozen in containers which can be put into the oven, remove the cover, place in a moderate oven, 350°–375°F., and heat to serving temperature. The time for reheating will depend on the amount of food, but for family-size portions, usually allow 1½–2 hr. Casseroles should be uncovered and may be sprinkled with buttered crumbs. Some dishes may be stirred occasionally, to heat uniformly. Bake meat and poultry pies with pastry topping at 400°F. for 45–60 min., depending on the size of pie.

Many of these dishes may be reheated on the top of the range. To do this without preliminary thawing, place the container with the food in it in a pan of water until the solid block can be removed. Then reheat in the top of the double boiler, or slowly over direct heat if there is no danger of burning. Stir occasionally to heat uniformly, but not so often or so vigorously as to break up the pieces of food.

Place fried foods on a baking sheet in the oven at 400°F. and heat to serving temperature.

Once these products have been completely thawed, they should not be refrozen.

Plate Meals

Since the main course for dinner usually includes meat, fish or poultry and two vegetables, when a plate meal is frozen, this combination is usually selected. These precooked foods are arranged on a plate just like the ones on which frozen dinners are sold, and the plate is covered with aluminum foil tucked down snugly over the edges, and sealed.

However, this presents several problems. The three foods must all require about the same time for reheating, otherwise the plate must be in the oven until the food requiring the longest time is hot, and by that time others may be overdone. The kind of food and its shape and size determine the time to reheat, so this needs to be considered in selecting the foods for a plate meal. But it is impossible to exclude air from these packages, and this fact shortens the time for which the foods will keep their high quality in freezer storage.

To avoid the problem of contact with air during freezer storage, here is a suggestion. The three foods may be frozen separately first, selecting suitable individual portions and freezing them in wrapping material or small containers. When frozen, several portions may be placed in larger containers for freezer storage, excluding as much air as possible.

The meal must be used after it has been stored for the time suitable for the food with the shortest recommended storage period.

Time for Freezer Storage

It is impossible to give as definite storage periods for many of these products as for most foods going into the freezer. This is because there can be so much difference in the quality of the ingredients used, the degree of cooking, the kind and amount of seasoning, and the speed of chilling and freezing after the products are prepared.

Following are merely suggested storage periods for some of these products. Under carefully controlled laboratory conditions, some of these have been stored for considerably longer periods. If very

Recommended Storage Periods for Prepared and Cooked Main Course Foods at 0°F.

Storage period in months	Kind of prepared or cooked food
4–6	Roast beef, lamb, veal and chicken; oven-baked beans
2–4	Roast pork and turkey; beef, lamb and veal stews; cooked vegetables; foods precooked in sauces and gravies, including chicken à la king and casserole dishes; chop sueys and chow meins; chicken and meat pies; meat balls and meat loaves; hash and scrapple; creoles; gravies and sauces
1–2	Turkey pies; stuffings; chili con carne
1	Left-overs not frozen within about an hour of preparation; fried foods; Newburgs and thermidors; macaroni, rice, spaghetti and noodle dishes

carefully prepared in the home, the storage periods may be longer, too. But it is safer to use them within the recommended periods.

SOUPS

A wide variety of soups can be successfully frozen. Those which require considerable time to prepare are especially suited to freezing, since a large amount can be made without much more effort than enough for one or two meals.

Those with a base of meat or poultry stock, or fish chowders, navy bean or split pea or vegetable soups are all satisfactory. Do not add potatoes until reheating for serving, and select vegetables which freeze well, including carrots, peas and lima beans. Barley, macaroni, spaghetti, noodles or converted rice can be added. It is better to add salt, pepper and other seasonings at the time of reheating for serving. Frozen vegetable purées are splendid for use in frozen soups.

Since soups are so bulky, it is better to freeze them in concentrated form whenever convenient. Concentrates of carrot, asparagus, celery and other vegetables can be prepared with all ingredients except seasonings and liquid to be added at the time of reheating. You can place these concentrates in quick-release ice cube trays and when they are frozen, remove them from the tray and store them in freezing containers. Then you can use as many of these cubes as you need for one meal, adding the cubes to hot milk or water or other hot liquid, with other ingredients as desired.

When you have removed most of the meat (either raw or cooked) from a carcass or bird, simmer the bones (with meat remaining on them) for 3 or 4 hr., or a shorter time in a pressure saucepan. Boil it down to make it concentrated, strain it, and when cool skim off excess fat. This stock is very convenient for many purposes.

The chief precaution in freezing these is that once the soup is cooked it should be chilled and frozen promptly. For directions for this, see pp. 155–156.

The maximum recommended storage period for soups is six months.

CHAPTER 10

Freezing Baked Goods and Desserts

FREEZING BAKED GOODS

An assortment of flour mixtures in your freezer, baked or unbaked, is one of the many advantages your freezer offers. As for main-course dishes, and other foods, you can prepare a large portion at one time, freezing what you do not need at present. Or you can prepare some of these ahead for use at holiday or party occasions, making the event a pleasant rather than a hurried one. Some of these are convenient to prepare ahead as gifts, too.

Yeast Breads and Rolls, Quick Breads, Cookies and Cakes

Baked Before Freezing.—There is practically no kind of baked product which is not thoroughly satisfactory when baked and then frozen. Popovers are never quite as good as when freshly baked, piping-hot out of the oven, but left-over ones can be frozen.

Preparation for Freezing.—Any baked cake may be frozen, including all those made with shortening and also angel food and sponge cake. Rich fruit cakes (like Christmas cakes) grow more mellow on storage, and these are fine to prepare ahead or as gifts. Cream puffs and éclairs freeze well, and are convenient to prepare ahead for parties. These may be filled with ice cream, but cream fillings are better added at the time of serving. Baked (hard) meringues can be frozen, but should not be stored longer than a couple of weeks. Baked fruit or nut loaves, and quick breads may be frozen, and a supply of baked cookies, doughnuts and waffles in your freezer is helpful.

Prepare any of these from your favorite recipe. But synthetic vanilla may acquire a bitter flavor during freezer storage, so use pure vanilla extract. Bake the products as usual, and immediately after baking, remove from the pan and cool on a rack. The product must be cool to the center before wrapping, otherwise it will be soggy.

Products which are rather firm, like fruit cakes and fruit and nut loaves are easily wrapped in moisture-vapor-proof material, using the drug store method of wrapping. Small items like rolls, cup cakes,

166

muffins, baking powder biscuits, doughnuts and waffles may be packed in bags or rigid containers. If you freeze them first, you can pack them tightly together in the bag or container, without danger of crushing them. For wrapping cookies and large cakes, see suggestions below. If the products are to be reheated for serving, it simplifies reheating if they are frozen in wrappers or containers which can be put into the oven.

Courtesy of The Dow Chemical Co.

Cakes and cookies can be prepared long before Christmas and kept in the freezer, ready as Christmas gifts. Samples of your own baking are especially welcome gifts

Preparation for Serving.—For any of these products to be served without reheating, just allow them to stand at room temperature, in the unopened container, until completely thawed. If they are unwrapped while still cold, moisture may condense on the surface. making the product soggy.

Suggestions for Some Products.—Yeast breads. If you bake your own bread, you can bake as many loaves as you like at one time, and freeze those you do not want to use right away. Then later, when you take a loaf out of the freezer, it will be almost like a loaf of freshly baked bread and it is not much more work to prepare a number of loaves at one time. Or you can buy day-old bread at bargain prices, and store the loaves in your freezer. If used within

Courtesy of General Foods Kitchens

When angel food is baked in a loaf pan, it takes less space in the freezer. After thawing, it may be sliced and served with thawed fruit and ice cream or whipped cream

a week or two, the store wrapper is satisfactory, otherwise overwrap with moisture-vapor-proof material. To make toast, you only need to thaw frozen sliced bread long enough to separate the slices, and put the cold slices in your toaster.

Yeast rolls, muffins, baking powder biscuits and doughnuts.—Thaw these in their wrappers for 15–30 min. Or to freshen them, they may be reheated in the oven at 300° F. for 10–15 min. For this, leave them in the original wrapper if it can be placed in the oven, otherwise transfer them to a paper bag.

Chocolate Nut Tortes like these are fine to have in the freezer. Trim the crusts from pound cakes and cut the cake lengthwise into four slices. Then put the layers together with uncooked, chocolate frosting between them and over the cake. Sprinkle with chopped nuts, wrap and freeze

Waffles. Place the frozen waffles, without thawing, in the toaster, to reheat.

Unfrosted cakes. Large, whole cakes, especially soft ones like angel food and sponge cake, are easier to wrap if they are frozen first. In either case, place the cake on a piece of cardboard covered with wrapping material, and wrap with moisture-vapor-proof material by the drug store method. Or for angel food and sponge cake, place a rather large piece of cellophane under the cake and a second sheet over it, then heat-seal around the edges. Or if you have a box just a little larger than the cake, put the cake in it and overwrap with moisture-vapor-proof material.

On thawing, cakes which were frozen may dry out somewhat more quickly than freshly prepared ones. So you may want to cut a large cake into portions, putting in one container only the amount to be used in one day. And slices of cake in the freezer are handy for lunch boxes, too.

Cup cakes and unfilled layer cakes will thaw in about an hour, whole angel food, sponge cakes and loaf cakes in about 2 hr. and filled layer cakes in about 3 hr. Do not remove the wrapper until the cake is thawed. If unwrapped while cold, moisture may condense on the surface and make the cake soggy.

Frosted cakes. Confectioner's butter-sugar frostings are best, especially when made with plenty of fat to keep them moist. Fudge or penuchi-type frostings can be used, but they may crack or crumble during freezer storage, though using part corn syrup or honey or molasses helps prevent this. Boiled or seven-minute frostings become frothy or "weep" when thawed, so should not be used. An assortment of petits fours in your freezer will be a big help in preparing for a party. Layer cakes may be filled, but cream fillings soak into the cake, making it soggy, so other kinds are better. If the frosting or filling is a cooked one, do not wrap the cake until it is cold.

Placing the frosted cake in the freezer an hour or two before wrapping helps to prevent the frosting sticking to the wrapper. Or inserting toothpicks at intervals, just far enough into the frosting so the wrapper does not touch it is a help. Then wrap as for unfrosted cakes, as described above.

Cakes which are either frosted or filled are better if thawed in the refrigerator, since at room temperature the frosting or filling may become grainy. If the wrapping material is near the frosting, you may want to loosen it so it will not stick as it thaws. But do not remove the wrapper until the cake is thawed, since moisture may condense on the surface when cold. If there is not space in the refrigerator for a large cake, thaw it at room temperature, covered. If you remove the original wrapper, the cover which you use for storing cakes in the kitchen is good for this purpose.

As for unfrosted cakes, you may wish to cut a large cake into portions or slices for freezing (see p. 169).

Cookies. Most cookies need to be packed into containers in such a way as to avoid having them broken when the containers are handled in the freezer. For crisp cookies, pieces of crumpled, waxed paper between layers will help, and soft cookies and brownies may be separated by two thicknesses of waxed paper. These may be packed in metal containers with tight lids, or plastic containers or paperboard cartons (not now avialable).

Most thin cookies can be removed from their containers without thawing, and placed on serving plates, and they are ready to use in a few minutes. Some crisp ones lose their crispness when treated this way, and should be left in their containers to thaw. Larger ones like bar cookies should be thawed in their unopened containers for about an hour.

Baked After Freezing.—There are a number of batter and dough products which can be baked after freezing, but special precautions are necessary for these. For any of them to be leavened with baking powder, use a double-acting baking powder to make it rise better.

*Yeast Roll Dough.—*If plain yeast dough is prepared as usual, shaped into rolls and then frozen, the dough does not rise at all well, even after a short time in the freezer. It helps to double the amount of yeast and to make a rich dough (plenty of sugar, shortening and egg) but even this does not give assurance of good rolls if stored more than a couple of weeks.

There is one way, however, in which satisfactory rolls can be made from frozen dough. Prepare a rich dough with double the usual amount of yeast, knead it and freeze it immediately after kneading. You can make a substantial amount of dough and freeze it in cartons of such a size as to give the amount of dough to use at one time. A pint carton of dough will provide a dozen large rolls. Freeze the dough quickly, to stop yeast action. The carton may be left in the refrigerator overnight to thaw; or the dough may be transferred from the carton to a greased bowl at room temperature, allowing 2 or 3 hr. for a quart of dough to thaw. Then knead it, shape it and place to rise, finishing as for fresh dough. Even after a couple of months in the freezer, such dough will rise well.

However, if you have definite plans to use "fancy" yeast dough products within a couple of weeks, and want to have them shaped, ready for the final rising, this can be done. Prepare rich dough with extra yeast (as described above), allow it to rise, then knead and shape it into raisin or pecan cinnamon buns, French breakfast ring, Stollen coffee cake, or as you wish, and freeze it as soon as it is shaped. On taking it from the freezer, place the dough in its pan over a pan of water just hot enough to be slightly steaming. It may take 2–3 hr. for the dough to thaw and rise, but it needs no attention and is a convenient arrangement on a busy day.

Partially baked rolls can be frozen, too, and these are similar to the "brown and serve" ones which you buy. Prepare these as usual, but bake at 275°–300°F. for 20–30 min. Stop baking when the rolls are still pale and are not fully risen, but are baked to the center. Cool before freezing, and wrap carefully to avoid crushing. Allow the rolls to thaw 10–15 min. in the unopened container to prepare for serving; then remove from container and bake at 400°F. for 5–10 min. If the under-side of the thawed rolls seems moist, place them on a rack instead of a baking sheet in the oven.

Muffin Batters.—Place muffin batter in paper baking cups and put the cups in muffin pans to freeze. When frozen, transfer to freezing containers. Thaw at room temperature about an hour to prepare for serving, then bake as for fresh muffins. Or if not thawed, bake at 300°F. until well risen, then finish at 425°F.

Baking Powder Biscuit Dough.—There is not much advantage in freezing this dough before baking, but it can be done. Put the shaped biscuits in the freezer until frozen, then pack in freezing containers. Prepare for serving as for muffins, but if these are to be thawed before baking, remove from the container so they will not stick together during thawing.

Cookie Dough.—Dough for drop cookies can be packed in bulk in freezing containers, and to prepare for baking you only need to thaw the dough enough to break off pieces. Or you can drop the freshly prepared dough as cookies on a pan, freeze them and then pack them into containers. This latter method eliminates the need for thawing, since the frozen cookies can be placed directly into the oven for baking.

Refrigerator-type cookies can be shaped into cylinders or bars, as usual, wrapped and frozen. When ready to bake, thaw only enough to slice off as many cookies as you want, and put the remaining dough back into the freezer at once.

Rolled cookies can be cut and packed in containers with two thicknesses of wrapping material, and these can be baked without thawing.

Cake Batters.—It is much easier to be sure of good quality in cakes which are baked before freezing, but the batter takes less space in the freezer and it can be frozen for cakes made with shortening. Angel food and sponge cakes should always be baked before freezing, however, since these batters are too fragile to freeze well.

Courtesy of Aluminum Company of America

Refrigerator-type cookies keep far longer in the freezer than in the refrigerator. Thaw the bar barely enough to slice the cookies you need, then put the bar back in the freezer

Turn the batter into a greased baking pan for freezing, if the pan can be spared, or else into a freezer carton. To prepare for baking, thaw the batter in the carton just long enough to transfer the batter to a greased baking pan. When thawed, bake as for freshly prepared batter. If the batter is baked before it is thawed, it will have a hump in the center unless a very slow oven is used until the cake is well risen; but if not baked immediately on thawing, some of the leavening gas will be lost so the cake will have small volume.

Pie Dough and Pies

Many different kinds of pies can be successfully frozen, and prove a great asset in the freezer. Some need only to be thawed for serving, others need to be reheated or baked. Pie dough and baked pie shells can be frozen, too. One essential for all of these is that the shortening be of high quality. All pies should be thoroughly cooled before wrapping. For directions for wrapping pies for freezing, see p. 96.

Pie Dough and Pie Shells.—Unbaked pie dough may be frozen in bulk, but this needs to be thawed in the refrigerator overnight. Or the dough may be cut into circles which thaw very quickly on removal from the freezer. The circles can be stacked in freezing containers, with two thicknesses of wrapping material between the circles. Pie shells may be baked before freezing, and if they are not too thin or fragile, they may be stacked on a pie plate, with two thicknesses of wrapping material between them.

One-Crust Pies.—Most one-crust pies freeze very well. These include all chiffon pies, cream pies, pumpkin and pecan pie. Custard pies should not be frozen, since they are apt to curdle when thawed. Allow chiffon pies to set in the refrigerator before freezing them.

Chiffon and cream pies may be topped with sweetened, whipped cream before freezing. But meringues should not be prepared until time for serving, since these shrink and "weep" when frozen. If egg yolks were used in making the filling, the whites can be frozen (see p. 153) for making the meringue when the pie is thawed. Thaw these pies in the refrigerator, allowing 4–5 hr. for a 9-inch pie. Then top with meringue, if desired.

Pumpkin, winter squash and sweet potato pies can be frozen, and are best if baked after freezing. Omit cloves in the filling, since they may become bitter during freezer storage. Pecan pies freeze well, too. Put the uncooked filling in the unbaked, lower crust, then put the pie on a level place in the freezer. When it is frozen it can be wrapped without danger of spilling. Uncooked fillings for these pies may be frozen in containers, for later use.

Two-Crust Pies.—Fruit pies and mincemeat pies freeze very satisfactorily. Lattice-top ones should not be stored long in the freezer, because the filling is exposed to air in the container.

The chief problem in these pies is that the lower crust is apt to be rather soggy. Using up to 20 per cent soy flour in making the pie dough helps to prevent this. Roll the dough for the lower crust thin, and when it is fitted into the pie plate, sprinkle it with flour or brush it with raw egg white or melted fat. From this standpoint, there is an advantage in freezing deep-dish pies without a lower crust, and these made with meat or poultry are fine. Do not cut holes in the top crust of pies to be frozen unbaked.

These pies are best if they are baked after freezing. Those baked before freezing are inclined to taste like day-old ones, and they take almost as long to reheat for serving, as those which are frozen raw take to bake. A mincemeat pie is especially appropriate for freezing unbaked, for then you can bake it and have it piping hot in time for a holiday dinner. However, when these pies are baked before freezing, they may be cut into serving pieces, and are ready in the freezer for use in lunch boxes. If these are frozen in wedge-shaped, plastic containers, seal the lid to its container with freezer tape.

Recommended Storage Periods for Baked Goods at 0° F.

Storage period	Kind of baked product
2 weeks	Unbaked baking powder biscuit dough, muffin batter and yeast dough not to be kneaded after thawing; baked (hard) meringues
2 months	Cake batters; yeast dough to be kneaded after thawing; baked baking powder biscuits, muffins, waffles, cream puffs, éclairs, angel food, sponge cake, pies and pie shells; chiffon and cream pies
4–6 months	Frosted cakes; fruit and nut loaves; fried doughnuts; pie and cookie dough; unbaked pumpkin, winter squash and sweet potato pies
6–8 months	Baked and partially baked yeast rolls; baked yeast bread, fruit cakes, unfrosted cakes, and cookies; unbaked fruit pies.

Juicy fruit fillings may need extra thickening in pies to be frozen. An extra tablespoon of flour or tapioca, combined with the sugar or an extra ½-tbsp. of cornstarch, should be satisfactory.

If fruit pies are to be baked before freezing, light-colored fruits like apples, peaches and apricots present no problem. If you are using your own, home-frozen fruits and they were treated before freezing, according to the directions for preventing darkening, these are fine in unbaked pies. But otherwise, these fruits for unbaked pies need to be treated to prevent them from darkening during freezer storage. Over the fruit for a pie, sprinkle either 1–2 tbsp. lemon juice or 1 tbsp. water in which ¼ tsp. powdered ascorbic acid has been dissolved. Cover each piece of fruit with this solution.

If baked, two-crust pies need to be reheated for serving, remove the wrapper and reheat in an oven at 375°F. for 30–40 min. For unbaked pies, remove the wrapper and bake at 400°F. about an hour for 8-inch pies and 1¼ hr. for 9-inch ones, cutting dents in the upper crust as soon as it is thawed.

FREEZING DESSERTS

It is evident from the preceding pages, that a wide variety of pies, cakes and other baked goods including cream puffs may be frozen for desserts. There are other desserts which may be frozen, too.

Cooked Fruits

Any fruit sauce may be frozen, using your favorite recipe. This includes apple sauce, apricot sauce, cranberry sauce and many others. Cool, and pack in containers, leaving headspace. Storage period, 9–12 months. Thaw in unopened container.

Fruit purées may be frozen, and directions for some of these are given in connection with the directions for freezing the fruit.

Prepare baked apples as for serving fresh, and cool. Pack in containers, adding syrup in which they were baked and leaving head-space. Glazed apples may be frozen, too. Storage period, 9–12 months. Thaw in unopened containers. If desired, they may be reheated in the oven or in a steamer.

Dessert Sauces

Any of your favorite dessert sauces such as chocolate, fruit, butter-scotch or caramel may well be kept in the freezer. It is good to have an assortment of these on hand. Hard sauces may be stored in the freezer, too.

Puddings

Steamed or baked puddings may be frozen. Steam or bake, as usual, in either individual or family-size portions, and cool. Storage period, 9 months. Reheat for serving, in the steamer or the oven, the time depending on the size of the pudding.

Ice Creams and Sherbets

You can make any number of your own frozen desserts and keep a variety of them in your freezer. If they are to be frozen in the

freezer, use the type of recipe which is suitable for freezing in the
ice cube compartment of your refrigerator. Or freeze the ice cream
or sherbet in a crank freezer and store it in your freezer. Frozen
fruit purées are convenient to use in making your own ribbon or
ripple or revel type of ice cream. For storing these frozen desserts
in the freezer, see directions on p. 151.

Frozen Fruit Salads

Rich, frozen fruit salads keep very well in the freezer. These are
usually made with mayonnaise and whipped cream, often including
cottage cheese. As an example, see p. 393. These are better if
taken from the freezer long enough before serving for the pieces of
fruit not to be too hard.

CHAPTER 11

Freezing Sandwiches, Canapés and Hors d'Oeuvres—and "Extras" for Your Freezer

SANDWICHES

Homemakers who need to prepare sandwiches for lunch boxes five days a week will welcome a plan for making a supply for a week or two all at one time. Choose a time of day when the kitchen table can be cleared for action, and set up an assembly line. Make a supply for a week or two and put them in your freezer. Then each morning, take out enough for the lunch boxes, and the sandwiches will be thawed in time for lunch.

A supply of sandwiches in your freezer also is handy for impromptu summer picnics and for many other purposes.

However, sandwiches should not be stored in the freezer more than two weeks, so make only the number and assortment for use within that time.

Wrapping, Freezing and Thawing

If the sandwiches are to be in the freezer only a few days, a double thickness of heavy waxed paper is satisfactory for wrapping them. But for longer than this, they must be stored in moisture-vapor-proof material or containers. As a rule, it is better to wrap each sandwich individually, and an easy method is to use moisture-vapor-proof cellophane and heat-seal. After freezing, a number of the same kind of sandwiches can be stored tightly together (without danger of crushing them) in a bag or carton, marked for identification. If preferred, a number can be stored in a freezing carton and then frozen, but so many must not be stacked on top of each other that the ones underneath are crushed.

Sandwiches should be kept away from the walls or bottom of the freezer and from freezing plates or shelves to avoid sogginess in sand-

178

wiches. This is because when they are in contact with these cold, metal surfaces, ice crystals form on the coldest part of the bread which then becomes soggy when thawed. This is, of course, contrary to directions for freezing most foods.

To prepare for serving, just remove the sandwiches from the freezer and keep them several hours in their wrappers; then they will be thawed.

Courtesy of The Dow Chemical Co.

Set up an assembly line for yourself, prepare a supply of sandwiches to last a week or two, and freeze them. Then the early morning rush to make sandwiches is at an end

Kind of Bread

Any kind of bread may be used, but day-old bread is usually better than very fresh loaves, especially if the bread is the fluffy type. The thickness of the slices is entirely a matter of choice.

Kind of Filling

There is a tendency for moist fillings to make the bread soggy in frozen sandwiches. To prevent this, spread both slices of bread generously, right out to the edge, with soft (not melted) butter or margarine.

Only a few ingredients are unsuitable for fillings for sandwiches to be frozen. Certain salad dressings separate when frozen, and when thawed they soak into the bread, making it soggy. To test a dressing you would like to use, place a small amount of it in a tightly covered jar and leave it overnight in the freezer. If it separates on thawing, do not use it in sandwiches to be frozen.

Hard-cooked egg whites become tough and rubbery when frozen, so should not be used, but hard-cooked egg yolks freeze very well.

Crisp salad greens, such as lettuce, watercress, cucumbers and celery lose their crispness when frozen, so should not be used in these sandwiches. Any of these, or tomatoes, can be added to the sandwiches after thawing, if desired.

Jellies and jams tend to soak into bread during thawing, and it is better not to use them unless the bread is spread very generously with butter or margarine first.

Any kind of cold meat, fish or poultry can be used in making these sandwiches, so can American Cheddar cheese, either sliced or ground and combined with other ingredients. Left-over meats can be ground and combined with pickles, horseradish or other seasonings. In fact, any favorite sandwich spread may be used, provided it does not include any of the unsuitable ingredients listed above.

You can freeze a sandwich loaf, too, and place "icing" on it before freezing or after thawing, as you wish. The "icing" may be a blend of cream cheese with heavy cream to give just the right consistency for spreading.

The following recipes for sandwich spreads are particularly good. Just combine the ingredients thoroughly, and spread on buttered bread slices. One cup of filling will make from 4 to 8 sandwiches, depending on how generously it is spread.

Beef and Ketchup

1¼ c. cooked ground beef (or other cold meat)
½ tsp. salt

1 tsp. Worcestershire sauce
⅓ c. ketchup
1 tbsp. softened butter or margarine

Beef, Gravy and Onion

1 c. cooked ground beef (or other cold meat)
½ c. gravy

1 tbsp. minced onion
½ tsp. salt (more or less, as desired)

Beef, Relish and Onion

1 c. cooked ground beef (or other cold meat)
½ c. salad dressing
2 tbsp. pickle relish

2 tsp. minced onion
½ tsp. celery salt (more or less, as desired)

Cream Cheese, Chipped Beef and Horseradish

½ c. shredded chipped beef rinsed in hot water and drained
1 pkg. (3 oz.) cream cheese

1 tbsp. horseradish
1 tbsp. minced onion
1 tbsp. salad dressing

Cream Cheese and Prunes

4 medium size prunes scalded, pitted and cut finely
1 pkg. (3 oz.) cream cheese
½ tsp. sugar

¼ tsp. cinnamon
2 tsp. light cream
2 tbsp. chopped nuts

Walnut and Date

½ c. pitted dates and
¾ c. walnuts (put through food chopper twice)

¼ tsp. salt
½ c. top milk (more or less as desired)

Cream Cheese, Date and Orange

1 pkg. (3 oz.) cream cheese
½ c. dates, sliced or chopped
½ tsp. grated orange rind

3 tbsp. orange juice (more if desired)

Cream Cheese and Chipped Beef

½ c. shredded chipped beef, rinsed in hot water and drained

1 pkg. (3 oz.) cream cheese
¼ c. top milk or enough to moisten

Liverwurst with Relish and Cheese

½ c. liverwurst
¼ c. pickle relish

½ c. grated American cheese
6 tbsp. salad dressing

Deviled Ham and Chili

1 can (3 oz.) deviled ham
1 tbsp. softened butter or margarine
1 tsp. prepared mustard

2 tbsp. chili sauce
½ tsp. horseradish

Ham and Pickle

½ c. finely chopped ham (¼ lb.)
2 tbsp. chopped sweet pickle

¼ c. salad dressing

Tongue and Mustard

½ c. minced tongue
2 tbsp. butter or margarine

1 tbsp. prepared mustard

Peanut Butter and Dill Pickle

½ c. peanut butter

½ c. chopped dill pickle (sour or sweet pickle may be used)

Peanut Butter, Bacon and Olive

½ c. peanut butter
10 slices bacon, cooked crisp,
    drained, chopped

12 small olives, chopped

Peanut Brittle and Butter

1 c. peanut brittle, crushed

¼ c. softened butter or margarine

Cream and Bleu Cheese

1 pkg. (3 oz.) cream cheese
3 oz. bleu cheese

1 tbsp. minced onion
¼ c. top milk (more if desired)

Cream Cheese and Liverwurst

½ c. liverwurst
1 pkg. (3 oz.) cream cheese

3-4 tbsp. milk to moisten

Tongue, Pickle and Horseradish

²/₃ c. minced tongue
2 tbsp. salad dressing
2 tsp. horseradish

½ tsp. prepared mustard
2 tbsp. chopped sour pickle
pepper and salt

Peanut Butter, Date and Honey

½ c. peanut butter
½ c. finely cut, pitted dates

¼ c. honey
5 tsp. lemon juice

Shrimp and Olive

½ c. chopped shrimp
¼ c. butter or margarine, softened
½ tsp. minced onion

2 tbsp. minced stuffed olives
2 tbsp. salad dressing

Shrimp and Capers

½ c. chopped shrimp
3 tbsp. salad dressing

½ tbsp. chopped capers

Sardines with Chili Sauce and Dill Pickle

½ c. mashed sardines
½ c. dill pickles
¹/₃ c. chili sauce

2 tbsp. softened butter or margarine
1 tsp. prepared mustard

Sardines with Lemon

½ c. mashed sardines
4 tsp. lemon juice

¼ tsp. Worcestershire sauce
1 tbsp. softened butter or margarine

CANAPÉS

These tiny delicacies, so time-consuming to prepare, can be made ahead and frozen, to take the last-minute hurry out of party prepara-

Aluminum Company of America

Many types of canapés and hors d'oeuvres may be frozen in preparation for a party, also "dips" and sauces to be served with them

tions in your own home, for weddings or for other functions. Like sandwiches, they should not be stored in the freezer more than a week or two. But this way, you have a week or so to get ready for the party, so you can make a larger variety of them than if they all needed to be prepared in one day.

If you are serving canapés on bread, the spread can be placed on the bread before freezing. But to use crackers, it is better to freeze the spread by itself and place it on the crackers just before serving.

You can make the usual, open-faced canapés, or rolled, ribbon or loaf canapés. Any fillings suitable for sandwiches (see above) can be used for canapés. Cream cheese is a good basic ingredient for them; so are anchovy, fish, avocado and egg yolk spreads.

For garnish, olives, pickles, egg yolks (not whites), pimientos, green peppers and mushrooms may be used. But do not add crisp vegetables like radishes, cucumbers, parsley or water cress until time for serving.

For freezing, the canapés can be arranged on a baking sheet or on a cardboard covered with wrapping material. If it is necessary to have several layers, place wrapping material between them, but do not pile them more than a couple of layers deep, and if space permits, a single layer is better. Then overwrap the entire arrangement with moisture-vapor-proof material, excluding as much air as possible.

The wrapper should not be removed from these until they are thawed, but when left at room temperature, they thaw quickly. A good plan, however, is to transfer them from the freezer to the refrigerator a couple of hours before they are to be used.

HORS D'OEUVRES

As for canapés, many of these can be prepared ahead and stored in the freezer for a week or two (see above). But those made with crisp vegetables (such as stuffed celery) cannot be stored in the freezer, for the vegetables would lose their crispness. For these, the spreads can be frozen, ready for use on the day of the occasion.

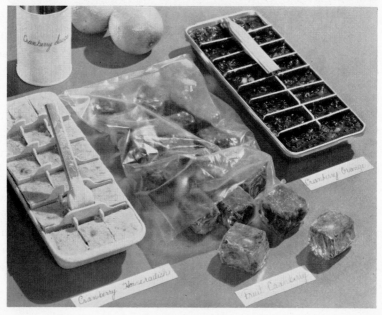

Courtesy of The Dow Chemical Co.

Cranberry and other sauces may be frozen in quick-release ice cube trays, removed from the trays, then wrapped and frozen.   Or soup concentrates, or fruit or vegetable purées may be frozen this way.   These "extras" are a boon in the freezer

Rich pastry hors d'oeuvres filled with meat, fish, cheese and other spreads may be frozen unbaked. When ready to use these, remove the wrapper and place them right into an oven at 400°F. and bake until done.

To wrap hors d'oeuvres, follow the directions given above for wrapping canapés.

"EXTRAS" FOR YOUR FREEZER

There are many "extras" which you will find convenient to have in your freezer.

A good supply of ice cubes or chopped ice, stored in plastic bags, comes in handy for use on short notice. In the summer, blocks of ice may be frozen in ½-gallon or quart containers, to use as a beverage cooler for picnics.

There is nothing the children will like better in the summer than a supply of popsicles. Make these from any frozen fruit juice or ade or punch, reconstituted according to instructions. Popsicle molds with sticks can be purchased. Or freeze the juice in a quick-release ice cube tray, inserting a popsicle stick in each cube. When they are frozen, separate the cubes and store them in a plastic bag in the freezer.

Most candies can be kept fresh by storing them in frozen food containers in the freezer. Marshmallows, fudges, chocolates, caramels and others may be kept for 6-12 months, though chocolate covered nuts and others with hard centers may chip. Do not remove the wrapper from any candy until it is thawed, except marshmallows which may be sliced, if desired, while still frozen. Brown sugar does not become dry or lumpy when stored in frozen food containers in the freezer. Coconut and caramel corn keep their crispness in a freezer.

Except when in unopened, vacuum-pack cans, coffee gradually loses its flavor if it is stored at room temperature. The best way to prevent this is to keep on hand in the kitchen only enough for your current use, and keep the remainder in your freezer. Or if you buy coffee in bags, keep the bulk of the coffee in its bag in the freezer. If you buy tea in large amounts, the best place for the bulk of it, too, is in the freezer.

Left-over cake or bread crumbs, or croutons, crackers and pretzels all keep well at 0°F. You can break bread into cubes for use in stuffings, and keep the cubes in a freezer bag or vegetable crisper until you are ready to make the stuffing. Unsalted nuts keep fresh at 0°F. for 8–12 months, but salted ones may acquire off-flavors after 6 months. Raisins keep well in the freezer.

SECTION IV

How to Use Frozen Foods

CHAPTER 12

How to Use the Recipes and Menus in This Book

All the recipes in this book require standard, level measurements. Each one includes temperatures and time periods whenever necessary for success. Follow them accurately, step by step, and you are sure to have success. Good cooking is no longer dependent on "good luck."

ABBREVIATIONS

tsp. = teaspoon

tbsp. = tablespoon

c. = cup

pt. = pint

qt. = quart

gal. = gallon

oz. = ounce

lb. = pound

bu. = bushel

pkg. = package

F. = Fahrenheit

sec. = second

min. = minute

hr. = hour

in. = inch

HOW TO MEASURE

Modern tools for measuring include: standard 8-oz. measuring cups, a nest of single-capacity measuring cups (holding $\frac{1}{4}$, $\frac{1}{3}$, $\frac{1}{2}$ and 1 c., respectively); pint (2 c.) measures, quart (4 c.) measures, and standard measuring spoons; thermometers to measure temperatures for baking, roasting, deep-fat frying, and for making candies and frostings. You may also have an electric timer to measure cooking periods.

Cups for measuring liquids have the 1-c. mark *below* the rim of the cup. Cups for measuring dry ingredients have the 1-c. mark *at* the rim.

Flour

For all recipes for baked products (cakes, pastry, baking powder biscuits and so on), the flour is sifted once before it is measured. Spoon the sifted flour into the measuring cup without shaking or jarring the cup. Fill the cup heaping full, then level it off with the back of a case knife or spatula. Throughout this book, the measurement of flour in these recipes assumes that the flour was sifted before measuring. Unless cake flour is specified, the flour in these recipes is all-purpose flour.

To measure flour for use as a thickening agent (in sauces, gravies and so on), measure the flour as above, but without sifting it.

Brown Sugar

Pack firmly into cup—so firmly that it will come out in one piece. If it is lumpy, roll before measuring.

Fats and Shortenings

Single-capacity cups provide the easiest way to measure solid fats in fractions of a cup. Pack solidly, then scoop out with a spatula.

The water-level method may be used. If you need $1/3$ c. shortening, fill the cup with water to the $2/3$ c. mark. Then add shortening, pushing it under the water until the water level reaches the 1-c. mark. And so on, for other fractions. For use in making pastry dough or other products where the exact amount of water is important, drain the shortening thoroughly before using it.

Liquids

Set the cup on a level surface and pour liquid into it until it reaches the mark for the required measurement. Have your eye on a level with the mark.

Syrups

Secure a level rather than rounded measure of these, and scrape the portion sticking to the cup. If you grease the cup first, the syrup will slide out without any waste. Single-capacity cups are best.

Spoonfuls

Dip measuring spoons in dry ingredients to be measured, lift out heaping full and level off with back of case knife or spatula.

SOME EQUIVALENTS

"Speck," "dash," "pinch or "few grains" = less than 1/8 tsp.

3 tsp. = 1 tbsp.   2 c. = 1 pt.
4 tbsp. = 1/4 c.   2 pt. = 1 qt.
5 tbsp. plus 1 tsp. = 1/3 c.   4 qt. = 1 gal.
8 tbsp. = 1/2 c.   8 qt. = 1 peck
10 tbsp. plus 2 tsp. = 2/3 c.   4 pecks = 1 bu.
12 tbsp. = 3/4 c.   16 oz. = 1 lb.

SOME SUBSTITUTIONS

1 tbsp. flour = 1/2 tbsp. cornstarch or 3/4 tbsp. quick-cooking tapioca, for thickening purposes
1 c. sifted all-purpose flour = 1 1/8 c. (1 c. plus 2 tbsp.) sifted cake flour
1 c. sifted cake flour = 7/8 c. (1 c. less 2 tbsp.) sifted all-purpose flour
1 square (1 oz.) unsweetened chocolate = 3 tbsp. cocoa plus 1 tbsp. fat
1 tsp. baking powder = 1/4 tsp. baking soda plus 1 tsp. cream of tartar; or = 1/4 tsp. baking soda plus 1/2 c. fully soured milk or buttermilk; or = 1/4 tsp. baking soda plus 1/2 tbsp. vinegar or lemon juice used with 1/2 c. sweet milk
1 c. bottled sweet milk = 1/2 c. evaporated milk plus 1/2 c. water
1 c. sour milk = 1 c. sweet milk plus 1 tbsp. lemon juice or vinegar; or = 1 c. buttermilk
1 c. butter = 1 c. margarine; or 7/8 c. hydrogenated fat plus 1/2 tsp. salt; or 7/8 c. lard plus 1/2 tsp. salt.

SOME BASIC RECIPES

Throughout the following pages, are recipes featuring commercially available meats, fish and shellfish, poultry, vegetables, fruits and fruit juices. For the recipes, the amount of frozen food is usually given as the weight of the package. To use a package of different weight, calculate the proportions of different ingredients to be used. And to use vegetables and fruits from "pour and store" bags, estimate the portion to use from the bag, to give the required weight.

A number of recipes throughout the book require the preparation of basic mixtures such as cream sauce, gravy, baking powder biscuits, pastry, muffins and cakes. These basic recipes are given here, and reference is made to them in the recipes using them.

Of course, the modern homemaker will take advantage of the wide variety of prepared mixes on the market, and in many cases will use them rather than combine the ingredients in her own kitchen. She will also use products which are already baked and frozen, available on the market.

Cakes

Plain "Butter" Cake, Conventional Method.—Following are the amounts of ingredients to use for baking plain "butter" cakes made by the conventional method, in different pans.

Amounts of Plain "Butter" Cake Batters for Baking in Different Pans

	Amount of ingredients							
Type of cake	Cake flour, c.	Baking powder, tsp.	Salt, tsp.	Shortening, c.	Sugar, c.	Egg	Milk, c.	Vanilla, tsp.
Cup cakes (1 doz., 2½ in. diameter)	1	1¼	⅛	¼	½	1	⅜	½
Loaf cake (8½ x 4½ x 2½ in. or 6 x 10 x 1½ in.)	1½	2	¼	⅜	¾	1	½	¾
Layer cake (two 8 in. layers) or square loaf (8 x 8 x 2 in.)	2	2½	¼	½	1	2	¾	1
Layer cake (two 9 in. layers) or square loaf (9 x 9 x 2 in.)	2½	3	¼	⅝	1¼	2	1	1

Preparation of Batter.—Have shortening at room temperature, and cream until very soft; add sugar gradually, creaming until well blended and the consistency of hard sauce.

Add egg; beat vigorously until light and fluffy.

Sift flour, baking powder and salt together and add to first mixture alternately with milk to which vanilla has been added. Begin and end with addition of dry ingredients, mixing lightly after addition of milk and more vigorously after adding dry ingredients.

Turn batter into pan, as follows:

(1) For cup cakes: use greased muffin pans or paper baking cups, filling only ½–⅔ full of batter.

(2) For layer cakes, loaf cakes or cakes baked in shallow pan: grease sides and bottom of pan. Sprinkle the bottom of the pan lightly with flour or cut waxed paper to fit the bottom. Fill pan not more than ½–⅔ full of batter, piling the batter slightly higher near the sides than in the center of the pan, so cake will be only slightly rounded when baked.

Baking the Cake.—Test any cake for doneness, as follows: cake springs back when touched gently with finger; toothpick or cake tester inserted into center comes out clean and cake has loosened from sides of pan. When done, let pan stand on wire rack 5–10 min., then remove cake and cool on wire rack.

(1) Cup cakes: bake in moderate oven, 375°F., 25–30 min.
(2) Layer cake and other shallow cakes: bake in moderate oven, 350°F., 25–40 min.
(3) Loaf cakes: bake in slow oven, 325°F., 40–60 min.

Quick Mix Plain Cake

1¼ c. cake flour
1½ tsp. baking powder
¼ tsp. salt
¼ c. sugar

½ c. milk
½ c. vegetable shortening
½ tsp. vanilla
1 egg

Take milk, shortening and egg out of refrigerator at least an hour before preparing batter, so they will be at room temperature.

Sift flour, baking powder, salt and sugar together into mixing bowl. Add shortening, vanilla and 5 tbsp. milk to dry ingredients and beat 2 min., either vigorously by hand using 150 strokes per min., or with an electric mixer using medium speed, scraping well down sides and bottom of bowl during mixing. Add egg and remaining milk and beat 2 min., as before.

Pour batter into greased pan, 6 x 10 x 1¾ in., or a round pan about this size. Bake in moderate oven, 350°F., for 25–40 min.

Note: This batter is especially appropriate for Upside Down cakes.

Cake Roll

¾ c. cake flour
1 tsp. baking powder
¼ tsp. salt
4 egg whites
¾ c. sugar

Yield: 10 servings
4 egg yolks
1 tsp. vanilla
2 tbsp. water
powdered or confectioner's sugar

Sift flour, baking powder and salt together twice. Beat egg whites until foamy, add 6 tbsp. sugar gradually, beating after each addition. When sugar is all added, the whites should hold good peaks.

Beat egg yolks until thick and lemon-colored, add remaining sugar (6 tbsp.) gradually, with vanilla, beating after each addition. When sugar is all added, egg yolk mixture should be very stiff. Add water and beat well.

Carefully fold egg yolk mixture into egg white mixture until well blended. Sift one-third of dry ingredients over egg mixture and fold in gently. Repeat until all dry ingredients are added.

Line shallow, rectangular baking pan (about 10 x 15 in.) with waxed paper, greasing pan and side of paper next to batter. Turn batter into pan, distributing evenly, and well out to corners. Bake in moderate oven, 375°F., 15–20 min.

Sprinkle powdered or confectioner's sugar generously over heavy waxed paper slightly larger than the baking pan. When cake is baked, quickly turn it out on sugared paper and remove waxed paper from bottom of cake. Trim off edges (crust) from cake. Roll paper and cake together from narrow end and place on rack to cool. When cool, unroll gently and use according to recipe.

Whipped dessert topping may be spread over cake and the cake rolled up again, then cut crosswise into serving pieces and topped with thawed, frozen fruit.

True Sponge Cake   *Yield:* 10–12 servings

1 c. cake flour   1½ tbsp. water
5 eggs   ¼ tsp. salt.
1 c. finely granulated sugar   ½ tsp. cream of tartar
1½ tbsp. lemon juice

Sift the flour twice after measuring it. Separate egg whites from yolks. Beat egg yolks with rotary or electric beater until very thick and lemon-colored. Sprinkle 2 tbsp. sugar over them and beat until mixture thickens. Add three more portions of sugar (8 tbsp., or ½ c. in all), beating after each addition. Mixture should then be so thick it will hold its shape. Combine lemon juice and water and add this mixture to egg yolks in three portions, beating after each addition.

Sift half the remaining sugar (¼ c.) with flour and sprinkle 3 tbsp. of this mixture over egg yolks, then fold in until flour has disappeared. Repeat until all the flour-sugar mixture has been added.

Add salt and cream of tartar to egg whites and beat until frothy, gradually add remaining sugar (¼ c.) and beat until mixture holds good peaks. Add one-third of egg white mixture to egg yolk mixture, folding carefully until well blended. Repeat until all of egg white mixture has been added. Extra folding may be necessary at end to blend well.

Turn into 9-inch ungreased tube pan and bake in slow oven,

325°F., 50 min. to 1 hr. When done, cake should be delicately browned and should spring back when lightly pressed with finger tips.

Invert pan on wire rack, letting stand until cake is thoroughly cooled. Then loosen sides with slender spatula and remove from pan.

Angel Food Cake   *Yield:* 10–12 servings
1 c. cake flour   ¼ tsp salt.
1½ c. finely granulated sugar   1 tsp. cream of tartar
1¼ c. egg whites (about 10 whites)   ½ tsp. vanilla

Sift the cake flour after measuring it and sift the sugar separately. Then sift about two-thirds of the sugar (about 1 c.) with the flour.

Add salt and cream of tartar to egg whites and beat until foamy. Then sprinkle the sugar which is not combined with the flour, over the egg whites in 2-tbsp. portions, beating after each addition until sugar has disappeared from sight (about 10 sec.), and adding vanilla.

Beat egg whites until just stiff enough to hold good peaks. Sift a *thin* layer (about 2 tbsp.) of flour-sugar mixture over entire surface of whites and fold until flour mixture is lost from sight. Repeat, adding the flour-sugar mixture in 2-tbsp. portions until it has all been used. After last addition, fold for 30 sec.

Turn into 9- or 10-inch ungreased tube pan and bake in slow oven, 325°F., for 50 min. to 1 hr. When done, cake should be delicately browned and should spring back when lightly pressed with the finger tips. Invert pan on wire rack and let stand until cake is thoroughly cooled. Loosen sides with slender spatula and remove from pan.

Muffins

The following proportions of ingredients will yield about a dozen, medium-size plain muffins.

2 c. flour   ¼ c. oil or melted shortening
¼ c. sugar   1 egg, well beaten
3 tsp. baking powder   1 c. milk
½ tsp salt.

Sift dry ingredients (including sugar) into mixing bowl. Combine oil or melted shortening, egg and milk, thoroughly. Add the oil, egg and milk mixture all at once to a "well" in the center of the dry ingredients, and combine only until dry ingredients are all dampened (25–30 strokes). The batter should not be smooth.

Fill greased muffin pans about two-thirds full and bake at 425°F. 15–25 min., or until golden brown and baked to the center.

For *whole-wheat muffins,* use the above recipe but with 1 c. white flour and 1 c. whole-wheat flour.

For *cornmeal muffins.* Prepare as above for *muffins,* but use only 1 c. flour to sift with baking powder, sugar and salt, then add ½ c. yellow cornmeal and combine well. Use only ¾ c. milk.

Baking Powder Biscuit Mixtures

A wide variety of products are based upon the preparation of baking powder biscuit doughs. They include meat pie toppings, dumplings, coffee cakes, cobblers and shortcakes. These differ somewhat in the proportion of ingredients and in the method used. On p. 197 is a summary of the ingredients and methods for these products. The amounts are based on the use of one cup of flour, and to make more than this, increase the amounts as necessary.

Pies

Preparation of Pie Dough.—*Ingredients.*—Following are the amounts of ingredients to use in preparing dough for different sizes of pies.

Amounts of Ingredients for Different Sizes of Pies

Amount of pastry	Flour, c.	Salt, tsp.	Shortening	Water (approximate amount), tbsp.
For 2-crust pie, 7 or 8 in.	1¾	¾	½ c. plus 1 tbsp.	3½
For 2-crust pie, 9 in. (or 1 doz. tarts)	2½	1	¾ c.	4½
For 1-crust pie, 7 or 8 in.	1	½	⅓ c.	2
For 1-crust pie, 9 in.	1¼	½	½ c. minus 1 tbsp.	2½

Method for Preparing Dough.—Sift flour and salt together; cut in cold shortening with pastry blender or two knives, until fat-flour mixture is size of small peas. Add ice-cold water by teaspoonfuls. Each time, drop water on a dry portion of ingredients and toss with a fork to dampen some of the dry ingredients. Finally, collect the dough in a ball. The amount of water is important and only enough should be used to hold the dough together without making it sticky. If too

Baking Powder Biscuit Mixtures

(Amounts based on 1 cup of flour)

Ingredients	Biscuit doughs		Dumpling and cobbler doughs		Shortcake doughs	
	Plain biscuit dough (4–6 biscuits)	*Biscuit dough for fruit coffee cake* (for 8 x 8 in. pan double the recipe)	*Meat dumplings* (for 4–6 dumplings)	*Fruit cobblers* (topping for qt. casserole) or fruit dumplings (4–6 dumplings)	*Regular shortcake* (4–6 small biscuits; for 2-layer short-cake in 8 in. pan, double the recipe)	*Golden shortcake* (makes same portions as shortcake)
Flour	1 c.	1 c.	1 c.	1 c.	1 c.	1 c.
Baking powder	1½ tsp.	1½ tsp.	2 tsp.	2 tsp.	1½ tsp.	1½ tsp.
Salt	½ tsp.	½ tsp.	½ tsp.	½ tsp.	½ tsp.	½ tsp.
Sugar	.....	1 tbsp.	.....	0–2 tbsp.	0–2 tbsp.	1–2 tbsp.
Shortening	2–4 tbsp.	1½ tbsp.	1 tbsp.	1 tbsp.	¼ c.	3 tbsp.
Liquid[1]	⅓–⅜ c.	⅓–⅜ c.	⅜–½ c.	⅜–½ c.	⅓–⅜ c.	3–4 tbsp.
Egg	.....	½ egg	.....	.....	.....	½ egg
Method of Preparation	Sift flour, baking powder and salt together. Cut in shortening. Make "well" in center of ingredients, add liquid (including egg, if used) all at once and stir until dry ingredients are dampened and thickened (about 20 sec.). Turn on floured board, knead quickly 20 sec., roll and cut into biscuits. Bake at 425°–450°F., 12–15 min., or until golden brown and done. May be used for meat pie topping, rolling in one piece to fit baking dish if preferred to cutting as biscuits.		Prepare as for plain baking powder biscuit dough. If sugar is used, sift it with other dry ingredients, or sprinkle it over them before adding shortening. Dough for cobblers should be slightly softer than for biscuits; for dumplings, dough should be still softer. Use dough according to recipe.		Prepare as for plain baking powder biscuit dough, sifting sugar with other dry ingredients or sprinkling it over them before adding shortening. Roll out, cut into biscuits and bake as for baking powder biscuits. Or roll out as 2 large "cakes"; brush one side with melted shortening, place second "cake" on top and bake in moderate oven, 350°–375°F. about 30 min.	

1 Liquid is usually milk, and amount required varies with the flour.

little is used, the dough and the baked pastry will be crumbly. If too much is used, the dough will be sticky and so will require additional flour and the baked crust will be tough. The exact amount of water differs according to the flour used. If convenient, chill the dough in the refrigerator thoroughly before rolling it. This will make it easier to roll, and is especially important if the crust is to be rolled thin.

Two-Crust Pies.—Using slightly more than half the dough, roll out the lower crust to a circle about ⅛-inch thick, using as little flour on the board as possible. Line pie plate with circle and sprinkle lightly with flour, or brush with egg white or oil to prevent sogginess.

Roll out top crust and slash several times to allow steam to escape during baking. (If preferred, top crust may be pricked with a fork after it is placed on the pie.) Place fruit or other filling in lower crust. Moisten the entire edge of the lower crust with cold water. Place upper crust on top and crimp edges together firmly, making a good seal between the upper and lower crusts. Trim edges beyond rim of pie plate.

Bake in hot oven, 450°F., 15 min., then reduce heat to moderate oven, 350°F. Seven or 8-inch pies require 40–45 min. total baking time, and 9-inch ones require about 10 min. longer.

Pie Shells.—Roll out circle of dough as for a two-crust pie. Place in pie plate and fit it firmly into the plate without stretching the dough. Trim the edge, leaving pastry well out to the rim of the plate, and make a fluted rim if desired. Prick the entire surface of the unbaked shell with a fork before placing it in the oven and again after about 5 min. of baking (when pastry has puffed and before it is set). If preferred, another pie plate slightly smaller in diameter may be set inside the pastry shell when it is put in the oven; remove the second plate a few minutes before the end of baking, to allow the shell to finish browning. These precautions are to prevent excessive shrinkage or an unshapely shell which is almost bound to result in a shell without such measures. Bake at 450°F. for 12–15 min.

Lattice Top Pies.—Fit pastry into pie plate and add filling, as for two-crust pie. Cut remaining dough into strips ½ in. wide and about 2 in. longer than the diameter of the pie pan. Arrange strips criss-cross fashion over the filling, sealing each strip to the edge of lower crust with cold water. Trim off excess pastry and crimp edges. Bake as for two-crust pies, above.

Pie Meringues.—Following are the proportions of ingredients to use:

	For 7 or 8 in. pies	*For 9 in. pies*
Egg whites	2	3
Salt	pinch	⅛ tsp.
Sugar	¼ c.	6 tbsp.

Add salt to egg white in mixing bowl and beat with rotary or electric beater until foamy. Add sugar gradually (1 tbsp. at a time), beating well after each addition. Continue beating until meringue is thick and glossy and holds good peaks. Spread over pie filling, swirling well out around entire rim of crust. For attractive browning, leave top in peaks or swirls. Bake in slow oven, 325°F., for 15–20 min., or until golden brown. Let stand out of drafts to cool, before cutting.

Gravies

Pan Gravy.—Remove meat from roasting pan and skim off all but about ¼ c. fat, leaving all the meat juices in the pan.

Add ¼ c. flour, 1 tsp. salt and $^1/_{16}$ tsp. pepper to the pan. Cook over high heat until mixture is a good brown but not burned, stirring to brown evenly. The mixture will not brown further after water has been added.

Remove from heat and add 2 c. broth or water, slowly, stirring constantly to prevent lumping. When water has been added, cook mixture until it thickens, stirring constantly. For giblet gravy, use broth in which giblets were cooked. For milk gravy (especially good for chicken or ham) use milk in place of water. *Yield:* about 2 c. gravy.

Pot Roast Gravy (or Pressure Saucepan Gravy).—Remove meat and rack from pan and blend in a smooth paste prepared from 2 tbsp. flour and 2 tbsp. cold water. This much will thicken 1 c. liquid and more or less should be used according to the amount of liquid in pan. Stir mixture constantly over low heat until it thickens, and season to taste.

Sauces

Recipes for a number of sauces are given in connection with the recipe in which they are used, and these are listed in the index. Following are some additional sauce recipes.

Cream (White) Sauce.—Cream sauce, or white sauce as it is sometimes called, is used as the basic mixture for many soups, sauces and creamed luncheon or supper dishes. These sauces are classified as *thin* sauce (used in preparing soups), *medium* sauce (used in preparing sauces to be served over vegetables, croquettes, etc.), and *thick* sauce (used as the base for croquettes, soufflés, etc.). The difference between the sauces is the proportion of flour and fat to liquid. The liquid for any of them may be entirely milk, or in some sauces some other liquid such as meat or vegetable stock is used in place of part of the milk.

Proportions for Cream Sauce

Ingredient	*Thin sauce*	*Medium sauce*	*Thick sauce*
Milk	1 c.	1 c.	1 c.
Butter or margarine	1 tbsp.	2 tbsp.	4 tbsp.
Flour	1 tbsp.	2 tbsp.	3–5 tbsp.
Salt	½ tsp.	½ tsp.	½ tsp.

To Combine Ingredients.—Melt butter or margarine in top of double boiler, add flour and salt and blend thoroughly. Add hot milk slowly, stirring to avoid lumps. Cook over hot water, stirring, until sauce is thickened. If sauce needs to stand before using, turn off heat and keep covered. Sauce may be prepared over direct heat if it is cooked slowly, with constant stirring to prevent scorching or lumping. The sauce may be prepared in advance, cooled quickly and stored in a covered jar in the refrigerator.

To Use Canned, Condensed Soups.—The mildly flavored, canned condensed soups are fine in many cases, for making "quick and easy" cream sauces. Cream of celery and cream of mushroom are especially appropriate and some of the others will blend well with other ingredients in your recipes.

Using one can (10½ oz.) of condensed soup, make the "cream sauce" as follows:

Thick sauce. The undiluted soup is equivalent to thick cream sauce, so just use the amount required. In one can there is about $1^1/_3$ c. soup.

Medium sauce. To the can of condensed soup, add $^1/_3$–$^1/_2$ c. milk and this gives 1¾–1⅞ c., or enough for serving over a pound meat loaf or 6 croquettes or 2 c. vegetables.

Thin sauce. Dilute the can of soup according to the directions on the can for using it as soup. This gives about 2²/₃ c. thin sauce.

Cheese Sauce

¼ lb. (1 c.) grated Cheddar cheese | 2 c. hot medium cream sauce, see above

Add grated cheese to hot cream sauce and heat only long enough to melt cheese. Serve at once.

Egg Sauce

2 hard cooked eggs, sliced | 1½ c. hot medium cream sauce, see above

Add sliced eggs to hot sauce a short time before serving.

Custard Sauce

2 egg yolks and 2 whole eggs, beaten together slightly
¼ c. sugar

⅛ tsp. salt
2 c. milk, scalded
½ tsp. vanilla

Combine eggs, sugar and salt in small bowl. Add a little of the scalded milk to this mixture and combine well. Then add this mixture to the rest of the hot milk in the top of a double boiler. Cook over water just below the boiling point, stirring gently to cook evenly, until mixture is thick enough to coat a spoon (about 10 min.). Add vanilla, remove from heat immediately and pour custard into cold bowl.

If custard is overcooked, it will curdle. If curdling is only slight, it may be removed by beating with a rotary or electric beater.

Tomato Sauce

1 No. 2 can (2½ c.) tomatoes, or 5–6 medium, fresh tomatoes
½ tsp. salt
1 slice onion
2 peppercorns

2 whole cloves
2 tbsp. butter or margarine
1½ tsp. flour
¼ tsp. salt

Simmer tomatoes, salt, onion, peppercorns and cloves together about 10 min., then rub through sieve. Blend butter, flour and salt together, add seasoned tomato juice and cook over low heat until thickened, stirring.

Italian Tomato Sauce

¼ c. olive oil
1 clove garlic, minced
1 medium onion, chopped
½ green pepper, chopped
1 No. 2 can (2½ c.) tomatoes
1 can (8 oz.) tomato sauce

1½ tsp. monosodium glutamate
¼ tsp. pepper
½ tsp. oregano
¼ c. Parmesan cheese
1 bay leaf

Sauté garlic, onion and green pepper in hot olive oil in large skillet, for about 5 min. Add remaining ingredients and simmer, uncovered, about 15 min. Before serving, remove bay leaf.

Cucumber Sauce

½ c. heavy cream or dessert topping
1 tbsp. lemon juice or vinegar
¼ tsp. salt

⅛ tsp. paprika
1 medium cucumber

Beat cream or dessert topping, add lemon juice slowly and season with salt and paprika. Pare cucumber, remove seeds, cut finely and drain well. Add cucumber to whipped cream. Sour cream may be used, and in that case omit lemon juice or vinegar.

Tartar Sauce

1 c. mayonnaise
1½ tsp. grated onion
1½ tsp. chopped parsley

1 tbsp. chopped sour pickle
1 drop Tabasco sauce
2 tsp. capers

Combine ingredients just enough to blend.

Maitre d'Hotel, or Parsley Butter

¼ c. butter or margarine
½ tsp. salt
dash cayenne

1 tbsp. finely chopped parsley
2 tsp. lemon juice

Cream butter until soft, add salt, cayenne and parsley, then add lemon juice very slowly, beating constantly.

Drawn Butter Sauce

¼ c. softened butter or margarine
2 tbsp. flour
¼ tsp. salt
dash cayenne

1 c. hot water or stock
1 tsp. lemon juice (more if sauce is
   to be served with fish)

Melt 2 tbsp. butter, blend in flour, salt and cayenne, then add hot water gradually and simmer 5 min., stirring. Beat in remaining 2 tbsp. butter (adding it in teaspoon portions) and finally beat in lemon juice.

Caper Sauce

drawn butter sauce (see directions
  above)

3 tbsp. drained capers

Add capers to drawn butter sauce and heat just before serving.

Parsley Sauce

drawn butter sauce (see directions
  above)

2 tbsp. chopped parsley

Add parsley to drawn butter sauce.

Lemon Butter

1/4 c. softened butter or margarine

1 tbsp. lemon juice

Cream butter and beat lemon juice in slowly.

Salad Dressings

Recipes for some salad dressings are given in connection with the recipe in which they are used, and these are listed in the index. Following are additional salad dressing recipes.

French Dressing

1 tsp. sugar
1/2 tsp. salt
1 tsp. paprika
1/4 tsp. dry mustard
1/8 tsp. pepper

1/4 c. mild vinegar or lemon juice,
  or a combination of these
3/4 c. salad oil
few drops onion juice or 1/2 tsp.
  grated onion (omit for fruit
  salads)

Beat all ingredients together with rotary beater, or shake well in a tightly covered jar. Keep in covered jar in refrigerator, and shake each time before using. Proportion of seasonings may be varied to taste.

Non-Separating French Dressing

4 tsp. sugar
1/2 tsp. salt
1/4 tsp. pepper
1/2 tsp. dry mustard

1/2 c. salad oil
1/4 c. vinegar
$1/3$ c. canned, condensed tomato
  soup (undiluted)

Combine all ingredients except vinegar and tomato soup and shake well. Add the vinegar and tomato soup and shake thoroughly.

Chiffonade Dressing

½ c. French dressing (see above)
1 tbsp. shredded, ripe olives

1 tbsp. shredded green pepper
white of 1 hard cooked egg, sieved; yolk of 1 hard cooked egg, mashed

Combine all ingredients.

Roquefort Dressing

½ c. French dressing (see above)
¼ c. Roquefort or bleu cheese

⅛ tsp. Worcestershire sauce, if desired

Crumble Roquefort or bleu cheese into French dressing, and add Worcestershire sauce if desired.   Shake well.

Fruit Salad Dressing

¹/₃ c. reconstituted frozen orange juice
1½ tbsp. lemon juice
1 egg or 2 egg yolks, slightly beaten

½ c. sugar
1 c. whipping cream or dessert topping
few grains salt

Mix fruit juices, add egg and sugar.   Cook in top of double boiler about 2 min., stirring.   Cool, then add cream which has been beaten but not stiff.   Add salt and continue beating until well blended.

Russian Dressing

1 c. mayonnaise
¼ c. chopped pimiento
¼ c. chopped celery
1 tsp. grated onion

½ c. chili sauce
¼ c. chopped green pepper
½ tsp. salt

Mix all ingredients thoroughly.

Thousand Island Dressing

Russian dressing (see above)
4 stuffed olives, chopped
1 finely chopped hard cooked egg

¼ c. sweet piccalilli
¼ c. heavy cream or dessert topping, if desired

Combine Russian dressing with all other ingredients, whipping cream and adding just before serving, if desired.

Cooked Salad Dressing

¼ c. sugar
2 tbsp. flour
½ tsp. salt
¾ tsp. dry mustard
2 eggs

¾ c. milk
¼ c. vinegar
2 tbsp. butter or margarine
few grains cayenne

Blend dry ingredients (except cayenne) in top of double boiler, add eggs and milk and beat thoroughly. Add vinegar slowly, stirring, and cook over simmering water, stirring constantly until thickened. Remove from heat and stir in butter and cayenne.

Chill in covered container in refrigerator. When ready to use, thin with fruit juice, milk or sweet or sour cream, if desired.

MENUS IN THIS BOOK

Throughout this book, menus are provided, including the use of frozen foods. In each menu, the words in italics represent the foods which were purchased frozen. When these frozen foods have been used in the preparation of a recipe in the book, the page for the recipe is inserted. The menus do not usually include the beverage, and they do not always include the bread or hot-bread. They are not designed to be complete menus, but rather to provide ideas for combinations of dishes to help in planning family and other meal-times or refreshments.

CHAPTER 13

Frozen Meats

METHODS OF MEAT COOKERY

The method of cooking which may be used for a cut of meat depends on its tenderness. Tender cuts are cooked by dry heat and need only to be cooked long enough to give the desired color and flavor. Less tender cuts have more connective tissue and need to be cooked in the presence of moisture for a longer time, to make them tender. Following are the usual methods of cookery.

For Tender Cuts

Roasting.—The roast may be seasoned with salt and pepper at any stage during cooking. Since the seasonings do not penetrate much beneath the surface, there is no special advantage in seasoning at the beginning.

Place the meat, fat side up, on a rack in a shallow roasting pan. Insert the meat thermometer so that the bulb is in the center of the largest muscle, not touching the bone or resting in the fat.

Do not add water, and do not cover the pan. Roast in a slow oven, 300°F. for all meats except fresh pork, and roast it at 350°F. For a roast with a good coating of fat, no basting is necessary. Roast until the thermometer indicates the desired degree of doneness. Pork should always be cooked to the well-done stage to avoid the possibility of trichinosis, and also to give it the best flavor.

Times for roasting different kinds of meats are given on page 208.

Broiling.—Tender beef steaks, lamb chops, ground beef or lamb patties, or sliced ham or bacon may be broiled.

To be satisfactory for broiling, steaks and chops should be at least 1 inch thick, and ham slices should be at least ½ inch thick. Slash the fat around the edges of the meat, to prevent curling. Turn the oven regulator to broil, preheating or not, according to the instructions for your range.

Place the meat on the broiling pan. Steaks or chops which are not more than 1 inch thick should be placed 2 inches from the heat,

206

thicker ones should be at least 3 inches. Broil until the top side is brown, sprinkle with salt and pepper (except for ham or bacon), turn and brown the other side and season. To determine the degree of doneness, cut a small slash in the meat and note the color.

Times for broiling different kinds of meat are given on page 209.

Pan-Broiling.—This method can be used for cuts suggested above for broiling, and it is preferred for thinner chops, steaks and ham slices. This is cooking in a skillet or griddle without added fat, and

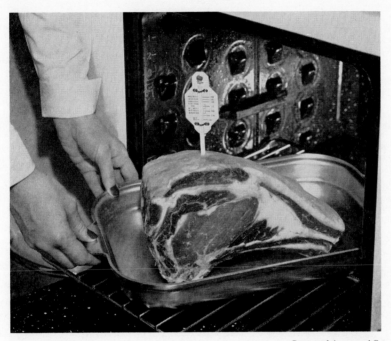

Courtesy of Armour and Co.

The best way to know when a roast is done is to test it with a meat thermometer with the bulb inserted into the center of the thickest muscle

any fat which accumulates during cooking is poured off. Preheat the skillet or not, as desired, and use constant, low or moderate heat. Cook uncovered, turning occasionally to cook evenly and to brown gradually on both sides. Season.

Pan-Frying.—Meats suitable for broiling or pan-broiling may be pan-fried, and those coated with flour, crumbs, meal or egg must be pan-fried. This is cooking in a skillet or griddle with a small amount

Timetable for Roasting Meats

Cut	Approximate weight, lbs.	Oven temperature constant, °F.	Interior temperature when removed from oven, °F.	Approximate time per pound, min.
Beef				
Standing rib	6 to 8	300	140	18–20
			160	22–25
			170	27–30
Rolled rib	5 to 7	300	140	32
			160	38
			170	48
Standing rump (high quality)	5 to 7	300	150–170	25–30
Rolled rump (high quality)	4 to 6	300	150–170	25–30
Pork—fresh				
Loin				
Center	3 to 5	350	185	35–40
Half	5 to 7		185	40–45
Ends	2 to 3		185	45–50
Picnic shoulder	5 to 8	350	185	30–35
Boned and rolled	3 to 5	350	185	40–45
Cushion-style	3 to 5	350	185	35–40
Boston butt	4 to 6	350	185	45–50
Fresh ham, whole	10 to 14	350	185	30–35
Pork—smoked				
Ham[1]				
Whole	10 to 14	300	160	18–20
Half	5 to 7	300	160	22–25
Shank or butt portion	3 to 4	300	160	35–40
Shoulder butt	2 to 4	300	170	35
Picnic shoulder	5 to 8	300	170	35
Lamb				
Leg	5 to 8	300	175–180	30–35
Shoulder (bone in)	4 to 6	300	175–180	30–35
Rolled	3 to 5	300	175–180	40–45
Cushion-style	3 to 5	300	175–180	30–35
Veal				
Leg	5 to 8	300	170	25–35
Loin	4 to 6	300	170	30–35
Rib (rack)	3 to 5	300	170	30–35
Shoulder (bone in)	5 to 8	300	170	25–35
Rolled	4 to 6	300	170	40–45

[1] Hams now on market which require shorter cooking period due to method of processing.
Courtesy National Live Stock and Meat Board, Chicago, Ill.

of fat. Unbreaded pork chops, ham, bacon or other fatty meats need no fat added, but for others add a small amount. Cook over moderate heat, uncovered, browning meat slowly on both sides and turning occasionally to cook evenly to desired degree of doneness.

Deep-Fat Frying.—Pieces of meat, raw or cooked, which are not too large may be deep-fat fried or cooked in fat to cover. For this, a deep kettle with a wire basket is necessary. The fat should be at 300°–350°F., depending on the size of piece and whether it is raw or cooked. Unless an automatically controlled fryer is used, a frying

Timetable for Broiling Meats

Cut	Weight	Approximate total cooking time[1], min. Rare	Approximate total cooking time[1], min. Medium
Beef			
Chuck steak—1 in.	1½ to 2½ lbs.	24	30
1½ in.	2 to 4 lbs.	40	45
Rib steak—1 in.	1 to 1½ lbs.	15	20
1½ in.	1½ to 2 lbs.	25	30
2 in.	2 to 2½ lbs.	35	45
Club steak—1 in.	1 to 1½ lbs.	15	20
1½ in.	1½ to 2 lbs.	25	30
2 in.	2 to 2½ lbs.	35	45
Sirloin steak—1 in.	1½ to 3 lbs.	20	25
1½ in.	2¼ to 4 lbs.	30	35
2 in.	3 to 5 lbs.	40	45
Porterhouse steak—1 in.	1¼ to 2 lbs.	20	25
1½ in.	2 to 3 lbs.	30	35
2 in.	2½ to 3½ lbs.	40	45
Ground beef patties			
1 in. thick by 3 in.	4 oz.	15	25
Pork—smoked			
Ham slice—tendered			
½ in.	¾ to 1 lb.	Ham always cooked	10–12
1 in.	1½ to 2 lbs.	well done	16–20
Canadian-style bacon			
¼ in. slices			6–8
½ in. slices			8–10
Bacon			4–5
Lamb			
Shoulder chops—1 in.	5 to 8 oz.	Lamb chops are not	12
1½ in.	8 to 10 oz.	served rare	18
2 in.	10 to 16 oz.		22
Rib chops—1 in.	3 to 5 oz.		12
1½ in.	4 to 7 oz.		18
2 in.	6 to 10 oz.		22
Loin chops—1 in.	4 to 7 oz.		12
1½ in.	6 to 10 oz.		18
2 in.	8 to 14 oz.		22
Ground lamb patties			
1 by 3 in.	4 oz.		18

[1] This timetable is based on broiling at a moderate temperature (350°F.). Rare steaks are broiled to an internal temperature of 140°F.; medium to 160°F.; well done to 170°F. Lamb chops are broiled from 170° to 175°F. Ham is cooked to 160°F. The time for broiling bacon is influenced by personal preference as to crispness.

Courtesy National Live Stock and Meat Board, Chicago, Ill.

thermometer is essential to success. Use enough fat so the food will float in it, but do not have the fat come so near the top of the kettle that there is any danger of fire.

Place a few pieces of food in the wire basket and carefully lower the basket into the fat at the required temperature. If the temperature of the fat (as given in a recipe) is satisfactory, the food will be heated or cooked to the center by the time it is golden brown. Then lift the basket from the fat, turn the food from the basket onto crumpled, absorbent paper to drain briefly, and serve.

After using, strain the fat, cool and cover it and store it in a cool place.

For Less Tender Cuts

Braising.—This is a good method for cooking many less-tender meats, and also for pork chops and some cutlets and pork liver.

By this method, the meat is first browned in hot fat on all cut surfaces, dredging first in seasoned flour if desired.   Then it is cooked, tightly covered, in the presence of a small amount of water. Water or other liquid may be added, or for rather tender meat which does not need long cooking, the steam provides sufficient moisture if the pan is very tightly covered.

Cook at low temperature (simmering, not boiling) until the meat is tender, adding extra liquid if necessary.   The liquid left in the pan contains flavoring materials and nutrients, so should be used for making sauce or gravy.   Pot roasts are cooked by this method.

Following is a timetable for braising meats.

Timetable for Braising Meats

Cut	Average weight or thickness	Approximate total cooking time
Beef		
Pot-roast	3 to 5 lbs.	3–4 hrs.
Swiss steak	1½ to 2½ in.	2–3 hrs.
Fricassee	2 in. cubes	1½–2½ hrs.
Beef birds	½ in. (x 2 x 4 in.)	1½–2½ hrs.
Short ribs	Pieces (2 x 2 x4 in.)	1½–2½ hrs.
Round steak	¾ in.	45–60 min.
Stuffed steak	½ to ¾ in.	1½ hrs.
Pork		
Chops	¾ to 1½ in.	45–60 min.
Spareribs	2 to 3 lbs.	1½ hrs.
Tenderloin		
Whole	¾ to 1 lb.	45–60 min.
Fillets	½ in.	30 min.
Shoulder steaks	¾ in.	45–60 min.
Lamb		
Breast—stuffed	2 to 3 lbs.	1½–2 hrs.
Breast—rolled	1½ to 2 lbs.	1½–2 hrs.
Neck slices	¾ in.	1 hr.
Shanks	¾ to 1 lb. each	1–1½ hrs.
Shoulder chops	¾ to 1 in.	45–60 min.
Veal		
Breast—stuffed	3 to 4 lbs.	1½–2½ hrs.
Breast—rolled	2 to 3 lbs.	1½–2½ hrs.
Veal birds	½ in. (x 2 x 4 in.)	45–60 min.
Chops	½ to ¾ in.	45–60 min.
Steaks or cutlets	½ to ¾ in.	45–60 min.
Shoulder chops	½ to ¾ in.	45–60 min.
Shoulder cubes	1 to 2 in.	45–60 min.

Courtesy National Live Stock and Meat Board, Chicago, Ill.

Cooking in Liquid.—Large and small pieces of less tender meats may be cooked this way. This is similar to braising, but the meat is covered with liquid. If full flavor and color are desired, brown the meat on all cut surfaces, dredging first in seasoned flour if desired. Then cover the meat with hot or cold water or stock, adding seasonings as desired. Cover tightly and simmer until tender, adding more liquid if necessary.

This is basically the method for making stews, and vegetables are added toward the end of cooking, in time so they will be tender by the time the stew is served, and the liquid is thickened. To cook lamb for stew, allow 1½–2 hrs., for veal for stew, 2–3 hrs., and for beef, 2½–3½ hrs. Soups are prepared this way, too, usually adding cold liquid to cover the meat so as to extract the maximum amount of flavor from the meat.

Cooking in Pressure Saucepans.—For cooking meats in pressure saucepans, follow the instructions provided by the manufacturer.

COOKING FROZEN MEATS

Is it Necessary to Thaw Meat First?

In many cases, meat can be successfully cooked from the hard-frozen state. Often, the decision as to thaw first or not will depend on whether a longer cooking period is more convenient than thawing ahead of time. However, many homemakers prefer to thaw meat before cooking, because cooking methods are then exactly the same as the familiar ones for fresh meats, and so your favorite recipes can be used exactly as they always have been. Nevertheless, it is good to know with a few exceptions, meats can be cooked from the hard-frozen state.

In the following instances, meat must be thawed before cooking:

(1) If pieces like steaks, chops or patties in one package have not been separated before freezing, with *two* thicknesses of wrapping material.

(2) If meat is to be cut into pieces, ground, shaped or stuffed, before cooking.

(3) If meat is to be dredged in flour or crumbs, or rolled in batter or eggs, since these will not stick to frozen meats.

(4) If meat is to be deep-fat fried.

How to Thaw Meats

Leave the meat in the unopened wrapper until you are ready to use it. Thawing in the refrigerator is recommended because it is more uniform. When thawed at room temperature, it will still be frozen at the center by the time it is thawed near the outside. The meat will thaw still more quickly in front of an electric fan, but this is poor practice for a large roast, because there is apt to be excessive "drip" from the outer portion of the roast before it is thawed to the center. Meat should never be thawed in cold water, even when left in the wrapper.

The most important precaution is to cook the meat as soon as it is thawed, and when it is still cold (as cold as it would be in the re-frigerator). After this, it begins to "drip," or "leak" or lose juice, and when this has happened the meat will be dry when served. In the leaked juices there are nutrients and flavoring materials, so these should be used in cooking the meat.

The following timetable serves as a guide to help in planning the time for thawing steaks and roasts.

Approximate Times to Thaw Meats

Where thawed	Steaks 1 in. thick	Roasts
In refrigerator (preferred method)	12–18 hrs.	3–5 hrs. per lb. for small roasts (less than 4 lbs.) 4–7 hrs. per lb. for large roasts
At room temperature	2– 3 hrs.	1–2 hrs. per lb. for small roasts 2–3 hrs. per lb. for large roasts
In front of electric fan	1–1½ hrs.	1 hr. (or less) per lb. for small roasts Not recommended for large roasts

How to Cook Frozen Meats

If meat is thawed, cook it exactly as you would cook similar fresh meat. Directions for basic methods of meat cookery are given in the preceding pages.

Meats can be roasted without thawing. Do not try to insert the meat thermometer until about half the anticipated cooking time has elapsed, for you may break the bulb of the thermometer. It is all the more important to put these roasts in a low-temperature oven to allow them plenty of time to thaw before they get crusty.

Following is a timetable giving the approximate minutes per pound to allow for thawed roasts and for roasts cooked from the frozen state. The time for roasting from the frozen state is usually from one and a half to two times as long as for similar roasts which have been thawed. For cooking roasts not listed in the timetable, allow this much extra time for cooking without thawing. In general, the larger the roast, the more the additional time required to roast it from the frozen state. It is all the more important to use a meat thermometer when roasting meats without preliminary thawing, since roasting times are not always so precise.

Approximate Times for Roasting Frozen Meats

Kind	How cooked, roast at	Degree of doneness	Thawed before cooking Minutes per pound	Cooked from frozen state Minutes per pound
Standing rib roast	300 °F.	Rare	18–20	43
	300 °F.	Medium	22–25	47
	300 °F.	Well-done	27–30	55
Rolled rib roast	300 °F.	Rare	32	53
	300 °F.	Medium	38	57
	300 °F.	Well-done	48	65
Pork-loin roast center cut rib or shoulder	350 °F.	Well-done	35–40	50–55
ends	350 °F.	Well-done	45–50	70–75
Leg of lamb	300 °F.	Well-done	30–35	40–45
Boneless lamb shoulder	300 °F.	Well-done	40–45	50

Courtesy National Live Stock and Meat Board, Chicago, Ill.

If steaks or chops are to be broiled from the frozen state, place them 1 to 2 inches farther from the source of heat than the recommendation for fresh or thawed ones, until they are thawed. Then move them closer to the heat, to brown. Allow about twice as long to broil as for similar fresh or thawed steaks or chops.

To pan-broil or pan-fry chops or steaks, start to cook over very low heat until thawed, then finish as for fresh or thawed meats. Allow from one and a half to two times as long to cook these as the recommended time for similar fresh or thawed meats.

With a little experience, excellent roasts, steaks and chops can be cooked from the frozen state. This is particularly true for those who like rare steaks or roasts with a crusty surface. This does not mean that such roasts and steaks always have this quality, but it is easy to learn to prepare them this way if it is the family preference.

Hard-frozen meats which are braised or cooked in liquid do not need as much extra cooking time, because the meats will thaw more quickly in steam or hot water.

For meats which are partially but not completely thawed, it is impossible to give any general recommendation for time of cooking. Such meat may be only slightly or almost completely thawed, and so the time may resemble one extreme or the other.

RECIPES AND MENUS

BEEF

Prepared this way, Yorkshire Pudding is as light as a popover:

Roast Beef with Yorkshire Pudding

Yield: 2–3 servings per pound of standing rib roast, or 3–4 servings, per pound of rolled rib roast

1 frozen roast of beef (at least 4 lbs. rolled or 6 lbs. standing rib)
1 c. flour
½ tsp. salt
1 c. milk
2 eggs, well beaten

For directions for cooking roast, see p. 206. Cook roast early enough to remove it from oven before baking pudding, since Yorkshire Pudding requires a very hot oven.

For pudding, sift flour and salt together, add milk and eggs and beat with rotary beater until smooth (about 2 min.). Pour batter into piping hot shallow baking dish, 8 x 12 in., containing ½ c. beef drippings. Bake in very hot oven, 450°F., about 30 min., reducing heat toward end, if necessary to prevent burning. Serve at once with roast beef.

Or, if preferred, bake pudding as for popovers. Pour batter into preheated muffin pans or custard cups, each containing 2 tsp. beef drippings, filling each cup only one-third full. Bake at 450°F. about 20 min., then turn oven down to 350°F. and bake 15–20 min. longer. Serve at once.

Dinner: *Standing Rib Roast* with Yorkshire Pudding, Gravy
Buttered *Broccoli*, Creamed Onions, *Grapefruit* and Avocado Salad,
p. 368—*Chocolate Cake.*

Without a doubt, the top favorite for men:

Broiled Steak with Mushrooms   *Yield:* 3–4 servings per lb. of steak

1 frozen porterhouse or   ½ lb. (2 c.) mushrooms, sliced,
   sirloin steak   or 1 can (8 oz.)
¼ c. butter or margarine

Broil steak (see directions, p. 206). Meanwhile, heat butter in frying pan until bubbling but not browned, add mushrooms, cover

Courtesy of Armour and Co.

A juicy, flavorsome steak, cooked to a turn...is not to be surpassed on any American table

pan tightly and simmer 2 min. Stir well, cover again and simmer until tender. Cook uncovered an additional few minutes to brown slightly.

Arrange hot steak on hot serving platter, add sautéed mushrooms with their juices and pour over steak the rich, brown juice (not fat) from broiler pan.

Dinner: Broiled *Porterhouse Steak* with Mushrooms, *French-Fried Onion Rings, Stuffed Baked Potato, Brussels Sprouts* with Celery, p. 344—*Blueberry* Dumplings, p. 379.

For the gourmet . . . a dish of great distinction:

Steak in Red Wine

Yield: 4–6 servings

1 frozen tender steak (1–1½ lbs.)
½–1 c. red wine (Burgundy,
   Chianti, or other dry, red wine)

1 can (4 oz.) mushrooms

Panbroil steak until half done (see directions, p. 207), then add mushrooms and wine and simmer gently until steak is done. To serve, pour wine gravy and mushrooms over steak.

Dinner: *Sirloin Steak* in Red Wine, *French-Fried Potatoes,* Piquant *Peas,* p. 359, *Green Bean* and Carrot Salad, p. 334—*Strawberry* Shortcake, p. 420.

Delicious steak, bacon and vegetable kabobs:

Saybrook Kabobs

Yield: 6 servings

2 lbs. frozen, tender beef steak,
   thawed
8 strips bacon
3 medium onions

8 stalks celery
split frankfurter rolls
prepared mustard or ketchup

Cut bacon crosswise into 1-inch pieces, dice onions into ½-inch pieces and cut celery crosswise into ½-inch slices. Cut beef into 1-inch cubes.

String on metal skewers, alternating beef, bacon, onion and celery, and beginning and ending with beef. Broil (preferably over charcoal), turning to cook on all sides.

Slip off skewers into split frankfurter rolls and serve with mustard or ketchup.

Luncheon or Supper: Saybrook Kabobs (*Tender Steak*), Lattice Potatoes, Cole Slaw with Tomato Wedges—*Blueberry* Pie, p. 380.

Cooked on the range at home, or simmered over glowing coals, this spicy, savory dish is a year 'round treat:

Barbecued Rump Roast   *Yield:* 6 servings

2 lbs. frozen beef rump roast, partially thawed	1 tbsp. vinegar
	1 tsp. mustard seeds
¼ c. olive or salad oil	3 whole allspice berries
1½ tbsp. Worcestershire sauce	pepper
3 tbsp. lemon juice	2 tbsp. fat

Place roast in bowl. Combine all remaining ingredients except oil and heat them together thoroughly. Pour this sauce over the meat and let stand several hours, turning several times to have the meat well covered with sauce. Drain, saving sauce.

Brown the meat in hot oil, then pour sauce over it and cover closely. Cook slowly until tender, about 3 hrs., adding water if necessary. Serve sauce with meat. Or use for making sandwiches, placing meat slices and sauce between slices of toast.

> **Luncheon or Supper:** Barbecued *Rump Roast* Sandwiches, Pickle Relish, Cole Slaw—*Mixed Fruit* Cup.

It's a favorite with everyone, everywhere:

Pot Roast of Beef with Vegetables   *Yield:* 2–3 servings per lb. unboned beef, or 3–4 servings per lb. boned beef

1 frozen beef chuck (about 5 lbs.), or other pot roast, partially thawed	¼ c. hot water
	6–8 small potatoes
3 tbsp. fat	4–8 carrots, cut lengthwise
2 tsp. salt	8 small onions
⅛ tsp. pepper	1 pkg. (10 oz.) frozen broccoli

Brown pot roast in Dutch oven in hot fat, then sprinkle with salt and pepper and add hot water. Cover very tightly and cook over very low heat, adding more water if necessary. About 30 min. before meat is done, add potatoes, carrots and onions, and place broccoli on top of vegetables for the last 15 min. of cooking.

When vegetables and meat are done, pour off drippings and make gravy (see directions, p. 199). Put meat in center of hot serving platter, arrange vegetables attractively around it, and serve with gravy.

If desired, spread ¼ c. horseradish over top of meat when serving. And for variation, omit broccoli, cook 1 pkg. (10 oz.) frozen cauliflower and 1 pkg. (10 oz.) frozen peas separately and add these at time of serving.

> **Dinner:**   *Pot Roast of Beef* with Vegetables, Hot *Baking Powder Biscuits,* Tossed Vegetable Salad with Dressing——*Cherry Upside Down Cake.*

Inexpensive, but quite fine enough for a company dinner:

Stuffed Round Steak   *Yield:* 6–8 servings

1 lb. frozen round steak, thawed	½ c. chopped celery and leaves
¼ c. fat	1½ c. soft bread crumbs
½ c. hot water	½ tsp. salt
1 small onion, chopped	speck pepper

To prepare stuffing, sauté onion and celery in 2 tbsp. fat, add bread crumbs, salt and pepper to taste.   If steak is in one piece, spread stuffing over it, roll up like a jelly roll, and fasten securely with string or skewers.   If steak is in two pieces, put stuffing between them and fasten securely.   Brown meat on all sides in remaining 2 tbsp. fat, add hot water and cover, closely.   Bake in moderate oven, 375°F. about 1½ hrs. or until tender, adding more water if necessary.

> **Dinner:**   Stuffed *Round Steak, Asparagus Spears,* Buttered *Carrots, Grapefruit* and *Artichoke* Salad, p. 327——Coconut *Peach* Pie, p. 400.

An American version of a Chinese specialty:

Chinese Beef with Tomatoes   *Yield:* 4–6 servings

1 lb. frozen round steak, partially thawed	4 tomatoes, each cut in sections, or 2 c. canned tomatoes
2 tsp. cornstarch	2 tbsp. sugar
½ tsp. salt	⅓ c. water
2 tbsp. soy sauce	1 tbsp. vinegar
2 tbsp. fat	fried Chinese noodles
1 medium onion, sliced	
1 small green pepper, cut in strips	

Cut the meat into thin slices, 1½ x 1 x ¼ in. Combine half the cornstarch with half the soy sauce and add the salt, then combine this with the beef. Sauté in skillet in hot fat until meat is barely done, then remove meat from skillet. Brown onion and green pepper in hot fat, then add tomatoes and boil about 2 min., or until some of the juice has cooked from the tomatoes, if fresh ones were used. Add the meat.

Combine remaining cornstarch and soy sauce with sugar, water and vinegar, add to meat mixture and cook until sauce has thickened and is clear, stirring constantly. Serve over fried Chinese noodles.

Dinner: *Cream of Shrimp Soup*—Chinese *Beef* with Tomatoes and Fried Chinese Noodles, Assorted Relishes and Pickles—Toasted *Cherry* Chiffon Pie, p. 382.

Tender steak, with an air of elegance:

Steak with Mushroom Sauce

Yield: 3–4 servings

1 tender steak (1 lb., 1¼–1½ in. thick)

mushroom sauce (see below)

Broil steak (see directions, p. 206). Meanwhile, prepare mushroom sauce. Serve hot sauce over broiled steak on hot platter.

Mushroom Sauce

1 can (8 oz.) mushrooms
2 tbsp. butter or margarine
½ c. top milk
½ c. mushroom liquid
½ tsp. salt

speck pepper
⅛ tsp. paprika
½ tsp. Worcestershire sauce
1 tbsp. flour
2 tbsp. cold water

Drain mushrooms, reserving liquid, and sauté them in hot butter, then add top milk, mushroom liquid, salt, pepper, paprika and Worcestershire sauce. Combine flour and cold water to make a smooth paste, add to mushroom mixture and bring slowly to boil, stirring, and cook until thickened.

Dinner: *Steak* with Mushroom Sauce, *Squash* Mallow, p. 445, *French-Fried Potatoes*, Chef's Salad—*Apple Cobbler.*

Seasoned to perfection . . . Swiss steak at its finest:

Swiss Steak   *Yield:* 4–6 servings

1–1½ lbs. frozen round steak,   1 tsp. salt
    thawed   2 tbsp. fat
6 tbsp. flour   ½ c. water
½ tsp. dry mustard   1 c. sliced onions

Combine flour, dry mustard and salt and pound this mixture into the steak until it is well absorbed.   Brown steak in hot fat, add water and arrange onions on top of steak.   Cover tightly and bake in slow oven, 300°F., for about 2 hrs., or cook slowly on top of range until tender.   Add more water during cooking, if necessary.

Dinner: Swiss *Steak, Potatoes au Gratin, Broccoli* with Garlic Butter, p. 342, *Bran Muffins,* Tomato and Cucumber Salad— *Blueberry* Pie, p. 380.

Flavor appeal in a one-dish meal:

Steak with Kidney Beans   *Yield:* 4–6 servings

1½–2 lbs. frozen round steak,   12 small white onions
    thawed   4 whole cloves
¹/₃ c. flour   1 tsp. salt
2–3 tbsp. fat   ½ c. water, or red wine, if preferred
1 can (16 oz.) kidney beans

Pound flour into steak until it is well absorbed, then brown steak well in hot fat in Dutch oven or skillet.   Add kidney beans, onions, cloves, salt and water (or wine), cover and simmer gently 1½ hrs., or until steak is tender.   Add water or wine during cooking, if necessary.

Dinner: *Steak* with Kidney Beans, Buttered *Asparagus, Pineapple* Orange Gelatin Salad, p. 403—*Devil's Food Cake.*

Strips of tender beef, in a luscious, sour cream sauce:

Beef Stroganoff

Yield: 4 servings

1½ lbs. frozen fillet of beef, or
  sirloin steak, thawed
¼ c. flour
½ tsp. salt
speck pepper
¼ c. butter or margarine
1 c. (¼ lb) thinly sliced mushrooms
  (or 1 can, 4 oz.)
½ c. chopped onion

1 garlic clove, minced
1 tbsp. ketchup
1½ c. beef stock (or dissolve 2
  bouillon cubes in hot water)
2 tbsp. sherry or white wine
3 c. cooked rice, preferably part
  wild and part white
1 c. sour cream

Trim beef and cut into strips ¼ inch wide. Dredge in 2 tbsp. flour to which salt and pepper have been added, coating all strips of beef. Sauté in 2 tbsp. hot butter in skillet, turning strips to brown on all sides. When brown, add mushrooms (drained, if canned), onion and garlic, and simmer 3–4 min., or until onion is golden.

Remove beef and mushrooms from skillet. Add remaining 2 tbsp. butter and remaining 2 tbsp. flour, beef stock and ketchup. Bring to boil and simmer until thickened, stirring constantly. Return beef and mushrooms to skillet, stir in sour cream and wine and heat briefly.

Serve beef in rice ring, and sauce in gravy boat.

> **Dinner:** *Beef Stroganoff* in Rice Ring, Buttered *Baby Carrots*, *Succotash*, Head Lettuce with Russian Dressing—*Orange* Charlotte Russe, p. 396.

Chili powder and olives make this an exotic dish:

Chili Steak

Yield: 6 servings

2 lbs. frozen round steak, thawed
½ c. seasoned flour
2 tbsp. fat
3 c. hot water

1 tbsp. chili powder
¼ c. cold water
1 c. sliced ripe olives

Cut steak into strips 4 inches long and 2 inches wide, and dredge in flour. Brown on all sides in hot fat in skillet, add hot water, cover and simmer about 1 hr. Blend chili powder with cold water and add to meat, and add olives. Simmer ½ hr. longer, or until tender.

> **Dinner:** Chili *Steak*, Baked Potatoes, Buttered *Spinach*, Mixed Vegetable Salad—*Boysenberry* Shortcake, p. 420.

A touch of the old world . . . the lavish use of paprika:

Beef Paprika   *Yield:* 8 servings
2 lbs. frozen round steak, thawed   1 tbsp. paprika
1 garlic clove, minced   2¼ c. water
4 c. sliced onions   3 tbsp. cornstarch
¼ c. fat   ½ green pepper, cut in rings
1 tbsp. salt

Cut steak into 2-inch cubes. Sauté garlic and onions in hot fat in skillet until tender but not brown. Remove garlic and onion, add steak cubes and brown well. Add salt, paprika and 2 c. water, cover tightly and simmer gently about 1½ hrs. Add cooked garlic and onion and simmer 30 min. longer, or until meat is tender. Blend cornstarch with remaining cold water (¼ c.) and add to meat mixture, combining well. Cook, stirring until thickened.

When serving, garnish with green pepper rings.

Dinner: *Grape Juice—Beef* Paprika, *French-Cut Green Beans,* Mashed Potatoes, Sliced Tomatoes—*Apple Pie.*

A Japanese dish which is also popular among Americans:

Sukiyaki   *Yield:* 4 servings
1 lb. frozen steak, round or other,   2 stalks celery, cut in very thin
   tender   slices
¼ c. suet, butter or margarine   ¼ lb. mushrooms (1 c. sliced) or 1
1 c. beef stock (or dissolve 1   can (4 oz.)
   bouillon cube in 1 c. boiling   2 tbsp. soy sauce
   water)   1 tsp. salt
1 c. bamboo shoots, or 1 can (5 oz.)   ⅛ tsp. pepper
10 young, green onions, cut in very   1 tbsp. sugar
   thin slices   cooked rice
½ green pepper, cut in very thin
   slices

For the Japanese style, vegetables should be sliced very thin, as indicated. If preferred, they may be "sliced" by cutting them on a coarse grater.

Cut meat into *very thin* slices across the grain, and brown in hot fat in skillet. If raw mushrooms are used, they may be sautéed with the beef. Boil beef stock and add to meat. Add remaining ingredients except rice, and cook, covered, for 15 min. At this time, the vegetables are "crunchy," and this is correct for the Japanese dish. For vegetables to be more thoroughly cooked, continue to cook 10–15 min. longer. Serve with rice.

Dinner: *Egg Drop Soup*—Sukiyaki *(Beef)* with Rice, *French-Cut Green Beans,* Tossed Green Salad—*Strawberry* Shortcake, p. 420.

A new version of chili con carne, and can be prepared over a picnic fire, too:

Mexican Rolls   *Yield:* 6 servings

1½ lbs. frozen round steak, thawed   5 tsp. chili powder
½ tsp. salt   1 No. 2 can (2½ c.) tomatoes
3 tbsp. flour   1 No. 2 can (2½ c.) kidney beans
¼ c. fat   split, toasted rolls
¹/₃ c. chopped onion
1 garlic clove

Cut steak into ½-inch cubes, sprinkle with salt and pepper and add to skillet with hot fat. Add chopped onion and garlic clove and cook until browned, stirring occasionally. Add chili powder and tomatoes, cover and simmer about ½ hr., or until meat is tender. Remove garlic, add kidney beans and heat thoroughly. Serve on split, toasted rolls.

Luncheon or Supper: Mexican Rolls *(Round Steak),* Green Pepper Cole Slaw, Pickled Onion—*Strawberries* in Sponge Cake Shells.

Poems have been written about perfect stews:

Old Fashioned Beef Stew   *Yield:* 4–6 servings

1 lb. frozen beef stew meat,   4–6 small onions
   partially thawed   1 pkg. (10 oz.) frozen peas and
2 tbsp. fat   carrots
2 tsp. salt   3 tbsp. flour
2 c. hot water   ¼ c. cold water
4–6 medium potatoes

Brown cubed meat in hot fat in Dutch oven, add 1 tsp. salt and hot water, cover tightly and simmer until tender. About ½ hr. before meat is done, add potatoes and onions, and 15 min. before it is done add peas and carrots.

Blend flour with cold water and remaining salt and slowly add this mixture to the stew, stirring. Cook until gravy is thickened, stirring constantly.

> **Dinner:** Old Fashioned *Beef* Stew, *Baking Powder Biscuits,* Tomato and Cucumber Salad—*Raspberry* Tapioca Pudding, p. 405.

An old favorite in a new guise:

Open-Faced Hamburgers

Yield: 4 servings

1 lb. frozen ground beef, thawed
4 slices bread

salt
pepper
melted butter or margarine

Toast one side of each slice of bread and spread raw beef on untoasted side, spreading it well out to the edges. Broil or bake in oven until beef is cooked to desired degree of doneness. Season with salt, pepper and melted butter.

> **Luncheon or Supper:** Open-Faced Hamburgers (*Beef*), Grilled Tomatoes, Sliced Cucumber and Onion Salad—*Orange* Cake Pudding, p. 395.

When winter appetites are keen, serve this hearty goulash:

Beef Goulash Supreme

Yield: 6–8 servings

1–1½ lbs. frozen ground beef, thawed
2–3 tbsp. fat
1 can (10½ oz.) condensed tomato soup
3 c. water
1 can (10½ oz.) condensed mushroom soup
1 tsp. salt

¼ tsp. pepper
¼ tsp. paprika
1 tsp. garlic salt (or 1 garlic clove)
4 oz. spaghetti (uncooked)
1 can (4 oz.) mushrooms, if desired
¼ c. chopped green peppers
1 c. diced celery
1 c. thinly sliced onion
1 pkg. (10 oz.) frozen cut corn

Brown meat in hot fat in skillet or Dutch oven. Add remaining ingredients except green peppers, celery, onion and corn, and mix well. Cover tightly and cook slowly about 1 hr., stirring occasionally. Add remaining ingredients about 15 min. before serving.

> **Dinner:** *Pineapple Juice*—*Beef* Goulash Supreme, Baked Potato, *Honey Nut Muffins*—*Cherry Ice Cream.*

"South of the Border" in origin . . . popular everywhere:

Chili Con Carne *Yield:* 8 servings

1 lb. frozen ground beef, partially
    thawed
1 c. chopped onions
1 small section garlic, minced
2 tbsp. fat
2 tsp. salt
1 tsp. sugar

⅛ tsp. pepper
1 can (20 oz.) tomatoes, or 2½ c.
1 can (6 oz.) tomato paste
1 can (16 oz.) kidney beans
¾ c. water
1–2 tbsp. chili powder

Sauté onions and garlic in hot fat in skillet, then add beef and brown slowly. Add remaining ingredients, cover and simmer until flavor is well blended, 30–45 min.

    Dinner: Chili Con Carne *(Beef)* on Rice, Pickles, Vegetable Salad —*Orange* Charlotte Russe, p. 396.

Fare for the whole family, but especially for the teen-agers:

Ground Beef in Barbecue Sauce *Yield:* 6–8 servings

1½ lbs. frozen ground beef, thawed
2 tbsp. fat

barbecue sauce, p. 338

Brown meat in hot fat in skillet, keeping it soft and crumbly. Add barbecue sauce, cover tightly and simmer gently about 30 min., adding a small amount of water during cooking, if necessary.

    Luncheon or Supper: Ground *Beef* in Barbecue Sauce, Savory Baked Corn, p. 353, Grilled Tomatoes—Mixed Fruits with Whipped *Dessert Topping, Cookies.*

This recipe from sunny Italy is popular throughout the world:

Italian Spaghetti with Meat Balls *Yield:* 6 servings

1 lb. frozen ground beef, thawed
¼ c. bread crumbs
2 eggs, slightly beaten
1 tsp. salt
1/₃ c. grated cheese (preferably
    Parmesan)
2 cloves garlic, minced

1 tbsp. chopped parsley, or 1 tsp.
    dried parsley, if desired
2 tbsp. salad or olive oil
1 can (No. 2½) tomatoes (3½ c.)
1 can (6 oz.) tomato paste
1 c. water
1 lb. spaghetti, cooked and drained
grated cheese, preferably Parmesan

Combine tomatoes, tomato paste, water, 1 minced garlic clove, and ½ tsp. salt, in skillet, cover and simmer about an hour.

Meanwhile, make meat balls. Add bread crumbs, eggs, ½ tsp. salt, $^1/_3$ c. grated cheese, remaining minced garlic and parsley to meat, mix until well blended and form into balls 1½ inch in diameter. Sauté balls lightly in oil, until brown on all sides. After sauce has simmered an hour, add the meat balls, cover and simmer for about 30 min. longer, adding more water if necessary.

Serve on spaghetti and top with grated cheese.

Dinner: Italian Spaghetti with Meat Balls (*Beef*), Tossed Green Salad with French Dressing, Relishes, *Rolls—Peach Strawberry Compote*, p. 401, *Cookies.*

For outdoor gourmets:

Broiled Stuffed Hamburgers　　*Yield:* 6 servings

2 lbs. frozen ground beef, thawed　　¼ c. chopped celery
3 tbsp. minced onion　　1 tsp. salt
2 tbsp. butter or margarine　　speck pepper
3 c. soft bread crumbs　　¾ tsp. poultry seasoning
2 tbsp. water

Form ground beef into 12 very thin patties. To make stuffing, brown onion lightly in hot butter, add remaining ingredients and combine well.

Place a layer of stuffing between two hamburg patties, sandwich-fashion. Broil about 10–15 min., turning once.

Supper or Luncheon: Broiled Stuffed Hamburgers (*Beef*), *Green Bean* and Carrot Salad, p. 334, Pickled Beets—*Rhubarb* Special, p. 409.

The old world joins hands with the new, in this recipe:

Hamburgers en Brochette　　*Yield:* 6 servings

2 lbs. frozen ground beef, thawed　　2 eggs
2 tsp. salt　　3–4 strips bacon
½ c. bread crumbs　　1 medium onion
speck pepper

Combine salt, bread crumbs, pepper and eggs, without packing crumbs tightly. Combine this with beef, keeping mixture spongy and form into balls. Cut bacon strips crosswise, and slice onion very thin.

String on metal skewers, alternating meat balls, bacon and onion, beginning and ending with meat balls. Broil about 10 min., turning once.

Supper or Luncheon: *Orange Juice*—Hamburgers en Brochette *(Beef), French-Fried Potatoes,* Mustard Pickles, Celery—*Pineapple Chunks, Cookies.*

A fine recipe for picnics, or for a family dinner at home:

Frying-Pan Barbecue

2 lbs. frozen ground beef, thawed	*Yield:* 8 servings
1 medium onion, finely chopped	1 c. ketchup
1 tsp. salt	¼ c. sugar
speck pepper	¼ c. Worcestershire sauce
¼ c. fat	2 tbsp. vinegar

Add ½ tsp. salt, pepper and onion to ground beef and mix well. Form into patties and brown on both sides in hot fat in skillet. Combine remaining ingredients, and pour over patties. Cover and cook about 10 min.

Luncheon or Supper: Frying-Pan Barbecue *(Beef), Green Bean* and *Cauliflower* Salad, p. 335, Dill Pickles, Radishes—*Sliced Peaches* and *Blueberries, Cookies*

Hamburgers with sour cream gravy you'll long remember:

Hamburgers Supreme

2 lbs. frozen ground beef, thawed	*Yield:* 8 servings
12 slices bread	¼ tsp. nutmeg
2 c. milk	2 large onions, sliced
2 tsp. salt	¼ c. fat
speck pepper	2 c. sour cream

Trim crusts from bread, pour milk over slices and let stand 15 min. Add bread mixture to beef, add seasonings and form into 16 patties.

Brown patties and onions in hot fat, add sour cream and simmer 10 min.

> **Dinner:** Hamburgers Supreme *(Beef)*, *French-Fried Potatoes*, Butttered *Asparagus*, Tomato Salad—*Cherry Pie* with *Ice Cream*.

Or serve this flavorsome loaf as cold slices:

Meat Loaf   *Yield:* 8 servings

1 lb. frozen ground beef, thawed	1 egg, slightly beaten
½ lb. frozen ground veal, thawed[1]	1 c. milk
½ lb. frozen ground pork, thawed[1]	2 tbsp. grated onion
1 c. fine, dry bread crumbs	1½ tsp. salt
	¼ tsp. pepper

Combine all ingredients well, but without packing meat tightly. Turn into greased loaf pan 8½ x 4½ x 2½ in. and bake in moderate oven, 350°F. about 1¼ hr.   Let stand in pan about 10 min. after removing from oven, then turn out on serving platter.

> **Dinner:** *Grapefruit Juice*—Meat Loaf *(Beef, Veal, Pork)* with Tomato Sauce, p. 201, Parsley Buttered *New Potatoes*, p. 361, Succotash—*Peach Strawberry* Compote. p. 401.

This hash is really something to sing about:

Raw Potato Beef Hash   *Yield:* 4 servings

2 c. cooked beef, diced or ground	⅛ tsp. pepper
2 c. grated raw potato	1 c. beef broth (or 1 bouillon cube
2 tbsp. chopped green pepper	dissolved in 1 c. boiling water)
2 tbsp. minced onion	3 tbsp. fat
½ tsp. salt	cheese-paprika sauce (see below)

Add vegetables, salt, pepper and broth to beef and combine well. Add to hot fat in skillet, cover and simmer about 30 min.   Uncover and bake in moderate oven, 350°F., about 15 min. or until browned. Serve with cheese-paprika sauce.

Cheese-Paprika Sauce

½ lb. American or processed cheese	2 tsp. paprika
2 tbsp. butter or margarine	1 egg, well beaten
1 tbsp. Worcestershire sauce	

[1] If preferred, omit veal and pork and use 2 lbs. beef.

Melt cheese and butter in top of double boiler, add Worcestershire sauce and paprika, and add egg just before serving.

Luncheon or Supper: Raw Potato *Beef* Hash with Cheese-Paprika Sauce, Poached Egg, Pickles, Carrot Curls—*Raspberry* Sherbet, p. 407, *Cookies.*

A little left-over, cooked beef goes a long way in this:

Southern Beef Roll with   *Yield:* 4 servings
  Cheese-Paprika Sauce

1 c. cooked, ground beef
¾ c. gravy
2 tbsp. minced onion
2 tbsp. chopped green pepper
½ tsp. salt
¼ tsp. pepper

1½ c. flour
2 tsp. baking powder
¾ tsp. salt
3 tbsp. shortening
½ c. milk
Cheese-paprika sauce, p. 228

Combine beef, gravy, onion, green pepper, salt and pepper. Prepare baking powder biscuit dough from remaining ingredients (see directions, p. 197), or use 1½ c. biscuit mix and ½ c. milk. Roll dough into rectangle about $1/3$-inch thick and spread dough with beef mixture. Roll up as for jelly roll, sealing the edges and placing edges down on baking pan.

Bake in hot oven, 400°–425°F., about 30 min. or until done.

Dinner: Southern *Beef* Roll with Cheese-Paprika Sauce, *French-Fried Onions,* Buttered *Peas,* Head Lettuce with French Dressing—*Strawberry* Whip, p. 419

A soufflé with a difference . . . try it and see why:

Beef Soufflé with Tomato Sauce   *Yield:* 5–6 servings

2 c. cooked ground beef, or other
  meat
2 tbsp. melted butter or margarine
2 tbsp. flour
¾ tsp. salt
speck pepper
2 c. milk

½ c. soft bread crumbs
1 tbsp. chopped parsley, or 1 tsp.
  dried parsley
1 tsp. grated onion
1 tsp. celery salt
2 eggs, well beaten
tomato sauce, p. 201

Combine butter, flour, salt, pepper, add milk slowly and cook over low heat until thickened, stirring.   Add bread crumbs, parsley, onion, and celery salt and mix well.   Add meat and combine, then stir in eggs.

Turn into greased 1½ qt. casserole and bake in moderate oven, 350°F., 40 min., or until set.   Serve at once with tomato sauce.

Dinner: *Beef* Soufflé with Tomato Sauce, *Corn on the Cob, Green Bean* and *Cauliflower* Salad, p. 335, *Blueberry Muffins—Butterscotch Ice Cream* with Marshmallow Sauce, p. 432.

The French feature of these is the toast:

French Beefburgers
1 c. cooked ground beef
¼ c. gravy
¼ tsp. celery salt
¼ tsp. onion salt
⅛ tsp. sage, if desired

Yield: 3 sandwiches
6 slices of buttered bread
2 eggs
¼ c. milk
¼ c. fat

Combine beef, gravy, celery salt, onion salt and sage and spread this between slices of bread, making three sandwiches.   Beat the eggs and milk together and dip each sandwich in this mixture, first on one side, then on the other.

Sauté both sides of the sandwiches in hot fat, until golden brown.

Luncheon or Supper: French *Beef*burgers, Tossed Vegetable Salad —Tapioca Pudding with Sliced *Strawberries.*

Feathery-light fritter batter makes left-over beef a conversation piece:

Beef Fritters
2 c. cooked beef, cut into pieces 1½
    x 1½ x ¹/₂ in.
1 c. flour
½ tsp. salt
1 tsp. baking powder

Yield: 6 servings
1 egg, well beaten
½ c. milk
2 tbsp. melted butter or margarine
fat for frying

Sift flour, salt and baking powder together.   Combine egg and milk, then add milk mixture to flour mixture and stir until smooth. Stir in butter.

Dip cubed meat in batter and fry until golden brown in deep fat at 375°F.

> **Brunch:** *Cream of Pea and Ham Soup—Beef* Fritters, *Succotash,* Head Lettuce with French Dressing—*Pineapple* Upside Down Cake, p. 404.

A modification of an Italian favorite:

Yankee Lasagna   *Yield:* 6 servings

1 lb. frozen ground beef, thawed   ½ lb. ricotta cheese (well drained
Italian tomato sauce, p. 202   cottage cheese, if preferred)
¼ lb. lasagna noodles (broad, flat)
½ lb. Mozzarella cheese

Prepare Italian tomato sauce, but add beef to garlic and onion mixture to sauté and heat until beef is browned.   Then add tomatoes and other ingredients and finish sauce as usual.

Cook noodles until tender in boiling, salted water, and drain. Pour one-third of meat-tomato sauce into greased baking pan, 12 x 8 x 2 in., and cover with strips of noodles.   Over this, arrange slices of Mozzarella cheese and spoonfuls of ricotta cheese.   Repeat these layers, with meat-tomato sauce on top.   Bake, uncovered, in moderate oven, 350°F., about 40 min.

> **Dinner:** Yankee Lasagna *(Beef), Peas* with Tiny Onions, p. 359, Tossed Green Salad with Italian Dressing—*Grapefruit, Blackberry* and Orange Compote, p. 376.

A popular American adaptation of Mexican hot tamales:

Tamale Pie   *Yield:* 4–6 servings

1 c. chopped cooked beef, or other   1 c. frozen cut corn
   meat   1 c. canned tomatoes
1 c. cornmeal   1 pimiento, chopped
1¼ tsp. salt   1 tsp. chili powder
1 qt. boiling water   2 tbsp. chopped olives
1 green pepper, chopped   ½ c. grated cheese
1 small onion, chopped   paprika
2 tbsp. fat

Combine cornmeal, salt and boiling water in top of double boiler and cook over direct heat until cornmeal thickens, then over boiling water 30 min.

Meanwhile, sauté green pepper and onion in hot fat, add corn and cook 2 min., after boiling is resumed. Add to this mixture the meat and remaining ingredients except cheese and paprika.

Line sides and bottom of 1½-qt. casserole ½-inch thick with cornmeal mixture, then add meat mixture. Top with remaining cornmeal mixture. Sprinkle with cheese and paprika and bake in moderate oven, 375°F., about 30 min.

> **Dinner:** *Bean Soup*—Tamale Pie (*Beef*), Hearts of Lettuce with Thousand Island Dressing—*Red Raspberry* Shortcake, p. 420.

Savory fare for a chilly evening:

Beef Pie

2 c. cooked beef, cubed
½ c. chopped celery
½ c. chopped onion
½ green pepper, chopped
2 tbsp. fat
1 c. cubed, cooked potatoes
1 pkg. (10 oz.) frozen peas and
    carrots, thawed enough to
    separate pieces

Yield: 6 servings

1 c. gravy
salt
speck pepper
4 slices dry bread cut in cubes
3 tbsp. butter or margarine

Sauté celery, onion and green pepper in hot fat, until tender. Add remaining ingredients except bread cubes and butter, combine well and place in greased 1½-qt. casserole. Brown bread cubes lightly in hot butter and arrange the cubes on top of casserole.

Bake in moderate oven, 375°F., about 30 min.

> **Dinner:** *Vegetable Soup*—*Beef* Pie, Buttered *Brussels Sprouts, Rolls,* —*Strawberry* and *Rhubarb* Sherbet, p. 411.

OTHER BEEF RECIPES

Barbecued Beef Patties. *See p. 443*
Steak Sandwiches. *See p. 443.*
Hamburgers with Welsh Rarebit. *See p. 443.*
Quick Beef Stew. *See p. 443.*

LAMB

Bland lamb flavor, enhanced discreetly with garlic and wine:

Leg of Lamb Burgundy *Yield:* 8–10 servings

1 frozen leg of lamb (6–8 lbs.) 1 c. domestic burgundy
8 slivers of garlic (2 garlic cloves,
  peeled and quartered lengthwise)

Cut gashes along the length of the leg of lamb, and insert garlic slivers into the gashes. Insert a meat thermometer into the thickest part of the meat, and roast in a slow oven, 300°F. If lamb is roasted without preliminary thawing, cut gashes and insert garlic and thermometer as soon as meat is thawed in the oven. About 45 min. after meat has been in oven (or 45 min. after garlic has been inserted into thawed meat), remove garlic. Baste lamb at approximately ½ hr. intervals, using ¼ c. wine for each basting, and using approximately 1 c. wine altogether.

> **Dinner:** *Leg of Lamb* Burgundy, Savory *Peas* and Tomatoes p. 358. *Green Bean* and Carrot Salad, p. 334——Baked *Strawberry* Alaska, p. 412.

A brand new way with lamb chops:

Crumbed Lamb Chops *Yield:* 4 servings

4 frozen lamb chops, thawed 1 egg, beaten
salt fine cracker crumbs
speck pepper

Sprinkle each chop with salt and pepper, dip in egg and roll in cracker crumbs. Sauté chops in hot fat, about ¼-inch deep, in skillet, 12-20 min. or until cooked through to the center.

> **Dinner:** *Cream of Mushroom Soup*——Crumbed *Lamb Chops,* Mustard *Cauliflower* and *Peas,* p. 350——*Citrus* Banana Sherbet, p. 396.

Flavor affinities . . . lamb and curry . . . combined in a new fashion:

Lamb Curry Pie   *Yield:* 8 servings
2 lbs. frozen lamb (shoulder or   ¼ tsp. thyme
   brest), cut into 1-in. cubes   1½ tsp. salt
2 tbsp. fat   2 tbsp. flour
1 medium onion, chopped   1 tsp. curry powder
1½ c. water   3 c. cooked rice

Brown meat in hot fat with onion, in skillet, add ¾ c. water, salt and thyme, cover tightly and simmer 1½ hrs., or until meat is tender.

Combine flour and curry powder with remaining ¾ c. water, to make a smooth paste. Add this slowly to the lamb mixture and cook, stirring constantly, until thickened.

Line greased baking dish, sides and bottom, with rice, pressing firmly into place. Add lamb mixture and bake in hot oven, 425°F. for 15–20 min.

If preferred, place baking powder biscuit dough (cut into serving pieces) on top of lamb mixture in baking dish (without rice) and bake in hot oven, 450°F. for 15–20 min.

Dinner: *Lamb* Curry Pie with Rice, Buttered *Broccoli, Pineapple* Orange Gelatin Salad, p. 403—*Brownies.*

Lamb stew in a casserole, crowned with pimiento pinwheels:

**Lamb Stew with Pimiento   *Yield:* 8 servings
   Pinwheels**
2 lbs. frozen lamb (shoulder or   3 tbsp. fat
   breast), thawed   6 small white onions
1½ tsp. salt   6 stalks celery, diced
¼ tsp. pepper   1 pkg. (9 oz.) frozen cut green beans
flour   pimiento pinwheels (see p. 235)

Cut lamb into 2-inch cubes, season with salt and pepper and dredge in flour. Brown meat in hot fat and cover with boiling water. Cover tightly and simmer 1½ hrs., or until meat is almost tender. Add vegetables and cook until vegetables are almost done. Place mixture in casserole and top with pimiento pinwheels.

Pimiento Pinwheels

2 c. flour
3 tsp. baking powder
1 tsp. salt
¼ c. chopped parsley or 1 tbsp.
  dried parsley

$^2/_3$–¾ c. milk
½ c. shortening
$^1/_3$ c. coarsely cut pimiento

Prepare biscuit dough from flour, baking powder, salt, shortening and milk (see directions, p. 197), adding parsley to dry ingredients. Roll dough to rectangular shape, ½-inch thick, and sprinkle with pimiento. Roll up like jelly roll and cut crosswise into 1-inch slices (pinwheels).

Dinner: *Fruit Juice* Cocktail——*Lamb* Stew with Pimiento Pinwheels, Buttered *Asparagus*——*Strawberry* Chiffon Pie, p. 417.

The blending of many flavors into a perfect whole:

Lamb Stew

2 lbs. frozen lamb (shoulder or
  breast), thawed
¼ c. flour
2 tsp. salt
speck pepper
¼ c. chopped onion
2 or 3 garlic cloves, minced
3 tbsp. fat
3 c. boiling water

Yield: 8 servings

2 tsp. celery seed
12 small onions
1 bunch carrots, cut in quarters,
  length-wise
2 tsp. minced parsley or ½ tsp.
  dried parsley
2 tsp. Worcestershire sauce
1 pkg. (12 oz.) frozen peas

Remove lamb from bone, cut in 2-inch pieces and dredge in flour to which pepper and 1 tsp. salt have been added. Sauté chopped onion and garlic in hot fat in Dutch oven, then remove onion and garlic and brown meat in the fat. Add onion and garlic to meat, then add remaining 1 tsp. salt, boiling water and celery seed. Cover tightly and simmer gently 1½–2 hrs. or until meat is tender.

About 30 min. before meat is tender, add small onions and carrots. Cook frozen peas just in time to have them ready by the time the stew is done. Add parsley and Worcestershire sauce just before serving. Turn stew into serving dish and pour cooked peas over top.

Dinner: *Lamb* Stew, Parsley Potatoes, Tomato and Cucumber Salad ——*Raspberry* Cream Pudding, p. 405.

Hearty and colorful, tomato dumplings add a different touch:

Lamb and Lima Beans with   *Yield:* 8 servings
  Tomato Dumplings

2 lbs. frozen lamb (shoulder or   3 tbsp. fat
  breast), thawed   1 pkg. (10 oz.) lima beans
¼ c. flour   tomato dumpling dough (see
1 tsp. salt   below)
speck pepper

Remove meat from bone and cut it into 2-inch pieces. Dredge meat in flour to which salt and pepper have been added, and sauté in hot fat in Dutch oven or skillet. Add boiling water almost to cover lamb, cover kettle tightly and simmer gently 1½–2 hrs., or until almost tender.

Add frozen lima beans and cook until they are almost tender, then add tomato dumpling dough by spoonfuls to the stew, cover tightly and steam 12–15 min.

Tomato Dumpling Dough

2 c. flour   2 tbsp. shortening
4 tsp. baking powder   ¾-1 c. tomato juice
1 tsp. salt

Prepare dumpling dough (see directions, p. 197), using tomato juice as the liquid. Or if preferred, use biscuit mix with tomato juice as the liquid.

> **Dinner:** *Lamb* and *Lima Beans* with Tomato Dumplings, *Grapefruit* and Avocado Salad—*Brownies* á la Mode.

You can prepare these at home, carry them to the picnic, and broil them over charcoal:

Lamb Kabobs   *Yield:* 6 servings

2 lbs. frozen boneless lamb shoulder,   1 tsp. dry mustard
  thawed   1 tsp. Worcestershire sauce
slashed garlic clove   dash cayenne
½ c. salad oil   few drops Tabasco sauce
¼ c. vinegar

Cut lamb into 1-inch cubes. Rub bowl with garlic clove. Combine all other ingredients except meat, place them in the bowl, and add lamb cubes and let stand several hours. Then drain, and string the lamb on skewers. Broil about 20 min., turning to brown evenly. Slide off skewers, and for a picnic, serve in split frankfurter rolls.

Dinner: *Lamb* Kabobs, Baked Potato, Sliced Tomato and Cottage Cheese with Russian Dressing, Olives, Sweet Pickles—*Cherry Pie.*

The fragrant bouquet of herbs with cold lamb:

Pressed Lamb Shoulder *Yield:* 6–8 servings

2 lbs. frozen lamb shoulder, thawed ¼ tsp. thyme
¼ c. fat ½ tsp. rosemary
1 garlic clove, cut in slivers 1 tsp. salt
1 c. sauterne wine (or water) 1 small bay leaf
½ tsp. summer savory

Cut slits in lean of lamb, at intervals, and insert garlic slivers. Add remaining ingredients, place in Dutch oven, cover tightly and simmer slowly several hours or until tender enough to remove bone. Remove bones, place meat in dish barely large enough to hold it, cover meat with plate, and put weight on plate to press firmly down on meat. When cold, remove from dish, slice meat and serve.

Dinner: Sliced Pressed *Lamb* Shoulder, Parsley Buttered *New Potatoes,* p. 361, Southern *Okra,* p. 357, Tossed Green Salad—Frozen *Orange* Cream, p. 395.

So savory, you'd never guess it was a thrifty left-over:

Lamb Timbales *Yield:* 3–4 servings

1 c. finely chopped, cooked lamb 1 tsp. minced onion
2 tbsp. butter or margarine 1 tsp. celery salt
¼ c. dry bread crumbs ½ tsp. Worcestershire sauce
²/₃ c. milk speck pepper
½ tbsp. chopped, fresh parsley, or tomato sauce, p. 201 or mushroom
  ½ tsp. dried parsley   sauce, p. 219
2 eggs, slightly beaten

Melt butter, add bread crumbs and milk and cook 5 min., stirring constantly. Add remaining ingredients except tomato or mushroom sauce, and combine well.

Fill 3 or 4 greased custard cups or ramekins about two-thirds full of meat mixture and place dishes in pan of hot water. Bake in moderate oven, 350°F., about 20 min. or until firm. Unmold on serving plates and serve with tomato or mushroom sauce.

Dinner: *Lamb* Timbales with Tomato Sauce, Piquant *Peas,* p. 359, *Grapefruit* and Avocado Salad, p. 386,—*Pumpkin* Caramel Custard, p. 366.

Really regal, in looks and in flavor:

Lamb Croquettes   *Yield:* 4 servings
2 c. cooked, ground lamb   1 tsp. minced onion
1 c. milk   ½ tsp. lemon juice
3 tbsp. butter or margarine   ½ tsp. powdered sage
3 tbsp. flour   1 egg, slightly beaten
1 tsp. salt   1 tbsp. water
speck pepper   finely sifted bread crumbs
1 tbsp. minced parsley or 1 tsp.   fat for frying
   dried parsley

Prepare thick cream sauce from milk, butter, flour, ½ tsp. salt and pepper (see p. 200). Add parsley, onion, lamb, lemon juice, sage, and remaining salt, and chill in refrigerator until firm enough to shape. Shape into croquettes, cone-shaped or rolls.

Coat all sides of croquettes with flour, dip them in egg which has been combined with water, and roll in bread crumbs. Fry in deep fat at 375°F. until golden brown (about 2 min.)

Dinner: *Lamb* Croquettes with Mushroom Sauce, Parsley Buttered *New Potatoes,* p. 361, Buttered *Broccoli,* Waldorf Salad—*Pound Cake* with *Lemon* Sauce, p. 391.

A favorite trio, presented in a novel way:

Lamb Ring with Peas and Mint   *Yield:* 4–5 servings
  Sauce
2 c. cooked, ground lamb   ½ tsp. salt
1 c. crumbled soda crackers   ⅛ tsp. pepper
1 c. meat stock (or 1 bouillon cube ⅛ tsp. poultry seasoning
   dissolved in 1 c. boiling water)   ½ tsp. celery salt
1 egg, slightly beaten   2 tbsp. melted butter or margarine
1 tbsp. minced onion   1 pkg. (12 oz.) frozen peas
2 tbsp. chopped fresh parsley, or 2 mint sauce (see p. 239)
   tsp. dried parsley

Thoroughly combine all ingredients except butter, peas and mint sauce, and place them in a small, greased ring mold. Brush the top of the meat with melted butter and bake in hot oven, 425°F., about 30 min. Meanwhile, boil peas in salted water so they will be cooked and drained when meat mixture is baked. Turn lamb ring out on serving platter and fill center of ring with drained, hot peas. Serve with mint sauce.

Mint Sauce

2 tbsp. sugar	2 tbsp. water
6 tbsp. vinegar	¼ c. finely chopped mint leaves

Add water to vinegar and dissolve sugar in this mixture, adding more water if vinegar is strong. Pour this over mint leaves, and let stand in warm place 30 min.

Dinner: *Lamb* Ring with *Peas* and Mint Sauce, *French-Fried Potatoes,* Head Lettuce with French Dressing——*Raspberry Turnovers.*

Lamb Fritters *Yield:* 6 servings

Prepare as for Beef Fritters, p. 230, but using cooked lamb in place of cooked beef.

OTHER LAMB RECIPES

Lamb Chops with Currant Sauce. *See p. 442.*
Lamb Chops with Minted Pineapple. *See p. 442.*
Broiled Lamb Chops with Peach Slices. *See p. 442.*

PORK

A pleasant and attractive change from pork and applesauce:

Roast Loin of Pork with Peaches *Yield:* 6–8 servings

1 frozen pork loin (3–4 lbs.)	1 pkg. (12 oz.) frozen peaches,
½ tsp. salt	thawed
¼ tsp. pepper	½ tbsp. cornstarch
1 tsp. poultry seasoning	2 tbsp. cold water

Sprinkle seasonings over roast and place in oven at 350°F. Roast according to directions on p. 206.

Drain peaches. Blend cornstarch and cold water to make a smooth paste and add this to peach juice. Cook over low heat until thickened, stirring constantly. About ½ hr. before roast is done, cover

Roast pork is the feature of this meal-from-the-freezer which also includes peach garnish, broccoli, raisin bread and cherry tarts

top of roast with peaches. Add remaining peaches to thickened juice and serve as sauce with roast.

> **Dinner:** Roast *Loin of Pork* with *Peaches, Spinach* in Onion Sauce, p. 369, Parsley Buttered *New Potatoes,* Head Lettuce with Russian Dressing—Frozen *Lemon* Dessert, p. 389.

When the chill of winter sharpens the appetites, serve:

Roast Loin of Pork with Onion   *Yield:* 6 servings
  Stuffing
1 frozen loin of pork (about 4 lbs.),   Onion stuffing (see p. 241)
  thawed

Cut down along the length of the loin close to the backbone to separate meat from bone, making a pocket for the dressing. Place loin in roasting pan, rib side down, and roast according to directions, p. 206.

About 45 min. before roast is done, remove from oven and fill pocket with onion stuffing. Return to oven to finish roasting. (If stuffed at the beginning, the stuffing is overcooked.)

Onion Stuffing

2 c. peeled, tiny onions
6 slices day-old bread, diced
¾ tsp. salt

¼ tsp. sage
1 egg, slightly beaten
¼ c. fat from roasting pan

Cook onions until tender, and drain. Add bread and seasonings and toss together lightly. Add fat and mix lightly.

Dinner: Roast *Loin of Pork* with Onion Stuffing, Baked Potatoes, Brown Gravy, Buttered *Green Beans,* Endive Salad—Jellied *Raspberries,* p. 406, with Whipped *Dessert Topping.*

A famous trio . . . pork, sweet potatoes and apples:

Stuffed Pork Chops

6 frozen pork chops, thawed
2 c. mashed, sweet potatoes
1½ c. pared, chopped apples
1 tsp. salt

Yield: 6 servings

speck pepper
1 c. milk
crushed cornflakes or other crumbs

Cut chops lengthwise through center to bone, making pocket for the stuffing. Combine sweet potatoes and apples with ½ tsp. salt, pepper and ½ c. milk, and fill pockets with this mixture. Fasten edges of each chop securely with toothpicks or skewers. Dip chops in remaining milk to which remaining salt has been added, and roll them in cornflakes. Bake in greased baking pan in moderate oven, 350°F., about 1½ hrs. or until done.

Dinner: *Vegetable Soup*—Stuffed *Pork Chops, Broccoli* Hollandaise, p. 329, Cucumbers with Garlic Wine Vinegar—*Peach* Upside Down Cake, p. 415.

Such an easy recipe . . . so delicious a dish:

Pork Chop Dinner

6 frozen pork chops, thawed
2 tbsp. fat
1 tsp. salt
⅛ tsp. pepper

Yield: 6 servings

4 c. broad noodles
1 can (10½ oz.) condensed tomato
  soup
½ c. water

Sear chops well on both sides in hot fat in skillet, seasoning with salt and pepper. Parboil the noodles in boiling, salted water for 5 min. and drain. Place the noodles in casserole and add tomato soup and water. Arrange pork chops over noodles and cover tightly. Bake in moderate oven, 350°F., for about 1½ hrs.

Dinner: *Pork Chop* Dinner, Deviled *Brussels Sprouts, p. 344—Blueberry* Pinwheels, p. 419, *Ice Cream.*

Pork flavor combines especially well with barbecue flavors:

Pork Chops with Barbecue Sauce   *Yield:* 6 servings

6 frozen pork chops, partially thawed
¼ c. minced onion
1 c. tomato purée
¼ c. ketchup
2 tbsp. vinegar
1 tbsp. Worcestershire sauce
1½ tsp. salt
1 tsp. paprika
½ tsp. chili powder
¼ tsp. cinnamon
dash of ground cloves

Prepare sauce by combining all ingredients except pork chops. Place chops in hot skillet and sear on both sides. Reduce heat and pour about ½ c. sauce over chops, cover and cook slowly about 10 min., then turn chops, and add another ½ c. sauce. Cover and cook slowly about 1 hr., or until chops are tender. Add remaining sauce to chops about 5 min. before serving.

Dinner: *Pork Chops* with Barbecue Sauce, *Baked Stuffed Potatoes, Spinach* in Onion Sauce, p. 369, *Mixed Fruit* Salad—*Pumpkin* Carmel Custard, p. 366.

Recommended for a winter party, this hearty dish:

Deviled Pork Chops   *Yield:* 6 servings

6 frozen pork chops, thawed
1 medium onion, minced
¾ c. chili sauce
3 tbsp. lemon juice
1 tsp. dry mustard
1½ tsp. Worcestershire sauce
$1/3$ c. water
salt
speck pepper

Trim most of the fat from the chops, and save it. Slash lean meat on both sides of each chop with sharp knife.

Combine remaining ingredients and pour them over the chops. Let chops stand 1 hr. in sauce, turning occasionally, then drain, reserving the sauce.

Brown chops on both sides, in fat trimmed from chops, then pour off the fat. Add sauce and simmer about 1 hr. tightly covered.

Dinner: Deviled *Pork Chops, French-Fried Potatoes,* Cole Slaw, Bread and Butter Pickles—*Apple Pie* with Cheddar Cheese.

Fine fare for a chill winter's evening:

Pork Chops with Peach Stuffing   *Yield:* 6 servings

12 frozen pork chops, thawed
1 pkg. (12 oz.) frozen peaches, thawed
1 small onion, minced
3 tbsp. fat

2 c. bread crumbs
1/4 tsp. salt
1/4 tsp. powdered savory
speck pepper

Drain peaches and chop them finely, reserving the syrup. Sauté onion in hot fat, combine remaining ingredients and chopped peaches, then add to onion and mix well.

Spread peach stuffing generously on 6 pork chops and top with remaining chops. Fasten the pairs of chops together with toothpicks, and place them in casserole. Add water to peach syrup to make 1 c. liquid, and pour this over the chops. Cover and bake in moderate oven, 350°F., 1 1/2 hrs.

Dinner: *Pork Chops* with *Peach* Stuffing, Baked Potatoes, Buttered *Green Beans,* Herb-Flavored *Carrots* in Cream, p. 347, Celery, Olives —*Raspberry Sherbet, Cookies.*

The Chinese way of making a little meat go a long way:

Pork Chop Suey   *Yield:* 6 servings

1 lb. frozen lean pork, thawed
2 tbsp. fat
1 can soy sprouts
1 c. thinly cut onion strips
2 tsp. salt
1/8 tsp. pepper
1 1/2 c. diced celery

3/4 c. coarsely cut green peppers
1 c. boiling water
2 tbsp. soy sauce
1 1/2 tsp. cornstarch
1 tbsp. hot water
fluffy rice or fried Chinese noodles

Cut pork into julienne strips, ¼ x 1 in. and sauté in hot fat, then cook slowly about 30 min., or until tender.

Add vegetables, salt and pepper and 1 c. boiling water and cook 10 min. after mixture returns to boil. Make a paste of soy sauce, corn-starch and hot water, add this slowly to meat mixture, and cook until thickened, stirring. Serve with fluffy rice or fried Chinese noodles.

Dinner: *Pork* Chop Suey, *Egg Rolls,* Fluffy Rice, Relishes—*Lemon* Chiffon Pie, p. 388.

Cornmeal muffins provide a fine foundation for:

Creamed Pork and Celery   *Yield:* 4–6 servings

1 lb. frozen lean pork, thawed   ¼ c. flour
1 medium onion, sliced   ¼ tsp. salt
½ tsp. salt   2 c. liquid (pork and celery liquid
1 c. diced celery   with milk to give 2 c.)
¼ c. butter or margarine   cornmeal muffins

Cut pork into ½-inch cubes (there should be about 2 c.). Place pork in skillet, add onions, ½ tsp. salt and enough water to cover pork. Cook until pork is tender, about 20 min. Drain pork, re-serving liquid. Cook celery in small amount of water and drain, reserving liquid. Prepare sauce from butter, flour, ¼ tsp. salt and liquids, then add meat and cooked celery to the sauce.

Serve on hot cornmeal muffins.

Dinner: Creamed *Pork* and Celery on *Cornmeal Muffins,* Parmesan *Broccoli,* p. 342, *Pineapple* Orange Gelatin Salad, p. 403— *Chocolate Cake.*

The best cooks are the ones who have a way with left-overs:

Scalloped Pork Hash   *Yield:* 4 servings

2 c. diced, cooked pork   1 tsp. Worcestershire sauce
2 c. diced, cooked potatoes   1 tbsp. chopped parsley, or 1 tsp.
    (preferably sweet)   dried parsley
2 tbsp. minced onion   1½ c. thin, left-over pork gravy
1 tsp. salt   2 chicken bouillon cubes dissolved
⅛ tsp. pepper   in 1½ c. boiling water

Thoroughly combine all ingredients except pork gravy and dissolved chicken bouillon cubes. Then add these remaining ingredients and mix well. Put into greased, 1½-qt. casserole, and bake in moderate oven, 350°F., about 1 hr.

Dinner: Scalloped *Pork* Hash, *Lima Beans in Butter Sauce,* Pickles and Relishes—*Strawberries* with *Cookies.*

A little left-over pork made into timbales, and with bechamel sauce:

Pork Timbales with Bechamel Sauce   *Yield:* 3–4 servings

1 c. finely chopped, cooked pork
2 tbsp. butter or margarine
¼ c. dry bread crumbs
²/₃ c. milk
½ tbsp. chopped parsley, or ½ tsp. dried parsley

2 eggs, slightly beaten
¼ tsp. salt
speck pepper
bechamel sauce (see below)
parsley garnish

Melt butter, add bread crumbs and milk and cook 5 min., stirring. Add pork, chopped parsley, eggs, salt and pepper and combine. Fill greased custard cups two-thirds full of mixture, and place in pan of hot water. Bake in moderate oven, 350°F., about 20 min. or until done. Let stand 5 min. before unmolding on serving plates. Serve with bechamel sauce, and garnish with parsley.

Bechamel Sauce
¾ c. stock or bouillon
1 slice onion
1 slice carrot
⅛ bay leaf
sprig of parsley
3 peppercorns

2 tbsp. melted butter or margarine
2 tbsp. flour
½ c. scalded milk
¼ tsp. salt
speck pepper

Simmer stock, onion, carrot, bay leaf, parsley and peppercorns together 20 min., covered, then strain, reserving stock. Blend flour with melted butter and add strained stock gradually, stirring. Add milk, salt and pepper and cook until thickened, stirring.

Dinner: *Pork* Timbales with Bechamel Sauce, *Potato Puffs,*
Succotash, Tossed Green Salad—*Blueberry* Crumb Pudding, p. 377.

Pork left from the roast? . . . here it is, in a new guise:

Pork en Casserole   *Yield:* 4–6 servings
2 c. diced, cooked pork   1 large apple, pared, cored and
6 tbsp. fat   diced
1½ tsp. salt   1 slice of onion
¼ tsp. poultry seasoning   5 tbsp. flour
6 small silverskin onions   2 c. liquid (use stock, or 2 chicken
1½ c. cooked macaroni   bouillon cubes and 2 c. boiling
1 large carrot, shredded   water)
1 green pepper, shredded   ⅛ tsp. pepper
                                    1 tsp. dry mustard

Brown pork in 3 tbsp. hot fat, sprinkling with 1 tsp. salt and poultry seasoning, then place in a greased 1½ qt. casserole. Cook silverskin onions until barely tender and add to pork. Add macaroni, carrot, green pepper and apple and mix well. Sauté onion slice in 3 tbsp. hot fat and blend in flour. Add liquid slowly to this and bring to boil, stirring constantly, and season with remaining salt, pepper and mustard.

Pour sauce over meat and vegetable mixture in casserole, and bake in moderate oven, 350°F., about 1 hr.

Luncheon or Supper: *Pork* en Casserole, Tossed Green Salad with French Dressing——Jellied *Raspberries,* p. 406.

A little left-over pork, for a delectable salad:

Pork, Apple and Celery Salad   *Yield:* 4 servings
1 c. cubed, cooked pork   ½ c. mayonnaise
½ c. diced celery   ½ tsp. salt
½ c. frozen peas, cooked   crisp lettuce cups
3 tbsp. chopped sweet pickle   2 hard-cooked eggs, quartered
½ c. diced, tart apples (unpared, if paprika
   red skinned)

Combine all ingredients except lettuce, eggs and paprika and toss lightly together. Arrange salad mixture on lettuce cups, garnish with quartered eggs and sprinkle with paprika.

Luncheon or Supper: *Clam Chowder——Pork,* Apple and Celery Salad, *Cornmeal Muffins——Blueberry* Cottage Pudding, p. 379.

Pork Fritters

Prepare as for Beef Fritters, p. 230, but using cooked pork in place of cooked beef.

Deviled Pork Chops and Vegetables. *See p. 443.*
Meat Loaf. *See p. 228.*

VEAL

The distinction that sour cream can lend to veal!

Veal Chops in Sour Cream   *Yield:* 6 servings

6 frozen veal chops, thawed   speck pepper
flour   paprika
2 tbsp. fat   1 c. sour cream
½ tsp. salt

Dredge veal chops in flour and brown them on both sides in hot fat in skillet. Season with salt, pepper and paprika and add sour cream.

Cover skillet tightly and simmer slowly about 45 min., or until tender. (If necessary, thicken gravy slightly, or thin it with water or stock, before serving.)

   Dinner: Tomato Juice—*Veal Chops* in Sour Cream, *Puff Potatoes,* Buttered *Asparagus Spears,* Raw Carrot Strips—*Apple Pie.*

A favorite with men everywhere:

Breaded Veal Cutlets in Tomato   *Yield:* 6–8 servings
  Gravy

2 lbs. frozen veal cutlets, thawed   ¼ c. fat
1 egg, slightly beaten   1 No. 2 can (2½ c.) tomatoes
1 tbsp. water   1 small onion, chopped
bread crumbs, seasoned with salt   ¼ c. chopped green pepper, if
  and pepper   desired

Cut cutlets into serving size pieces. Add water to egg, and beat slightly, then dip cutlets in egg, and roll them in bread crumbs. Brown cutlets on both sides in hot fat in heavy skillet. Add remaining ingredients, cover tightly and simmer about 1 hr., or until veal is tender. Serve cutlets with gravy poured over them.

Dinner: *Orange Juice*—Breaded *Veal Cutlets* in Tomato Gravy, *Peas* with Tiny Onions, p. 359, Avocado and Watercress Salad— Frozen *Boysenberry* Cream, p. 376.

Rosemary is for remembrance, and you'll remember this:

Veal Cutlet Rosemary   *Yield:* 6 servings

2 lbs. frozen veal cutlet, thawed   1 tsp. salt
flour   1 tsp. paprika
3 medium onions, sliced   ¼ tsp. powdered rosemary
2 tbsp. fat   1 c. sour cream

Cut veal cutlets into serving size pieces and dredge them in flour. Sauté onion in hot fat in skillet, add floured veal and brown thoroughly on all sides. Sprinkle with seasonings, add sour cream, cover and simmer about 1 hr., or until veal is tender.

Dinner: *Veal Cutlet* Rosemary, *Green Beans* with Mushrooms, p. 332, Baked Potato, Endive Salad—*Peach* Refrigerator Pie, p. 399.

Veal flavor with tart apples and curry:

Curried Veal Casserole   *Yield:* 4–6 servings

1 lb. frozen lean veal, thawed   ½ tsp. curry powder
2 tbsp. fat   ⅛ tsp. ginger
⅜ c. raw rice   2 tsp. salt
2 tart apples, pared and cubed   speck pepper
½ c. seedless raisins   2 c. water
1 medium onion, chopped   2 tbsp. butter or margarine

Cut veal into 1-inch cubes and sauté in hot fat until brown, then place in greased 1½-qt. casserole. Add remaining ingredients except butter and combine thoroughly. Dot with butter, cover and cook in moderate oven, 350°F., about 1¼ hrs., or until done.

Luncheon or Supper: Curried *Veal* Casserole, *Green Bean* and Celery Salad, p. 334—*Sliced Peaches, Brownies.*

A superb sauce, with many flavors blended:

Veal Supreme
Yield: 4 servings

1 lb. frozen lean veal, thawed
flour
2 tbsp. fat
1 tsp. salt
⅛ tsp. pepper
½ tsp. paprika

½ medium onion, chopped
½ garlic clove, chopped
½ lb. mushrooms (2 c. sliced) or 1
    can (8 oz.)
¼ c. sherry wine
1 c. top milk or cream

Cut veal into 1-inch cubes, dredge in flour and brown in hot fat in skillet. Add salt, pepper and paprika and mix well, then add remaining ingredients. Cook on high heat until steaming, then turn heat down, cover and cook about 40 min.

> **Luncheon or Supper:** *Veal* Supreme, Savory *Peas* and Tomatoes, p. 358, *Asparagus* Aspic Salad, p. 328—*Ice Cream, Cookies.*

As thrifty as its name implies . . . one cup of veal makes three or four servings:

Scotch Pancakes with Tomato Sauce
Yield: 3–4 servings

1 c. ground, cooked veal
1 c. cooked oatmeal
1 egg
½ tsp. salt

⅛ tsp. pepper
¼ tsp. Worcestershire sauce
tomato sauce, p. 201

Place all ingredients in mixing bowl and combine well. Drop by spoonfuls in hot, greased skillet, or on griddle. Bake until top is full of air bubbles and under side is golden-brown, then turn and bake until brown on other side. Serve with tomato sauce.

> **Luncheon or Supper:** Scotch Pancakes with Tomato Sauce (*Veal*), Tossed Vegetable Salad—*Raspberries* in Cream.

Veal Fritters
Yield: 6 servings

Prepare as for Beef Fritters, p. 230, but using cooked veal in place of cooked beef.

Veal, Apple and Celery Salad   *Yield:* 4 servings

Prepare as for Pork, Apple and Celery Salad, p. 246, but using cooked veal in place of cooked pork.

Veal Chop Suey   *Yield:* 6 servings
1 lb. frozen lean veal, thawed

Cut veal into strips ¼ x 1 in., then prepare chop suey as for Pork Chop Suey, p. 243, using veal instead of pork.

Meat Loaf. *See p. 228.*

CHAPTER 14

Frozen Fish and Shellfish

FISH

Is Thawing Necessary?

As for frozen meats, frozen fish and shellfish can be successfully cooked without thawing. Often, the question is whether it is more convenient to allow time for thawing, or extra time for cooking. But very soon after fish is completely thawed it begins to "drip" or lose moisture, and then the fish is dry and disappointing when it is served. To avoid this, it is well to cook it when it is only partially thawed, and fish must be at least partially thawed before cooking, in the following instances:

(1) If fish is to be dredged with flour or crumbs, or rolled in egg or batter, since these will not stick to frozen products.

(2) If fish is to be cut into pieces, shaped or stuffed, before cooking.

(3) If pieces like steaks or fillets have not been separated with two thicknesses of wrapping paper before freezing.

(4) Fish which is to be fried in deep fat must be completely thawed before frying.

Just How to Thaw

Leave fish in the unopened package until you are ready to use it. Thawing in the refrigerator is recommended, since it is more uniform. Allow 6 to 10 hrs. per lb. of fish, depending on the thickness of the package and on how solidly the fish is packed. It will thaw in about half this time at room temperature, and still more quickly in front of an electric fan.

Methods of Fish Cookery

Methods of cooking fish are, in general, similar to those for cooking tender cuts of meat. Since fish does not contain as much connective tissue as meat, there is no need for using methods to make fish tender, as is necessary for less tender cuts of meat. Regardless of the method of cooking, fish is done when it flakes apart readily with a fork. By this time, it no longer appears translucent.

The cooking times suggested in the following are for fresh or fully thawed fish. For fish cooked from the hard-frozen state, allow

251

half again or twice as long to cook. An exception to this is cooking in liquid, and thawing in this case occurs more quickly so not as much extra time is required. But test the fish to be sure it flakes readily, to decide when it is done.

Broiling.—This method is especially suited for fatty fish (for list, see pp. 253–254), since the fat melts and some of it drips off during cooking. It is also useful for any medium-sized fish split in half, or for fillets or steaks.

Preheat the broiler or not, according to the instructions for using your range. Place fatty fish on broiling rack; others may be placed on baking pan if preferred. Sprinkle with salt and pepper and other seasonings as desired, and brush lean (non-fatty) fish with melted fat. Place fully thawed pieces of medium size 2–3 inches from the heat and pieces that are thicker or only partially thawed, 4 inches. If skin is on fish, broil with skin side up first. Broil until golden brown, then turn carefully with a broad spatula or pancake turner, and again brush lean fish with fat or oil. Cook until browned, and fish flakes. Most thawed fish will broil in 10–20 min.

Pan-Frying.—Any small fish, or fillets or steaks may be pan-fried. Season with salt and pepper, or if desired, roll in seasoned flour, or fine bread crumbs.

Cook slowly in skillet in fat ⅛–¼ in. deep, skin side up first, if skin is on fish. Any table fat may be used, but many people prefer bacon fat for fish. When brown on under side, turn carefully with a broad spatula or pancake turner and brown other side. Cook until fish flakes well, usually 10–20 min.

Deep-Fat Frying (French Frying).—This is suitable only for small, lean fish, fillets or steaks cut into serving pieces not more than 1½ inches thick. Frozen fish must be completely thawed first. Dry fish thoroughly, roll in flour, then in egg and finally in bread crumbs or cornmeal. Or if preferred, dip in batter. Fry according to directions for deep-fat frying meat, p. 208, using fat at 360°–370°F. and fry until golden brown.

Baking.—Any fish may be baked, including whole fish, fillets or steaks, and this is a good method for cooking fish "chunks" (thick steaks). Dip fish into salted milk, using 1 tbsp. salt per cup of milk, then roll in fine bread crumbs. Place in well-greased, shallow baking pan. If fish is not fatty, sprinkle with melted fat or oil, and bake in moderate oven, 350°–375°F. for 20–30 min. (longer for large pieces), until done.

Cooking in Water.—This is sometimes called the way to prepare "boiled" fish, but the water should be simmering, not boiling. It is also called "poaching." Whole fish, fillets, steaks or chunks may be cooked by this method. Tie the fish loosely in cheesecloth or wrap it in parchment or place it in an oven-proof plate. Lower it into seasoned, boiling water, continue to keep the water simmering, not boiling. The water may be seasoned with 1 tbsp. vinegar or lemon juice, 1 small sliced onion, ½ c. chopped celery and leaves and 1 tsp. salt, or as preferred. Cover, and watch pan to be sure water keeps simmering but does not boil, and allow 10–20 min. per lb. When done, remove fish with bag or parchment or plate.

Fish may also be poached in milk. Place fish in skillet, add almost enough milk to cover the fish and seasonings as desired. Cover tightly and cook very gently until done.

Steaming.—Fish which may be cooked in water may also be steamed. Have water in lower compartment of steamer boiling vigorously. Tie fish loosely in cheesecloth bag or wrap it in parchment, or place on an oven-proof plate and lower it into the upper compartment. Cover tightly and keep water boiling vigorously. Allow 10–20 min. per lb. When done, remove with bag or parchment or plate.

In Pressure Saucepans.—To cook fish in pressure saucepans, follow the manufacturer's instructions.

Frozen Fish Available, and Methods of Cooking

Following is a list of the most commonly frozen fish, the forms in which each is sold, and recommended methods of cooking them.

Frozen Fish and Methods of Cooking Them

Kind of fish	Fat or lean	Frozen form available	Suggested methods of cooking
Cod	Lean	Fillets, steaks, pan-dressed	Broil, bake, boil or steam, deep-fat fry, pan-fry or pan-broil
Flounder	Lean	Fillets, pan-dressed	Broil, bake, boil or steam, deep-fat fry, pan-fry or pan-broil
Haddock	Lean	Fillets, steaks, pan-dressed	Broil, bake, boil or steam, deep-fat fry, pan-fry or pan-broil
Halibut	Lean	Fillets and steaks	Broil, bake or pan-broil
Mackerel	Fat	Pan-dressed	Broil, bake or pan-broil

Frozen Fish and Methods of Cooking Them (*continued*)

Kind of fish	Fat or lean	Frozen form available	Suggested methods of cooking
Pollock	Lean	Fillets, pan-dressed	Boil or steam, deep-fat fry, pan-fry, pan-broil
Ocean perch	Lean	Fillets	Broil, bake, deep-fat fry, pan-fry or pan-broil
Salmon	Fat	Steaks, pan-dressed	Broil, bake, boil or steam
Scrod (cod or haddock less than 2½ lbs.)	Lean	Fillets, pan-dressed	Broil, bake or pan-broil
Smelts	Fat	Pan-dressed	Broil, bake, deep-fat fry, pan-fry or pan-broil
Sole	Lean	Fillets, pan-dressed	Broil, bake, deep-fat fry, pan-fry or pan-broil
Swordfish	Lean	Steaks	Broil, bake or pan-broil
Trout, lake	Fat	Fillets, pan-dressed	Broil, bake, boil or steam, deep-fat fry, pan-fry or pan-broil
Tuna	Fat	Pan-dressed	Bake, broil, deep-fat fry, pan-fry, pan-broil
Whitefish	Fat	Fillets, pan-dressed	Broil, bake, deep-fat fry, pan-fry or pan-broil
Whiting	Lean	Pan-dressed, fillets	Broil, bake, pan-broil

Courtesy National Fisheries Institute, Inc.

Fish Accompaniments

While the rather bland flavor of most fish is one of their attractive features, it is a good idea to serve them with a flavorsome sauce. A colorful, tasty garnish is also appropriate. Here are suggestions for fish sauces and garnishes:

Sauces

Caper Sauce, p. 203
Cheese Sauce, p. 201
Cucumber Sauce, p. 202
Curry Mayonnaise, p. 326
Drawn Butter Sauce, p. 202
Egg Sauce, p. 201
Hollandaise Sauce, p. 329
Lemon Butter, p. 203

Maitre d'Hotel Butter, p. 202
Mustard Sauce, p. 350
Parsley Butter, p. 202
Parsley Sauce, p. 203
Spanish Sauce, p. 267
Tartar Sauce, p. 202
Tomato Sauce, p. 201
Vinaigrette Dressing, p. 326

Garnishes

Lemon slices or wedges
Paprika
Parsley
Pickles
Pickled beets
Pimiento strips

Radish "roses"
Sliced cucumbers
Sliced tomatoes
Water cress
Shredded green pepper

SHELLFISH

Clams and Oysters

If clams and oysters are to be served raw, they should be barely thawed and still ice-cold when served. If possible, they should be thawed slowly (in the refrigerator) for best quality. For use in cooking, this is somewhat less important.

Thawing.—Leave in unopened can as follows:

In the refrigerator overnight, or 7–9 hrs.
At room temperature 4–6 hrs.
In front of an electric fan about 3 hrs.
In cold water, 2 hrs.

When thawed, examine the clams and oysters carefully to be sure there are no particles of shell. Use them as soon as possible after thawing so as to avoid spoilage.

Scallops

Scallops as they are purchased frozen are already removed from their shells and they may be prepared in a number of ways. Thaw, remove any shell particles, and wash. Place in boiling water to cover, adding 1 tbsp. salt per lb. of scallops. Cover kettle and bring water back to boiling, then reduce heat and simmer 3–4 min., depending on size. Drain. One pound of scallops yields about 6 servings.

Or thaw and wash as above, then drain thoroughly and broil. Or coat drained scallops with egg and bread crumb mixture and pan-fry, or coat with similar mixture, or with batter, and fry in deep fat.

Shrimp, Lobster and Crabmeat

If cooked shrimp, lobster or crabmeat are to be used in cocktails, hors d'oeuvres or salads, it is important to keep them as tender as possible. Slow thawing in the refrigerator gives the best results. The time for thawing varies with the shape as well as the weight of package, but in general they do not require as long as the times given above, for thawing clams and oysters.

If shrimp are raw, immerse the solidly frozen block in rapidly boiling water to cover, to which 1 tbsp. salt has been added per pint of water. Bring the water rapidly back to a boil, then turn heat down so water simmers, and simmer 5 min. Plunge the shrimp into a pan of cold water to cool them rapidly, then slip shrimp out of their shells, remove veins and wash. One pound of raw shrimp in their shells gives ½ lb. shelled, cooked shrimp and yields 3–4 servings.

RECIPES AND MENUS

FISH

Here's a quickie that is as good to eat as it is easy to fix:

Jiffy Fish Fry   *Yield:* 3–4 servings
1 lb. frozen fish fillets or steaks,   drawn butter sauce, p. 202
   partially thawed   parsley
flour seasoned with ½ tsp. salt and   olive slices, if desired
   pepper
¼ c. fat

Separate the pieces of fish and dredge in seasoned flour. Pan-fry fish in hot fat (see directions, p. 252) over moderate heat. Place fish on hot platter. Pour hot sauce over it and garnish with parsley and olives.

> **Luncheon or Supper:** *Cream of Potato Soup*——Jiffy *Fish* Fry, Tomato, Green Pepper and Cabbage Salad——*Raspberries* with Cream, *Cookies*.

Mild-flavored, sea-fresh haddock, in pungent cheese sauce:

Baked Haddock in Cheese Sauce   *Yield:* 5–6 servings
1½ lbs. frozen haddock, fillets or   ½ tsp. salt
   steaks, partially thawed   cheese sauce, p. 201

Separate fillets or steaks and arrange in shallow baking dish. Sprinkle with salt and pour cheese sauce over fish. Bake in moderate oven, 350°F., 25–30 min., or until fish is done.

> **Dinner:** Cream of *Crabmeat* Soup, p. 271——Baked *Haddock* in Cheese Sauce, *Rissole Potatoes*, Panned *Spinach*, p. 369——*Apple Pie*.

Try this and you will find your family will ask for it again:

Baked Fish with Cheese Dressing   *Yield:* 4–6 servings

1 lb. frozen fish fillets or steaks,   ½ c. grated American cheese
  partially thawed   ¾ tsp. salt
½ c. sliced onion   speck pepper
¼ c. butter or margarine   ¾ c. top milk or light cream
1½ c. soft bread crumbs

Separate fillets or steaks and arrange them in greased baking dish. Sauté onion in hot butter until golden brown. Toss bread crumbs, cheese, salt and pepper together lightly until mixed, then combine with onions and spread on top of fish. Pour milk around fish and bake in moderate oven, 350°F., about 30 min. or until fish is done.

> **Dinner:** Baked *Fish* with Cheese Dressing, *French-Fried Onion Rings,* Buttered *Broccoli,* Pickled Beet Salad——*Strawberry-Rhubarb Pie.*

Quick and easy . . . but just taste it:

Baked Fish Fillets, Spencer   *Yield:* 3 servings

1 lb. frozen fish fillets, partially   2 tbsp. melted butter or bacon fat
  thawed   parsley
$^1/_3$ c. milk   any fish sauce
½ tsp. salt
sifted bread crumbs

Cut fillets into serving portions and dip into milk to which salt has been added. Roll in bread crumbs and place in well greased shallow baking dish. Pour butter or bacon fat over top and bake near top of very hot oven, 500°F., for 10–12 min. or until fish is done. Garnish with parsley and serve with fish sauce.

> **Luncheon or Supper:** Baked *Fish Fillets,* Spencer, with Caper Sauce, p. 203, Baked Potatoes, *Asparagus Spears——Strawberry* Whip, p. 419.

Tiny, flavorsome fish, fried and served with a piquant sauce:

Fried Smelts   *Yield:* 4 servings

1 lb. frozen smelts, partially thawed   3 tbsp. fat
flour seasoned with salt and pepper   tartar sauce, p. 202

Separate smelts and roll them in seasoned flour.   Fry in hot fat in heavy skillet until golden brown.   Serve immediately with tartar sauce.

> **Dinner:** *Pineapple-Orange Juice*——Fried *Smelts* with Tartar Sauce, Mashed Potatoes, Buttered *Peas,* Endive Salad——Coconut *Peach* Pie, p. 400.

Reminiscent of Creole cookery, is this flavorful recipe:

Fish Baked in Tomato Sauce   *Yield:* 4–6 servings

1 lb. frozen fish fillets or steaks, partially thawed	1 tbsp. flour
2 tbsp. chopped green pepper	1 c. canned tomatoes
2 tbsp. chopped celery	1 tbsp. chopped parsley, or 1 tsp. dried parsley
2 tbsp. chopped onion	½ tsp. salt
¼ c. fat	pepper

Separate fillets or steaks and arrange them in shallow greased baking dish.   Sauté green peppers, celery and onions in hot fat, add flour and blend well.   Add remaining ingredients slowly, bring sauce to a boil, stirring, then pour it over fish.   Bake in moderate oven, 350°F. about 30 min. or until fish is done.

> **Dinner:** *Vegetable Soup*——*Fish* Baked in Tomato Sauce, Mashed Potatoes, Parsley *Cauliflower*——*Raspberry* Tapioca Pudding, p. 405.

The recipe says wine "if desired" . . . and it is a fine addition:

"Boiled" Fish with Egg Sauce   *Yield:* 4 servings

1 pkg. (about 1 lb.) frozen fish, partially thawed	½ bay leaf
2 c. water	1 whole clove
2 tbsp. chopped celery	1 tsp. salt
2 tbsp. chopped onion	speck pepper
2 tbsp. chopped carrot	½ c. sauterne wine (if desired)
few sprigs parsley (or 1 tsp. dried parsley)	egg sauce, p. 201
	parsley garnish

Place all ingredients except fish, egg sauce and parsley garnish in saucepan, and simmer over low heat about 15 min.   If fish is in steaks or fillets, separate the pieces and tie loosely in cheesecloth bag or wrap it in parchment or place it on oven-proof plate.   Lower this arrangement with the fish into the hot liquid, cover tightly and simmer about 15 min. or until fish is done.   Remove fish and serve hot with hot egg sauce, and garnish with parsley.

> **Dinner:** *Grapefruit Juice*—"Boiled" *Halibut* with Egg Sauce, Buttered *Lima Beans,* Harvard Beets, Red Cabbage and Green Pepper Salad—*Mixed Fruit* Cup.

Fish baked with dressing over it is delicious:

Fish Baked with Dressing   *Yield:* 4–5 servings

1 pkg. (1 lb.) frozen fish fillets or steaks, partially thawed
2 tbsp. chopped onion
3 tbsp. butter or margarine
1 tsp. chopped parsley
1 tsp. salt
speck pepper
1 tbsp. water
1½ c. soft bread crumbs

Arrange fish pieces in greased, shallow baking dish.   Sauté onion in hot butter until light brown, then add remaining ingredients and combine well.   Arrange the crumb mixture over the fish and bake in moderate oven, 350°F., about 30 min., or until done.

> **Dinner:** Baked *Fish* with Dressing, Scalloped Potatoes, Buttered *Green Beans,* Sliced Tomatoes on Watercress—*Orange* Cake Pudding, p. 395.

Onion rings add savor to an old favorite:

Cod Baked in Milk   *Yield:* 3 servings

1 pkg. (1 lb.) frozen cod fillets, partially thawed
1 egg, beaten
fine cracker crumbs (or crumbled cornflakes)
2 large onion slices, separated into rings
½ c. milk
2 tsp. butter or margarine
paprika
parsley garnish

Dip fish in beaten egg, then roll it in crumbs or cornflakes and place in greased, shallow baking dish.   Arrange onion slices over fish, pour milk over it and dot with butter.   Sprinkle lightly with paprika and bake in moderate oven, 350°F., about 30 min. or until fish is done. Serve, garnished with parsley.

Dinner: *Cod* Baked in Milk, Potato Puffs, Deviled *Brussels Sprouts*, p. 344, *Sesame Seed Rolls*—Jellied *Raspberries*, p. 406.

Fish baked in sauce delicately flavored with curry:

Curry of Fish   *Yield:*   4–5 servings

1 pkg. (1 lb.) frozen fish fillets or   1 tsp. salt
  steaks, partially thawed   speck pepper
½ c. sliced celery   1 tsp. curry powder
½ c. sliced onion   ¾ c. top milk or light cream
3 tbsp. butter or margarine

Arrange fish in greased, shallow baking dish. Sauté celery and onion in hot butter until light brown, add salt, pepper and curry powder and mix well. Add milk slowly, stirring. Heat this sauce thoroughly, stirring, then pour it over the fish. Bake about 30 min. in moderate oven, 350°F., or until fish is done.

Dinner: Curry of *Fish, Baked Stuffed Potatoes, Corn on the Cob, Mixed Vegetables* in Tomato Aspic—*Ice Cream* with *Sliced Strawberries.*

This would be a talk-provoking dish for your next luncheon meeting:

Fish au Gratin   *Yield:*   6 servings

1 pkg. (1 lb.) seafood   ¾ c. water
2 slices onion, chopped fine   ¼ lb. American Cheddar cheese,
2 tbsp. chopped green pepper   grated (1 c.)
¼ c. butter or margarine   fine bread crumbs
¼ c. flour   butter
1 tsp. salt   paprika
1¼ c. evaporated milk

Use any seafood such as haddock, flounder, sole, cod or shellfish, and cook the fish by your preferred method, then flake it, coarsely. There should be about 1½ c. flaked fish.

Cook onion and green pepper in butter in top of double boiler, about 5 min., add flour and salt and mix well, then stir in evaporated milk and water. Cook until mixture thickens, about 10 min., stirring, then add flaked fish. Place in greased baking dish or ramekins. Combine grated cheese and bread crumbs (using enough crumbs to cover fish) and sprinkle this mixture over the fish. Dot top with butter and sprinkle with paprika. Bake in moderate oven, 375°F. about 15 min. or until crumbs are light brown.

Luncheon or Supper: *Snapper Soup—Fish* au Gratin, *French-Fried Potatoes,* Cold *Asparagus Spears* on Salad Greens with French Dressing—*Strawberry* Chiffon Pie, p. 417.

An attractive and tasty salad for summer fare:

Fish Salad Plate   *Yield:* 6–8 servings

1 lb. frozen fish, partially thawed   8 eggs, hard-cooked and quartered
1 tbsp. vinegar or lemon juice   head lettuce
1 small onion, sliced   dill or sweet pickle
½ c. chopped celery and leaves   Bermuda onion rings
1 tsp. salt   diced celery
1 pkg. (10 oz.) frozen peas and   mayonnaise
   carrots   parsley
French dressing, if desired   paprika

Into a saucepan, put enough water to cover the fish, add vinegar, sliced onion, chopped celery and salt, and bring to a boil. If fish is in fillets or steaks, separate the pieces before placing in loose cheesecloth bag or parchment or on an oven-proof plate, and lower this arrangement into the boiling liquid. Cover, and simmer until fish is done (about 15 min.). Remove fish from hot liquid, remove any skin and bone and chill well. Flake into rather large pieces.

Meanwhile, cook peas and carrots, drain and chill them. Marinate fish and vegetables together with French dressing, if desired. Prepare lettuce cups for individual salads and in each cup arrange fish, carrots and peas, pickles, onion rings (use chopped onion, if preferred) and diced celery.

Top salads with mayonnaise, garnish with egg quarters and parsley and sprinkle with paprika.

Luncheon or Supper: *Fish* Salad Plate, *French-Fried Potatoes, Asparagus Spears* Marinated in French Dressing—*Blueberry Pie.*

A delicious way of serving fish, for luncheon or dinner:

Creole Fish Supper   Yield: 4–6 servings

1½ lbs. frozen fish, partially thawed   ⅛ tsp. pepper
¼ c. chopped onion   1 bay leaf
¼ c. chopped green pepper   1 pkg. (10 oz.) frozen cut corn
2 tbsp. fat   2 tbsp. flour
1 c. cooked or canned tomatoes   3 tbsp. water
1 tsp. salt

Separate pieces of fish and arrange in greased, shallow baking dish. Sauté onion and green pepper in hot fat, add remaining ingredients except flour and water, and bring to a boil. Combine flour with water to make a smooth paste and add gradually to hot mixture, stirring. Cover fish with vegetable mixture and bake in moderate oven, 350°F., for about 30 min. or until fish is done.

> **Dinner:**   Creole *Fish* Supper, Parsley Buttered *New Potatoes*, p. 361, Tossed Salad with Russian Dressing—*Lemon* Chiffon Pie, p. 388.

So elegant, yet so easy to make, and not expensive, either:

Baked Flounder Thermidor   Yield: 4–5 servings

1 lb. frozen fillet of flounder,   2 tbsp. flour
    partially thawed   ¼ c. sherry wine
1 c. milk   ¼ c. grated American or processed
½ tsp. salt   cheese
speck pepper
2 tbsp. melted butter or margarine

Arrange fish in greased, shallow baking dish, cover with milk and sprinkle with salt and pepper. Bake in moderate oven, 350°F., about 30 min. or until fish is done.

Combine butter and flour. Pour hot milk off fish (keeping fish in warm place) and add flour and butter mixture to milk, cooking until thickened, with stirring. Add sherry wine and cheese to sauce, pour sauce over fish and just before serving, brown lightly under broiler.

> **Dinner:**   *Grape Juice*—Baked *Flounder* Thermidor, Buttered *Asparagus*, Duchess Potatoes—*Red Cherry* Roll-Ups, p. 385.

Courtesy of National Fisheries Institute

Tasty fish fillets, garnished with lemon wedges and served with buttered broccoli. . .a treat at any time

Broiled, and with mustard . . . especially good for fish:

Broiled Fish Fillets with Mustard Sauce

1 lb. frozen fish fillets, thawed
seasoned flour
melted butter or margarine
tomato halves

Yield: 3–4 servings
buttered crumbs
mustard sauce, p. 350, but omitting
lemon juice

Sprinkle one side of fish fillet lightly with flour which has been seasoned with salt and pepper. Place the fillet on greased baking pan or broiler rack, floured side up, and brush generously with melted butter. Broil (avoiding too high heat) until fish is lightly browned and flakes readily. About 5 min. before fish is done, place a ¼-inch layer of buttered crumbs on top of tomato halves and place on broiler rack. Allow crumbs to brown lightly, then remove fish and tomatoes to serving platter. Pour hot mustard sauce over fish.

Dinner: *Fish* Chowder, p. 264—Broiled *Fish Fillets* with Mustard Sauce and Broiled Tomatoes, *Cauliflower* with Almond Butter, p. 351—*Strawberry* Mousse, p. 412.

Beloved by Cape Cod fishermen, this is gaining national recognition:

Fish Chowder   *Yield:* 6–8 servings
1 lb. frozen fish, preferably   ½ c. water
   haddock or cod, partially thawed   3 c. milk
¼ c. diced salt pork   1 tbsp. butter or margarine
3 tbsp. chopped onion   1 tsp. salt
2 c. thinly sliced potatoes   paprika

Place fish in boiling water to cover, then turn heat down and simmer 10 min. Drain fish (reserving liquid), remove any skin and bone. Fry salt pork in heavy kettle until golden brown, add onion and cook in pork until golden brown. Combine fish, fish stock, pork and onion, add potatoes and water. Simmer about 15 min., covered. Add milk and bring just to boiling point. Add butter, salt and paprika just before serving.

Dinner: *Fish* Chowder—Broiled *Lobster Tails*, p. 275, with Lemon Butter, Baked Potato, Piquant *Peas*, p. 359—*Strawberry* Whip, p. 419.

"Down East," codfish cakes are a favorite Sunday morning special:

Codfish Cakes   *Yield:* 4–6 servings
1 lb. frozen cod   ½ tsp. onion juice
1½ c. mashed potatoes   1 egg
1 tbsp. butter or margarine   fat
¼ tsp. salt   tomato sauce p. 201
⅛ tsp. pepper

Cook the cod by your preferred method, and pull it apart into fine flakes with a fork. Add remaining ingredients except fat and tomato sauce, and beat mixture until smooth and fluffy. Shape lightly into balls or rolls. Sauté in hot fat in skillet about 5 min., or until golden brown. Or fry in deep fat at 375°F. about 3 min., or until golden brown. Serve hot with tomato sauce.

Luncheon or Supper: *Codfish* Cakes with Tomato Sauce, *Baby Lima Beans*, Sliced Cucumbers and Radishes—*Raspberry* Cream Pudding, p 405.

A really unusual fish recipe, and delicious:

Fish Fillets Baltimore

Yield: 6 servings

1½ lbs. (6 fillets) frozen fish fillets, thawed	½ tsp., salt
1 pkg. (6 oz.) frozen cooked crabmeat, thawed	1 tbsp. chopped parsley 1 tbsp. cut chives 3 tbsp. butter or margarine
2 c. soft bread crumbs	¾ c. milk
1 egg, beaten	

Arrange three fish fillets in greased, shallow baking dish.   Combine bread crumbs, egg, salt, parsley and chives, add crabmeat and mix well.   Cover three fish fillets with crabmeat mixture, then cover each fillet with a second fillet, fitting pieces well togther.   Dot with butter, and pour milk into baking dish.   Bake in moderate oven, 350°F., about 30 min. or until fish is done.   Transfer to serving dish, using broad spatula or pancake turner.

> **Dinner:**   *Fish Fillets* Baltimore, Baked Potato, *Broccoli* and Cheese Sauce, p. 201, Head Lettuce, French Dressing—*Mixed Fruit* Cup, *Cookies.*

Grapefruit juice adds a fine flavor to baked fish steaks:

Fish Baked in Grapefruit Juice

Yield: 6 servings

2 lbs. frozen fish steaks, about 1 in. thick, thawed	1 c. reconstituted, frozen grapefruit juice
1 medium onion, sliced	1½ tsp salt
1 small carrot, sliced	¼ tsp. pepper
1 sprig parsley	¼ tsp. ground thyme
1 small bay leaf	½ c. (2 oz.) grated American cheese
1 whole clove	½ c. fine bread crumbs
½ c. vinegar	

Arrange fish in shallow pan of a size so that the fish covers most of the bottom of the pan.   Cover steaks with vegetables, parsley, bay leaf, clove and vinegar and pour grapefruit juice over them.   Add water if grapefruit juice does not quite cover the steaks, and place in refrigerator a couple of hours.   Place pan over low heat, and slowly bring liquid to simmering point, then drain, reserving liquid.

Using a pancake turner, transfer the fish steaks to a shallow, greased baking dish and pour some of the liquid over the steaks. Sprinkle with salt, pepper and thyme.   Finally, combine bread crumbs and cheese and sprinkle on top.   Bake in hot oven, 425°F. about 15 min. or until crumbs are brown.

Dinner: *Fish* Baked in *Grapefruit Juice,* Mashed Potatoes, *Green Peas*—*Red Cherry* Pie, p. 383.

Something very different, for perch:

Baked Stuffed Perch Rolls

Yield: 3–4 servings

1 lb. frozen ocean perch fillets, thawed
paprika
¼ c. melted butter or margarine
1½ c. bread crumbs
¼ c. chopped celery
1 tsp. grated onion

1 tbsp. chopped parsley, or 1 tsp. dried parsley
¼ tsp. salt
melted butter or margarine
bacon strips, if desired
lemon wedges

Cut fillets, if necessary, so they fit into muffin pans or custard cups, and sprinkle lightly with paprika.   For the stuffing, combine ¼ c. butter, bread crumbs, celery, onion, parsley and salt, adding a little water if too dry to hold together.   Place a portion of stuffing on each fillet and roll each one, securing with toothpicks.   Place the rolled fillets in greased muffin pans or custard cups, brushing tops with melted butter, and if desired place a slice of bacon on top of each.

Bake in a moderate oven, 375°F., 25–30 min. or until fish flakes readily.   Remove fillets from pans or cups, remove toothpicks and serve with lemon wedges.

Luncheon or Supper: Baked Stuffed *Perch* Rolls, *Brussels Sprouts* in Pimiento Sauce, p. 346, *Cornmeal Muffins,* Assorted Relishes— *Lemon* Chiffon Pie, p. 388.

Ocean perch fillets with smooth tomato sauce:

Ocean Perch with Spanish Sauce *Yield:* 6–8 servings

2 lb. frozen ocean perch fillets,
  thawed
¼ c. chopped onion
3 tbsp. butter or margarine
2 tbsp. flour
2 c. canned tomatoes
¼ c. chopped green pepper

1 tsp. salt
½ tsp. sugar
speck pepper
1 bay leaf
1 whole clove
parsley

Arrange perch fillets in greased, shallow baking pan. Cook onion in hot butter until tender, then blend in flour. Add remaining ingredients except fillets and parsley, and cook until thick, stirring constantly. Remove bay leaf and clove, then cover fillets with sauce. Bake in moderate oven, 350°F., for 25–30 min. or until fish flakes readily with a fork. Serve hot, garnished with parsley.

Dinner: *Green Pea with Ham Soup—Ocean Perch* with Spanish Sauce, *Wax Beans, Corn* and Green Pepper, p. 339, *Rolls—Lemon Sherbet, Brownies.*

Surprise the family with an attractive molded fish salad:

Molded Fish Salad *Yield:* 6 servings

1 lb. frozen fish fillets
1 tbsp. (1 envelope) unflavored
  gelatin
¼ c. cold water
½ c. boiling water
½ c. mayonnaise or salad dressing
¼ c. ketchup
2 tbsp. lemon juice

½ c. chopped celery
2 tbsp. chopped sweet pickle
2 tbsp. chopped stuffed olives
¼ tsp. salt
salad greens

Cook fillets in hot water until fish flakes readily (see directions, p. 253). Pull fish apart into flakes with a fork, removing any skin or bone. Soften gelatin in cold water for 5 min., add boiling water and stir until gelatin is dissolved, turn into mold, then cool until gelatin begins to set. Blend mayonnaise, ketchup and lemon juice. Combine all ingredients except salad greens, fold into gelatin and chill until firm. Unmold on salad greens.

Luncheon or Supper: *Vegetable Soup—*Molded *Fish* Salad, Tomato and Cucumber Salad, Hot *Baking Powder Biscuits—Lemon* Meringue Pie, p. 388.

A Shepherd's Pie made with fish instead of meat:

Shepherd's Fish Pie   *Yield:* 6–8 servings

2 c. cooked fish   ½ tsp. salt
2 tbsp. chopped onion   ¼ tsp, paprika
2 tbsp. chopped parsley or green   ½ c. cooked green peas or green
  pepper   beans
3 tbsp. fat   ½ c. cooked, diced carrots
¼ c. flour   1–2 c. mashed potatoes
2 c. milk   milk or melted butter

Pull the fish apart into coarse flakes, removing all bones. Sauté onion and parsley (or green pepper) in hot fat, stir flour in carefully, add milk slowly and cook until thickened, stirring constantly. Add salt, paprika, peas (or beans), carrots and fish, and put mixture into greased casserole. Cover mixture with mashed potatoes and brush the top with milk or melted butter. Bake in moderately hot oven, 375°F., about 15 min. or until lightly browned.

> **Dinner:** Shepherd's *Fish* Pie, *Broccoli Spears* with Drawn Butter, Tossed Vegetables with Thousand Island Dressing—Frozen *Lemon* Dessert, p. 389.

"Soup of the evening, beautiful soup," so said the Mock Turtle:

Cream of Fish Soup   *Yield:* 6–8 servings

2 c. cooked fish   1 tsp. salt
¼ c. butter or margarine   ⅛ tsp. pepper
¼ c. sliced onion   1 tsp. caraway seed
1 c. chopped celery   1 or 2 tbsp. lemon juice or vinegar,
¼ c. flour   if desired
1 qt. scalded milk   paprika, minced chives, or parsley

Pull the fish apart into coarse flakes, removing any skin and bones. Melt butter in top of double boiler, add onion and celery and cook over direct heat until tender but not brown, then add flour and blend well. Add milk slowly, then cook over hot water until mixture thickens, stirring constantly. Add fish, salt, pepper and caraway seed and cook about 5 min. to heat thoroughly. If desired, add lemon juice just before serving. Serve in heated bowl with paprika, chives or parsley sprinkled over top.

> **Luncheon or Supper:** Cream of *Fish* Soup, Oyster Crackers, Brown Bread and Butter Sandwiches— Baked *Cherry* Pudding, p. 384.

OTHER FISH RECIPES

Jiffy Fish Fillets, *See p. 444.*
Fish Poached in Milk. *See p. 444.*

SHELLFISH

Clams

The salty flavor of clams, in a sauce of distinctive flavor:

Clams on Toast

1 pkg. (12 oz.) frozen clams,
  partially thawed
1 small green pepper, chopped
1 small onion, chopped
2 tbsp. fat
1 tbsp. flour

Yield: 4–6 servings

¼ tsp. salt
speck pepper
1 can (6 oz.) tomato paste or purée
parsley

Cut clams into small pieces, reserving liquor. Sauté onion and green pepper in hot fat, add flour, salt and pepper and blend well. Then add tomato paste or purée, clams and clam liquor and simmer about 10 min., stirring occasionally. Serve on toast, and garnish with parsley.

> **Luncheon or Supper:** *Clams* on Toast, Tossed Vegetable Salad with Vinaigrette Dressing—*Blueberry* Cream, with Custard Sauce, p. 380.

———————————

With the tang of the sea . . . and such a favorite:

New England Clam Chowder

1 pkg. (12 oz.) frozen clams,
  thawed
¼ c. finely diced salt pork
1 medium onion, thinly sliced
1 c. boiling water
½ tsp. salt

Yield: 4–6 servings

speck pepper
1 c. raw potatoes cut in small cubes
1 tbsp. butter or margarine
1 tbsp. flour
1½ c. milk

Drain clams (reserving liquor), cut hard parts away and keep them separate. Cook salt pork in heavy kettle until golden brown, add onion and sauté until light brown. Add hard parts of clams, and boiling water, salt, pepper and potatoes. Cover and simmer gently until potatoes are tender. Combine butter and flour and add slowly to chowder, stirring. Add soft parts of clams and clam liquor. Add milk just before serving and heat thoroughly, but do not boil. **Serve** with oyster crackers.

> **Dinner:** New England *Clam* Chowder—Broiled *Sirloin Steak,* *Brussels Sprouts* with Celery, p. 344, Tomato and Cucumber Salad —*Chocolate Cake.*

A sophisticated beginning for a dinner party:

Clam Cocktail   *Yield:* 6 servings

1 pkg. (12 oz.) frozen clams, thawed

¼ c. ketchup

1 tbsp. lemon juice

½ tsp. salt

6 drops Tabasco sauce

2 tsp. horseradish

½ tsp. Worcestershire sauce

¼ c. finely chopped celery

small, crisp lettuce leaves

lemon wedges

Drain clams. Combine remaining ingredients thoroughly (except lettuce and lemon wedges). Arrange lettuce leaves in cocktail dishes, add clams and top with sauce. Serve with lemon wedges.

> **Dinner:** *Clam* Cocktail—*Chicken* Marengo, p. 304, *French-Fried* *Potatoes,* Golden Cheese Topped *Wax Beans,* p. 339—*Raspberry* Pinwheels, p. 419.

A Jack Horner Pie, with its element of surprise:

Clam Pie   *Yield:* 4 servings

1 pkg. (12 oz.) frozen clams, thawed

2 tbsp. butter or margarine

½ tsp. salt

speck pepper

¼ tsp. thyme, if desired

¼ c. cracker crumbs

1 c. hot cream or top milk

pastry dough prepared from 1 c. flour (see p. 196)

Drain clams, reserving liquor. Cut hard parts away from clams and chop these, keeping them separate. Simmer hard parts about 5 min. in clam liquor, then remove from heat. Add soft parts of clams and remaining ingredients except pastry dough.

Place mixture in four individual baking dishes or in one small casserole. Cover with a layer of pastry dough. Prick the crust several times to allow steam to escape, and bake in hot oven, 425°F. for about 20 min., or until crust is browned.

Luncheon or Supper: *Pineapple Juice—Clam* Pie, *Green Bean* and *Corn* Salad, p. 334, Date and Nut Bread—*Peach* Mousse, p. 401.

Fried to a turn, shellfish are always popular:

Fried Clams *Yield:* 3–4 servings

1 pkg. (12 oz.) frozen clams, thawed
2 eggs
½ c. milk
1 c. flour

1 tsp. baking powder
1 tsp. salt
1 tsp. salad oil
fat for frying

Drain clams thoroughly and dry well on absorbent paper. To prepare batter, beat egg and stir in milk. Sift dry ingredients together and beat them into the egg mixture, then beat in salad oil.

Dip the clams, a few at a time, in the batter, and fry in deep fat at 375°F. for 3–4 min., or until golden brown.

Luncheon or Supper: *Pineapple-Orange Juice*—Fried *Clams* with Tartar Sauce, *Lima Bean* Casserole, p. 337, Cole Slaw—*Red Cherry* Upside Down Cake, p. 415.

Crabmeat

Epicurean in its delicate nuances of flavor:

Cream of Crabmeat Soup *Yield:* 6 servings

2 c. frozen, cooked crabmeat, thawed
2 tbsp. chopped onion
2 tbsp. butter or margarine
3 c. hot milk

1½ c. cream
½ tsp. salt
speck pepper
2 tbsp. sherry wine, if desired

Flake crabmeat into small pieces. Sauté onion in butter until tender, add crabmeat and simmer together about 1 min. Add hot milk to crabmeat in top of double boiler and cook over boiling water about 15 min. Stir in cream, salt and pepper and cook about 15 min. longer. If desired, add sherry wine just before serving.

Dinner: Cream of *Crabmeat* Soup—Broiled *Lamb Chops, Squash* New Orleans, p. 370, *Grapefruit-Pineapple* Salad, p. 387—*Red Cherry* Dumplings, p. 384, with Hot *Lemon* Sauce, p. 391.

Tasty, attractive bits for your cocktail party:

Crabmeat Celery Curls   *Yield:* 1–1½ doz. curls

½ c. frozen cooked crabmeat,   pinch salt
   thawed   celery curls
¹/₃ c. mayonnaise   paprika
2 tsp. lemon juice

For celery curls, cut 2-inch lengths of celery stalks, fringe both ends of each stalk with a sharp knife and let stand in ice water until the fringes curl.

Pull crabmeat apart in small flakes and combine with mayonnaise, lemon juice and salt. Fill the center of the celery curls with the crabmeat mixture, and sprinkle with paprika. Keep cold until serving time.

   Cocktail Party: *Crabmeat* Celery Curls, Cheese Sticks, Spiced *Pineapple* Appetizers, p. 402, Assorted Hors d'Oeuvres, Cocktails.

A super flavor combination:

Grapefruit and Crabmeat Cocktail   *Yield:* 8 servings

2 pkg. (13½ oz. each) frozen grape-   1 tbsp. vinegar
   fruit sections, thawed   2 tsp. lemon juice
sugar, if desired   2 tbsp. ketchup
1 pkg. (12 oz.) frozen, cooked   1 drop Tabasco sauce
   crabmeat, thawed   pimiento strips
1 c. mayonnaise   parsley

Drain grapefruit sections and add sugar to sweeten, if desired. Pull crabmeat apart in rather coarse pieces. Arrange grapefruit sections around sides of cocktail glasses and fill center with crabmeat. Combine remaining ingredients (except pimiento and parsley) and pour this sauce over crabmeat. Garnish each cocktail with thin strip of pimiento and a sprig of parsley.

   Dinner: *Grapefruit* and *Crabmeat* Cocktail—Roast *Leg of Lamb* with Mint Sauce, Browned Potatoes, Buttered *Carrots*—*Peach* Puff Pudding p. 418.

This recipe has such a nice amount of sophistication:

Crabmeat Newburg   *Yield:* 3–4 servings
1 c. frozen cooked crabmeat,   ¼ tsp. salt
  thawed   1 c. top milk or light cream
1 tbsp. butter or margarine   1 egg
1 tbsp. flour   2 tbsp. sherry wine
¼ tsp. paprika
¼ tsp. nutmeg

Melt butter in top of double boiler, add flour, paprika, nutmeg and salt and blend well. Add milk or cream slowly, and cook over direct heat, stirring, until thickened. To egg in small bowl, add a small portion of thickened sauce, mix well and add this to rest of sauce. Cook over hot water about 1 min. Add crabmeat and cook until thoroughly heated. Just before serving, add sherry wine.

Luncheon or Supper: *Grapefruit Juice——Crabmeat* Newburg on Toast, *Artichoke* Hearts with Curry Mayonnaise, p. 326, Assorted Relishes——*Strawberry* Whip, p. 419.

This is an exquisitely flavored crabmeat recipe:

Deviled Crabmeat   *Yield:* 8 servings
1 pkg. (12 oz.) frozen, cooked   2 egg yolks
  crabmeat, thawed   1 tsp. salt
2 tbsp. butter or margarine   speck cayenne
1 c. (¼ lb.) sliced mushrooms, or   2 tsp. dry mustard
  1 can (4 oz.)   2 tsp. Worcestershire sauce
2 tbsp. flour   buttered bread crumbs
2 c. top milk or cream

Melt butter, add mushrooms and heat, then add flour and blend well. Add milk or cream slowly, stirring. Combine remaining ingredients except bread crumbs and add these to milk mixture. Bring barely to a boil, then remove from heat. Add crabmeat which has been pulled apart into flakes, and mix well. Place in greased, individual baking dishes or shells. Sprinkle with bread crumbs and bake in moderately hot oven, 400°F., about 15 min. or until crumbs are browned.

Luncheon or Supper: *Grape Juice*——Deviled *Crabmeat, Asparagus* Aspic Salad, p. 328——*Ice Cream* with *Sliced Peaches.*

These are just as nice as their name implies:

Curried Crabmeat Fantasies

½ c. frozen, cooked crabmeat, thawed
½ tsp. minced onion
1½ tbsp. butter or margarine
½ tbsp. flour
½ tsp. curry powder

Yield: 12 canapes

⅛ tsp. salt
¼ c. top milk or cream
small toast squares
grated American or Parmesan cheese

Sauté onion in hot butter. Combine flour, curry powder and salt and blend well with onion. Add milk or cream slowly, stirring. Pull crabmeat apart in flakes, and add to milk mixture. Arrange on toast squares, sprinkle with cheese and broil until delicately browned. Serve hot.

Cocktail Party: *Asparagus* Rolls, p. 331, Curried *Crabmeat* Fantasies, Cheese Dips and Cocktail Crackers, Cocktails.

A dainty dish, made hearty with rice and leeks:

Crabmeat Riviera

2 lbs. frozen cooked crabmeat, thawed
2 c. cooked rice
2 c. cooked leeks
2 cans condensed mushroom soup

Yield: 8 servings

¾ c. light cream
¼ tsp. powdered tarragon
1 c. buttered crumbs
parsley

Pull crabmeat apart in coarse flakes and combine with rice and leeks. Combine mushroom soup, light cream and tarragon and add to crabmeat mixture. Turn into individual shells or baking dishes and top with buttered crumbs. Bake in moderate oven, 350°F., about 30 min. Garnish with parsley.

Dinner: *Crabmeat* Riviera, *French-Fried Potatoes, Green Beans* with Mushrooms, p. 332, Head Lettuce with French Dressing— *Pecan Pie.*

OTHER CRABMEAT RECIPES

Fish Fillets Baltimore. *See p. 265.*
Crabmeat Rarebit. *See p. 444.*
Broiled Cheese 'N Crabmeat Boats. *See p. 445.*

Lobster

Fit for king and his consort, this elegant dish for two:

Broiled Lobster Tails   *Yield:* 2 servings

1 pkg. (2 tails) frozen lobster tails,   butter or margarine
   thawed   lemon butter, p. 203

Using kitchen shears, clip and remove the under shell of the lobster tails. Arrange tails with shell side up, on broiler rack about 5 inches from source of heat.

Broil 4–6 min., then turn flesh side up, brush with butter. Broil about 5 min. longer and serve at once, with lemon butter.

> **Dinner:**   Broiled *Lobster Tails* with Lemon Butter, *French-Fried Potatoes, Broccoli* Hollandaise, p. 329, *Pineapple* Orange Gelatin Salad, p. 403—*Mixed Fruit* Cup with *Sherbet.*

An unusual combination which is superlative:

Lobster and Pineapple Salad   *Yield:* 6 servings

1 c. frozen cooked lobster meat,   ½ c. salted toasted almonds
   thawed   1 tbsp. chopped green pepper
1 pkg. (13½ oz.) frozen pineapple   ½ c. mayonnaise
   chunks, thawed   crisp lettuce cups
1 c. diced celery

Cut lobster meat into large pieces, removing bits of shell if necessary. Add celery, almonds, green pepper and mayonnaise to lobster. Drain pineapple thoroughly and add to lobster mixture, tossing ingredients together. Serve on crisp lettuce cups.

> **Luncheon or Supper:** *Lobster* and *Pineapple* Salad, Cream Cheese and Watercress Sandwiches—Frozen *Loganberry* Cream, p. 376.

An especially tasty sauce, lobster meat and mushrooms:

Baked Lobster and Mushrooms   *Yield:*   4–6 servings

1 c. frozen cooked lobster meat,   2 tbsp. sherry wine or sauterne
   thawed   1 tsp. grated lemon rind
2 tbsp. butter or margarine   1 tsp. chopped parsley, or ½ tsp.
1½ tbsp. flour   dried parsley
1 c. liquid (liquid from   1 can (4 oz.) mushrooms
   mushrooms, adding top milk to   2 hard cooked eggs, sliced
   make 1 c.)   ¼ c. buttered bread crumbs
¼ tsp. salt

Prepare cream sauce from butter, flour, liquid and salt (see directions, p. 200).   Add sherry, lemon rind and parsley.   Place lobster, mushrooms and egg slices in alternate layers in 1-qt. casserole, **cover** with sauce and top with bread crumbs.   Bake in hot oven, 450°F. about 10 min.

> **Dinner:** Baked *Lobster* with Mushrooms, Baked Potato, *Peas* with Tiny Onions, p. 359, Tossed Green Salad—*Blueberry* Shortcake, p. 420, with *Dessert Topping*.

Triple the recipe, and serve it from a chafing dish for a buffet party:

Lobster Newburg   *Yield:*   4 servings

1 c. frozen cooked lobster meat,   1 c. top milk or cream
  thawed   1 egg
1 tbsp. butter or margarine   2 tbsp. sherry wine
1½ tbsp. flour   2 tbsp. brandy (if desired)
¼ tsp. paprika
¼ tsp. nutmeg

Melt butter in top of double boiler, add flour, paprika and nutmeg and blend well.   Add milk or cream and cook over direct heat until thickened, stirring constantly.   To egg in small bowl, add a small portion of thickened sauce, mix well and add this to rest of sauce.   Cook over hot water, about 1 min.   Pull lobster meat apart into coarse flakes, add to sauce and heat thoroughly.   Just before serving, add wine and brandy, and salt if necessary.

> **Luncheon or Supper:** *Lobster* Newburg on Rice, *Grapefruit* and Avocado Salad, p. 386, — Hot *Baking Powder Biscuits* and Strawberry Jam.

A favorite for men, with lobster, curry, cheese and shortcake:

Curried Lobster Shortcake   *Yield:* 6 servings

1½ c. frozen cooked lobster meat,   6 large baking powder biscuits
  thawed   6 slices American Cheddar cheese
2 c. curry sauce (see p. 277)

Pull lobster meat apart into large pieces, and add curry sauce. Split baking powder biscuits in halves crosswise and arrange 6 halves on heatproof platter. Pour curried lobster over biscuits and top with remaining biscuit halves and slices of cheese. Broil slowly until cheese melts.

Curry Sauce

1 tbsp. onion	½ tsp. salt
2 tbsp. butter or margarine	⅛ tsp. paprika
2 tbsp. flour	1 tsp. curry powder
1 c. milk	1 tsp. lemon juice

Heat onion in hot butter until tender but not brown. Blend in flour, add milk slowly, stirring, and cook until thickened, stirring constantly. Add remaining ingredients and combine.

Dinner: Curried *Lobster* Shortcake, *Wax Beans* and Mushrooms, p. 341, *Grapefruit* Salad—*Vanilla Ice Cream* with Caramel Sauce

Creamed Shrimp and Lobster. *See p. 444.*

Oysters

A delicious dish for a brisk winter day:

Scalloped Oysters　　　　　　　　*Yield:* 4 servings

1 pkg. (12 oz.) frozen oysters, thawed	speck pepper
1 c. coarse cracker crumbs	½ tsp. salt
½ c. dry bread crumbs	¼ c. oyster liquor
½ c. melted butter or margarine	2 tbsp. top milk or cream

Drain the oysters thoroughly, reserving liquor. Combine cracker and bread crumbs with melted butter and put thin layer of crumb mixture on bottom of greased shallow baking dish or 8-inch pie plate. Cover crumbs with layer of oysters and sprinkle with salt and pepper. Combine oyster liquor and milk and pour half this liquid over oysters. Cover oysters with crumbs, add another layer of oysters, then remaining liquid and cover top with crumbs. Do not use more than 2 layers of oysters, or the oysters in the center will not be done.

Bake in hot oven, 450°F., 20–30 min.

Dinner: *Hawaiian Punch*—Scalloped *Oysters*, Buttered *Peas, Mixed Vegetables* in Tomato Aspic, Rolls—*Peach Turnovers.*

Oyster and baked potato flavor are fine together:

Oyster Baked Potato   *Yield:* 8 servings
1 pkg. (12 oz). frozen oysters,   1 tsp. salt
    thawed   ⅛ tsp. pepper
4 large baking potatoes   buttered crumbs
¹/₃ c. butter or margarine   paprika
½ c. hot milk   parsley

Scrub potatoes and brush skin with melted fat, then bake in hot oven, 425°F., 1 hr. or until done. Cut baked potatoes in halves, scoop out inside, reserving shells. Mash potato pulp and add butter, hot milk, salt and pepper, and beat until mixture is light and fluffy.

Return mixture to potato shells, and make a hollow in the center of each shell. Place oysters in hollows, top with crumbs and sprinkle with paprika. Put potatoes back into oven at 425°F. and bake 15 min. longer or until crumbs are browned. Garnish with parsley and serve at once.

> **Supper:** *Grape Juice—Oyster* Baked Potato, Tossed Vegetable Salad—*Ice Cream* Eclair with Butterscotch Sauce.

Off to a wonderful start . . . any dinner that begins with:

Oyster Cocktail   *Yield:* 6 servings
1 pkg. (12 oz.) frozen oysters,   ½ tsp. Worcestershire sauce
    thawed   ¼ c. finely chopped celery
¼ c. ketchup   small crisp lettuce leaves
1 tbsp. lemon juice   lemon wedges
½ tsp. salt
6 drops Tabasco sauce
2 tsp. horseradish

Drain oysters thoroughly. Combine remaining ingredients except lettuce and lemon wedges. Arrange small pieces of lettuce in cocktail glasses, add oysters and pour sauce over them. Garnish with lemon wedges.

> **Dinner:** *Oyster* Cocktail—Roast *Chicken* with Herb Stuffing, Candied Yams, Buttered *Broccoli,* Hearts of Celery, Radishes, Olives —*Vanilla Ice Cream* with Coffee Caramel Sauce, p. 435.

An all-American favorite, available now at all seasons:

Oyster Stew   *Yield:* 4 servings

1 pkg. (12 oz.) frozen oysters, thawed	speck pepper
2 tbsp. butter or margarine	3 c. scalded milk
½ tsp. salt	oyster crackers
½ tsp. celery salt, if desired	paprika

Heat oysters in their own liquor, just until their edges curl.   Add butter, seasonings and milk.   Serve immediately, with oyster crackers, sprinkling each serving with paprika.

> **Luncheon or Supper:** *Oyster* Stew, Crackers—Combination Vegetable Salad Plate—*Chocolate Cake.*

Especially fine for a luncheon party:

Oysters à la King   *Yield:* 6 servings

1 pkg. (12 oz.) frozen oysters, thawed	¼ c. flour
milk	2 tbsp. minced pimiento
½ c. chopped green pepper	1½ tsp. salt
½ lb. mushrooms, 2 c. sliced, or 1 can (8 oz.)	⅛ tsp. pepper
¼ c. butter or margarine	dash nutmeg
	toast or patty shells

Simmer oysters in their own liquor for 5 min., then drain, reserving liquor.   Add enough milk to oyster liquor to give 2½ c. liquid. Sauté green peppers and mushrooms (drained, if canned ones are used) in hot butter until lightly browned.   Blend in flour, add liquid, pimiento, seasonings and simmer until thickened, stirring constantly. Add oysters and heat thoroughly.   Serve on toast or in patty shells.

> **Luncheon or Supper:** *Grapefruit Juice—Oysters* à la King in Patty Shells, *Brussels Sprouts* with Wine Grapes, p. 346, Tomato Salad— *Peach* Shortcake, p. 420.

Seasoned to the best of taste:

Browned Oysters with Toast Points   *Yield:* 4–6 servings

1 pkg. (12 oz.) frozen oysters,   ¼ tsp. salt
  thawed   speck pepper
flour   parsley
6 tbsp. butter or margarine   toast points
1½ tbsp. flour   lemon wedges, if desired
3 tbsp. lemon juice
few drops Worcestershire sauce

Drain oysters thoroughly, reserving liquor, and dredge each one in flour. Brown oysters in ¼ c. hot butter, then remove oysters to serving dish and keep hot. To pan from which oysters were removed, add 2 tbsp. butter and 1½ tbsp. flour, blend well, then stir in liquor from oysters, add lemon juice, Worcestershire sauce, salt and pepper and heat until slightly thickened, stirring constantly. Pour this sauce over oysters in serving dish, garnish with parsley and toast points, and with lemon wedges if desired.

> **Luncheon or Supper:** Browned *Oysters* with Toast Points, *Cauliflower* and *Green Bean* Salad, p. 335——Baked Alaska Tarts, p. 426.

In season now, in June or January:

Scalloped Oysters and Corn   *Yield:* 4–6 servings

1 pkg. (12 oz.) frozen oysters,   ¼ tsp. dry mustard
  thawed   1 tsp. salt
1 pkg. (10 oz.) frozen cut corn   1 tsp. Worcestershire sauce
1/3 c. chopped green pepper   ¾ c. milk
1/3 c. minced onion   ½ c. buttered crumbs
2 tbsp. fat   1 tbsp. butter or margarine
1 egg, well beaten

Drain oysters, reserving liquor. Cook corn until tender. Sauté green pepper and onion in hot fat until light brown. Combine egg, mustard, salt, Worcestershire sauce and milk with 6 tbsp. oyster liquor. In a greased, 1-qt. casserole, arrange alternate layers of crumbs, oysters, corn, onion and pepper mixture, making only two layers of oysters.   Pour milk mixture over top, and dot with butter. Bake in hot oven, 400°F., about 30 min.

Luncheon or Supper: Scalloped *Oysters* and *Corn, Broccoli* with Garlic Butter, p. 342, Tomato and Endive Salad with Russian Dressing—*Raspberry* Cream Roll, p. 416.

Oyster and spinach flavor make a fine adventure:

Oysters Rockefeller

Yield: 3 servings

1 pkg. (12 oz.) frozen oysters, thawed
1 c. cooked spinach
2 tbsp. chopped onion
1 bay leaf
½ tbsp. chopped parsley
¼ tsp. celery salt

¼ tsp. salt
3 drops Tabasco sauce
3 tbsp. butter or margarine
½ c. bread crumbs
lemon slices

Drain oysters thoroughly and place them in deep shells or in small, shallow baking dish.   Put spinach, onion, bay leaf and parsley through food grinder, add seasonings and cook in butter 5 min.   Add bread crumbs and combine well.   Spread mixture over oysters and bake in hot oven, 400°F., about 10 min. or until heated to serving temperature.   Serve with lemon slices.

Dinner: Tomato Juice—*Oysters* Rockefeller, Mashed Potatoes, *Green Beans* with Mushrooms, p. 332—*Pineapple-Grapefruit* Salad, p. 387—*Ambrosia* Parfait, p. 429.

Fried Oysters. *Follow directions for* Fried Clams, *p. 271.*
Oyster Stuffing. *See p. 302.*
Oysters au Champignons. *See p. 445.*

Scallops

Delicately flavored scallops with a delicious sauce:

Savory Broiled Scallops

Yield: 3 servings

1 lb. frozen scallops, thawed
melted butter
3 slices bacon, diced
1½ tsp. minced onion
2 tbsp. lemon juice

1½ tsp. Worcestershire sauce
½ tsp. celery salt
2½ tbsp. ketchup
⅛ tsp. salt
speck cayenne

Drain scallops and to the liquor add enough water to make 1 c. liquid. Bring this liquid to a boil, add scallops and barely bring to a boil again. Drain scallops and dry them on absorbent paper. Dip scallops in melted butter, broil until lightly browned on both sides and keep them hot. Cook diced bacon until crisp, and drain on paper, reserving 1 tbsp. bacon fat in pan. Add remaining ingredients except toast to bacon fat, and heat well.

Arrange scallops on toast, add diced bacon to heated sauce and pour over scallops. Serve on toast.

> **Dinner:** *Corn* Chowder—Savory Broiled *Scallops* on Toast with Tartar Sauce, *French-Fried Potatoes,* Buttered *Spinach—Orange* Soufflé, p. 399, with *Lemon* Sauce, p. 391.

Scallops baked in mushroom sauce are delicious:

Scallops and Mushrooms   *Yield:* 4–5 servings

1 lb. frozen scallops, thawed	2 tbsp. flour
1 c. boiling water	$2/3$ c. milk
¼ c. chopped onion	¼ tsp. salt
2 tbsp. butter or margarine	⅛ tsp. pepper
1 c. sliced mushrooms, or 1 can (4 oz.)	buttered crumbs

Add scallops to boiling water, barely bring water back to a boil and drain, reserving liquor. Sauté onion in hot butter over low heat for 5 min., add mushrooms (drained, if canned ones) and sauté for 3 min. longer. Sprinkle flour over mushrooms and blend well, then add $2/3$ c. liquor drained from scallops, and cook until mixture thickens, stirring constantly. Add milk. Cut scallops into pieces about ½ x ¾ inch, add to sauce, add salt and pepper and combine well. Place in greased baking dish, cover with buttered crumbs and bake in hot oven, 400°F., about 15 min.

> **Dinner:** *Grapefruit, Pineapple* Ginger Cocktail, p. 402—*Scallops* and Mushrooms, Baked Potato, Buttered *Carrots—Citrus* Banana Sherbet, p. 396.

Scallops in a special cheese dish:

Scallops au Gratin

Yield: 4–5 servings

1 lb. frozen scallops, thawed
1½ c. soft bread crumbs
2 tbsp. melted butter or margarine
½ c. diced celery
1 small green pepper, diced

2 tbsp. fat
¼ c. grated American cheese
½ tsp. salt
speck pepper
1 c. top milk or light cream

Cover scallops with boiling water, bring water barely back to boiling, then drain scallops and cut in halves. Mix bread crumbs with melted butter.

Sauté celery and green pepper in hot fat for 5 min. In greased 1-qt. casserole, arrange alternate layers of crumbs, scallops, blended green peppers, celery and cheese, sprinkling each layer lightly with salt and pepper. Pour milk or cream over top and bake in moderate oven, 350°F., about 30 min.

Dinner: *Pineapple Juice*—*Scallops* au Gratin, Parsley Buttered *New Potatoes,* p. 361, Buttered *Peas,* Sliced Tomatoes—*Raspberry* Tapioca Pudding, p. 405.

Tomato sauce with a tang, poured over scallops:

Deviled Scallops

Yield: 4–5 servings

1 lb. frozen scallops, thawed
¼ c. melted bacon fat
flour, seasoned with salt
¾ c. canned tomatoes
¼ tsp. salt

¼ tsp. paprika
1 tbsp. minced onion
1 tbsp. lemon juice
½ c. buttered crumbs

Drain scallops thoroughly on absorbent paper. Dip each scallop in melted bacon fat and roll in seasoned flour, then place them in shallow baking dish.

Combine tomatoes, salt, paprika, onion and lemon juice and pour this mixture over scallops. Sprinkle with buttered crumbs and bake in moderate oven, 375°F., about 25 min.

Dinner: *Grape Juice*—Deviled *Scallops, French-Fried Potatoes, Lima Beans* in Sour Cream Sauce, p. 338—Toasted *Cherry* Chiffon Pie, p. 382.

For New Englanders . . . and lots of people, everywhere:

New England Scallop Supper   *Yield:* 3 servings

1 lb. frozen scallops, thawed   2 tbsp. flour
1 qt. water   1 c. milk
2 tbsp. salt   ½ tsp. salt
3 medium baking potatoes   ½ c. cooked peas, if desired
2 tbsp. fat   parsley

Wash potatoes, dry the skins, and brush with melted fat. Bake in hot oven, 450°F., 45–60 min. or until done.

Meanwhile, place scallops in boiling water to which 2 tbsp. salt have been added and simmer 3–4 min. Drain. If scallops are large, cut in halves. Make cream sauce from fat, flour, ½ tsp. salt and milk (for directions, see p. 200).

Cut a cross in top of baked potatoes and squeeze them so the interior is exposed. Add scallops and peas (if desired) to cream sauce and heat to serving temperature. Pour hot scallop mixture over hot potatoes, and garnish with parsley.

Dinner: *Pineapple-Grapefruit Juice*—New England *Scallop* Supper, *Green Bean* and Carrot Salad, p. 334, *Rolls*—*Blueberry* Crumb Pudding, p. 377.

A New England favorite, but in European style:

Scallop Kabobs   *Yield:* 6 servings

1 lb. frozen scallops, thawed   3 tbsp. butter or margarine
4 slices bacon, cut into squares   ½ tsp. salt
1 can (4 oz.) button mushrooms   speck pepper
1 green pepper, cut into 1-inch
  squares

Alternate scallops, bacon squares, mushrooms and green pepper squares on skewers about 7 inches long, beginning and ending with scallops. Place on greased broiler pan. Combine butter with seasonings, brush scallops with this mixture and broil about 3 inches from source of heat for 5 min. Turn carefully, brush other side with seasoned butter and broil 3–5 min. longer. Serve at once.

Dinner: *Grape Juice*—*Scallop* Kabobs, Baked Potato, *Spinach* in Onion Sauce, p. 369—*Pineapple* Upside-Down Cake, p. 404.

Fried Scallops. *Follow directions for* Fried Clams, *p. 271.*
Scallops Hurry Curry. *See p. 444.*

Shrimp

(Whenever frozen cooked shrimp are specified in these recipes, frozen raw shrimp may be used if they are first cooked and cleaned.)

Coral shrimp and green peas in a tasty cream sauce:

Creamed Shrimp and Peas   *Yield:* 4 servings

1 pkg. (12 oz.) frozen, cooked shrimp, thawed
1 pkg. (10 oz.) frozen peas
1/4 c. melted butter or margarine
1/4 c. flour
1 tsp. minced onion
1/2 tsp. salt

speck pepper
2 1/4 c. scalded milk
1/2 c. cooked, chopped celery
1 tsp. Worcestershire sauce
1 1/2 tsp. lemon juice
1 tsp. chopped parsley

Cook peas and drain them. Combine melted butter, flour, onion, salt and pepper until well blended, add hot milk slowly and cook until thickened, stirring constantly. Add cooked shrimp, peas and remaining ingredients, heat well and serve.

> **Luncheon or Supper:** Creamed *Shrimp* and *Peas* on Toasted English Muffins, *Green Bean* and *Cauliflower* Salad, p. 335—*Coffee Ice Cream* with Coffee Caramel Sauce, p. 435.

Savory and superb . . . a delightful treat:

Shrimp Rarebit on Toast   *Yield:* 5 servings

1 pkg. (12 oz.) frozen, cooked shrimp, thawed
1 tbsp. chopped onion
2 tbsp. chopped green pepper
6 tbsp. butter or margarine
1 tbsp. flour
1/2 c. milk
1/2 tsp. Worcestershire sauce

1/8 tsp. dry mustard
1/4 tsp. salt
speck pepper
1/4 lb. sharp Cheddar cheese, grated (1 c.)
toast

Cook onion and green pepper slowly in 5 tbsp. hot butter, add shrimp, mix carefully with a fork and cook until shrimp are hot. Melt remaining 1 tbsp. butter, combine flour with it, add milk slowly, stirring, then add Worcestershire sauce, mustard, salt and pepper and cook until thickened, stirring constantly. Add shrimp mixture, and just before serving, add grated cheese and heat only until cheese is melted. Serve on toast,

> **Luncheon or Supper:** *Shrimp* Rarebit on Toast, Tossed Green Salad, Hot *Baking Powder Biscuits—Rhubarb* Meringue Pie, p. 410.

Here are appealing combinations of color and flavor:

Shrimp Chili Mold

1 pkg. (1 lb.) frozen, cooked shrimp, thawed	*Yield:* 6–8 servings
1 pkg. lemon flavored gelatin	3 tbsp. chili sauce or ketchup
1½ c. hot water	½ c. chopped celery
speck pepper or cayenne	¹⁄₃ c. pickle relish
	¼ c. finely diced cucumbers

Dissolve lemon gelatin in hot water and add pepper, pickle relish and chili sauce. Chill this mixture until syrupy, then fold in shrimp and remaining ingredients. Chill in individual molds.

If preferred, pour a small amount of the gelatin mixture (before chopped ingredients are added) in bottom of molds, arrange part of shrimp in this, decoratively, and chill until firm. Then fill molds with remaining gelatin and other ingredients. One large mold may be used, if desired.

> **Dinner:** *Bean Soup*—Shrimp Chili Mold, *French-Fried Potatoes,* Buttered *Peas—Chocolate Cream Pie.*

A taste of this, and a taste of that . . . savory shrimp:

Savory Shrimp

1 pkg. (12 oz.) frozen, cooked shrimp, thawed	*Yield:* 4 servings
2 slices bacon, diced	¼ tsp. celery salt
1 tsp. minced onion	speck cayenne
4 tsp. lemon juice	1½ tbsp. ketchup
1 tsp. Worcestershire sauce	⅛ tsp. salt
	toast, or toast points or squares

Cook bacon until crisp, and drain on absorbent paper, leaving 1 tbsp. bacon fat in pan. Add shrimp and remaining ingredients, except bacon and toast, to the bacon fat in pan. Heat thoroughly, then

Courtesy of Shrimp Association of the Americas

Shrimp are not only flavorsome, they are also a colorful and decorative addition to many a meal

add cooked bacon. Serve on toast. Or serve as hors d'oeuvres on toast points or squares.

Luncheon or Supper: Savory *Shrimp, Artichoke* and *Grapefruit* Salad, p. 327, Hot *Baking Powder Biscuits—Raspberry* Cream Roll, p. 416.

This is just right for a crisp, fall evening:

Shrimp in Blankets

1 pkg. (12 oz.) frozen, cooked jumbo shrimp, thawed	*Yield:* 6–8 servings bacon hot, buttered toast
salt	lemon wedges
pepper	chopped parsley
paprika	

Sprinkle each shrimp with salt, pepper and paprika. Cut bacon to roll around shrimp, and wrap a piece around each, fastening with toothpicks.

Arrange shrimp in single layer on baking pan and bake in moderately hot oven, 400°F., about 10 min. or until bacon is crisp. Serve on hot, buttered toast, garnishing with lemon wedges and chopped parsley.

> **Luncheon or Supper:** *Shrimp* in Blankets, *Broccoli Spears* with Curry Mayonnaise, p. 326, Head Lettuce with French Dressing—— *Raspberry Peach* Compote.

Deviled eggs and a tasty sauce make this an unusual dish:

Deviled Egg and Shrimp on Toast   *Yield:* 8 servings

1 pkg. (12 oz.) frozen, cooked
    jumbo shrimp, thawed
4 deviled eggs (see below)
sherry wine sauce (see below)

paprika
toast
parsley

Prepare deviled eggs according to directions below. Arrange shrimp and deviled eggs in shallow baking dish. Cover with sherry wine sauce and sprinkle with paprika. Bake in moderate oven, 350°F., about 20 min. Serve on toast and garnish with parsley.

Deviled Eggs

4 hard-cooked eggs
2–3 tbsp. mayonnaise
1/4 tsp. salt
speck pepper

1/8 tsp. prepared mustard
1/2 tsp. minced onion
1 tsp. chopped parsley

Remove shells from eggs, cut in halves lengthwise and remove yolks. Mash yolks to a smooth paste with remaining ingredients. Pack this mixture back into the egg white cavities.

Sherry Wine Sauce

3 tbsp. butter or margarine
1 tsp. paprika
1/2 tsp. dry mustard
1/8 tsp. nutmeg

1/2 tsp. salt
3 tbsp. flour
2 c. homogenized milk
1/4 c. sherry wine

Melt butter, add seasonings and flour and blend well, then add milk slowly and heat slowly until thickened, stirring constantly.   Add sherry wine just before serving.

Luncheon or Supper: Deviled Egg and *Shrimp* on Toast, *Mixed Vegetables* in Tomato Aspic—*Blueberry* Pie, p. 380.

From New Orleans, where gumbo is so popular:

Shrimp Gumbo

Yield: 8 servings

2 pkg. (12 oz. each) frozen, cooked shrimp, thawed
4 strips bacon
1 large onion, minced
1 garlic clove, minced
½ c. diced green pepper
½ c. diced celery
3 c. consommé (or 3 bouillon cubes dissolved in hot water)
1 c. canned tomatoes
1 pkg. (10 oz.) frozen okra, preferably cut
½ tsp. powdered thyme
1 bay leaf
1 tsp. Worcestershire sauce
2 tbsp. cornstarch
¼ c. water
2 c. cooked rice

Dice bacon and cook until crisp.   Add onion, garlic, green pepper and celery and cook slowly about 5 min.   Add consommé, tomatoes, okra (thawed if desired), thyme, bay leaf and Worcestershire sauce, and combine.   Blend cornstarch and water to a smooth paste and add slowly to other ingredients.   Cover, and simmer about 45 min.   Add shrimp and continue to cook slowly only until shrimp are thoroughly heated (about 10 min.).

Serve in soup plates, topped with rice.

Luncheon or Supper: *Shrimp* Gumbo with Rice, Combination Vegetable Salad, *Cornmeal Muffins*—*Apple Pie.*

Hearty and delectable . . . another meal-in-a-dish:

Shrimp in Casserole

Yield: 6 servings

1 pkg. (12 oz.) frozen, cooked jumbo shrimp, thawed
1 c. uncooked rice
sherry and curry sauce (see p. 290)
paprika

Cook rice until barely done. Half fill individual casseroles (or one large casserole) with cooked rice and add shrimp. Cover with sherry and curry sauce and sprinkle top with paprika. Brown lightly in broiler and serve at once.

Sherry and Curry Sauce

3 tbsp. grated onion	¾ tsp. salt
6 tbsp. butter or margarine	speck pepper
1 tsp. curry powder	speck nutmeg
5 tbsp. flour	$1/3$ c. sherry wine
3 c. homogenized milk or light cream	

Sauté onion in hot butter, add curry powder and flour and blend well. Add milk or cream slowly and heat until thickened, stirring constantly. Season with salt, pepper, nutmeg and sherry wine.

Dinner: *Grapefruit Juice—Shrimp* in Casserole, *French-Fried Potatoes, Cauliflower* with Almond Butter, p. 351—*Ice Cream* with *Strawberries.*

Superb for a main course for luncheon, or for a dinner salad:

Shrimp and Grapefruit Salad

Yield: 8 servings

1 pkg. (12 oz.), frozen, cooked shrimp, thawed	2 tbsp. mayonnaise
1 pkg. (13½ oz.) frozen grapefruit sections, thawed	5 or 6 large stalks of crisp celery
1 pkg. (3 oz.) cream cheese	crisp lettuce
	French dressing

Drain grapefruit sections thoroughly. Combine cream cheese well with mayonnaise. Cut shrimp into small pieces, add to cheese mixture and mix. Pack the shrimp and cheese mixture tightly into celery stalks and cut stalks into ¾-inch slices. Arrange stuffed celery and grapefruit sections decoratively on crisp lettuce and serve with French dressing.

Dinner: Roast *Leg of Lamb,* Mashed Potatoes, Buttered *Peas.* *Shrimp and Grapefruit* Salad—*Raspberry* Sherbet, p. 407.

Pink shrimp and grapes in a jewel-like salad:

Shrimp and White Grape Salad　　*Yield:* 3–4 servings

1 pkg. (12 oz.) frozen, cooked jumbo shrimp, thawed	1 c. seedless white grapes
French dressing	crisp salad greens
½ c. diced celery	

Marinate shrimp in French dressing. Just before serving add celery, and grapes which have been washed and cut in halves. Arrange shrimp and celery on salad greens and top with grapes.

Luncheon or Supper: *Shrimp* and White Grape Salad, *Asparagus* Rolls, p. 331, Brown Bread Sandwiches—*Peach Turnovers.*

Beautiful to see, and delightful to eat:

Shrimp and Asparagus Salad　　*Yield:* 6–8 servings

1 pkg. (12 oz.) frozen, cooked shrimp, thawed	½ c. chopped celery
1 pkg. (10 oz.) asparagus spears	3 hard-cooked eggs, sliced
French dressing	mayonnaise
crisp lettuce	

Cook asparagus spears, drain and chill thoroughly. Marinate chilled shrimp in French dressing. Arrange asparagus on lettuce leaves, sprinkle celery over asparagus and add shrimp. Garnish with egg slices and serve with mayonnaise.

Luncheon or Supper: *Cream of Potato Soup*—*Shrimp* and *Asparagus* Salad, Cole Slaw, *Cornmeal Muffins*—Pecan Pie.

These are delicious party snacks or appetizers:

Spiced Shrimp　　*Yield:* 8–10 servings as party snacks

1 pkg. (12 oz.) frozen, cooked jumbo shrimp	1 tsp. whole cloves
2 bay leaves	1 qt. water
½ tbsp. whole allspice	1 can (12 oz.) beer, if desired
1 tsp. crushed red peppers	1 medium onion, sliced
1 tsp. whole black peppers	3 garlic cloves
1 tsp. peppercorns	1 lemon, sliced
	2 tbsp. salt

Tie spices loosely in cheesecloth bag. Add bag containing spices, onion, garlic, lemon, salt and beer (if desired) to water and bring to a boil. Add shrimp, cover saucepan and return to boiling point, then reduce heat and simmer 5 min. Drain thoroughly, and chill shrimp.

Cocktail Party: Spiced *Shrimp,* Cheese Sticks, *Asparagus* Rolls, p. 331, Cocktails.

Fried Shrimp. *Follow directions for* Fried Clams, *p. 271, using thawed, cooked jumbo shrimp.*
Easy Shrimp and Geen Peas. *See p. 444.*

CHAPTER 15

Frozen Poultry

THAWING POULTRY

Turkeys, or any other birds which are purchased already stuffed, should not be thawed before cooking. And while it is possible to cook other kinds of poultry from the hard-frozen state in most instances, thawing is preferred. It is often necessary to do some final cleaning of the bird, or to remove giblets from whole ones, and for this at least some thawing is needed. Cut-up poultry or poultry parts need to be thawed to separate the pieces, or to bread them or dredge in flour or roll them in egg or batter. And thawed birds may roast more uniformly than those which are not thawed.

Thaw the birds in the wrapper, preferably in the refrigerator, since it is more uniform than thawing at room temperature. For large birds, thawing may be started in the refrigerator, and to speed final thawing (if necessary) it may be completed in cold water. For thawing in cold water, it is best if the bird is in its watertight wrapper. Keep the cold-water tap running gently over the bird, or allow the bird to stand in cold water, changing the water frequently. Allow it to stand in cold water only until it becomes pliable.

Birds thaw more quickly at room temperature than in a refrigerator, and still more quickly in front of an electric fan. But these methods are not recommended for large birds like turkeys or geese, because they will be completely thawed near the outside while they are still frozen near the center.

Approximate times for allowing frozen chickens and turkeys to thaw are given in table on page 294. Allow the same time for other birds of the same weight.

Start cooking as soon as the bird is thawed, and while it is still cold (about refrigerator temperature). If this is impossible, hold it in the refrigerator until cooking time. With excessive thawing, there will be loss of juices and the bird when served will be dry. Use any juices in cooking.

Birds which are completely thawed should be cooked exactly as

Approximate Thawing Times for Frozen Poultry

	Chickens[1]		
	Whole	*Cut-up 5-lb. packages*	*Whole turkeys*[1]
In refrigerator	4–5 lbs., 15–30 hrs.	15–20 hrs., to separate pieces	4–10 lbs., 1–2 days 10–20 lbs., 2–3 days 20–24 lbs., 3–4 days
At room temperature	4–5 lbs., 6–8 hrs. (or 3–4 hrs. in front of electric fan)	4–5 hrs., to separate pieces	Not recommended
In cold water (in watertight wrapper)	4–5 lbs., 2–3 hrs.	Not recommended	4–10 lbs., 4–6 hrs. 10–20 lbs., 6–8 hrs. 20–24 lbs., 8–12 hrs.

[1] Allow the same time for other birds of the same weight.

Suggestions for Selection and Cooking of Frozen Poultry

Market description of bird	Forms available frozen	Average weight, lbs.	Amount to buy per serving, approximate	Suggested ways to cook
Chicken Broiler-fryer	Whole, quartered, halved or parts	1½ to 4	¾ lb.	Broil, fry, grill, roast, rotisserie, simmer or stew
Roaster	Whole	3½ and over	¾ lb.	Roast, rotisserie
Rock Cornish hen	Whole	1 to 2	½ to 1 bird	Broil, fry, roast, rotisserie
Squab	Whole	½ to 1	1 bird	Roast, rotisserie
Capon	Whole	4 to 9	¾ to 1 lb.	Roast
Stewing hen or fowl	Whole or cut-up	3½ and over	¼ to ¾ lb.	Braise, simmer, stew
Duckling	Whole	4 to 6	¼ to ½ bird	Braise, roast, rotisserie
Goose	Whole	4 to 14	1 to 1½ lbs.	Braise, roast
Turkey, small	Whole or cut-up	4 to 8	½ to 1 lb.	Broil, fry, grill, roast, rotisserie
Turkey	Whole, quartered, halved or parts	9 to 24	½ to ¾ lb. for over 12-lb. birds ¾ to 1 lb. for under 12-lb. birds	Braise, roast, rotisserie

Courtesy Poultry and Egg National Board, Chicago, Ill.

similar fresh ones. In emergencies, when the bird is cooked without complete thawing, extra cooking time must be allowed. The extra time needs to be estimated, according to whether the bird is only slightly or almost completely thawed, and this is not easy. Some authorities state that birds roasted from the hard-frozen state require about half again as long to cook as thawed ones. This may provide a basis for estimating the extra time to allow for partially thawed birds.

In the pages that follow, the times given for cooking poultry are all for fresh or thawed birds.

Courtesy of Swift and Co.

If turkey is roasted breast up from the beginning, a "tent" of aluminum foil keeps it moist.   Or cheesecloth dipped in oil or melted fat can be used for the same purpose

FROZEN POULTRY AND METHODS OF COOKING

A list of the kinds of poultry commonly frozen is given in table on page 294.   Included are the amounts to buy per serving and suggested ways of cooking them.

COOKING TENDER BIRDS

Roasting

Frozen, Stuffed Turkeys.—Turkeys which are purchased already stuffed should be cooked without thawing, though they may be allowed to stand overnight in the refrigerator before cooking.   Once roasting is started, it should be continuous—do not start it one day and finish it the next.   In such birds, the giblets are often found in a package on the back of the bird. If they are frozen to the turkey, remove them after the turkey has been in the oven about an hour. For roasting, follow the instructions accompanying the turkey.

Preparation and Care of Whole Birds for Roasting.—If the bird as you purchase it is not stuffed, the cavity is usually well cleaned, but before stuffing or cooking, thaw at least enough to do any final, necessary cleaning, then drain the cavity and pat it dry. Rub the body cavity lightly with salt, and stuff the bird lightly, if desired.

To truss, fasten the neck skin to the back and bring the wings to the back, "akimbo" style. Tie the drumsticks to the tail, except for ducklings and geese, and for these tie the drumsticks together but not attached to the tail.

In general, birds will brown more evenly if they are roasted breast down for the first two-thirds of the cooking time, then turned breast up for the remainder of the cooking. But for large birds this may not be practical, and for other reasons, it is not always recommended.

Turkeys.—These may be roasted breast down for the first two-thirds of the cooking time, then turned and finished breast up. Rub the skin with soft fat or oil, and place skin or body fat over the bird. Baste occasionally during roasting. If roasted breast up from the beginning, several thicknesses of cheesecloth dipped in melted fat may be placed over the bird. Or the bird may be covered loosely with a "tent" of aluminum foil, anchoring it at the drumsticks.

Geese.—Roast with breast down for the first two-thirds of cooking time, and finish breast up. Since geese contain plenty of fat, they should not be basted during roasting. Neither should they be covered with cheesecloth dipped in fat, or with aluminum foil. Spoon or siphon off fat as it accumulates in the pan (to keep the pan fat light in color), and use the fat in cooking.

Ducklings.—Roast breast up, throughout. Like geese, these are rather high in fat, so do not rub the skin with fat or cover the bird with cheesecloth dipped in fat or with aluminum foil. Do not baste during roasting.

Chickens and Capons.—Rub skin with softened fat or oil. If convenient, roast with breast down during first two-thirds of cooking and finish with breast up, basting occasionally with pan drippings.

Rock Cornish Hens and Squabs.—Brush skin with softened butter or margarine and roast breast up, throughout. Baste occasionally, adding more butter or margarine if necessary.

Temperature and Time for Roasting.—Large birds, like turkeys, geese, capons and ducklings, should be roasted in a slow oven at 325°F. in order to cook uniformly. Smaller birds like chickens, Rock Cornish hens and squabs have better color and flavor if roasted in a hot oven at 400°F.

For large birds, it is strongly recommended that the test for doneness be made by a meat thermometer. If the bird is roasted without complete thawing, insert the thermometer when about half the expected time to roast has elapsed. If the thermometer is inserted into the thickest part of the breast meat, or into the thigh muscle next to the body cavity, the temperature for doneness is 190°–195°F. If it is inserted into the stuffing, the temperature should be 165°F.

Birds are done when the thickest part of the drumstick feels very soft when pressed with protected fingers, or small birds are done when the drumstick twists easily out of the thigh joint.

Turkeys, Geese and Chickens.—See the following timetables for roasting these birds.

Timetable for Roasting Turkey

Purchased ready-to-cook weight (unstuffed), lbs.	Oven temperature, °F.	Internal temperature,[1] °F.	Approximate total time for stuffed turkey,[2] hrs.
6 to 8	325	190–195	3½ to 4
8 to 12	325	190–195	4 to 4½
12 to 16	325	190–195	4½ to 5½
16 to 20	325	190–195	5½ to 6½
20 to 24	325	190–195	6½ to 7

[1] Temperature with roast meat thermometer placed in center of thickest part of breast meat.
[2] Shorten time ½ to 1½ hrs. for unstuffed turkeys—the shorter time for birds up to 12 lbs., and the longer time for birds over 12 lbs.
Courtesy Poultry and Egg National Board, Chicago, Ill.

Timetable for Roasting Chicken

Ready-to-cook Weight, lbs.	Oven temperature, °F.	Approximate total time for unstuffed chicken,[1] hrs.
1½ to 2	400	¾ to 1[2]
2 to 2½	400	1 to 1½[2]
2½ to 3	400	1½ to 2[2]
3 to 4	400	2 to 2½[2]

[1] For stuffed chickens, add an additional 15 to 20 min. to the roasting time.
[2] Allow the same time for rotisserie cooking except for birds over 3 lbs.; reduce time slightly for heavier birds.
Courtesy Poultry and Egg National Board, Chicago, Ill.

Timetable for Roasting Goose

Because of the variation among geese, allow an extra half hour in case more cooking is needed—especially if the meal is planned for a set time

Ready-to-cook weight, lbs.	Oven temperature, °F.	Approximate total time, hrs.
4 to 6	325	2¾ to 3
6 to 8	325	3 to 3½
8 to 10	325	3½ to 3¾
10 to 12	325	3¾ to 4¼
12 to 14	325	4 to 4¾

Courtesy Poultry and Egg National Board, Chicago, Ill.

Ducklings.—Roast at 325°F. An unstuffed duckling of 4–5 lbs. requires 2½–3 hrs., and about ½ hr. longer if stuffed.

Capons.—Roast at 325°F., allowing 25–30 min. per lb. or about 2½ hr. for a 6 lb. capon, stuffed.

Rock Cornish Hens and Squabs.—Roast at 400°F. Allow about 1 hr. for a Rock Cornish hen weighing 1½–2 lbs., and 30–40 min. for a squab weighing ½–1 lb.

Roasting Half-Turkeys.—Tie the tail and leg of the half-bird together by stitching through the skin at end of leg, and then through meat of the tail. Place the bird skin down and sew loose skin at neck so it forms a pocket. Fill the pocket loosely with stuffing. Fill the body cavity with stuffing and cover stuffing with heavy paper or foil cut to fit the cavity, and lace across, catching the skin on both sides. Place the bird with stuffing down on rack in shallow pan and roast in slow oven, 325°F., uncovered and without adding water. After the first 1½ hrs. baste every 45 min. until done. A half-turkey weighing 7–9 lbs. requires 3¾–4½ hrs., a larger half-bird longer.

Rotisserie Cookery

Chickens of any weight (not fowl), ducklings, Rock Cornish hens, squabs and turkeys up to 6 lbs. may be cooked on a rotisserie. Or several Rock Cornish hens or squabs, or two larger birds, each weighing not more than 5 lbs. may be cooked at one time if the spit is long enough. Follow the manufacturer's instructions for operating the spit.

Rub the body cavity lightly with salt, stuffing the bird if desired. Tie or skewer the wing tips over the breast, fasten the neck skin to the back with a skewer, and tie the drumsticks (crossed) to the tail. If the bird is stuffed, place a piece of foil over the exposed stuffing, tucking edges in securely. With back of bird down, push spit from tail end of bird to front, so that the point emerges between branches of wishbone near tip. For halves of birds, pierce the spit through the thigh, then through breast meat. Tie bird firmly so it will not loosen or move on spit, and balance bird (or birds) so the spit rotates smoothly. With two birds, place breasts in opposite direction, for balance. Rock Cornish hens and squabs may be fastened on spit either lengthwise or crosswise.

Except for duckling, brush skin with soft fat or oil. Cook at 400°F. (*high*), or slightly lower for stuffed turkey. For birds weighing 3 lbs. or less, allow about the same time as for roasting, and for the time to roast each type of bird, see the preceding pages. For birds over 3 lbs., slightly less time is needed for rotisserie cooking than for roasting. The test for doneness is the same as for roasting, but without a meat thermometer. The drumstick is soft when pressed between protected fingers.

Broiling

Broiler-fryer chickens, Rock Cornish hens, 4 to 8-lb. turkeys, or turkey parts may be broiled. Split whole birds in half lengthwise, and hook the wing onto the back so as to expose the white meat to the heat. Place bird, skin side down, on broiler pan or shallow pan (not on the broiler rack). Brush with melted fat and season. Place turkey or chicken about 9 inches from the source of heat, or so that turkey begins to brown after 20 min. and is nicely browned and ready to turn in 40 min. Chicken should begin to brown in 15 min., and should be ready to turn in 25–30 min. Place Rock Cornish hen 7–9 inches from the source of heat, or so it is ready to turn in 15 min.

Then turn skin side up, baste with drippings or brush with additional fat and broil about as long as before turning, basting frequently to brown and cook evenly. The bird is done when the drumstick twists easily in the thigh joint and the breast meat near the shoulder is fork-tender. The total broiling time should be about 1¼–1½ hrs. for turkey, 45–60 min. for chicken, and 30 min. for Rock Cornish hen.

Pan-Frying

Rock Cornish hens (split in half lengthwise), cut-up chicken, duckling or turkey parts may be pan-fried. Shake several pieces of bird in a bag with seasoned flour. Chicken pieces may be dipped in milk before coating with flour, if desired, and the milk used later for preparing gravy.

Heat ¼ inch of fat in skillet (½ inch for turkey), add large pieces of bird first, and slip in smaller pieces as the large ones brown. Keep turning pieces to brown and cook them evenly. Pieces should be browned in 15–20 min. Then reduce heat and add 2 tbsp. water for turkey and also for other birds if the skillet cannot be very tightly covered. Reduce heat, cover tightly and cook until thickest pieces are fork-tender, turning once or twice to insure even cooking. After covering, turkey requires 45–60 min. cooking, young chicken 15–20 min. and Rock Cornish hen about 15 min. For a crisper serving, leave uncovered the last 10 min. of cooking for all birds except Rock Cornish hens, and the last 5 min. for these.

While poultry cooked this way is usually called "fried," this is really a braising method, since the skillet is covered during the second half of the cooking and so the bird is cooked in steam.

Oven-Frying

Chicken.—Coat pieces of chicken with seasoned flour and brown in hot fat, as for pan-frying (see above). When lightly browned, arrange pieces, one layer deep, in shallow baking pan. The pieces should cover the bottom of the pan but should not be crowded. For each chicken, spoon 2 tbsp. melted butter or margarine and 2 tbsp. broth or milk over it. Cook in moderate oven, 350°F. for 35–45 min., or until fork-tender, turning once or twice during cooking, to brown and crisp evenly.

Turkey.—Coat pieces of turkey with seasoned flour and brown in hot fat, as for pan-frying. For a 5-lb. turkey, melt 1 c. butter or margarine in shallow baking pan, in moderate oven, 350°F. Place turkey pieces in pan, turning to coat all sides with butter or margarine, then leave pieces with skin down. Pieces should cover bottom of pan but should not be crowded. Bake at 350°F. for 45 min., then turn skin side up and bake about 45 min. longer, or until thickest pieces are fork-tender.

Deep-Fat Frying

Only very tender chickens, not more than 1½ lbs., can be deep-fat fried. Coat chicken pieces in fritter batter or as desired, and lower a few pieces at a time into a kettle of deep fat at 350°F. Fry until golden brown, about 20 min., or until the thickest pieces are fork-tender. Drain on absorbent paper. It is advisable to hold the drained pieces in a single layer in a pan in a slow oven, 325°F. for about 20 min., to be sure the meat is cooked well to the bone.

COOKING LESS TENDER BIRDS

Fricassee or Stew

Stewing hens or fowl may be prepared this way, so may other mature birds. The bird may be cooked whole but it is usually disjointed.

For brown fricassee or stew, first dredge the pieces in seasoned flour and brown in hot fat in skillet, as for pan-frying (see p. 299).

Place pieces in kettle and cover with boiling water. Add ½ tsp. salt per pound of bird, and other seasonings as desired. Cover tightly, bring to boil, then reduce heat and simmer until thickest pieces are fork-tender, about 2 hrs. Vegetables may be added toward end of cooking, if desired. If pieces were not browned before simmering, they may be drained when tender, dredged in flour and browned in hot fat in skillet, and such pieces will be crisp for serving.

Strain broth if desired, and skim off excess fat. Add water or milk, if necessary to give the desired amount of stock for gravy, and thicken, using scant 2 tbsp. flour per cup of stock.

Braising

Any mature birds may also be braised. Follow instructions for pan-frying poultry, but allow extra time for cooking after skillet is covered, to have thickest parts fork-tender.

POULTRY GIBLETS

Liver may be broiled or fried to serve with broiled or fried poultry, but other giblets (heart and gizzard) should be cooked before combining with other ingredients for use in recipes.

Wash giblets thoroughly and place heart and gizzard (with neck, if desired) in saucepan, and cover with water, adding seasonings as desired. Bring rapidly to boil, skim off any froth, cover and turn heat low to keep water just simmering. Cook until fork-tender, 1½– 3 hrs., depending on size and tenderness of poultry. Add liver 10–30 min. before heart and gizzard are done.

Trim off any gristle, cool meat and broth separately, and chop or grind meat for use in recipes. Use broth for making gravy, sauce or soup.

COOKING POULTRY IN PRESSURE SAUCEPANS

For cooking poultry in pressure saucepans, follow the manufacturer's instructions.

RECIPES AND MENUS

Chicken

Company fare, or holiday feasting:

Roast Chicken with Oyster Stuffing   *Yield:* 5-6 servings
and Gravy

1 frozen, roasting chicken, thawed   oyster stuffing (see below)

Rub body cavity of the chicken with salt and prepare the bird for roasting. Fill the body cavity with oyster stuffing. Truss the chicken and place in roasting pan, breast side down. Roast according to directions, p. 297. Prepare gravy from pan drippings, p. 199.

Oyster Stuffing

1 can (12 oz.) frozen oysters, thawed   ⅛ tsp. pepper
4 c. soft bread crumbs, cut in cubes   2 tbsp. chopped onion
½ tsp. sage or poultry seasoning   ½ c. diced celery
½ tsp. salt   ⅓ c. butter or margarine

Drain oysters and cut them in small pieces. Combine bread crumbs with seasonings and mix well. Cook onion and celery in hot butter until tender, but not brown. Add oyster mixture to onion and celery mixture just long enough to heat through, then add to bread crumb mixture.

Dinner: *Pineapple-Grapefruit Juice*—Roast *Chicken* with *Oyster* Stuffing and Gravy, Buttered *Peas*, Mashed Potatoes, Assorted Relishes —*Strawberry* Cream Roll, p. 416.

A famous Italian recipe, to prepare in your own kitchen:

Chicken Cacciatore   *Yield:* 4–6 servings

1 frozen fryer (2–2½ lbs.) disjointed, thawed
¼ c. flour
1½ tsp. salt
speck pepper
3 tbsp. fat or salad oil
½ c. minced onion
½ c. chopped green pepper

2 peeled garlic cloves, minced
1 can (6 oz.) tomato sauce
1¾ c. canned tomatoes (or about 5 medium, fresh ones)
¼ tsp. thyme
dash cayenne
¼ c. Chianti wine
¼ tsp. ground allspice

Dredge pieces of chicken in flour seasoned with salt and pepper, and sauté in hot fat in skillet or Dutch oven, until golden brown on all sides. Add all remaining ingredients and mix. Cover and simmer gently 20–30 min., or until chicken is tender. Turn chicken out on serving plate and pour sauce over it.

Dinner: *Chicken* Cacciatore with Spaghetti, Tossed Green Salad with French Dressing, *Rolls—Strawberry* Chiffon Pie, p. 417.

Golden brown chicken, in luscious sour cream gravy:

Smothered Chicken   *Yield:* 4–6 servings

1 frozen fryer (2–2½ lbs.), disjointed, thawed
¼ c. seasoned flour

¼ c. fat
1 c. sour cream

Dredge chicken pieces in seasoned flour and brown in hot fat on all sides. Add sour cream and cover closely. Bake in moderate oven, 350°F. about 45 min., or until tender. If necessary, add flour or milk to gravy, before serving, to give desired consistency.

Dinner: Smothered *Chicken, Rissole Potatoes,* Buttered *Lima Beans,* Asparagus Aspic Salad, p. 328, with French Dressing—*Loganberry* Pinwheels, p. 419.

A recipe with a Latin flavor . . . exotic but easy:

Chicken Marengo   *Yield:* 4 servings

1 frozen fowl (4 lbs.), disjointed, thawed
½ c. flour
1½ tsp. salt
⅛ tsp. pepper
¼ c. fat
12 small, white onions, cooked until barely tender
2 garlic cloves, minced

¼ lb. mushrooms (1 c. sliced) or 1 can (4 oz.)
¼ c. butter or margarine
2 tbsp. flour
½ c. water
¼ c. sherry wine
4 fresh tomatoes, diced, or 1 c. drained canned tomatoes

Dredge chicken pieces in ½ c. flour seasoned with salt and pepper and saute in hot fat in skillet. Add a small amount of water, cover and simmer about 2 hrs., or until chicken is tender. Combine onions, garlic cloves, mushrooms and butter in small saucepan and cook slowly about 15 min., stirring occasionally. Add flour to mushroom mixture and blend well, then add water, sherry wine and tomatoes and cook until thickened, stirring. Cover and simmer about 10 min.

Turn chicken out on serving platter and cover with sauce.

Dinner: *Chicken* Marengo, Buttered *Squash, Asparagus* Hollandaise, p. 329, Celery and Carrot Strips—*Peach* Melba, p. 426.

A golden sauce, delicate and savory, makes this a favorite:

Chicken à la King   *Yield:* 8 servings

1 frozen fowl (4 lbs.)
3 tbsp. butter or margarine
¼ lb. mushrooms (1 c. sliced), or 1 can (4 oz.)
1 tbsp. green pepper, cut in strips
¼ c. flour
½ tsp. salt
few grains cayenne

1 c. chicken broth
1 c. milk (or part cream)
2 egg yolks, slightly beaten
1 tbsp. chopped pimiento
1 tbsp. chopped parsley, or 1 tsp. dried parsley
2 tbsp. sherry wine, if desired

Cook chicken in simmering water until tender, remove meat from bones and cut into cubes. (Or use left-over chicken.) There should be about 3 c. cubed chicken. Place butter in top of double boiler, melt it over direct heat, add mushrooms and green pepper and cook for 5 min. Add flour, salt and cayenne and mix well. Add chicken broth and milk slowly, stirring, and cook over low heat, stirring until thickened. Pour a little of this hot mixture over egg yolks, then return to double boiler and cook over hot water about 2 min., stirring. Add chicken, pimiento, parsley and sherry wine, stirring enough to distribute ingredients evenly. Serve as soon as chicken is heated.

Luncheon or Supper: *Chicken* à la King in *Patty Shells, Green Peas,* Watercress Salad and French Dressing—*Ice Cream* with *Blueberries.*

Herbs, spices and red wine give flavor to a meal-in-a-dish:

Chicken Country Style   *Yield:* 6 servings

1 frozen fowl (4–5 lbs.), disjointed, thawed
⅛ tsp. powdered marjoram
few grains mace
seasoned flour
1½ c. frozen, diced carrots, thawed
¼ c. fat
1 pkg. (10 oz.) frozen lima beans, thawed
½ bunch celery, diced
1 lb. small white onions, peeled
½ lb. mushrooms (or 8-oz. can mushrooms, with liquid)
1 c. water
2 whole cloves
1 tsp. salt
1 bay leaf
1 c. domestic Burgundy wine
pinch of thyme

Dredge each piece of chicken in seasoned flour and brown all sides in hot fat until golden. Transfer chicken to large casserole or baking dish and add celery and onions. Drain fat from pan in which chicken was browned, add water, cloves, bay leaf, thyme, marjoram and mace and boil 5 min. Strain and pour the liquid over the chicken. Cover and bake in slow oven, 300°F. about 1½ hrs. Remove any excess fatty layer from top.

Add vegetables, salt and wine and return to oven but increase temperature to 400°F., cover and bake 1 hr. longer or until chicken and vegetables are tender.

Dinner: *Chicken* Country Style, Hot *Baking Powder Biscuits,* Cucumber and Red Onion Salad—*Peach Ice Cream* with *Raspberries.*

———————————

Curry biscuits transform an old favorite into a gourmet's delight:

Chicken Pie with Curry Biscuits   *Yield:* 6-8 servings

1 frozen fowl (4 lbs.), disjointed, thawed
½ tsp. salt per lb. of chicken
2 medium onions, sliced
1 c. diced celery
3 tbsp. minced parsley, or 1 tbsp. dried parsley

¼ lb. mushrooms (1 c. sliced) or 1 can (4 oz.)
3 tbsp. fat
3 tbsp. flour
curry biscuit dough (see below)
    parsley or water cress

Place chicken in pan, add salt and boiling water to cover. Cover tightly and simmer until tender, about 2 hrs. Drain, cool slightly and bone chicken. Add onions, celery and parsley to stock and simmer 15 min., then strain and reserve stock. Sauté mushrooms in hot fat 5 min., stir in flour carefully, add 2½ c. stock gradually and cook until thickened, stirring. Add chicken and vegetables and bring to a boil, then pour into greased, large casserole or baking dish.

Top with curry biscuit dough (see below) and bake in hot oven, 425°F. 15–20 min., or until biscuits are done, and garnish with parsley.

Curry Biscuit Dough

2 c. flour
2 tsp. curry powder
3 tsp. baking powder
1 tsp. salt

½ c. shortening
$^2/_3$–¾ c. milk
paprika

Prepare biscuit dough (see directions, p. 197), sifting curry powder with other dry ingredients. (Or if preferred, stir curry powder

A rich cream sauce including mushrooms and chives, topped with fried chicken breasts and served with rice . . . delicious party fare

into 2 c. biscuit mix and add milk.) Roll dough to about ½-inch
thickness and cut into 12–16 biscuits. Sprinkle each biscuit with
paprika.

Luncheon or Supper: *Chicken* Pie with Curry Biscuits, *Green Bean*
and Celery Salad, p. 334—*Raspberry* Cream Pudding, p. 405.

An especially fine salad for a company luncheon:

Chicken Salad de Luxe   *Yield:* 6-8 servings

1 frozen fowl (4 lbs.), disjointed,   2 tbsp. chopped, mixed pickles
  thawed   2 hard cooked eggs, sliced
1 c. sliced celery   ¾ c. mayonnaise
½ c. toasted almonds, sliced   2 tbsp. capers, if desired
2 tbsp. chopped, stuffed olives   lettuce or other salad greens
2 tbsp. chopped, ripe olives

Cook chicken in simmering water until tender, remove meat from
bones and cut into small cubes. There should be about 3 c., and
left-over chicken can be used, if preferred. Chill thoroughly. Add
remaining ingredients except salad greens, and mix lightly. Serve
on salad greens.

Luncheon or Supper. *Cream of Potato Soup*—*Chicken* Salad de
Luxe, Spiced Crab Apple, Hot *Baking Powder Biscuits*—Coconut
Peach Pie, p. 400.

Hearty and savory, a chicken stew which is a meal in itself:

Brunswick Stew   *Yield:* 6 servings

1 frozen fowl (4–5 lbs.), disjointed 1 pkg. (10 oz.) frozen okra (prefer-
  and thawed   ably cut), thawed
2 tsp. salt   speck pepper
¼ c. chopped onion   1 tsp. Worcestershire sauce
1 No. 2 can tomatoes (2½ c.)   ½ tsp. marjoram
1 pkg. (10 oz.) frozen lima beans,   3 tbsp. flour
  thawed   ¼ c. water
1 pkg. (10 oz.) frozen cut corn,
  thawed

Barely cover fowl with water, add salt, cover, and simmer 1 hr.
Add onion and tomato and simmer about ½ hr. longer.

Lift chicken from hot stock, remove meat from bones, keeping it in fairly large pieces. Return meat to kettle with stock and add remaining ingredients except flour and water and cook ½ hr. longer, or until vegetables are cooked. Blend flour with water, add to stock and cook until thickened, stirring.

Dinner: Brunswick Stew (*Chicken, Lima Beans, Cut Corn, Okra*), *French-Fried Potatoes,* Tossed Green Salad—*Peach Strawberry* Compote, p. 401.

Here is a chow mein with chicken and pork . . . it is good, too, with shrimp or beef:

Chicken Chow Mein   *Yield:* 6-8 servings

1 frozen fowl (4 lbs.), disjointed, thawed
½ c. chopped celery
½ c. chopped green pepper
½ c. sliced onion
¼ lb. (1 c. sliced) mushrooms or 1 can (4 oz.)
¼ c. fat
1 c. sliced, cooked pork
⅛ tsp. pepper

2 tbsp. soy sauce
1 tsp. Worcestershire sauce
2 pkg. (16 oz. each) frozen chow mein vegetables, or 2 cans, 16 oz. each
1 c. chicken stock
1/3 shredded, blanched almonds, if desired
fried Chinese noodles

Cook chicken in simmering, salted water until tender. Then remove meat from bones and cut into small cubes. (There should be about 3 c. cubed meat.)

Cook celery, green peppers and onions in hot fat until tender. Add remaining ingredients except almonds and noodles, and simmer, covered, about 30 min., adding more liquid if necessary. Serve chow mein over noodles, sprinkle with almonds and serve additional soy sauce if desired. Or, if preferred, serve chow mein in deep platter, surrounded with noodles.

Dinner: *Cream of Shrimp Soup*—*Chicken* Chow Mein with Fried Noodles, Buttered *Broccoli,* Head Lettuce with Thousand Island Dressing—*Strawberry* Chiffon Pie, p. 417.

Named for the famed Tetrazzini, and delicious, as anticipated:

Chicken Tetrazzini   *Yield:* 6-8 servings

1 frozen fowl (4 lbs.), disjointed,   2 c. hot chicken broth
  thawed   1 c. light cream or top milk
½ c. slivered almonds, if desired   2 tbsp. sherry wine, if desired
½ lb. spaghetti   ¼ tsp. salt
½ lb. mushrooms (2 c. sliced), or 1   ⅛ tsp. pepper
  can (8 oz.)   ½ c. grated, Parmesan cheese
$1/_3$ c. fat   paprika
3 tbsp. flour   parsley

Cook chicken in simmering water until tender, remove meat from bones and cut it in small cubes. (There should be about 3 c.). Add almonds to chicken, if desired. Cook spaghetti in boiling salted water and drain thoroughly.

Sauté mushrooms in hot fat, add flour and blend well, then add hot chicken broth slowly and cook until thickened, stirring constantly. Add cream, sherry wine, salt and pepper.

Add half the sauce to the chicken and half to the spaghetti. Place spaghetti in greased casserole, and pour the chicken mixture into a "hole" made in the center of the spaghetti. Bake in moderate oven, 375°F. about 20 min., then sprinkle grated cheese over top of casserole and continue baking until cheese is browned and mixture is bubbly. Sprinkle with paprika and garnish with parsley.

Dinner: *Onion Soup—Chicken* Tetrazzini, *Mixed Vegetables* in Tomato Aspic Salad—Brandied *Peach* Parfait, p. 428.

Rich chicken flavor in a delicious soup:

Chicken Bisque   *Yield:* 3-4 servings

½ c. finely slivered cooked chicken   ⅛ tsp. salt
1 tbsp. butter or margarine   ⅛ tsp. paprika
1 tbsp. flour   whip topping whipped, or whipped
1½ c. chicken broth   cream
½ c. scalded milk

Melt butter, add flour and blend well, then add chicken broth and cook until thickened, stirring constantly. Add chicken, milk, salt and paprika and top with whipped cream.

> **Dinner:** *Chicken* Bisque—Broiled *Lamb Chops, Stuffed Baked Potatoes, Brussels Sprouts* in Pimiento Sauce, p. 346—*Orange* Charlotte Russe, p. 396.

A popular and fine use for left-over chicken:

Chicken Croquettes

Yield: 6 servings

2 c. cooked, ground (or finely chopped) chicken	approximately 1 c. thick cream sauce (see p. 200)
½ tsp. salt	flour
¼ tsp. celery salt	1 egg
1 tsp. lemon juice	1 tbsp. water
few drops onion juice	sifted, dry bread crumbs
1 tsp. finely chopped parsley	

To chicken add salt, celery salt, lemon juice, onion juice and parsley, then add just enough cream sauce so mixture can readily be shaped. Divide into 12 portions and shape as desired.

Roll each croquette in flour. Combine egg and water and roll croquettes in this mixture, and finally in bread crumbs. Cover the complete surface of the croquettes with each coating before rolling in the next one. Chill for at least 30 min.

Fry in deep fat at 375°F., a few croquettes at a time, 2–4 min., or until golden brown. Drain on absorbent paper.

> **Luncheon or Supper:** *Cream of Shrimp Soup*——*Chicken* croquettes with Mushroom Sauce, *Artichokes* Vinaigrette, p. 326, Assorted Relishes—*Orange* Soufflé, p. 399.

Refreshingly tart, this is perfect for a midsummer menu:

Jellied Chicken Salad

Yield: 6-8 servings

1 c. cooked, cubed chicken	1 tbsp. pimiento, cut in strips
1 pkg. lemon flavored gelatin	¼ c. sliced olives
2 c. hot water	2 hard cooked eggs, sliced
4 tsp. vinegar	crisp lettuce or water cress
½ c. chopped celery	

Dissolve gelatin in hot water and add vinegar, then chill until gelatin is syrupy. Add chicken, celery, pimiento, olives and eggs. Pour into individual molds or ring mold and chill until set. Unmold and serve on lettuce or water cress.

If preferred, chill a small amount of gelatin in bottom of mold first, then add slices of hard cooked egg and pimiento in decorative arrangement, and enough gelatin to cover. When set, add remaining ingredients and let stand until firm.

Luncheon or Supper: Jellied *Chicken* Salad in Individual Molds, Potato Chips, *Green Bean* and *Corn* Salad, p. 334—*Raspberry* Cream Roll, p. 416.

A special dish for a special luncheon:

Chicken Livers à la King   *Yield:* 6 servings
1 pkg. (8 oz.) chicken livers, thawed   1 c. chopped celery, cooked
¼ c. fat   1 tbsp. sherry wine, or ½ tsp. Wor-
¼ c. flour   cestershire sauce
2 c. milk (or 1 c. stock and 1 c.   ¼ c. stuffed olives, sliced
  cream)   3 hard cooked eggs, diced
½ tsp. salt   Melba toast baskets (see below)
¼ tsp. paprika   parsley

Dice livers and sauté them in hot fat, then add flour and blend well. Add milk, salt and paprika and cook until thickened, stirring constantly. Add celery, sherry and mix, then add olives and egg and combine lightly. Serve in Melba toast baskets and garnish with parsley.

Melba Toast Baskets

Cut very thin slices of fresh, white bread, remove crusts and butter lightly on both sides. Press slices into 3-inch muffin pans to make baskets, letting the corners protrude slightly. Toast in very slow oven, 250°–300°F. until crisp and delicately browned, 25–30 min.

Luncheon or Supper: *Chicken Livers* à la King in Melba Toast Baskets, Tossed Green Salad—*Cherry Upside Down Cake.*

Chicken livers and mushroom sauce with wine . . . fit for royalty:

Chicken Livers in Toast Baskets   *Yield:* 4 servings

½ c. thawed chicken livers
1 c. sliced mushrooms (or 1 can 4 oz.)
2 tbsp. butter or margarine
½ tbsp. flour
½ c. liquid (chicken or mushroom broth or both)

½ tsp. salt
speck pepper
2 tbsp. Madeira wine, if desired
Melba toast baskets (see p. 312)
parsley

Sauté chicken livers and mushrooms (drained, if canned) in hot fat, then blend in flour. Add liquid, salt and pepper and simmer 5 min., stirring. Add Madeira wine and serve in Melba toast baskets, garnishing with parsley.

Luncheon or Supper: *Chicken Livers* in Toast Baskets, Buttered *Broccoli Spears,* Head Lettuce with Thousand Island Dressing— *Chocolate Cake.*

Just right for an after-theater snack or Sunday night supper:

Chicken Livers in Scrambled Eggs   *Yield:* 4 servings

1 pkg. (8 oz.) chicken livers, thawed
2 tbsp. finely chopped onion
2 tbsp. fat
6 eggs
½ c. top milk or light cream

1 tsp. salt
¼ tsp. thyme
toast points
parsley
paprika

Sauté onion in hot fat until tender but not brown, add chicken livers and cook until livers are done (about 5 min.). Combine eggs, milk, salt and thyme and beat slightly.

Pour the egg mixture over livers, and cook over low heat, stirring gently and lifting cooked egg portions to allow uncooked portion to run under and cook. Serve on toast points, garnish with parsley and sprinkle with paprika.

Luncheon or Supper: *Chicken Livers* in Scrambled Eggs on Toast Points, *Green Peas, Asparagus* Aspic Salad, p. 328—*Mixed Fruit Cup, Brownies.*

This recipe has elegant simplicity:

Chicken Livers Provence   *Yield:* 4 servings

1 pkg. (8 oz.) chicken livers, thawed	speck pepper
2 tbsp. butter or margarine	4 eggs
¼ tsp. powdered basil	salt and pepper
½ tsp. salt	butter or margarine
	paprika

Sauté chicken livers in hot butter and while cooking add basil, ½ tsp. salt, and pepper. Chop livers slightly. Grease 4 shirred egg dishes or custard cups and put layer of chicken livers in each. Break an egg carefully into each dish, sprinkle with salt, pepper and paprika and dot with butter. Bake in slow oven, 300°F. until eggs are set (15–20 min.). Serve immediately.

> **Luncheon or Supper:** *Chicken Livers* Provence, Buttered *Artichoke Hearts,* Relishes, *Parkerhouse Rolls—Red Cherry* Pie, p. 383.

Fried Chicken with Cranberry-Orange Relish. *See p. 443.*

TURKEY

Sausage and cornflakes as the base for the dressing:

Roast Turkey with Sausage Stuffing *Yield:* About 1 serving per pound

1 frozen turkey (10–12 lbs.), thawed	of turkey
sausage stuffing (see below)	pan gravy, p. 199

Rub the body cavity of the turkey with salt and fill the cavity with sausage stuffing. Truss the turkey and roast according to directions, p. 297. Serve with pan gravy.

Sausage Stuffing

½ lb. sausage	1 tsp. salt
⅔ c. chopped onion	1 tsp. poultry seasoning
1½ c. diced celery	1 tsp. sage
6 c. cornflakes	1 c. chopped Brazil or other nuts
¼ tsp. pepper	

Sauté sausage, breaking up meat as it cooks, add onion and celery and cook until softened. Combine cornflakes and sausage with a fork, add remaining ingredients and toss lightly to mix well.

> **Dinner:** Roast *Turkey* with Sausage Stuffing, Gravy, Mashed Potatoes, *Peas and Carrots, Crookneck Squash, Cranberry-Orange Relish —Pumpkin* Chiffon Pie, 364.

A dinner menu combining turkey and rhubarb . . . winter and spring:

Turkey Casserole   *Yield:* 6 servings

2 c. coarsely diced, cooked turkey
3 c. left-over turkey stuffing
2 tbsp. flour
¾ tsp. salt

2 c. turkey broth (or 2 chicken
   bouillon cubes dissolved in 2 c.
   boiling water)

Spread half the turkey stuffing in the bottom of a casserole, add diced turkey and top with remaining stuffing. Prepare sauce from remaining ingredients and pour over stuffing. Bake in moderate oven, 350°F. about 30 min.

Dinner: *Turkey* Casserole, *Squash* Baked with *Pineapple,* p. 371, *Broccoli* with Vinaigrette Dressing, p. 326—*Rhubarb* Meringue Pie, p. 410.

A famous dish, for turkey or chicken, as you wish:

Turkey Divan   *Yield:* 4 servings

4 servings, sliced, cold turkey
1 pkg. (10 oz.) frozen broccoli spears
4 slices bread
melted butter or margarine
2 tbsp. butter or margarine

2 tbsp. flour
1 c. milk
½ tsp. salt
¼ tsp. paprika
¼ lb. sharp cheese, (1 c.) grated

Cook broccoli and drain. Meanwhile, toast bread slices on one side, place turkey slices on untoasted side of bread, and sprinkle with melted butter. Also, prepare cream sauce from butter, flour, milk and salt (see directions, p. 200).

Place bread slices with turkey on them under broiler and when turkey is heated, top it with broccoli. Just before serving, add paprika and cheese to cream sauce, heat just long enough to melt cheese; pour sauce over broccoli and turkey, and serve at once.

Luncheon or Supper: *Turkey* Divan with Broiled Tomatoes, *Grapefruit* and Avocado Salad, p. 386—*Devils Food Cake.*

With the authentic touch . . . apples and raisins . . . superb:

Curried Turkey in Rice Ring

Yield: 6 servings

2 c. coarsely diced, cooked turkey
   meat
3 tbsp. butter or margarine
2 medium apples, diced
½ c. chopped onions
1 medium carrot, cubed
½ c. coarsely diced celery
1 tsp. curry powder
1½ tbsp. flour

½ tsp. ginger
½ c. raisins
½ tsp. salt
1½ c. turkey broth (or 2 chicken
   bouillon cubes dissolved in 1½ c.
   boiling water)
1 tbsp. lemon juice
hot rice ring

Melt butter, add apples and vegetables and cook until tender. Add seasonings, raisins and flour and blend thoroughly, then add hot turkey broth slowly and cook until thickened, stirring. Add turkey and lemon juice and continue cooking until turkey is thoroughly heated. Serve in hot rice ring.

Luncheon or Supper: *Pineapple-Grapefruit Juice*—Curried *Turkey* in Rice Ring, *Peas* with Tiny Onions, p. 359—Frozen *Boysenberry* Cream, p. 376, *Chocolate Cookies.*

A delicious combination of flavors in a turkey salad:

Turkey Salad

Yield: 4 servings

1½ c. coarsely diced cooked turkey
   meat
1½ c. halved white grapes
½ c. slivered almonds, toasted and
   salted

¹/₃ c. mayonnaise
1 avocado pear, sliced, if desired
1 pimiento, cut in strips
crisp lettuce cups

Combine turkey meat, grapes, almonds, mayonnaise and half the avocado pear slices, and arrange in lettuce cups on serving plates. Decorate with remaining avocado slices and garnish with pimiento strips.

Luncheon or Supper: *Clam Chowder*—*Turkey Salad,* Potato Chips, *Cranberry-Orange Relish*—*Strawberry* Shortcake, p. 420.

Turkey Croquettes

Follow directions for Chicken Croquettes, p. 311, using cooked. ground turkey in place of chicken.

DUCKLING

For an extra special occasion, with reward for a little extra time in preparation:

Roast Duckling with Browned Rice Stuffing and Orange Sauce

Yield: 4 servings

1 frozen duckling (4–5 lbs.) thawed
1½ tsp. salt
browned rice stuffing (see below)
½ c. reconstituted, frozen orange juice

½ c. reconstituted, frozen grape juice
orange sauce (see below)

Rub cavity of duckling lightly with salt, and fill the cavity lightly with browned rice stuffing. Truss the duckling, place on rack breast side up and roast according to directions on p. 298. After 40 min. roasting, drain fat from pan, reserving it. Combine orange and grape juices, and baste the duckling occasionally with this juice, during remainder of roasting. Serve with orange sauce.

Browned Rice Stuffing

2 tbsp. chopped onion
2 tbsp. fat
1 c. raw rice
3 c. soup stock (water or bouillon cubes dissolved in boiling water may be substituted)

1½ tsp. salt
1 tsp. poultry seasoning
2 eggs, if desired

Sauté onion in hot fat, add rice and heat, stirring until rice is golden brown. Add remaining ingredients, cover, and cook slowly about 30 min. Remove from heat, and if desired, add slightly beaten eggs and mix lightly.

Orange Sauce

2 tbsp. duck fat (from roasting pan)
2 tbsp. flour
1½ c. liquid (use pan juices, not fat, and make up to 1½ c. with water)

½ c. reconstituted, frozen orange juice
½ tsp. salt
speck pepper

Place duck fat in small saucepan, add flour and blend well. Then add remaining ingredients and cook until thickened, stirring.

Dinner: *Shrimp* Cocktail—Roast *Duckling* with Browned Rice Stuffing and *Orange* Sauce, Buttered *Broccoli,* Mashed Potatoes, Tossed Green Salad with French Dressing—Butterscotch-Marshmallow Parfait, p. 428.

A fine holiday dinner for four:

Roast Duckling, Potato Stuffing and Sherry Wine Currant Sauce

Yield: 4 servings

1 frozen duckling (4–5 lbs.) thawed
½ tsp. salt
potato stuffing (see below)
¼ c. butter or margarine
1 tbsp. flour

4 oranges
1 c. reconstituted, frozen orange juice
sherry wine currant sauce (see below)

Rub body cavity of duckling lightly with salt, fill the cavity lightly with potato stuffing and truss the duckling. Place in roasting pan, breast side up and roast according to directions, p. 298. Melt 2 tbsp. butter, add flour, blend well and cook until this mixture bubbles. About 40 min. after putting duckling in oven, remove fat from roasting pan and spread the mixture of butter and flour over surface of duckling. Cut 2 oranges in ½-inch slices and fasten them over breast of duckling with toothpicks. Add orange juice to roasting pan, and every 15 or 20 min. during remainder of roasting, baste with pan drippings. Fifteen minutes before duckling is done, remove orange slices from top of duckling and baste every 5 min.

Cut remaining 2 oranges into ⅓-inch slices and sauté them in remaining 2 tbsp. butter. Serve duckling garnished with sautéed orange slices and with sherry wine currant sauce.

Potato Stuffing

1 qt. cold, diced baked potatoes (avoid overbaking)
½ c. melted butter or margarine

1 medium onion, grated
1 tsp. salt
pepper

Combine ingredients and toss lightly together.

Sherry Wine Currant Sauce

1 c. currant jelly
1 c. sherry wine
⅛ tsp. thyme

½ small bay leaf
1 tbsp. cornstarch
2 tbsp. water

Melt currant jelly in top of double boiler and add sherry wine, thyme and bay leaf. Blend cornstarch and water to smooth paste and add to other ingredients. Cook until slightly thickened and there is no flavor of raw starch. Remove bay leaf and serve.

Dinner: Roast *Duckling* with Potato Stuffing and Sherry Wine Currant Sauce, *Brussels Sprouts, Rolls—Lemon* Chiffon Pie, p. 388.

Braised duck in red wine . . . a special savor:

Braised Duck

	Yield: 4 servings
1 frozen duckling (4–5 lbs.), thawed	1½ c. red wine
2 tbsp. fat	4 carrots, cut in fingers
¼ tsp. poultry seasoning	4 onions, sliced
1 clove garlic	½ lb. (2 c.) mushrooms, sliced, or
1½ tsp. salt	1 can (8 oz.)

Cut duckling into serving pieces and brown in hot fat in large skillet. Add poultry seasoning, garlic, 1 tsp. salt, and wine, cover tightly and simmer until duckling is almost tender (about 1 hr.). Remove garlic. About 20 min. before serving, add carrots, onions and remaining salt and continue to cook. Add mushrooms about 10 min. before serving (draining the mushrooms if canned). Skim off excess fat and serve.

Dinner: *Cream of Potato Soup*—Braised *Duck,* Mustard *Cauliflower* and *Peas,* p. 350, *Sesame Seed Rolls*—*Raspberry* Sherbet, p. 407.

Try this with left-over turkey or chicken, too:

Duck Pilau

	Yield: 4 servings
left-over duck carcass, with meat	¾ c. finely chopped celery
5 c. water	1 tsp. grated onion
1 medium onion, chopped	1 c. thickened stock
celery leaves from half bunch	salt
⅔ c. rice	paprika
2 tbsp. butter or margarine	frozen peaches, thawed, if desired

Remove meat from left-over duck, and cut into small cubes (there should be 2 c.). Break the duck carcass apart and add water, chopped onion and celery leaves, cover and simmer about an hour. Strain, and bring stock to boil, then add rice and cook until tender. Strain, reserving stock and thickening 1 cup of it.

Melt butter, add chopped celery and grated onion and cook (covered) 5 min., then add thickened stock. Add cooked rice and duck, season with salt and paprika. Serve with peaches, if desired.

Dinner: *Duck* Pilau with *Peaches, Broccoli* with Curry Mayonnaise, p. 326, Tomato and Endive Salad—*Lemon* Soufflé, p. 390.

The French have their word for it . . . not stew or goulash, but ragoût:

Ragoût of Duck

Yield: 4 servings

2 c. cubed, cooked duck meat
1½ c. left-over gravy
½ tsp. Worcestershire sauce
½ c. chopped green peppers
¼ c. sliced stuffed olives

salt, if necessary
1 tbsp. currant jelly
¼ c. sherry or Madeira wine
hot toast, cornbread or muffins

Combine duck and gravy, add Worcestershire sauce, green peppers and olives, adding salt if necessary. Simmer 10 min., add currant jelly and stir until dissolved. Add wine and serve on toast, cornbread or muffins, as desired.

Dinner: Ragoût of *Duck* on Hot Cornbread, *Spinach* Soufflé, p. 368, Sliced Cucumbers in Sour Cream Dressing—*Strawberry* Chiffon Pie, p. 417.

Duck Croquettes

Follow directions for Chicken Croquettes, p. 311, using cooked, ground duck in place of chicken.

CHAPTER 16

Frozen Vegetables

COOKING FROZEN VEGETABLES

The secrets of success in cooking frozen vegetables are to cook them only until they are tender, and in the smallest amount of water that is practical. In this way, they keep their best flavor, texture and color, and have the maximum nutritive value. Vegetables are blanched in preparation for freezing, and this short precook softens them somewhat. Then the process of freezing, itself, softens them a little, too. As a result, the time to cook frozen vegetables is usually only about half as long as the time to cook corresponding fresh ones. According to modern standards of vegetable cookery, they should be tender but rather firm.

When frozen vegetables reach the table, they can have as high nutritive value as corresponding fresh ones. For a discussion of their nutritive value, see Chapter 2.

Boiling

One of the best innovations of recent years for frozen vegetables on the market is the "cook-in-bag" (or pouch) kind of pack. The unopened bag containing the frozen vegetables is immersed into boiling water, so the vegetables do not come in contact with the cooking water and no flavoring materials or nutrients are dissolved into it. And no flavors are lost from the bag during cooking.

There is another rather new, convenient style of vegetable pack on the market, called the "pour and store." These are bags containing vegetables in "loose pack"; and you can "pour" the amount you want from the bag directly into the boiling water, then reclose the bag and put it back in the freezer. To use these in recipes requiring certain weights or measures, estimate the portion to take from the bag.

In the more usual carton, the vegetables may be frozen as a "loose pack," but more often they are in a solid block. If these solid blocks are immersed into boiling water and given no further attention, the vegetables near the outside of the block will thaw and cook quickly, before those toward the center of the block are done. And by the time the pieces toward the center are done, the rest are overcooked. This can be prevented by gradually separating the pieces with a fork during the first 2 or 3 min. after adding the vegetables to the water. This is fairly easy to do with vegetables which are small pieces, like peas, lima beans, cut corn, mixed vegetables and others. It is more difficult to do with larger pieces like broccoli and asparagus spears without injuring the spears. And it is difficult to do with spinach and other greens.

Do Vegetables Need to Be Thawed?—Except for corn on the cob, frozen vegetables can be immersed into boiling water without thawing. If this is done, those frozen in a solid block must be separated in the early stages of heating, to insure uniform cooking, as described above.

Preliminary treatment of these solid blocks is often recommended. For vegetables which are in small pieces, like peas, cut corn, lima beans, mixed vegetables, okra and many others, you can knock the package several times against a hard surface, to separate the pieces.

Vegetables which are in larger pieces, like broccoli and asparagus spears and cauliflower, are best if thawed for an hour at room temperature or four hours in the refrigerator. Spinach and other greens are best if thawed this way, too. Then they will separate easily when immersed in boiling water.

Corn on the cob is the one vegetable which must be completely thawed before it is cooked. Otherwise, when the corn is tender and ready to eat, the cob itself is very cold. To thaw it, leave it in the unopened package at room temperature for 5 or 6 hrs.

How Much Water to Use?—The amount of water necessary for boiling frozen vegetables is very small, and this helps greatly in avoiding loss of flavor and nutrients, since the larger the proportion of water to vegetable, the larger the loss by solution into the water. The frost clinging to the vegetables provides some moisture, and in the short time of cooking not so much water is lost during evaporation, hence the recommended small amount. Use only as much as necessary to avoid the possibility of the vegetables going dry before they are cooked. For most vegetables, from 1/4 to 1/2 c. water is sufficient for boiling a pint (pound) of vegetables. More is needed for lima beans, since the starch in these absorbs a good deal of water. More is needed for soybeans, for some greens and for a few other vegetables. See the timetable for boiling vegetables.

Just How to Boil Them?—If the vegetables are in a solid block, select a saucepan of such a size and shape that the block will rest on the bottom of the pan, for this will hasten cooking. Immerse the vegetables into the recommended amount of boiling, salted water and cover the pan, keeping the heat turned high until the water has resumed boiling (this takes 3–6 min.), separating the pieces if necessary. Count the cooking time from when the water throughout the pan (not just around the edges) has resumed boiling. Then turn the heat down so that the water will boil gently, keeping the pan tightly covered to hold in the steam. Test for doneness and drain. Any remaining cooking water contains nutrients and flavoring materials dissolved from the vegetables, so use it, if you can, in sauces, gravies or soups. If the vegetables are

Time for Boiling Frozen Vegetables[1]

Vegetable	*Minutes to boil after water resumes boiling*[2]	Vegetable	*Minutes to boil after water resumes boiling*[2]
Artichoke hearts	5–10	Greens	
Asparagus		Beet	6–12
Cuts	4–8	Chard	8–10
Spears	8–10	Collard	18–22
Beans		Kale	10–20
Green	8–12	Mustard	10–15
Lima, large	12–16	Spinach	4–6
Lima, small	16–20	Turnip	15–20
Soy, green	10–15	Kohlrabi	8–10
Wax	5–8	Mixed vegetables	15–20
Broccoli		Okra	5–8
Cuts	4–7	Peas	
Spears	5–8	Black-eyed	40–45
Brussels sprouts	4–8	Green	5–8
Carrots		Peas and carrots	5–8
Diced	4–6	Potatoes, new	7–10
Sliced	10–12	Squash, crookneck, sliced	10–12
Baby, whole	10–12	Succotash	15–20
Cauliflower	4–6		
Corn			
Cut and whole kernel	2–5		
On the cob	3–8		

[1] For packages of 10–16 oz. add ½ tsp. salt. And add ¼–½ c. water except for: some greens, ½–1 c.; cauliflower, mixed vegetables, green soybeans and succotash, ½–1 c.; lima beans, 1–1½ c.; black-eyed peas, 2 c.; corn on the cob, water to cover.
[2] Allow 3–6 min. for water to resume boiling after vegetables are added. Times given are for boiling at sea level; slightly longer times are required at higher altitudes.

done before you are ready to serve them, drain and reheat them rather than cooking them beyond the time they are just tender.

If two packages of unthawed or partially thawed vegetables are to be cooked at one time, do not place one block on top of another, for this would delay thawing and cooking. Instead, place them both flat, on a pan with a large bottom (like a skillet), with a tightly fitting cover. You will not need double the amount of water for the two packages.

For a guide to the time for boiling vegetables, see chart on p. 323.

Steaming

Most vegetables can be cooked satisfactorily in a steamer if it has a very tightly fitting cover. Spinach and other greens should not be steamed, however, since they mat and do not cook uniformly. Vegetables need to be thawed enough to separate them into pieces before being placed in the steamer. Have the water in the lower part of the steamer boiling vigorously, count the cooking time from when the vegetables are placed in the steamer, cover tightly and keep the heat turned high to provide plenty of steam in the upper compartment.

The time for boiling vegetables in the above chart is also a guide to the time for steaming. But for steaming, allow at least as long as the maximum time for boiling each vegetable.

Cooking in a Pressure Saucepan

There are two advantages in cooking frozen vegetables in a pressure saucepan—the short time of cooking, and the very small amount of water required. However, even when boiled, frozen vegetables do not take long to cook, so some authorities feel there is not much to be said in favor of using a pressure saucepan. Also, there is no way of testing the vegetables to know exactly when they are done, and an extra minute in the pressure saucepan overcooks them more than an extra minute in boiling water.

For directions for cooking frozen vegetables in pressure saucepans, follow the instructions provided with your pressure saucepan.

Pan-Frying

For this method, it is well to thaw any vegetables which are frozen in a solid block, enough to separate the pieces. Place the vegetables in a heavy skillet to which 1–3 tbsp. fat have been added, cover and cook over moderate heat, stirring occasionally. Cook until tender. For some vegetables the cover may be removed toward the end of cooking, to allow excess water to evaporate.

Baking

This is a good method to use for any frozen vegetable, and it is especially convenient if you happen to be using the oven at 350° or 375°F. for other purposes. It is best to thaw the vegetables so they can be separated into pieces, then place them in a greased casserole. Add 2–3 tbsp. butter or margarine and ½ tsp. salt per pint (pound) package. Cover and bake at 350° or 375°F. At 350°F., most vegetables require 45–60 min., and at 375°F., 35–50 min. For green soybeans, lima beans, and succotash, allow the maximum time, and to these add ½ c. water. Stir several times during baking, to heat evenly, and test the vegetables to decide when they are done.

Frozen corn on the cob is best when cooked in the oven. It needs to be completely thawed first (allow 5–6 hrs. at room temperature in the unopened package). Then remove any frost from the ears, brush them with softened butter or margarine and place them on a baking sheet or pan or foil, in the oven at 400°F. Allow about 20 min. to bake, turning the cobs once or twice during baking. They will really "roast" and be slightly browned, and in the oven the corn dries out just enough to lose any tendency to sogginess. Cobs of corn which were frozen individually in aluminum foil can be baked in the foil, and in this way they retain their full flavor.

In a Double Boiler

Frozen vegetables which were cooked and mashed before freezing are best when reheated in the top of the double boiler. This includes winter squash, pumpkin, mashed potatoes or sweet potatoes. If these are not thawed, cutting them into 1-inch cubes will hasten heating. Some other cooked vegetables like Harvard beets should be reheated in the top of the double boiler. If reheated without thawing, allow about 40 min., stirring occasionally and seasoning as desired. For emergencies, squash may be thawed in a small, covered skillet or saucepan over low heat in 10–15 min., or in a hot oven, 400°F., in about 30 min.

RECIPES AND MENUS

ARTICHOKE HEARTS

Artichokes in a sauce that makes any vegetable elegant:

Artichoke Hearts in Curry   *Yield:* 3–4 servings
Mayonnaise

1 pkg. (9 oz.) artichoke hearts   curry mayonnaise (see below)

Boil artichoke hearts until tender, and drain. Turn vegetables into serving dish, and add curry mayonnaise.

Curry Mayonnaise

2 tbsp. butter   ½ c. mayonnaise
⅛ tsp. finely minced garlic   1 tsp. lemon juice
½ tsp. curry powder

Melt butter in top of double boiler and stir in garlic and curry powder. Add mayonnaise and keep over hot water until ready to serve. Just before serving, add lemon juice.

Note: This sauce is particularly suited, too, for serving over broccoli or asparagus spears, cauliflower, green beans and many other vegetables.

> **Dinner:** Broiled *Lobster Tails,* p. 275, Mashed Potatoes, *Artichoke Hearts* in Curry Mayonnaise, Curly Endive and Bermuda Onion Salad—Toasted *Cherry* Chiffon Pie, p. 382.

Vinaigrette sauce . . . a perfect companion for vegetables, hot or cold:

Artichoke Hearts Vinaigrette   *Yield:* 3–4 servings

1 pkg. (9 oz.) frozen artichoke   vinaigrette dressing (see below)
hearts

Boil artichoke hearts until tender and drain. Serve with vinaigrette dressing. The vegetable and the dressing may both be either hot or cold.

Vinaigrette Dressing

½ c. salad oil   1 tbsp. chopped pimiento
½ tsp. salt   1 tbsp. chopped cucumber pickle
⅛ tsp. pepper   1 tbsp. chopped green pepper
speck cayenne   ½ tbsp. chopped parsley
¼ tsp. paprika   ½ tbsp. chopped onion or chives
3 tbsp. vinegar

Combine salad oil, salt, pepper, cayenne and paprika and add vinegar slowly, beating thoroughly. Add chopped vegetables. Serve cold, or heat in top of double boiler and serve hot.

Note: This dressing is suited for serving over many cold vegetables, as salad, or for serving hot over hot vegetables.

> **Dinner:** *Cream of Shrimp Soup*—Broiled *Lamb Chops, French-Fried Potatoes,* Hot *Artichoke Hearts* Vinaigrette——*Strawberry* and *Rhubarb* Sherbet, p. 411.

This is light and very tasty fare:

Artichoke Hearts and Grapefruit Salad

Yield: 6–8 servings

1 pkg. (9 oz.) frozen artichoke hearts

1 pkg. (13½ oz.) grapefruit sections, thawed

pimiento strips
French dressing
crisp lettuce cups

Boil artichokes until tender. Drain and chill thoroughly, and if convenient, marinate them in French dressing in the refrigerator 1–2 hrs. before serving.

Drain grapefruit sections thoroughly. Arrange artichoke hearts alternately with grapefruit sections in crisp lettuce cups. Garnish with pimiento strips and serve with French dressing.

> **Dinner:** *Chicken* Cacciatore, p. 303, Buttered *Carrots, Artichoke Hearts* and *Grapefruit* Salad——*Chocolate Cream Pie.*

Artichoke Hearts Hollandaise. *See p. 329.*

ASPARAGUS
(Spears and Cuts)

A delightful combination of two favorites:

Asparagus in Mushroom Sauce

Yield: 6 servings

1 pkg. (10 oz.) asparagus spears or cuts

mushroom sauce, p. 328

½ c. grated Cheddar cheese
buttered crumbs

Cook asparagus and drain, reserving the liquid. Place asparagus in shallow, greased baking dish, cover asparagus with mushroom sauce, sprinkle with cheese and top with buttered crumbs. Bake in moderate oven, 375°F., until heated through and crumbs are brown (about 10 min.)

Mushroom Sauce

¼ lb. (1 c.) sliced mushrooms, or 1 can (4 oz.)
5 tbsp. butter
5 tbsp. flour

1 tsp. salt
2 c. liquid (use liquid from asparagus and mushrooms, and milk to give 2 c.)

Sauté mushrooms in hot butter 2–3 min. Add flour and salt and blend well, then add liquid slowly, stirring. Cook gently until mixture thickens, stirring constantly.

Dinner: Savory Broiled *Scallops*, p. 281, Baked Potato, *Asparagus* in Mushroom Sauce, Cole Slaw——*Raspberry* Pie, p. 406.

Aspic, always a favorite, is very special with asparagus:

Asparagus in Aspic Salad

1 pkg. (10 oz.) frozen asparagus spears or cuts
1 pkg. (10 oz.) frozen mixed vegetables
1 pkg. lemon flavored gelatin
1 c. hot water

Yield: 8 servings

3 tbsp. vinegar
¾ c. water
½ tsp. salt
¼ c. pimiento, cut in shreds
crisp lettuce
French dressing or mayonnaise

Cook and drain asparagus and mixed vegetables. Dissolve gelatin in hot water, then add vinegar, cold water and salt. Chill until slightly thickened, in a large ring mold or in individual molds. Add pimiento and fold in asparagus and mixed vegetables. The gelatin at this time should be thick enough to keep the vegetables distributed through it. If asparagus spears are used, they may need to be cut to fit the mold. Chill until firm. Then unmold on lettuce and serve with French dressing or mayonnaise.

If preferred, pour about one-fourth of the gelatin mixture into the bottom of the mold first, and when partly set arrange some of the asparagus and pimiento decoratively in it. Chill until firm, then add the rest of the gelatin and vegetables.

Dinner: Pan-Broiled *Club Steaks, French-Fried Potatoes,* Buttered *Cauliflower,* Asparagus Aspic Salad——Frozen *Orange* Cream, p. 395.

Buttered asparagus spears and stuffed tomatoes, served with a tasty shrimp sauce make an attractive luncheon menu

An infallible recipe for Hollandaise Sauce:

Asparagus Hollandaise   *Yield:* 4 servings
1 pkg. (10 oz.) asparagus spears   Hollandaise sauce (see below)

   Cook asparagus until tender, and drain.   Serve it hot, with Hollandaise sauce.

Hollandaise Sauce
½ c. butter or margarine   ¼ tsp. salt
2 egg yolks   speck cayenne
½–1 tbsp. lemon juice

   Divide butter into three portions.   Place one portion in heavy bowl over hot water and add egg yolks and lemon juice.   Stir constantly with wire whisk or fork until butter melts. Keep water hot but not boiling, and do not let hot water touch bottom of bowl. Add a second portion of butter and stir until thick, and as mixture thickens further, add third portion of butter. At once remove from heat, and beat with wooden spoon until glossy. Season and serve at once.

Note: This sauce is also appropriate for serving with broccoli spears, cauliflower, green beans and many other vegetables.

Dinner: Pan-Fried *Ham Slices, Potato Puffs, Asparagus* Hollandaise, Relishes—*Strawberries* with Custard Sauce.

A subtle blending of delicious flavors:

Asparagus with Egg Sauce   *Yield:* 4–6 servings

1 pkg. (10 oz.) frozen asparagus   1 c. liquid (use water from cooking
   spears or cuts   asparagus, and make up to 1 c.
2 tbsp. melted butter or margarine   with milk)
2 tbsp. flour   2 hard-cooked eggs, diced
1/4 tsp. salt   1 tbsp. pickle relish or capers
1/8 tsp. paprika

Cook asparagus and drain, reserving liquid. Combine butter, flour, salt and paprika and add liquid slowly, stirring. Cook sauce until thickened, stirring constantly. Add hard-cooked eggs and pickle relish or capers. Pour egg sauce over hot asparagus and serve at once.

Dinner: Broiled *Ham Slices*, Baked Sweet Potatoes, *Asparagus* with Egg Sauce, Waldorf Salad—*Orange* Cake Pudding, p. 395.

An Irish name . . . but it is French-fried, just the same:

Asparagus Shillelaghs   *Yield:* 4 servings

1 pkg. (10 oz.) asparagus spears   1/2 tsp. salt
3/4 c. flour   1 egg
1/2 tsp. baking powder   5/8 c. milk

Cook asparagus and drain. Sift flour, baking powder and salt together. Beat egg and milk together, add to flour mixture, and beat until smooth. Dip separate cooked asparagus spears into batter and fry in deep fat at 375°F., 3 or 4 at a time. Serve piping hot.

Dinner: *Pork* en Casserole, p. 246, *Asparagus* Shillelaghs, Tossed Salad——*Pound Cake* with *Peaches.*

An elegant way to treat asparagus:

Asparagus in Almond Sauce

1 pkg. (10 oz.) frozen asparagus spears or cuts	*Yield:* 3–4 servings
	2 tbsp. flour
1 can (4½ oz.) blanched almonds, chopped	½ tsp. salt
	speck pepper
2 tbsp. butter or margarine	milk

Cook asparagus and drain, reserving liquid. Brown almonds lightly in hot butter, blend in flour, salt and pepper. To liquid drained from asparagus, add milk to give 1 c. liquid and add this to almonds. Stir over low heat until thickened and serve over hot asparagus.

Dinner: *Corn Chowder,* p. 352—Broiled *Sirloin Steak,* Mashed Potatoes, *Asparagus* in Almond Sauce——*Deep Dish Apple Pie* à la Mode.

The perfect tea accompaniment, easy to prepare:

Asparagus Rolls

1 pkg. (10 oz.) frozen asparagus spears	*Yield:* 8–10 servings
	softened butter or margarine
	mayonnaise
1 thin slice of bread for each spear of asparagus	melted butter or margarine

Cook and drain asparagus. Trim crusts from bread, making slices square. Spread softened butter on one half of each slice, and spread mayonnaise on other half.

Cut asparagus spears to fit slices of bread, and place one spear on the end of slice which is spread with mayonnaise. Roll up as for rolled sandwiches (butter helps hold bread together in rolling). Fasten with toothpicks, if necessary. Brush outside of bread with melted butter and broil rolls until delicately browned. Remove toothpicks and serve hot.

Afternoon Tea: Assorted Tea Sandwiches, *Asparagus* Rolls, Hot Tea, *Raspberry Sherbet,* Mints and Nuts.

OTHER ASPARAGUS RECIPES

Shrimp and Asparagus Salad. *See p. 291.*
Asparagus with Curry Mayonnaise. *See p. 326.*
Asparagus Vinaigrette. *See p. 326.*

GREEN BEANS
(French Style and Cut)

Bland green beans, with a deviled sauce:

Deviled Green Beans
1 pkg. (9 oz.) frozen green beans
¾ c. sliced onion
3 tbsp. fat

Yield: 4–6 servings
1 tbsp. prepared mustard
1 tbsp. horseradish

Cook green beans until tender, and drain. Sauté onion in hot fat, add cooked green beans, mustard and horseradish. Combine well and serve hot.

Dinner: Broiled *T-Bone Steak, French-Fried Potatoes,* Deviled *Green Beans, Rhubarb* Salad Ring, p. 409—*Cake* and *Ice Cream.*

Mushrooms and green beans make good partners:

Green Beans with Mushrooms
1 pkg. (9 oz.) frozen green beans
¼ lb. mushrooms (1 c. sliced), or 1 can (4 oz.)

Yield: 4 servings
2 tbsp. butter or margarine
¼ tsp. salt

Cook green beans until tender and drain. Meanwhile, sauté mushrooms (drained if canned) in hot butter, adding salt. Combine hot green beans and sautéed mushrooms and serve.

Dinner: *Beef* Paprika, p. 222, *Corn on the Cob, Green Beans* with Mushrooms, Tossed Vegetable Salad—*Pineapple Pie.*

A succotash of corn with green beans instead of lima beans:

Kentucky Succotash in Casserole *Yield:* 6 servings

1 pkg. (10 oz.) frozen cut corn, 1 tsp. salt
  thawed speck pepper
1 pkg. (9 oz.) frozen green beans, 1 c. canned tomatoes
  thawed

Place corn in greased 1½-qt. casserole and sprinkle with half the salt. Add green beans and sprinkle with remaining salt, and pepper. Heat tomatoes and pour them over the vegetables. Cover casserole and bake in moderate oven, 350°F., until vegetables are tender, about 45 min. Stir about 15 min. before end of cooking, to combine vegetables well.

> **Dinner:** Stuffed *Round Steak,* p. 218, *CrinkleCut Potatoes,* Kentucky Succotash in Casserole *(Green Beans, Corn)*—*Blueberry* Pie, p. 308.

Even those who "don't like vegetables" will like this:

Green Bean Casserole *Yield:* 6 servings

1 pkg. (9 oz.) frozen cut green 1 tbsp. butter or margarine
  beans, thawed ½ tsp. salt
4 medium onions, chopped ⅛ tsp. paprika
2 medium green peppers, chopped buttered crumbs

Place vegetables in greased 1-qt. casserole, alternating layers of green beans and other vegetables. Include dots of butter, salt and paprika between layers, and dot the top with butter. Cover casserole and bake in moderate oven, 350°F., about 45 min. or until green beans are tender. About 15 min. before cooking is completed, remove cover and sprinkle buttered crumbs over vegetables. Finish baking uncovered, until crumbs are brown.

> **Dinner:** *Pork Chops* with Barbecue Sauce, p. 242, Mashed Potatoes, *Green Bean* Casserole, Tomatoes Stuffed with Cottage Cheese and Bermuda Onion—*Lemon* Soufflé, p. 390.

A happy combination, enlivened by an unusual dressing:

Green Bean and Celery Salad   *Yield:* 6 servings

1 pkg. (9 oz.) frozen green beans $^1/_3$ c. non-separating French
1 c. chopped celery   dressing
1 pimiento, cut in strips   hard-cooked eggs, quartered
2 tbsp. minced onions   crisp lettuce

Cook green beans until tender, drain and chill them. Add celery, pimiento and onion and marinate with French dressing. Serve on crisp lettuce, garnishing with hard-cooked eggs.

Luncheon or Supper: Tomato Juice——French *Beef*burgers, p. 230, *Green Bean* and Celery Salad——Baked *Cherry* Pudding, p. 384.

Contrasting colors and flavors make this appealing:

Green Bean and Carrot Salad   *Yield:* 6 servings

1 pkg. (9 oz.) frozen green beans   ½ c. sliced, raw young carrots
French dressing   ½ c. diced celery
1 medium onion, sliced   crisp lettuce

Cook green beans until tender, drain and chill them. When thoroughly chilled, marinate them with French dressing, adding onions, carrots and celery. Serve on lettuce.

Dinner: *Orange-Grape* Cocktail, p. 398——Broiled *Lamb Chops* with Mint Sauce, Parsley Buttered *New Potatoes,* p. 361, *Green bean* and Carrot Salad——*Pumpkin Pie.*

An unusual combination of vegetables with tangy dressing:

Green Bean and Corn Salad   *Yield:* 8 servings

1 pkg. (9 oz.) frozen green beans   ½ c. chopped celery
1 pkg. (10 oz.) frozen cut corn   1 pimiento, cut in strips
$^1/_3$ c. French dressing   ¼ c. chopped green pepper
1 tbsp. vinegar   crisp lettuce
1 tsp. minced onion

Cook green beans and corn separately, drain them and chill thoroughly. Combine remaining ingredients, then add green beans and corn, mix well, and chill. Serve on crisp lettuce.

Note: Lima beans may be used in place of green beans, if desired.

> **Dinner:** *Vegetable Soup—Loin End Pork Roast,* Browned Potatoes, *Apple Sauce, Green Bean* and *Corn* Salad—Baked *Cherry* Pudding, p. 384.

A fine blending of vegetable flavors:

Green Bean and Cauliflower Salad   *Yield:* 6 servings

1 pkg. (9 oz.) frozen green beans	tomato wedges
1 pkg. (10 oz.) frozen cauliflower	hard-cooked or deviled eggs
½ c. chopped celery	mayonnaise
French dressing	crisp lettuce

Cook green beans and cauliflower separately, until tender, drain and chill them thoroughly. Combine the chilled vegetables, add celery and marinate with French dressing. Serve on crisp lettuce with mayonnaise, and garnish with tomato wedges and egg.

> **Dinner:** Broiled *Rib Steak, French-Fried Potatoes, Squash* Baked with *Pineapple,* p. 371, *Green Bean* and *Cauliflower* Salad— *Lemon* Meringue Pie, p. 388.

Lamb Stew with Pimiento Pinwheels. *See p. 234.*

LIMA BEANS

Lima beans and corn, one of the American favorites:

Succotash   *Yield:* 6–8 servings

1 pkg. (10 oz.) frozen lima beans   butter or margarine
1 pkg. (10 oz.) frozen cut corn

Boil lima beans and corn separately, until tender, and drain. Then combine, add butter and additional seasoning if necessary, and serve.

> **Dinner:** Chinese *Beef* with Tomatoes and Noodles, p. 218, Succotash (*Lima Beans* and *Corn*), Spinach, Lettuce and Cheese Salad with Thousand Island Dressing—*Peach* Shortcake, p. 420.

Scalloped tomatoes with luscious lima beans:

Lima Beans and Tomatoes   *Yield:* 5–6 servings

1 pkg. (10 oz.) frozen lima beans   2 tsp. sugar
½ tbsp. chopped onion   ½ tsp. salt
2 tbsp. fat   speck pepper
1½ c. canned tomatoes   ⅔ c. soft bread crumbs

Cook lima beans until tender and drain. Sauté onion in hot fat until light brown. Add tomatoes, sugar, salt, pepper and bread crumbs, reheat and serve.

Dinner: Ham Loaf with Horseradish Sauce, Mashed Potatoes, *Lima Beans* and Tomatoes, Cole Slaw——*Strawberry* and *Peach* Compote.

This is a tasty, colorful combination:

Lima Beans and Celery   *Yield:* 5–6 servings

1 pkg. (10 oz.) frozen lima beans   ½ c. top milk or light cream
2½ c. diced celery   ½ tsp. salt
2 tbsp. chopped onion   ⅛ tsp. pepper
2 tbsp. chopped green pepper   1 tbsp. pimiento, cut in strips
2 tbsp. fat

Boil lima beans until tender and drain. Meanwhile, cook celery in boiling water until tender and drain. Also, sauté onion and green pepper in hot fat until light brown. Add lima beans and celery to sautéed vegetables. Add remaining ingredients, combine well and reheat.

Luncheon or Supper: *Chicken Livers* in Toast Baskets, p. 313, *Lima Beans* and Celery, Tomato and Cucumber Salad——*Ice Cream* with crisp *Lemon* Cookies, p. 391.

This is a quick and tasty scalloped vegetable:

Scalloped Lima Beans   *Yield:* 4 servings

1 pkg. (10 oz.) frozen lima beans   1 c. liquid (liquid from cooking
2 tbsp. flour   lima beans and enough milk
2 tbsp. butter or margarine   to make 1 c.)
½ tsp. salt   buttered bread crumbs

Boil lima beans until tender and drain, reserving liquid. Make medium cream sauce from flour, butter, salt and liquid (see directions, p. 200). (Or use canned condensed celery or mushroom soup, diluting to give consistency of medium sauce.)

Put layer of lima beans in 1-qt. casserole, add some of the cream sauce and cover with layer of buttered crumbs. Add alternating layers of lima beans, sauce and bread crumbs, topping with bread crumbs. Bake in moderately hot oven, 400°F., 20 min., or until crumbs are brown.

Dinner: *Pork Sausage Patties, Baked Stuffed Potato,* Scalloped *Lima Beans—Blueberry* Cottage Pudding, p. 379, with *Lemon* Sauce, p. 391.

Quickly prepared, and piping hot and savory, out of the oven:

Lima Bean Casserole　　　　　*Yield:* 6 servings

1 pkg. (10 oz.) frozen lima beans	1 tsp. salt
2 tbsp. minced onion	¼ tsp. pepper
2 tbsp. ketchup	1 c. soft bread crumbs
3 tbsp. melted butter or margarine	¼–½ c. chopped nuts, if desired
1 egg, beaten	crisp bacon, if desired

Boil lima beans until tender, drain and place in 1-qt. casserole. Combine remaining ingredients except bacon, then mix them with lima beans. Garnish top with crisp bacon, if desired. Bake in moderate oven, 350°F., about 25 min.

Dinner: Roast *Loin of Pork* with Gravy, Roast Brown Potatoes, *Lima Bean* Casserole, Tomato and Cucumber Salad—*Apple Pie* with Cheddar Cheese.

Flavored with originality . . . and curry:

Curried Lima Beans　　　　　*Yield:* 4 servings

1 pkg. (10 oz.) frozen lima beans	1 tsp. curry powder
1 medium onion, minced	2 tbsp. flour
2 tbsp. butter or margarine	½ tsp. salt
½ tsp. lemon juice	1 c. milk

Boil lima beans until tender and drain. Meanwhile, cook onion slowly in butter until tender. Combine lemon juice, curry powder, flour and salt and add these slowly to onion, blending until smooth. Add milk gradually, stirring, and cook until thickened, stirring constantly. Add sauce to hot lima beans and serve at once.

Dinner: Sautéed *Ocean Perch,* Baked Sweet Potatoes, Curried *Lima Beans,* Tossed Green Salad——*Raspberry* Shortcake, p. 420.

If you like a real peppery sauce try this one:

Barbecued Lima Beans   *Yield:* 4 servings

1 pkg. (10 oz.) frozen lima beans thawed

½ c. chopped onion

½ c. chopped green pepper

¼ c. fat

2 tbsp. brown sugar

2 tsp. prepared mustard (less if preferred)

1 tsp. Worcestershire sauce

1 tsp. salt

¾ c. ketchup

Heat onion and green pepper in hot fat, 2–3 min. Combine remaining ingredients, except lima beans, add to onion and green pepper mixture and simmer about 5 min.

Place lima beans in greased 1-qt. casserole, pour sauce over them and stir gently. Cover and bake in moderate oven, 350°F., about 40 min., uncover and stir gently, and continue baking, covered, until lima beans are done (total baking time about 1 hr.).

Dinner: Braised *Pork Chops,* Mashed Potatoes, Barbecued *Lima Beans,* Carrot and Raisin Salad——*Cherry Turnovers.*

This sauce will make lima beans the family favorite:

Lima Beans in Sour Cream Sauce   *Yield:* 3–4 servings

1 pkg. (10 oz.) frozen lima beans   sour cream sauce (see below)

Boil lima beans until tender, and drain. Meanwhile, prepare sour cream sauce. Pour hot sauce over hot lima beans and serve at once.

Sour Cream Sauce

2 tbsp. butter or margarine

½ tsp. salt

¾ tsp. dry mustard

1 tsp. molasses

¼ c. sour cream

2 tbsp. milk

¼ tsp. onion juice

Combine all ingredients in small saucepan, and just before serving time, heat to serving temperature.

> **Dinner:** Roast *Leg of Lamb,* Parsley Buttered Potatoes, *Lima Beans* in Sour Cream Sauce, *Grapefruit* and Avocado Salad, p. 386 *Neapolitan Ice Cream.*

OTHER LIMA BEAN RECIPES

Lamb and Lima Beans with Tomato Dumplings. *See p. 236.*
Chicken Country Style. *See p. 305.*
Brunswick Stew. *See p. 308.*
Welsh Rarebit Lima. *See p. 445.*

WAX BEANS

To arouse dormant appetites, try:

Golden Cheese Topped Wax Beans   *Yield:* 3–4 servings
1 pkg. (9 oz.) frozen wax beans $^1/_3$ c. grated American cheese
½ c. top milk or light cream

Boil the wax beans until tender and drain. Place beans in shallow baking dish, add milk and sprinkle cheese over them. Bake in hot oven, 425°F., about 15 min. or until cheese is melted and lightly browned.

> **Dinner:** *Grapefruit Juice*——Broiled *Lamb Chops,* Mashed Potatoes, Parsley Garnish, Golden Cheese Topped *Wax Beans,* Head Lettuce with Thousand Island Dressing——*Blueberry Pie.*

An unusual combination, seasoned to perfection:

Wax Beans, Corn and Green   *Yield:* 6–8 servings
  Pepper
1 pkg. (9 oz.) frozen wax beans   ¼ c. chopped onion
1 pkg. (10 oz.) frozen cut corn   ¼ c. chopped green pepper
3 tbsp. butter or margarine   ¼ tsp. salt

Cook the wax beans and corn separately, until tender, and drain. Sauté onion and green pepper in hot butter until tender. Then combine all ingredients, heat well and serve.

Dinner: *Vegetable Soup*——Braised *Pork Chops,* Rissole Potatoes, *Wax Beans,* Corn and Green Pepper——*Cherry* Cobbler, p. 381.

Bits of crisp bacon add savor to a bland vegetable:

Wax Beans with Bacon   *Yield:* 3–4 servings
1 pkg. (9 oz.) frozen wax beans   3 slices bacon, diced

Cook wax beans until tender, and drain.   Meanwhile, cook bacon until crisp and drain on absorbent paper.   Add bacon and 2 tbsp. bacon fat to hot wax beans, toss together lightly and serve.

Dinner: *Tangerine Juice*——Meat Loaf (*Beef*), *Potatoes au Gratin, Wax Beans* with Bacon, Tomato Aspic Salad——*Butterscotch Cream Pie.*

All delicate flavors, but blending for a fine recipe:

Creamed Wax Beans, Eggs and   *Yield:* 5 servings
   Mushrooms
1 pkg. (9 oz.) frozen wax beans   2 c. top milk or light cream
½ lb. mushrooms (2 c. diced), or   4 hard-cooked eggs, quartered
   1 can (8 oz.)   1 tsp. salt
¼ c. butter or margarine   toast baskets, p. 312
¼ c. flour

Cook wax beans and drain.   Meanwhile, sauté mushrooms (drained, if canned) in hot butter, then sprinkle flour over them and blend well.   Add milk to mushrooms and bring to boil, stirring, and heat until thickened, stirring constantly.   Add wax beans, eggs and salt.   Serve in toast baskets.

Dinner: Tomato Juice——Jiffy *Fish* Fry, p. 256, Creamed *Wax Beans,* Eggs and Mushrooms, Cole Slaw with Green Pepper Garnish——*Lemon Turnovers.*

This is certainly a quick and easy one, and delicious, too:

Wax Beans and Mushrooms   *Yield:* 4 servings
1 pkg. (9 oz.) frozen wax beans   3 tbsp. butter or margarine
½ lb. mushrooms (2 c. sliced), or   ¼ tsp. salt
   1 can (8 oz.)

Cook wax beans until tender, and drain. Meanwhile, sauté mushrooms (drained, if canned) in hot butter. Add hot wax beans to mushrooms, add salt and serve hot.

> **Luncheon or Supper:** Savory *Shrimp*, p. 286, *Wax Beans* and *Mushrooms, Artichoke Hearts* and *Grapefruit* Salad, p. 327— *Brownies* á la Mode.

From Louisiana kitchens to you:

Creole Wax Beans   *Yield:* 4 servings
1 pkg. (9 oz.) frozen wax beans   1 small carrot, grated
2 tbsp. butter or margarine   1¼ c. canned tomatoes
1 medium onion, chopped   ¾ tsp. salt
1 stalk celery, chopped   speck pepper

Melt butter in saucepan, add onion, celery and carrot and cook slowly until tender, about 5 min. Add tomatoes, salt, pepper and wax beans and cook until beans are tender.

> **Dinner:** Smothered *Chicken*, p. 303, *Crinkle-Cut Potatoes*, Buttered *Spinach*, Creole *Wax Beans*, *Bran Muffins—Vanilla Ice Cream* with *Raspberry* Sauce, p. 430.

BROCCOLI
(Spears and Cuts)

Broccoli with a bit of onion and lemon juice . . . very tasty:

Broccoli with Onion Sauce   *Yield:* 3–4 servings
1 pkg. (10 oz.) frozen broccoli   speck salt
1 tbsp. minced onion   speck pepper
3 tbsp. butter or margarine   1 tbsp. lemon juice

Cook broccoli and drain. Meanwhile, sauté onion in hot butter until lightly browned and add salt, pepper and lemon juice. Add the cooked broccoli to the onion mixture and heat about 1 min., then remove broccoli to serving dish and pour onion sauce over it.

Dinner: *Veal Chops* in Sour Cream, p. 247, *French-Fried Potatoes, Broccoli* with Onion Sauce, Jellied *Grapefruit* and Avocado Salad, p. 386—*Chocolate Cake.*

Another "quickie" that is delicious:

Parmesan Broccoli   *Yield:* 3–4 servings
1 pkg. (10 oz.) frozen broccoli   2 tbsp. melted butter or margarine
   spears   grated Parmesan cheese

Cook and drain broccoli, and add melted butter.   Turn onto hot serving dish and sprinkle generously with grated cheese.

Dinner: *Pork Chops* with Barbecue Sauce, p. 242, Mashed Potatoes, Parmesan *Broccoli,* Cabbage Salad—Devonshire Tarts *(Fruit,)* p. 420.

A bit of garlic, onion or chives, to point up the flavor:

Broccoli with Garlic Butter   *Yield:* 3–4 servings
1 pkg. (10 oz.) frozen broccoli   1 tbsp. lemon juice or vinegar
   spears   ¼ c. toasted, shredded almonds, if
3 tbsp. butter or margarine   desired
¼ tsp. minced garlic or 2 tbsp.
   grated onion or chopped chives

Cook broccoli and drain.   Meanwhile, cook garlic, onion or chives in hot butter until lightly browned, and add lemon juice or vinegar. Pour butter mixture over hot broccoli in serving dish and sprinkle with almonds if desired.

Luncheon or Supper: *Fish* Baked in Tomato Sauce, p. 258, *Broccoli* with Garlic Butter, Head Lettuce with Russian Dressing—*Pumpkin Pie* with Ginger Meringue, p. 363.

A new and interesting treatment for broccoli:

Broccoli in Celery Sauce   *Yield:* 6–8 servings

2 pkgs. (10 oz.) frozen cut broccoli   3 tbsp. butter or margarine
1 can condensed cream of celery   1 tbsp. chopped onion
  soup   ½ c. grated cheese
¹/₃ c. milk

Cook broccoli until tender, and drain. Place in greased 1½-qt. casserole. Add milk to celery soup and combine well, then pour this over broccoli. Dot with butter and sprinkle with grated cheese and chopped onion. Bake in moderate oven, 350°F., covered, until bubbly, about 25 min.

> **Dinner:** Broiled *Lamb Chops,* Parsley Buttered *New Potatoes,* p. 361, *Broccoli* in Celery Sauce, Tossed Salad——Layer Cake with Creamy *Orange* Frosting, p. 398.

For broccoli and other vegetables, a sauce both sweet and nippy:

Broccoli with Horseradish Sauce   *Yield:* 3–4 servings

1 pkg. (10 oz.) frozen broccoli,   horseradish sauce (see below)
  spears or cuts

Cook broccoli until tender and drain. Serve hot, with horseradish sauce.

Horseradish Sauce

1½ tsp. sugar   2 tbsp melted butter or margarine
½ tsp. paprika   ½ tsp. prepared horseradish
2 tbsp. lemon juice

Blend ingredients thoroughly.

> **Dinner:** Shepherd's *Fish* Pie, p. 268, *Broccoli* with Horseradish Sauce, *Grapefruit* and *Peach* Salad——*Chocolate Ice Cream* with Coffee Caramel Sauce, p. 435.

OTHER BROCCOLI RECIPES

Pot Roast of Beef with Vegetables. *See p. 217.*
Turkey Divan. *See p. 315.*
Broccoli with Curry Mayonnaise. *See p. 326.*
Broccoli Hollandaise. *See p. 329.*
Broccoli Vinaigrette. *See p. 326.*

BRUSSELS SPROUTS

Two "strong juiced" vegetables combined, with epicurean results:

Brussels Sprouts with Onions

1 pkg. (10 oz.) frozen Brussels
    sprouts
about 1 doz. very small onions
salt

Yield: 4–5 servings

pepper
butter or margarine
paprika

Cook Brussels sprouts until tender, and drain. Meanwhile, boil onions until tender (about 7 min.). When onions are almost done, add Brussels sprouts to reheat them. Drain, season with salt and pepper, add butter and sprinkle generously with paprika, and serve.

> **Dinner:** *Chicken* Tetrazzini, p. 301, *Brussels Sprouts* with Onions, Tossed Green Salad with French Dressing——Angel Food à la Mode.

This sauce has a zest which gives the sprouts a fine flavor:

Deviled Brussels Sprouts

1 pkg. (10 oz.) frozen Brussels
    sprouts
¼ c. melted butter or margarine
2 tsp. prepared mustard

Yield: 3–4 servings

1 tsp. Worcestershire sauce
¾ tsp. salt
speck cayenne

Cook Brussels sprouts until tender. Combine remaining ingredients together thoroughly, for the sauce. Pour sauce over hot Brussels sprouts and serve at once.

> **Luncheon or Supper:** *Clam* Pie, p. 270, Deviled *Brussels Sprouts,* Cole Slaw with Tomato Wedges——*Peach* Brown Betty, p. 400.

Brussels sprouts and celery blend especially well:

Brussels Sprouts with Celery

1 pkg. (10 oz.) frozen Brussels
    sprouts
3 tbsp. butter or margarine
1½ c. coarsely chopped celery

Yield: 4 servings

3 tbsp. flour
1½ c. milk
salt
speck pepper

Cook Brussels sprouts until tender and drain. Meanwhile, cook celery in butter over low heat about 5 min., blend in flour and add

Combination vegetable plates are always popular, and with so many frozen vegetables available all year, a good selection can always be made

hot milk slowly, stirring.   Heat just to boiling, stirring constantly.
Add Brussels sprouts to celery, season with salt and pepper, and serve.

Dinner: Baked *Lobster* and Mushrooms, p. 275, Parsley Buttered
New Potatoes, p. 261, *Brussels Sprouts* with Celery—*Strawberry*
Sundae.

Speaking of color . . . just picture this one:

Brussels Sprouts in Pimiento Sauce   *Yield:* 4 servings

1 pkg. (10 oz.) frozen Brussels sprouts	½ tsp. salt
2 tbsp. butter or margarine	1 c. milk
2 tbsp. flour	½ pimiento, cut in small pieces

Cook Brussels sprouts until tender, and drain.   Meanwhile, prepare cream sauce from butter, flour, salt and milk (see directions, p.
200).   Add pimiento to sauce, add hot sauce to Brussels sprouts, heat
if necessary, and serve.

Dinner: Baked *Ham Slice, Squash* Baked with *Pineapple,* p. 371,
Brussels Sprouts in Pimiento Sauce—*Citrus* Banana Sherbet, p. 396.

The grapes give an exotic touch:

Brussels Sprouts with Grapes   *Yield:* 4 servings

1 pkg. (10 oz.) frozen Brussels sprouts	½ c. seedless grapes
	2 tbsp. butter or margarine

Cook Brussels sprouts until tender, and drain.   Meanwhile, cut
grapes in halves and heat in butter until hot but not boiling.   Pour
hot, buttered grapes over hot Brussels sprouts in serving dish.

Dinner: *Chicken* Bisque, p. 310—*Steak* in Red Wine, p. 216,
Mashed Potatoes, *Brussels Sprouts* with Grapes—*Peach* Melba,
p. 426.

Tomato and cheese flavors serve to complement sprouts:

Brussels Sprouts in Tomato   *Yield:* 4 servings

1 pkg. (10 oz.) frozen Brussels   ½ tsp. salt
   sprouts   1½ c. tomato juice
2 tbsp. butter or margarine   ¹/₃ c. grated, sharp Cheddar cheese
2 tbsp. flour

Cook Brussels sprouts until tender, and drain. Blend butter, flour and salt in small saucepan, add tomato juice slowly, stirring, and cook until thickened, stirring constantly. Place Brussels sprouts in greased 1-qt. casserole, add tomato sauce and sprinkle with cheese. Bake in moderate oven, 350°F., about 20 min.

> **Dinner:** *Oyster* Cocktail, p. 278—Roast *Loin of Pork* with Onion Stuffing, p. 240, Mashed Potatoes, *Brussels Sprouts* in Tomato—*Raspberry Turnovers.*

This simple sauce adds just the right touch:

Brussels Sprouts with Lemon Butter   *Yield:* 3–4 servings

1 pkg. (10 oz.) frozen Brussels   lemon butter, p. 203
   sprouts

Cook Brussels sprouts and drain. Serve with lemon butter.

> **Luncheon or Supper:** Deviled Egg and *Shrimp* on Toast, p. 288, *Brussels Sprouts* with Lemon Butter, Tomato and Cucumber Salad *Peach* Mousse, p. 401.

OTHER BRUSSELS SPROUTS RECIPES

Brussels Sprouts Hollandaise. *See p. 329.*
Brussels Sprouts with Curry Mayonnaise. *See. p. 326.*
Golden Brussels Sprouts. *See p. 339.*

CARROTS
(Diced, Sliced, and Baby Whole)

A dash of thyme . . . and try rosemary and oregano:

Herb-Flavored Carrots in Cream   *Yield:* 4 servings

2 c. frozen, diced or sliced carrots   ¹/₃ c. light cream
¼ tsp. thyme

Cook carrots until tender, and drain. Sprinkle with thyme, add cream and combine. Bring barely to boil and serve.

> **Dinner:** *Minestrone*—Stuffed *Pork Chops,* p. 241, Baked Potato, Herb-Flavored *Carrots* in Cream—*Pineapple* Upside Down Cake, p. 404.

Lyonnaise potatoes at other times . . . this time with carrots:

Lyonnaise Carrots   *Yield:* 4 servings

2 c. frozen, diced or sliced carrots   salt
½ c. sliced onion   pepper
¼ c. butter or margarine

Cook carrots until tender, and drain. Meanwhile, sauté onion in 2 tbsp. hot butter in skillet, until light brown. Add remaining butter and carrots, and sauté until onions are slightly deeper brown. Season to taste, with salt and pepper.

> **Dinner:** *Grape Juice*—Breaded *Veal Cutlets* in Tomato Gravy, p. 247, Mashed Potatoes, Lyonnaise *Carrots–Strawberry* Mousse, p. 412.

Pascal celery, crisp and green, pairs well with carrots:

Scalloped Carrots and Celery   *Yield:* 6 servings

2 c. frozen, diced or sliced carrots   1 tsp. salt
1 c. diced, pascal celery   2 c. milk
¼ c. butter or margarine   ½ c. grated American cheese
¼ c. flour   buttered bread crumbs

Cook carrots until tender, and drain. Cook celery in small amount of boiling salted water, and drain. Meanwhile, prepare medium cream sauce from remaining ingredients (see directions, p. 200). Add cheese to sauce.

Place vegetables in 1½-qt. casserole in alternating layers with sauce, and top with buttered crumbs. Bake in hot oven, 425°F., about 15 min., or until crumbs are browned.

> **Dinner:** *Vegetable Soup*—Pressed *Lamb Shoulder,* p. 237, Scalloped *Carrots* and Celery, Tomato Salad—*Cherry* Whip, p. 382, with Custard Sauce.

Candied, baby carrots are especially sweet and tasty:

Candied Baby Carrots   *Yield:* 4 servings
15–20 frozen, baby whole carrots   3 tbsp. butter or margarine
$^1/_3$ c. water   6 tbsp. brown sugar
½ tsp. salt

Bring water, salt, butter and sugar to boil in saucepan, and add carrots. Cover and simmer until carrots are tender, 10–12 min., stirring occasionally. Serve syrup with carrots.

> **Dinner:** *Grape Juice*—Ragout of *Duck*, p. 320, Mashed Potatoes, Candied *Baby Carrots,* Head Lettuce with French Dressing—*Apple Pie.*

Try carrots, mushroom flavor and cheese together:

Carrots in Casserole   *Yield:* 5–6 servings
15–20 frozen, baby whole carrots   ½ tsp. salt
1 can condensed mushroom soup,   speck pepper
  undiluted   ½ c. grated American cheese

Stir mushroom soup well, to distribute mushrooms uniformly. Place about half the carrots in greased, 1-qt. casserole and add half the soup. Add the remaining carrots, then the remaining soup and seasonings and top with grated cheese. Cover and bake in moderate oven, 350°F., about 1 hr. or until carrots are tender.

> **Dinner:** *Pineapple Juice*—Fried *Smelts,* Mashed Potatoes, *Carrots* in Casserole, Tomato and Lettuce Salad—*Strawberry* Chiffon Pie, p. 417.

Carrot and pineapple flavor blend to make a fine combination:

Hawaiian Carrots   *Yield:* 6 servings
15–20 frozen, baby whole carrots   2 tbsp. cornstarch
1 pkg. (13½ oz.) frozen pineapple   ½ tsp. salt
  chunks, thawed   1 tbsp. butter or margarine

Drain pineapple chunks and add enough water to juice to make 1½-c. liquid. Add cornstarch to small amount of the liquid, to make a smooth paste, then add to remaining liquid already heated. Bring slowly to boil, stirring constantly. Add carrots, pineapple chunks and salt and bring to boil. Cover and simmer gently about 12 min., or until carrots are tender, stirring occasionally. Add butter, and serve sauce with carrots and pineapple.

Dinner: *Cream of Potato Soup—Duck* Pilau, p. 319, Hawaiian *Carrots, Artichoke Hearts* Vinaigrette, p. 326, Head Lettuce with French Dressing—Raspberry Sherbet, p. 407.

OTHER CARROT RECIPES

Chicken Country Style. *See p. 305.*

Creamed Carrots with Bacon. *See p. 446.*

CAULIFLOWER

Cauliflower with a tangy mustard sauce, and peas:

Mustard Cauliflower and Peas   *Yield:* 6–8 servings
1 pkg. (10 oz.) frozen cauliflower   mustard sauce (see below)
1 pkg. (10 oz.) frozen peas

Cook the cauliflower and peas, separately, until tender, drain and combine them. Turn into serving dish and pour mustard sauce over them.

Mustard Sauce
1 tbsp. melted butter or margarine   1 egg yolk
1 tbsp. flour   ¾ c. milk
1 tbsp. prepared mustard   1 tbsp. lemon juice
1 tsp. salt

Combine butter, flour, mustard and salt in top of double boiler, add milk slowly and cook over direct heat until thickened, stirring constantly. Pour a small amount of this into the egg yolk, combine well, then put back in top of double boiler over hot water and cook only a minute or two. Add lemon juice just before serving.

Dinner: Broiled *Swordfish*, Rissole Potatoes, Mustard *Cauliflower and Peas—Blueberries* and Cream.

Crunchy bits of almonds add a novel touch to cauliflower:

Cauliflower with Almond Butter   *Yield:* 3–4 servings
1 pkg. (10 oz.) frozen cauliflower   ¼ c. choppped, toasted almonds,
¼ c. butter or margarine   slightly salted

Cook cauliflower until tender, and drain.   Melt butter over low heat, add almonds and heat.   Pour almond butter over cauliflower in serving dish and serve at once.

Dinner: *Grape Juice*——*Shrimp* in Casserole, p. 289, *French-Fried Potatoes, Cauliflower* with Almond Butter, Assorted Relishes—— *Pineapple* and *Strawberry* Compote.

Cauliflower with a sparkle:

Cauliflower Polonaise   *Yield:* 3–4 servings
1 pkg. (10 oz.) frozen cauliflower   1 tbsp. chopped parsley
¼ c. melted butter or margarine   2 hard-cooked eggs, chopped

Cook cauliflower until tender, and drain.   Arrange cauliflower in serving dish with flowerets upward.   Pour butter over it, sprinkle with hard-cooked egg and parsley.

Dinner: Broiled *Lamb Chops,* Delmonico Potatoes, *Cauliflower* Polonaise, *Rhubarb* Salad Ring, p. 409——*Ice Cream* with Coffee Caramel Sauce, p. 434.

You will wish you had tried this sooner:

Cauliflower in Chipped Beef Sauce   *Yield:* 4 servings
1 pkg. (10 oz.) frozen cauliflower   ¼ tsp. garlic salt
¼ c. butter or margarine   2 c. milk
¼ c. flour   2 oz. chipped dried beef (more if
speck pepper   desired)

Cook cauliflower until tender, and drain.   Meanwhile, melt butter in skillet, blend in flour, pepper and garlic salt.   Add milk slowly, stirring, and cook until sauce is thickened, stirring constantly.   Add beef and keep over heat about 2 min., then pour sauce over cauliflower in serving dish.

Dinner: Jiffy *Fish* Fry, p. 256, *Puff Potatoes, Cauliflower* in Chipped Beef Sauce, Stuffed Tomatoes——*Lemon* Chiffon Pie, p. 388.

OTHER CAULIFLOWER RECIPES

Green Bean and Cauliflower Salad. *See p. 335.*

Cauliflower with Cheese Sauce. *See p. 446.*

CORN
(Cut, Whole Kernel and Cream-Style)

A hearty dish for wintertime:

Casserole of Corn and Sausage   *Yield:* 4–6 servings

1 pkg. (10 oz.) frozen cut corn,   ¼ c. butter or margarine
   thawed   ¼ c. flour
6–8 Vienna sausages   1 tsp. salt
½ green pepper, chopped   2 c. milk
seasonings   1½ c. buttered cracker crumbs

Cut sausages in thirds, crosswise, then combine sausages, green pepper and corn, and add seasonings. Prepare cream sauce from butter, flour, salt and milk (see directions, p. 200). Place alternating layers of corn mixture, crumbs and cream sauce in greased 1-qt. casserole and top with buttered crumbs. Bake in moderate oven, 350°F., for 30–40 min. or until corn is done and crumbs are golden brown.

> **Luncheon or Supper:** Casserole of *Corn* and Sausage, *Apple Sauce, Mixed Vegetables* in Aspic Salad—*Fruit* Cup with *Sherbet, Brownies.*

A hearty and delicious chowder:

Corn Chowder   *Yield:* 4–5 servings

1 pkg. (10 oz.) frozen cut corn   2 c. boiling water
¼ c. finely cubed, salt pork   1 tsp. salt
1 medium onion, sliced   ⅛ tsp. pepper
1 c. finely diced potatoes   2 c. milk

Cook salt pork in large kettle until crisp, then add onion and cook until golden brown. Add potatoes, boiling water, and salt and pepper and boil until potatoes are almost tender. Add corn and cook until it is tender. Finally, add milk and cook until thoroughly heated.

Luncheon or Supper: *Corn* Chowder——Cheese Slices on Crackers, *Shrimp* and *Asparagus* Salad, p. 291——*Raspberry* Whip, p. 419.

As American as Yankee Doodle, and an all-time favorite:

Corn Pudding   *Yield:* 4–6 servings

1 pkg. (10 oz.) frozen cut corn, thawed	⅛ tsp. pepper
	1½ c. top milk
1 tbsp. melted butter or margarine	1 tsp. grated onion
1 tbsp. flour	1 tbsp. chopped pimiento
1 tsp. salt	2 eggs, slightly beaten
½ tsp. sugar	

Make cream sauce from butter, flour, salt, pepper and milk, (see directions, p. 200), adding sugar to sauce. Remove from heat, add onion, pimiento, eggs and corn. Mix well and turn into baking dish. Set baking dish in pan of hot water and bake in moderate oven, 350°F., about 1 hr. or until set.

Luncheon or Supper: *Scallops* and Mushrooms, p. 282, *Corn* Pudding, Tomato and Shredded Spinach Salad——*Peach* and *Strawberry* Compote, p. 401.

A delicious corn casserole:

Savory Baked Corn   *Yield:* 4–6 servings

1 pkg. (10 oz.) frozen cut corn	½ tsp. salt
milk	½ tsp. mustard
1 green pepper, chopped	1 egg, slightly beaten
1 tbsp. butter or margarine	1 tbsp. chopped pimiento
2 tbsp. flour	½ c. buttered crumbs
	4 slices bacon, cut in halves

Simmer corn in small amount of milk until tender, then drain, reserving milk. Sauté green pepper in butter 5 min., blend in flour and ½ c. milk (use milk from cooking corn and add enough to make ½ c.). Heat to boiling, stirring constantly. Add corn, salt, mustard and pimiento. Add a small amount of this to the egg, then put egg into hot mixture. Pour into greased 1-qt. casserole and top with buttered crumbs and bacon strips. Set casserole in pan of hot water and bake in moderate oven, 350°F., for 30–40 min.

> **Dinner:** *Pineapple Juice*—Braised *Pork Chops,* Mashed Potatoes, Savory Baked *Corn,* Tossed Green Salad—Jellied *Raspberries,* p. 406.

A splendid main course dish for luncheon:

Corn Souffle

Yield: 4–6 servings

1 pkg. (10 oz.) frozen whole kernel corn
scalded milk
1 tbsp. melted butter or margarine
2 tbsp. flour

½ tsp. salt
speck pepper
2 egg yolks
2 egg whites
paprika

Drain corn, reserving liquid. To the drained liquid, add enough milk to make 1 c. liquid. Blend butter with flour, salt and pepper, add enough liquid to make a smooth paste, then add the rest of the liquid and cook, stirring constantly until thickened. Add corn, then add beaten egg yolks and combine slowly, stirring well. Beat egg whites until stiff, then fold them carefully into the corn mixture. Spoon into greased 1½-qt. casserole, place in pan of hot water and bake in moderate oven, 350°F., for 45–60 min. or until firm. Sprinkle with paprika and serve at once.

> **Luncheon or Supper:** Tomato Juice—*Corn* Soufflé, *Spinach* in Onion Sauce, p. 369, *Grapefruit* Salad—*Ice Cream* with *Raspberries.*

The flavor of harvest-ripe corn, in a steaming soup:

Cream of Corn Soup

Yield: 4–5 servings

1 pkg. (10 oz.) frozen cut corn, thawed
1 tbsp. chopped onion
½ c. chopped celery
2 c. boiling water
2 c. scalded milk

2 tbsp. flour
2 tbsp. melted butter or margarine
1 tsp. salt
⅛ tsp. paprika
chopped parsley

Chop the corn finely, then add onion, celery and boiling water and simmer, covered, about 20 min. Put mixture through colander or coarse sieve or food mill. Combine flour, butter, salt and paprika, add a little of the scalded milk and make a smooth paste. Add rest of milk slowly, then add sieved mixture and cook until thickened, stirring constantly. When serving, sprinkle with chopped parsley.

> **Luncheon or Supper:** Cream of *Corn* Soup—*Macaroni and Beef with Tomatoes,* Head Lettuce with French Dressing—*Strawberries, Cookies.*

A novel and delightful way to serve corn:

Corn Fritters
Yield: 8–10 servings

1 pkg. (10 oz.) frozen cut corn, thawed
1¼ c. flour
1 tsp. baking powder
1 tsp. salt
¼ tsp. paprika
2 egg yolks
2 egg whites

Drain corn thoroughly. Sift baking powder, salt and paprika together, add corn and combine well. Beat egg yolks until thick and add to corn mixture. Beat egg whites until they hold peaks and fold them into corn mixture, blending well. Lower fritter mixture by spoonfuls into deep fat at 375°F., a few at a time, and fry until delicately browned. Drain on unglazed paper.

> **Luncheon or Supper:** *Cream of Potato Soup—Pork Sausage Patties, Corn* Fritters, Chef's Salad—*Fruit* Surprise Dessert, p. 394.

OTHER CORN RECIPES

Creole Fish Supper. *See p. 262.*
Kentucky Succotash in Casserole. *See p. 333.*
Green Bean and Corn Salad. *See p. 334.*
Succotash. *See p. 335.*
Wax Beans, Corn and Green Pepper. *See p. 339.*
Savory Okra and Corn. *See p. 357.*
Squash and Corn Pudding. *See p. 372.*
Scalloped Oysters and Corn. *See p. 280.*
Beef Goulash Supreme. *See p. 224.*
Tamale Pie. *See p. 231.*
Chicken Country Style. *See p. 305.*
Scrambled Maize. *See p. 446.*
Corn and Mushroom Soup. *See p. 446.*

GREENS¹

For greens, southern style try:

Greens with Bacon or Salt Pork   *Yield:* 3–4 servings
1 pkg. (10 oz.) greens   speck pepper
4 strips bacon or 2 oz. salt pork   vinegar or lemon juice
2 tbsp. chopped onion   2 hard-cooked eggs, sliced
½ tsp. salt

Cut bacon or salt pork into small pieces and fry until crisp. Remove bacon or pork from pan, add onion and sauté in hot fat until light brown. Add greens, bacon or pork and seasonings, cover tightly and steam until greens are tender, stirring occasionally. If much liquid is left in pan, boil rapidly, uncovered, a minute or two until it has evaporated. Add vinegar or lemon juice and serve, garnished with egg slices.

> **Dinner:** *Pineapple Juice*—Southern Fried *Chicken, Candied Yams, Greens* with Salt Pork, Tomato Salad—*Cherry Pie.*

Greens Italian style make an interesting variation:

Greens in Italian Tomatoes   *Yield:* 4 servings
1 pkg. (10 oz.) greens   ½ tsp. salt
¼ c. chopped onion   ⅛ tsp. pepper
3 tbsp. fat   ⅓ c. grated Cheddar cheese or ¼ c.
¾ c. Italian tomato sauce, p. 202   grated Parmesan cheese

Sauté onion in hot fat until golden color. Add greens, cover and simmer until greens are thawed and separated. Add Italian tomato sauce, salt, pepper and grated cheese. Blend well, cover and cook over moderate heat until greens are tender.

> **Dinner:** *Orange Grape* Cocktail, p. 398—Broiled *Rib Steak,* Mashed Potatoes, Collards in Italian Tomatoes—*Strawberry* Shortcake, p. 420.

---

¹ These recipes are for use with turnip, mustard and other greens. Also, recipes for spinach are suited for use with any greens.

OKRA

(Whole or Cut)

Okra served in a peppy tomato sauce:

Southern Okra

1 pkg. (10 oz.) frozen okra
1 medium onion, chopped
1 green pepper, chopped
1/4 c. fat
1 c. canned tomatoes

Yield: 4–6 servings

2 tsp. sugar
1 tbsp. flour
1/4 tsp. salt
speck pepper

Cook okra until tender and drain.   Meanwhile, brown onion and green pepper in hot fat in skillet. Combine flour, sugar, salt and pepper and add to onion mixture, blending well. Add tomatoes and cook slowly, stirring until thickened. Add okra and heat to serving temperature.

Luncheon or Supper: *Chicken* à la King, p. 304, *French-Fried Potatoes,* Southern *Okra—Raspberry* Puff Pudding, p. 418.

An especially good introduction to okra:

Savory Okra and Corn

1 pkg. (10 oz.) frozen okra,
   preferably cut
1 pkg. (10 oz.) frozen cut or whole
   kernel corn
1/4 c. fat

Yield: 6–8 servings

1 tsp. salt
speck pepper
1 c. canned tomatoes
$1/_3$ c. grated sharp Cheddar cheese

Add corn to hot fat in skillet and heat, stirring, until corn is delicately browned, then add okra, salt and pepper. Cover, and cook over low heat until okra is tender, stirring occasionally. Add tomatoes and cheese and heat until cheese melts. Blend well and serve.

Dinner: Raw Potato *Beef* Hash, p. 228, Savory *Okra* and *Corn,* Tomato Aspic Salad—*Peaches* and Cream.

OTHER OKRA RECIPES

Shrimp Gumbo. *See p. 289*
Brunswick Stew. *See p. 308.*

GREEN PEAS

Peas and salmon, creamed, make a delicious luncheon dish:

Creamed Salmon and Peas

Yield: 6 servings

1 pkg. (10 oz.) frozen green peas, thawed
1 c. canned salmon (or tuna fish)
½ tsp. salt

1 c. medium cream sauce (see p. 200, or dilute condensed celery or mushroom soup)
buttered crumbs

Flake the salmon apart, add thawed peas and salt and combine well. Turn into 1-qt. greased casserole, add cream sauce and top with buttered crumbs. Bake in moderate oven, 350°F., for 40–50 min. or until peas are tender and crumbs are brown.

> **Luncheon or Supper:** *Pineapple* Orange Mint Cocktail, p. 402— Creamed Salmon and *Peas,* Buttered *Broccoli, Bran Muffins—Blueberry* Cottage Pudding, p. 379, with *Lemon* Sauce, p. 391.

A delicious blend of peas and tomatoes in rice:

Savory Peas and Tomatoes

Yield: 4–5 servings

1 pkg. (10 oz.) frozen green peas
½ c. chopped onion
½ c. chopped celery
3 tbsp. butter or margarine

1½ c. canned tomatoes
1½ c. cooked rice
1 tsp. sugar
crisp cooked bacon strips

Cook peas until tender and drain. Meanwhile, sauté onion and celery in hot butter, add tomatoes, rice and sugar. Add peas and heat to serving temperature. Garnish with bacon.

> **Dinner:** *Vegetable* Soup—Baked *Lobster* and Mushrooms, p. 275, *Crinkle-Cut Potatoes,* Savory *Peas* and Tomatoes—*Orange* Cake Pudding, p. 395.

For a gala luncheon or dinner, or a wedding breakfast:

Creamed Peas and Mushrooms in Toast Baskets

Yield: 8 servings

1 pkg. (10 oz.) frozen green peas
garlic, if desired
3 tbsp. butter or margarine
¼ c. mushrooms (1 c. sliced) or 1 can (4 oz.)
2 tbsp. flour
¼ tsp. salt

⅛ tsp. paprika
1 c. liquid (liquid drained from peas and mushrooms, with milk to make 1 c.)
toast baskets, p. 312
additional paprika
parsley

Cook and drain peas, reserving liquid. Meanwhile, rub skillet with garlic, if desired. Melt butter in skillet, add mushrooms (drained if canned) and cook about 5 min. Sprinkle flour, salt and paprika over mushrooms and blend well. Add liquid, stirring, and cook until thickened, stirring constantly. Add peas and heat to serving temperature.

Serve in toast baskets, sprinkle with additional paprika and garnish with parsley.

Dinner: *Grapefruit* and *Crabmeat* Cocktail, p. 272—Broiled *Delmonico Steaks* with Broiled Tomatoes, Creamed *Peas* and Mushrooms in Toast Basket—Brandied *Peach* Parfait, p. 428.

Tender green peas, harvested in the summer, yours all year:

Piquant Peas

Yield: 3–4 servings

1 pkg. (10 oz.) frozen green peas
1/4 c. minced onion
2 tbsp. butter or margarine

1/2 tsp. sugar
1 tsp. celery seed
speck pepper

Cook peas until tender and drain. Meanwhile, sauté onion in butter until light brown, add sugar, celery seed, and pepper. Combine hot onion mixture with hot peas and serve, adding salt if necessary.

Luncheon or Supper: *Chicken Livers* á la King, p. 312, Piquant *Peas, Cornmeal Muffins*—Frozen *Fruit* Salad, p. 393.

Onions to enhance this vegetable favorite:

Peas with Tiny Onions

Yield: 4–6 servings

1 pkg. (10 oz.) frozen green peas
6–8 tiny white onions
2 tbsp. butter or margarine

or
1/4 c. heavy cream
2 tbsp. chopped parsley

Cook peas and onions separately, and drain thoroughly. Combine vegetables. Melt butter or heat cream and pour over vegetables. Sprinkle with parsley and serve.

> **Dinner:** *Shrimp* in Casserole, p. 289, *Peas* with Tiny Onions, Tossed Green Salad—Toasted *Cherry* Chiffon Pie, p. 382.

This makes an unusually tasty combination:

Tasty Peas and Rice Casserole   *Yield:* 4–5 servings

1 pkg. (10 oz.) frozen green peas, thawed
¾ c. celery cut in 1-inch pieces
2 tbsp. minced onion
¾ c. quick-cooking rice

1½ c. water
2 chicken or beef bouillon cubes
1 tsp. soy sauce
½ tsp. sugar
½ tsp. salt

Combine peas, celery and onion and rice in 1-qt. greased casserole. Add bouillon cubes, soy sauce, sugar and salt to water in small saucepan and bring to a boil. Pour this mixture over vegetables in casserole and bake in moderate oven, 350°F., covered, about 30 min. Then remove cover and bake about 15 min. longer, or until peas are done.

> **Dinner:** Tomato Juice—*Steak* with Mushroom Sauce, p. 219, Tasty *Peas* and Rice Casserole, Curly Endive Salad—*Orange* Cake Pudding, p. 395.

Here is a new, interesting salad:

Peas and Cheese Salad   *Yield:* 4–6 servings

1 pkg. (10 oz.) frozen green peas
1 c. cubed American cheese
½ c. finely chopped sweet pickle
¼ tsp. salt

$1/3$ c. cooked salad dressing or mayonnaise
crisp lettuce

Cook peas, drain them and chill thoroughly. Combine with cheese, pickle, salt and dressing. Serve on crisp lettuce.

> **Luncheon or Supper:** Tomatoes Stuffed with *Peas* and Cheese Salad, Cole Slaw, Deviled Eggs, Potato Chips—*Red Cherry* Roll-Ups, p. 385, with *Ice Cream*.

OTHER GREEN PEA RECIPES

Mustard Cauliflower and Peas. *See p. 350.*
Casserole of New Potatoes and Peas. *See p. 361.*
Creamed Shrimp and Peas. *See p. 285.*
Lamb Stew. *See p. 235.*
Lamb Ring with Peas and Mint Sauce. *See p. 238.*
Easy Shrimp and Peas. *See p. 444.*

NEW POTATOES

Delicious little potatoes, with a touch of green:

Parsley Buttered New Potatoes   *Yield:* 4 servings
1 doz. frozen new potatoes   2 tbsp. finely chopped parsley
2 tbsp. melted butter or margarine

Boil potatoes until tender and drain thoroughly, then replace over heat a minute to evaporate excess moisture. Turn into serving dish and pour melted butter over them, turning them so each potato is coated all over with butter. Sprinkle with parsley and serve at once.

> **Dinner:** *Crabmeat* Newburg, p. 273, Parsley Buttered *New Potatoes*, Parmesan *Broccoli*, p. 342, Tossed Salad—*Peach, Grapefruit* and *Strawberry* Compote.

In this case, two vegetables are better than one:

Casserole of New Potatoes and Peas   *Yield:* 4–8 servings
6–8 frozen new potatoes   1 c. medium cream sauce, p. 200,
1 pkg. (10 oz.) frozen green peas   (or dilute condensed cream of
¼ c. chopped onion, preferably   mushroom or celery soup)
  green   ½ c. grated sharp cheese

Boil potatoes and peas separately until tender, adding onion to peas during cooking. Drain vegetables. Place potatoes in greased 1-qt. casserole, add peas with onions and pour sauce over them.

Sprinkle with cheese and bake in hot oven, 400°F., about 20 min. or until top is delicately browned.

Dinner: Deviled *Pork Chops,* p. 242, Casserole of *New Potatoes* and *Peas,* Buttered *Carrots, Fruit* Salad—*Mince Pie.*

To have at home or to carry with you to a picnic:

Potato Salad   *Yield:* 3 servings

8 frozen new potatoes   2 tbsp. chopped onion
½ tsp. salt   1 tbsp. juice from pickles
¼ tsp. celery seed   1 tsp. prepared mustard
6 radishes, sliced   ¼ c. mayonnaise or cooked salad
½ c. diced cucumbers or chopped   dressing
   celery   2 hard-cooked eggs, diced
2 tbsp. diced sweet pickle

Boil potatoes until tender, drain and chill thoroughly. Cut potatoes in cubes (there should be about 2 c.). Add salt, celery seed, radishes, cucumbers, pickles and onion. Combine pickle juice and mustard and add this mixture to potatoes, combining lightly with a fork until each piece of potato is coated. Add mayonnaise and combine. Add diced eggs and toss together lightly so as not to break pieces. Chill thoroughly before serving.

Picnic Dinner: Hamburbers Supreme (*Beef*), p. 227, *Potato* Salad, Cheese Slices, Assorted Relishes—*Pineapple* Upside Down Cake, p. 404, *Dessert Topping.*

An old favorite, but not everyone has tried it:

Hot Potato Salad   *Yield:* 5–6 servings

13–15 frozen new potatoes   1 tsp. salt
4 slices bacon   1 tbsp. sugar
¼ c. finely chopped onion   ½ c. water
1 tbsp. flour   1 egg, beaten
1 tsp. dry mustard   ¼ c. vinegar

Cook potatoes until tender, drain and dice them. Meanwhile, cook bacon in skillet until crisp, remove from skillet and chop. Remove all bacon fat from skillet except about 2 tbsp., add onions to this and sauté them until golden color. Blend flour, mustard, salt and sugar and add this mixture to onions, stir in water and boil about

2 min., stirring. Add a small amount of this hot mixture to egg, then add egg to hot mixture, add vinegar and reheat.

Pour hot dressing over hot, diced potatoes, add hot bacon and combine. Serve hot.

> **Luncheon or Supper:** Frying Pan Barbecue (*Beef*), p. 227, Hot *Potato* Salad, Salad of *Asparagus Spears* and Tomato, with Mayonnaise——*Peach* Mousse, p. 401.

PUMPKIN

You don't have to wait until "the frost is on the punkin" to make a pumpkin pie nowadays:

Pumpkin Pie with Ginger Meringue

Yield: 9-inch pie

1 pkg. (16 oz.) frozen pumpkin, thawed
½ c. sugar
2 tbsp. molasses
2 tbsp. melted butter or margarine
2 tsp. ginger

1 tsp. cinnamon
½ tsp. salt
2 egg yolks
1½ c. milk
9-inch unbaked pie shell
ginger meringue (see below)

Add sugar, molasses, butter, ginger, cinnamon and salt to pumpkin and combine well. Beat egg yolks with milk and add to pumpkin mixture. Pour into unbaked pie shell in pie plate and bake in hot oven, 450°F., for 15 min., then reduce heat to moderate, 350°F., and bake about 1 hr. longer, or until done.

Let pie stand about 1 hr. at room temperature to cool, then cover with ginger meringue. Bake in slow oven, 325°F., 15–20 min. or until delicately browned. Let stand to cool several hours before serving.

Ginger Meringue

3 egg whites
6 tbsp. sugar

3 tbsp. finely chopped preserved ginger
2 tbsp. ginger syrup

Beat egg whites until foamy, then add 3 tbsp. sugar gradually (1 tbsp. at a time) with continued beating until whites are thick and glossy. Fold remaining sugar, chopped ginger and ginger syrup into meringue.

> **Dinner:** *Oyster* Cocktail, p. 278——Smothered *Chicken*, p. 303, Mashed Potatoes, Piquant *Peas*, p. 359,——*Pumpkin* Pie with Ginger Meringue.

Courtesy of Aluminum Company of America

*With a pumpkin chiffon pie and a few interesting table decorations,
you are ready for a Hallowe'en dessert party*

A delicacy for Thanksgiving, or for midsummer:

Pumpkin Chiffon Pie   *Yield:* 9-inch pie

1 pkg. (16 oz.) frozen pumpkin,   ½ c. milk
   thawed   ½ tsp. ginger
1 tbsp. (1 envelope) unflavored   ½ tsp. nutmeg
   gelatin   ½ tsp. cinnamon
¼ c. cold water   ½ tsp. salt
3 egg yolks   3 egg whites
²/₃ c. sugar   9-inch pie shell, baked and cooled

Soak gelatin in cold water about 5 min. Meanwhile beat egg
yolks slightly, add ¹/₃ c. sugar, milk, pumpkin and seasonings and
cook over hot water until mixture coats a spoon (as for custard). Re-

move from heat, add softened gelatin, stirring until it is dissolved. Allow to cool until mixture begins to stiffen.

Beat egg whites until foamy, and gradually add remaining $1/3$ c. sugar while continuing to beat until whites are thick and glossy, as for a meringue. Fold the partially set pumpkin mixture into egg whites, blending well. Pour into baked and cooled pie shell. If mixture is not stiff enough to stand up well in center of pie, chill one-third of it further before adding it to pie. Chill pie until filling is firm.

Dinner: *Duck* Pilau, p. 319, *Broccoli* with Garlic Butter, p. 342, Glazed Onions, Cottage Cheese and Tomato Wedges—*Pumpkin* Chiffon Pie.

For Hallowe'en feasting . . . or any time of year:

Pumpkin Orange Spice Cake   *Yield:* 10–12 servings

1 pkg. (16 oz.) frozen pumpkin, thawed	1 tsp. baking powder
½ c. shortening	1 tsp. baking soda
1¼ c. sugar	¼ tsp. salt
1 egg	1 tsp. cinnamon
1 c. raisins	½ tsp. ground cloves
1 c. finely chopped nuts	juice of ½ large or 1 medium
grated rind of 1 orange	orange
1¾ c. cake flour	1½ tbsp. lemon juice

Cream shortening and gradually cream in 1 c. sugar until thoroughly combined. Add egg and beat well. Put raisins through food grinder and combine them with pumpkin, nuts and grated orange rind. Add this pumpkin mixture to shortening-sugar-egg mixture and combine well. Sift flour with baking powder, baking soda and seasonings, add to pumpkin mixture and mix well.

Pour batter into two greased baking pans, 8 inches square, and bake in moderate oven, 350°F., about 35 min. or until done.

As soon as cake comes out of oven, combine orange juice and lemon juice with remaining ¼ c. sugar and stir until sugar is dissolved. Pour this syrup over cake.

This cake needs no frosting, but a delicious topping may be prepared by beating cream cheese with a small amount of cream, adding grated orange rind to taste.   Or cut cake into serving pieces and top with whipped dessert topping.

Dinner: Braised *Duck,* p. 319, Savory Creamed *Spinach,* p. 368, *Whipped Potatoes,* Cranberry Sauce——*Pumpkin* Orange Spice Cake.

Muffins with a delicious flavor . . . and moistness:

Pumpkin Muffins   *Yield:* 1 doz. muffins
¾ c. frozen pumpkin, thawed   ¼ c. brown sugar
2 c. flour   ½ c. raisins or chopped nuts, if
3 tsp. baking powder   desired
1 tsp. salt   1 egg, beaten
1 tsp. cinnamon $1/_3$ c. milk
¼ tsp. ginger   ¼ c. molasses
¼ tsp. nutmeg $1/_3$ c. melted shortening or oil
¼ tsp. allspice

Sift flour, baking powder and seasonings together.   Stir in brown sugar and raisins (or nuts).   Combine milk, pumpkin, egg, molasses and shortening thoroughly.   Add the pumpkin mixture to a well in the center of the dry ingredients and stir only until dry ingredients are all moistened.   Fill greased muffin pans about two-thirds full of batter and bake in hot oven, 400°F., about 25 min. or until done.

Dinner: *Chicken Livers* in Scrambled Eggs, p. 313, *Asparagus* Aspic Salad. p. 328, *Pumpkin* Muffins——*Mixed Fruit* Cup with *Lemon Sherbet.*

There never was a custard like this one . . . superb flavor:

Pumpkin Caramel Custard   *Yield:* 6 servings
1 pkg. (16 oz.) frozen pumpkin,   ½ tsp. cinnamon
   thawed   ¼ tsp. salt
2 eggs   1 tbsp. melted butter or margarine
¼ c. granulated or light brown   1 c. undiluted evaporated milk or
   sugar   top milk
1 tbsp. molasses   ¼ c. granulated sugar
½ tsp. ginger   ¼ c. water

Beat eggs slightly and add to pumpkin. Add ¼ c. granulated or brown sugar, molasses, seasonings and butter to pumpkin mixture and mix well, then add evaporated milk and combine thoroughly.

Place remaining ¼ c. sugar in heavy skillet and caramelize it (see directions, p. 434). Then remove from heat, slowly add ¼ c. water and stir until caramel is all dissolved, heating if necessary.

Pour caramel syrup into bottom of custard cups or ring mold, tilting the cups or mold to coat the sides with caramel. Add custard mixture and set cups or mold in pan of hot water. Bake in moderate oven, 350°F., about 35 min. (a ring mold may require longer). Custard is done when a knife inserted into it (half way between the center and edge of the custard) comes out clean.

Cool and unmold. The caramel runs down the sides of the custard and provides a sauce.

Luncheon or Supper: *Pineapple-Orange Juice*—Scotch Pancakes (*Veal*) with Tomato Sauce, p. 249, Tossed Vegetable Salad—*Pumpkin* Caramel Custard.

An unusual and delicious flavor for ice cream:

Harvest Ice Cream   *Yield:* 6 servings

²/₃ c. frozen pumpkin, thawed   ½ tsp. cinnamon
¼ c. sugar   ⅛ tsp. nutmeg
¼ c. light corn syrup   ¼ tsp. salt
1 tsp. vanilla   ⅛ tsp. ginger, if desired
2 c. light cream   1 pkg. vanilla rennet custard
¹/₃ c. brown sugar   (Junket)

Combine granulated sugar, corn syrup, vanilla and light cream well, then add brown sugar and seasonings and mix thoroughly. Gradually add this mixture to pumpkin in saucepan, and mix well. Heat slowly to lukewarm temperature (not warmer) and remove from heat. Add vanilla rennet custard and stir until custard is dissolved but not more than 1 min. Pour into ice cube tray or other mold and let stand at room temperature until firm (about 10 min.). Then place in freezer.

Put bowl and beater in refrigerator or freezer to chill. When pumpkin mixture is consistency of a firm mush, put it in cold bowl and quickly beat it with rotary or electric beater until smooth, but without letting it melt.　Quickly return it to mold and to freezer, and freeze until firm.　For a still smoother mixture, beat again during freezing, if desired.

Dinner:　Roast **Turkey** with Sausage Stuffing, p. 314, Gravy, **Candied** *Yams,* Buttered *Spinach, Cranberry-Orange Relish*——Harvest Ice Cream (*Pumpkin*).

SPINACH[2]
(Leaf and Chopped)

Everyone will enjoy spinach in a fluffy soufflé:

Spinach Soufflé　　　　　　　*Yield:* 6 servings

1 pkg. (10 oz.) frozen, chopped spinach
2 tbsp. chopped onion
3 tbsp. fat
3 tbsp. flour
1 c. liquid (liquid from cooking spinach and milk to make 1 c.)

¾ tsp. salt
speck pepper
½ tsp. Worcestershire sauce
3 egg yolks
3 egg whites

Cook spinach until tender and drain, reserving liquid.　Sauté onion in fat until light brown, add flour and liquid and blend well. Add spinach, salt, pepper and Worcestershire sauce and well beaten egg yolks and combine.　Beat egg whites until they hold good peaks, then fold spinach mixture carefully into them.　Turn into greased 1½-qt. casserole, place casserole in pan of hot water and bake in moderate oven, 350°F., for 45–60 min. or until firm.　Serve at once.

Dinner:　Breaded *Veal Cutlet,* p. 247, Fluffy Rice, *Spinach* Soufflé, *Pineapple*-Orange Gelatin Salad, p. 403——*Ice Cream* with Praline Sauce, p. 434.

———————

The zest of horseradish gives this its savoriness:

Savory Creamed Spinach　　　*Yield:* 5 servings

1 pkg. (10 oz.) frozen spinach
½ c. top milk or light cream
1 tbsp. flour
1 tbsp. butter or margarine

½ tsp. salt
speck pepper
2 tbsp. prepared horseradish
hard-cooked eggs, sliced

[2] Recipes for use with greens may also be used with spinach.

Cook spinach and drain, chopping it if leaf spinach was used. Prepare cream sauce from milk, flour, butter, salt and pepper (see directions, p. 200, or if preferred, dilute canned condensed cream of celery or mushroom soup. Add horseradish and spinach, and reheat to serving temperature. Serve, garnished with hard cooked eggs.

Dinner: Stuffed *Round Steak,* p. 218, *French-Fried Potatoes,* Savory Creamed *Spinach*——Frozen Fruit Salad *(Mixed Fruit),* p. 393, *Brownies.*

Just the right amount of onion enhances spinach:

Spinach in Onion Sauce   *Yield:* 4–5 servings

1 pkg. (10 oz.) frozen spinach   ¼ c. flour
1 small onion, minced   ½ tsp. salt
3 tbsp. butter or margarine   speck pepper
          1½ c. milk

Cook spinach until tender and drain (if leaf spinach, chop it). Cook onion in butter until tender, stir in flour, salt and pepper and blend well, then add milk slowly. Cook slowly until thickened, stirring constantly. Fold in spinach and reheat if necessary.

Dinner: Broiled *Steak* with Mushrooms, p. 215, Mashed Potatoes *Spinach* in Onion Sauce, Tomato Salad——*Strawberry* and *Rhubarb* Sherbet, p. 411.

A subtle combination of flavors with spinach:

Panned Spinach   *Yield:* 4 servings

1 pkg. (10 oz.) frozen spinach,   ½ tsp. salt
    thawed   speck pepper
1 garlic clove, minced   ½ c. milk
1 tbsp. fat (preferably bacon fat)   1 tsp. lemon juice
1 tbsp. flour

Sauté garlic in hot fat until golden, add spinach and cook, covered, about 5 min., or until spinach is tender. Combine flour, salt and pepper and add milk and lemon juice slowly. Pour milk mixture over spinach and cook gently until thickened, tossing spinach with a fork.

> **Luncheon or Supper:** *Chicken* à la King, p. 304, with Rice, Panned *Spinach,* Tossed *Fruit* Salad with Mayonnaise—*Chocolate Chip Cream Pie.*

Here is perfection in a casserole:

Spinach and Cheese Casserole   *Yield:* 4 servings

1 pkg. (10 oz.) frozen chopped   2 hard-cooked eggs, quartered
    spinach, thawed   1 c. cheese sauce, see p. 201
½ tsp. salt   2 strips bacon, finely chopped and
speck pepper   cooked crisp

Place thawed spinach in 1-qt. casserole, add salt and pepper and hard-cooked eggs. Cover with cheese sauce (cooked only until cheese is barely melted). Top the spinach with chopped bacon strips and bake in moderate oven, 350°F., about 25 min.

> **Dinner:** *Minestrone—Swiss Steak,* p. 220, Baked Potato, *Spinach* and Cheese Casserole—*Strawberry* and *Peach* Compote.

OTHER SPINACH RECIPES

Oysters Rockefeller. *See p. 281.*
Poached Eggs on Spinach. *See p. 446.*

COOKED SQUASH

A wonderful way to serve squash:

Squash New Orleans   *Yield:* 4–6 servings

1 pkg. (14 oz.) cooked squash,   ¾ tsp. salt
    thawed   2 slices bread, preferably whole
4 strips bacon, diced   wheat
1 clove garlic, minced   2 eggs, beaten
¼ c. chopped onion   buttered bread crumbs
¼ c. melted butter or margarine

Cook bacon until crisp, then drain on absorbent paper, reserving about 2 tbsp. fat in pan. Add garlic and onion to bacon fat and sauté until delicate brown. Combine squash, bacon, garlic and onion, add butter and salt. Soak bread slices in cold water a few minutes, then squeeze out excess moisture and add bread to squash. Add beaten eggs, mix well and place in greased 1-qt. casserole. Top with buttered crumbs and bake in moderately hot oven, 400°F., 30–40 min.

> **Dinner:** Broiled *Swordfish* with Mustard Sauce, p. 263, *Crinkle-Cut Potatoes, Squash* New Orleans, Tomato Wedges on Lettuce— *Raspberry* Sundae.

A festive dish for serving with turkey, ham or pork:

Squash Baked with Pineapple
1 pkg. (14 oz.) frozen cooked squash, thawed
1 pkg. (13½ oz.) frozen pineapple chunks, thawed

Yield: 4–6 servings
¾ tsp. salt
3 tbsp. butter or margarine
¼ c. brown sugar

Add salt and 2 tbsp. butter to squash and place half the squash in 1-qt. casserole. Drain pineapple thoroughly, add half of it to squash in casserole, dot with ½ tbsp. butter and sprinkle with 2 tbsp. brown sugar. Add remaining squash, then remaining pineapple, dot with remaining butter and sprinkle with remaining brown sugar. Bake in moderate oven, 350°F., 45–50 min.

> **Dinner:** Broiled Ham Steak, *French-Fried Potatoes, Squash* Baked with *Pineapple—Ice Cream* with Chocolate Peppermint Sauce p. 434.

Another meal-in-a-dish recipe, and a tasty one:

Squash Pudding with Sausage
1 pkg. (14 oz.) frozen cooked squash, thawed
2 tbsp. butter or margarine
1 egg, well beaten
½ c. top milk or light cream

Yield: 4 servings
2 tbsp. brown sugar
¼ tsp. nutmeg
¾ tsp. salt
speck pepper
½ lb. link sausages

Add all ingredients except sausages to squash, combine thoroughly and place in 1-qt. casserole. Prick sausages with a fork, place in pan and put in moderately hot oven, 400°F., for about 10 min. Place sausages on top of squash and bake at 400°F. for about 15 min.

> **Dinner:** *Pineapple Juice—Squash* Pudding with Sausage, Buttered *Broccoli Spears, Cornmeal Muffins,* Pickled Beet and Sliced Onion Salad—Rhubarb Puff Pudding, p. 418.

An autumn dish, but good all year:

Squash and Corn Pudding

Yield: 6–8 servings

1 pkg. (14 oz.) frozen cooked
squash, thawed
1 pkg. (10 oz.) frozen corn,
cream-style, thawed
1 small onion, chopped
1 tbsp. fat

1 egg, beaten
1 tsp. salt
speck pepper
1 c. fine bread crumbs
1 tbsp. butter or margarine

Brown onion lightly in hot fat. Then thoroughly combine squash, corn, onion, salt, pepper and egg. Add ¾ c. bread crumbs and combine lightly. Place in 1½-qt. casserole, dot with butter and cover with remaining bread crumbs. Bake in moderate oven, 350°F., until corn is tender and top is browned, about 40 min.

> **Dinner:** Roast *Turkey* with Sausage Stuffing, p. 314, Baked Potato, *Squash* and *Corn* Pudding, *Cranberry-Orange Relish—Pumpkin* Chiffon Pie, p. 364.

Squash Muffins

Prepare as for Pumpkin Muffins, p. 336, using ¾ c. frozen, thawed squash instead of pumpkin.

Squash Mallow. *See p. 445.*

VERSATILE RECIPES FOR VEGETABLES

This always lends interest to the main course:

Vegetable au Gratin

Yield: 4–5 servings

1 pkg. frozen vegetable[3]
2 tbsp. flour
2 tbsp. butter
½ tsp. salt
speck pepper
⅛ tsp. Worcestershire sauce

dash cayenne
1 c. liquid (use liquid from cooked
vegetable and milk to give 1 c.)
½ c. buttered, soft bread crumbs
½ c. grated sharp Cheddar cheese
paprika

Cook vegetable until tender and drain. Prepare cream sauce from remaining ingredients except bread crumbs, cheese and paprika (see directions, p. 200, or make medium sauce from condensed

---

[3] Almost any kind of vegetable can be used, e.g., cut asparagus, chopped broccoli, Brussels sprouts; cauliflower, lima beans, green beans or wax beans are especially good. Left-over vegetables can be used, combining several if desired, using about 1½ c. vegetable. Or for serving a larger number, use two packages of different kinds of vegetable, doubling the other ingredients in the recipe.

canned soup, following directions given with those for preparation of cream sauce).

Place vegetable and sauce in alternating layers in greased 1-qt. casserole. Combine bread crumbs with cheese and top casserole with this mixture and sprinkle with paprika. Bake in moderate oven, 375°F., until nicely browned, about 15 min.

A quick and easy way to make a welcome soup:

Cream of Vegetable Soup   *Yield:* 3–4 servings

1–2 c. frozen vegetable, cooked and drained

1 c. thin cream sauce, p. 200

seasonings as desired

paprika or chopped parsley or chives

Almost any kind of freshly cooked or left-over vegetable can be used. In place of making your own cream sauce, you can use condensed cream of celery or cream of mushroom soup, adding milk according to instructions on the can for making soup. If you use the contents of the entire can (10½ oz.), diluted according to instructions, you will need 2–3 c. cooked vegetable, yielding 6–8 servings.

Or if a large proportion of vegetable is used, milk may be used in place of cream sauce, since the vegetables give "body" to the soup.

Place the vegetable and seasonings in the electric blender, adding part of the cream sauce or milk, if desired, and blend thoroughly. Heat all ingredients except paprika or parsley to serving temperature and serve, sprinkling with paprika or chopped parsley.

CHAPTER 17

Frozen Fruits and Fruit Juices

HOW TO USE FROZEN FRUITS AND FRUIT JUICES

Fruits

Most frozen fruits are fine when served the way you would serve fresh ones, as fruit cup or fruit cocktail, in salads, or as dessert toppings and in many other ways. They are also entirely satisfactory for use in many recipes.

Thawing Frozen Fruits.—The fruit should always be left in its unopened container until the time it is used, chiefly to retain its full flavor. Turn it several times during thawing, if convenient, to insure uniform thawing and also to keep the pieces of fruit covered with the syrup which protects them.

Thawing in the refrigerator is best, since it is more uniform and there is less change in the texture of the fruits. For emergencies, they can be thawed more quickly at room temperature, or in front of an electric fan, or in cold water if the container is watertight. But when thawed by these quick methods, the quality of the fruit is not as fine.

The following are the times required to thaw fruits which are packed in syrup or sugar. Those packed without sweetening thaw more slowly.

Time to Thaw Pint (Pound) Packages of Fruits Packed in Syrup or Sugar

In refrigerator	At room temperature	In front of electric fan	In cold water
5–8 hrs.	2–4 hrs.	1 hr.	30–60 min.

For Use in Fruit Cup or Salads, and as Toppings.—For such uses as these, the fruit should be served when barely thawed and still icy cold. After that, the fruit loses some of its flavor and begins to collapse. This effect is less evident in fruits which are packed in heavy syrups than in light ones, since the heavy syrups help the fruits to keep their good texture.

374

Fruits intended for use at breakfast can be placed in the refrigerator the night before. An hour or two extra time in the refrigerator is not as detrimental as extra time by quicker methods of thawing.

Light colored fruits, even when treated with ascorbic acid, will darken if allowed to stand long after thawing, especially after the container has been opened. Frozen fruits do not become dangerous to eat on standing, any more than fresh ones do, but they gradually lose their best flavor and texture, and the ascorbic acid content may become lower. If they are not to be used soon, it is best to cook them.

So for these reasons, it is important to thaw at one time only as much as you will use at one meal.

For Other Uses.—As a rule, frozen fruits to be used in cooking need to be thawed only enough to be able to separate the pieces, and this takes about half as long as the time given in the above chart for complete thawing. For instance, frozen fruits for use in pies need to be thawed only enough to spread the fruit over the lower crust.

For use in recipes, take into account the sugar which has been added when the fruit was frozen. Packages of frozen fruits often have more juice than is called for in recipes for baked products, and so they may need extra thickening. For the amount of extra thickening to use in making fruit pies, p. 175. Or in some cases, you may prefer to use the extra juice as a beverage or in some other recipes. On the other hand, if there is not enough juice for a recipe, or enough to prevent scorching, add water as needed.

Some frozen fruits are splendid for making uncooked jams. When packed in sugar or syrup, the juice provides the necessary liquid, so cooking to extract juice (as in making jams from fresh fruits) is not necessary. These jams have the natural color and flavor of the fresh fruit.

Fruit Juices

Most frozen fruit juices are now sold as concentrates in cans, and these are easy to thaw. Place the can in a pan of water for a few minutes until the juice around the edges of the can is thawed, then pour the concentrate into a large container and add cold water as recommended. Let stand until all the juice is thawed, stirring occasionally. The flavor of the reconstituted juice is often improved by incorporating air into it. If the juice does not fill the container, cover the container and shake it vigorously. Or pour it back and forth several times from one container to another, or aerate it in your electric blender.

For these juices to be served at breakfast, leave the unopened can in the refrigerator overnight, and by morning, the concentrate will be thawed and ready to be reconstituted.

It is better not to reconstitute more of these juices than you will use at one time, but if there is some left, it can be stored in a tightly covered container in the refrigerator, for a day or two.

For a discussion of the cost of frozen orange juice compared with the cost of freshly squeezed juice, see p. 35. And for statements concerning the ascorbic acid contents of these juices, see p. 26.

RECIPES AND MENUS

BLACKBERRIES—BOYSENBERRIES—LOGANBERRIES

A frozen delight . . . an easy dessert that the family will enjoy:

Frozen Boysenberry or Loganberry Cream   *Yield:* About 1½ qts.

1 pkg. (10 oz.) frozen boysenberries or loganberries, partially thawed
¾ c. sugar
⅛ tsp. salt

1 can (14½ oz.) thoroughly chilled evaporated milk
1 tbsp. lemon juice

Add sugar and salt to berries and heat just long enough to dissolve the sugar. Put the mixture through a coarse sieve. Whip evaporated milk until stiff and fold lemon juice into it. Add fruit mixture and combine. Pour into ice cube tray or other freezing mold, and put into freezer to freeze. Do not stir during freezing.

> **Luncheon or Supper:** Curried *Veal* Casserole, p. 248, *Green Bean* and Celery Salad, p. 334, *Cornmeal Muffins*——Frozen *Loganberry* Cream.

An exotic flavor and a lovely color in a quickly made dessert:

Blackberry, Grapefruit and Orange Compote   *Yield:* 8 servings

1 pkg. (10 oz.) frozen blackberries, thawed
1 pkg. (13½ oz.) frozen grapefruit sections, thawed

1½ c. orange sections and juice
¾ c. grenadine syrup
1½ tbsp. lemon juice

Combine berries and grapefruit sections (with their juices), add remaining ingredients and hold an hour or so in refrigerator before serving, so flavors will be blended.

Dinner: *Chicken* Tetrazzini, p. 310, Buttered *Broccoli,* Tossed Green Salad—*Blackberry, Grapefruit* and Orange Compote, *Cookies.*

OTHER BLACKBERRY, BOYSENBERRY OR LOGANBERRY RECIPES

Blackberry, Boysenberry or Loganberry Cream Roll. *See p. 416.*

Blackberry, Boysenberry or Loganberry Meringue Glacé. *See p. 416.*

Blackberry, Boysenberry or Loganberry Puff Pudding. *See p. 418.*

Blackberry, Boysenberry or Loganberry Pinwheels. *See p. 419.*

Blackberry, Boysenberry or Loganberry Whip. *See p. 419.*

Blackberry, Boysenberry or Loganberry Shortcake. *See p. 420.*

Blackberry, Boysenberry or Loganberry Devonshire Tarts. *See p. 420.*

Blackberry, Boysenberry or Loganberry Sauce. *See p. 430.*

Cooked Blackberry, Boysenberry or Loganberry Jam. *See p. 421.*

BLUEBERRIES

It couldn't be easier . . . it couldn't taste better:

Blueberry Crumb Pudding   *Yield:* 4 servings

1 pkg. (12 oz.) frozen blueberries, partially thawed
1 c. zwieback crumbs
¼ c. sugar

¼ tsp. cinnamon
3 tbsp. melted butter or margarine
dessert topping

Combine zwieback crumbs, sugar, cinnamon and melted butter. Place ²/₃ c. drained blueberries in small greased casserole and cover with one-third of crumb mixture. Add remaining blueberries and crumb mixture in alternating layers, making 3 layers of blueberries and topping with crumbs. Press down firmly with spoon. Bake in moderate oven, 350° F., about 30 min. Cool for about 5 min., then unmold on serving plate and top with whipped dessert topping.

Dinner: *Chicken* Marengo, p. 304, *Asparagus* Hollandaise, p. 329, Celery and Carrot Strips, Radish Roses—*Blueberry* Crumb Pudding.

Try these, and find a new, delicious pancake:

Blueberry Pancakes   *Yield:* about 1 doz. cakes, 4–5 in.
                             in diameter

1 pkg. (12 oz.) frozen blueberries,   1 tbsp. sugar
  thawed   1 egg, well beaten
1¼ c. flour   1 c. milk
1½ tsp. baking powder   2 tbsp. oil or melted shortening
½ tsp. salt

Drain blueberries thoroughly. Sift dry ingredients together. Combine egg, milk and oil thoroughly, and add these all at once to a "well" in the center of the dry ingredients. Combine only until dry ingredients are all dampened. Fold in blueberries carefully, without crushing them. If preferred, blueberries may be sprinkled over each pancake as soon as the batter is dropped on the griddle.

Bake on griddle iron or heavy skillet which has been evenly heated, greasing or not, according to instructions for using the griddle (usually a skillet needs to be lightly greased). Drop batter on hot griddle from tip of spoon. Turn the cakes with pancake turner as soon as they are full of bubbles, and continue cooking until brown on underside. Turn only once during baking.

Brunch: *Orange Juice––Blueberry* Pancakes with Sausage Links *––Mixed Fruit* Cup, Coffee.

———

Muffins with blueberries in them are always a treat:

Blueberry Muffins   *Yield:* 1 doz. medium muffins
¾ c. thawed, drained blueberries   3 tbsp. sugar
2 c. flour   1 egg
¾ tsp. salt   ¾ c. milk
3 tsp. baking powder   ¼ c. oil or melted shortening

Drain blueberries very thoroughly. Sift dry ingredients together into mixing bowl. Beat egg slightly, add milk and oil and combine well. Add liquid ingredients all at once, to a "well" in center of dry ingredients and combine only until dry ingredients are all dampened. Fold in blueberries carefully, without crushing them. Turn into greased muffin pans, filling pans about two-thirds full. Bake in hot oven 425°F., 15–20 min. or until done.

Luncheon or Supper: *Chicken Livers* in Scrambled Eggs, p. 313, *Grapefruit* and *Pineapple* Salad, p. 387, *Blueberry* Muffins— *Chocolate Ice Cream*, Cookies.

This is a luscious blueberry dessert, for any meal:

Blueberry Cottage Pudding   *Yield:* 6 servings
1 pkg. (12 oz.) frozen blueberries,   ¾ c. milk
  thawed   1½ c. flour
2 tbsp. flour   2 tsp. baking powder
¹/₃ c. shortening   ½ tsp. salt
1 egg, well beaten   lemon sauce, p. 391, if desired

Drain blueberries, and combine 2 tbsp. flour with them, coating each berry with flour without crushing them. Sift remaining dry ingredients together. Cream shortening until soft, gradually cream in sugar until mixture is consistency of hard sauce. Add egg and beat thoroughly. Add milk and dry ingredients alternately, as in making cake. Finally, fold in blueberries gently, avoiding crushing them. Turn into greased 8 x 8 x 2 in. cake pan and bake in moderate oven, 350°F., 40–45 min. or until done. Serve with lemon sauce, if desired.

> **Dinner:** Broiled *Steak* with Mushrooms, p. 215, Mashed Potatoes, *Spinach* in Onion Sauce, p. 369, Tomato Salad—*Blueberry* Cottage Pudding with *Lemon* Sauce.

These will be a favorite, any time, anywhere:

Blueberry Dumplings   *Yield:* 6–8 servings
1 pkg. (12 oz.) frozen blueberries,   3 tsp. baking powder
  thawed   ¾ tsp. salt
¼ tsp. salt   3 tbsp. sugar
¹/₃ c. sugar   1½ tbsp. shortening
1 tbsp. cornstarch   ²/₃–¾ c. milk
1 tbsp. butter or margarine   dessert topping
1½ c. flour

Drain blueberries. To the juice, add enough water to give 2 c. liquid. Place blueberries in 2- or 3-qt. kettle with tight-fitting lid, add liquid and salt and bring to boil. Combine ¹/₃ c. sugar with cornstarch, stir into hot mixture slowly, and cook until slightly thickened, stirring. Add butter. Prepare fruit dumpling dough from remaining ingredients except dessert topping (see directions, p. 197). Drop dumplings by spoonfuls on hot berry mixture, cover kettle tightly and boil gently 12—15 min., or until dumplings are done. Serve with whipped dessert topping.

Luncheon or Supper: *Vegetable Soup*—Cold Pressed *Lamb Shoulder*, p. 237, Cole Slaw, Tomato and Cucumber Salad— *Blueberry* Dumplings.

Cinnamon adds a good flavor to blueberries:

Blueberry Cream   *Yield:* 5 servings

1 pkg. (12 oz.) frozen blueberries   ¼ tsp. cinnamon
1 c. water   1 tbsp. lemon juice
¼ c. cornstarch   custard sauce (see p. 201) or
¼ c. sugar   dessert topping, whipped
¼ tsp. salt

Add water to blueberries and bring slowly to boiling point. Combine cornstarch, sugar, salt and cinnamon thoroughly and add slowly to blueberries, stirring. Cook until thickened, stirring constantly. Simmer about 5 min., then remove from heat. Add lemon juice and pour into serving dishes and chill thoroughly. Serve with custard sauce or whipped dessert topping.

Luncheon or Supper: New England *Scallop* Supper, p. 284, *Broccoli* with Garlic Butter, p. 342—*Blueberry* Cream with Custard Sauce.

A treasured, blueberry favorite:

Blueberry Pie   *Yield:* 8-inch pie

1 pkg. (12 oz.) frozen blueberries,   speck salt
   packed in syrup, partially thawed   ½ tsp. lemon juice
1½ tbsp. cornstarch   butter or margarine
¹/₃ c. sugar (brown preferred)   pastry dough for 2-crust, 8-inch pie
⅛ tsp. nutmeg   (see p. 196)
⅛ tsp. cinnamon

Combine cornstarch, sugar and seasonings thoroughly. Add lemon juice to blueberries, then add the dry ingredients and combine well.

Arrange lower crust in pie plate and put filling into it.   Dot with butter and put upper crust in place.   Seal the upper and lower crusts together and prick the upper crust to allow steam to escape.   Bake in hot oven, 450°F. for 15 min., then reduce heat to 350°F. and bake about 25 min. longer or until done.

Note: For Blueberry Tarts, the same filling as above may be used.

Dinner: *Cream of Shrimp Soup*—*Chicken* Salad de Luxe— p. 308, *Asparagus Spears* on Lettuce with French Dressing— *Blueberry* Pie.

OTHER BLUEBERRY RECIPES

Blueberry Cream Roll. *See p. 416.*
Blueberry Meringue Glacé. *See p. 416.*
Blueberry Puff Pudding. *See p. 418.*
Blueberry Pinwheels. *See p. 419.*
Blueberry Whip. *See p. 419.*
Blueberry Shortcake. *See page 420.*
Blueberry Devonshire Tarts. *See p. 420.*
Blueberry Sauce. *See p. 430.*
Cooked Blueberry Jam. *See p. 421.*

RED SOUR PITTED CHERRIES

A favorite for generations . . . and now you can make it any time of the year:

Cherry Cobbler

	Yield: 4–5 servings
1 pkg. (10 oz.) frozen red sour pitted cherries, partially thawed	1½ c. flour
2 tbsp. sugar	3 tsp. baking powder
1 tbsp. cornstarch	¾ tsp. salt
⅛ tsp. salt	3 tbsp. sugar
¼ c. water	1½ tbsp. shortening
1 tbsp. butter or margarine	$^2/_3$–¾ c. milk

Combine 2 tbsp. sugar, cornstarch, ⅛ tsp. salt and water and add this mixture to cherries, stirring together gently.   Place in greased, shallow baking dish, 6 x 10 inches, and dot with butter.

Prepare cobbler dough from remaining ingredients (see directions, p. 197).   Or use 1½ c. biscuit mix and add milk.

Drop dough on cherries, by spoonfuls. Bake in hot oven, 425°F., about 30 min. or until done.

Luncheon or Supper: New England *Clam* Chowder, p. 269, Crackers —*Green Beans* and *Cauliflower* Salad, p. 335—*Cherry* Cobbler.

Gorgeous color, and wonderful flavor:

Cherry Whip   *Yield:* 6 servings
1 pkg. (10 oz.) frozen red sour   3 tbsp. water
   pitted cherries, partially thawed   2 egg whites
½ c. sugar   ⅛ tsp. salt
1 tbsp. (1 envelope) unflavored   custard sauce (see p. 201)
   gelatin

Drain cherries. Add water to juice to make 1 c. liquid and add sugar. Add cherries and cook together about 3 min., then drain off juice. Add water to gelatin and soak about 5 min. Then add hot cherry juice to gelatin and stir until gelatin is dissolved. Chill until the mixture thickens to about the consistency of raw egg white. Then beat with a rotary or electric beater until very light and fluffy. Add salt to egg whites and beat until stiff, then fold them into the gelatin mixture. Pour part of the whip into mold, then add some cherries and add remaining whip and cherries in alternating layers. Chill until set. Serve with custard sauce.

Dinner: Baked *Fish* Fillets, Spencer, p. 257, Mashed Potatoes, *Peas* with Tiny Onions, p. 359—*Cherry* Whip with Custard Sauce.

The very name is intriguing . . . and just try the pie:

Toasted Cherry Chiffon Pie   *Yield:* 8-inch pie
1 pkg. (10 oz.) frozen red sour   2 egg whites
   pitted cherries, partially thawed   1 tbsp. sugar
2½ tbsp. cornstarch   8-inch pie shell, baked and cooled
¼ c. sugar

Drain cherries, and to juice add water to make ¾ c. liquid. Combine sugar and cornstarch, blend with juice and cook until thickened, stirring constantly. Add cherries to cornstarch mixture and cook about 3 min. Cool until lukewarm.

Courtesy of General Foods Kitchens

For a change, prepare an attractive lattice top for cherry pie, or for any other two-crust pie

Beat egg whites until foamy, then add 1 tbsp. sugar gradually while beating until whites are stiff. Fold egg whites into cherry mixture and pour into baked pie shell. Bake in slow oven, 325°F., for about 20 min. or until lightly browned.

Dinner: Broiled *Ham Slices,* Baked Potato, *Squash* Baked with *Pineapple,* p. 371, Tomato Salad—Toasted *Cherry* Chiffon Pie.

"Can she make a cherry pie, Billy Boy" . . . *Oh, yes, for it is really easy to do:*

Cherry Pie

1 pkg. (10 oz.) frozen red sour
   pitted cherries, partially thawed
½ c. sugar
2 tbsp. cornstarch
⅛ tsp. salt

Yield: 7-inch pie

1½ tbsp. butter or margarine
pastry for 2-crust, 7-inch pie (see
   p. 196)

Combine sugar, cornstarch and salt, add to cherries and blend well. Roll out lower crust and line pie plate with it. Add cherry mixture and dot with butter. Cover with top crust and seal upper and lower crusts together. Prick upper crust and bake in hot oven, 450°F., 15 min., then reduce heat to moderate, 350°F., and bake 30 min. longer, or until done.

Luncheon or Supper: *Lobster* Newburg on Toast Points, p. 276, *Broccoli* with Garlic Butter, p. 342, Green Salad—*Cherry* Pie.

Mix this right in the baking pan, to save time:

Baked Cherry Pudding   *Yield:* 6 servings

1 pkg. (10 oz.) frozen red sour   1½ tsp. baking powder
   pitted cherries, partially thawed   ½ c. milk
6 tbsp. butter or margarine   ½ c. boiling water
½ c. sugar   ½ tsp. vanilla
1½ c. flour   dessert topping, whipped, if desired
½ tsp. salt

In 1-qt. greased loaf pan, cream ¼ c. butter until soft and gradually cream in sugar. Sift flour, salt and baking powder together. Add flour mixture to creamed butter and sugar, alternately with milk, blending well. Spread mixture lightly in bottom of baking pan. Combine cherries, boiling water, vanilla and remaining 2 tbsp. butter and bring this mixture to a boil, then pour it over the batter. Bake in moderate oven, 350°F., about 30 min. Serve with whipped dessert topping, if desired.

Dinner: *Steak* with Kidney Beans, p. 220, Baked Potato, *Brussels Sprouts* with Lemon Butter, p. 347, Cottage Cheese and Onion Salad—Baked *Cherry* Pudding.

Beautiful to see, luscious to taste:

Red Cherry Dumplings   *Yield:* 6–8 servings

1 pkg. (10 oz.) frozen red sour   1½ c. flour
   pitted cherries, partially thawed   3 tsp. baking powder
1½ c. water   ¾ tsp. salt
¼ c. sugar   3 tbsp. sugar
1 tbsp. cornstarch   1½ tbsp. shortening
⅛ tsp. salt   ⅔–¾ c. milk
1 tbsp. butter or margarine

Add water to cherries and bring to boil in deep kettle. Blend sugar, cornstarch and salt and add to cherry mixture, then cook until clear and thickened, stirring constantly. Add butter.

Prepare fruit dumpling dough from remaining ingredients (see directions, p. 197). Drop dumplings by spoonfuls on hot cherry mixture. Cover tightly and boil gently about 15 min., or until dumplings are done.

> **Dinner:** *Turkey Tetrazzini,* Mashed Potatoes, *Asparagus* Hollandaise, p. 329, Relishes—*Red Cherry* Dumplings.

Try this for a breakfast sweet, or for dessert with cream:

Red Cherry Roll-Ups

1 pkg. (20 oz.), or 2 pkgs. (10 oz. each) frozen red sour pitted cherries, partially thawed
½ c. sugar
2 c. flour
4 tsp. baking powder

Yield: 6–8 servings
1 tsp. salt
¼ c. sugar
2 tbsp. shortening
¾–1 c. milk
cream

Drain cherries. Add ½ c. sugar to cherry juice and pour this into greased baking pan, 8 inches square. Place baking pan in hot oven, 425°F., while preparing biscuit dough. Prepare biscuit dough from remaining ingredients except cream (see directions, p. 197). Roll dough to shape of rectangle.

Spread drained cherries evenly over dough and roll up dough as for jelly roll. Cut roll into 1-inch pieces, using sharp knife. Place rolls in hot syrup in pan, with cut edges turned up, and bake in hot oven, 425°F., for about 35 min. or until browned and syrup bubbles around them. Serve warm, with cream.

> **Dinner:** *Scallops* with Mushrooms, p. 282, Mashed Potatoes, Buttered *Spinach, Green Bean* and Carrot Salad, p. 334—*Red Cherry* Roll-Ups.

OTHER RED SOUR PITTED CHERRY RECIPES

Red Cherry Sauce. *See p. 430.*
Cherry Upside Down Cake. *See p. 415.*

GRAPEFRUIT SECTIONS

The bland, smooth avocado pear is perfect with grapefruit:

Grapefruit and Avocado Salad   *Yield:* 4 servings

1 pkg. (13½ oz.) frozen grapefruit   crisp lettuce or watercress
sections, thawed   French dressing
1 avocado pear   paprika, or pimiento strips

Drain grapefruit sections. Pare avocado pear and cut in length-wise slices. Arrange grapefruit sections and avocado pear slices alternately on lettuce or watercress. Add French dressing and sprinkle with paprika or garnish with pimiento strips.

Dinner: Baked *Lobster* and Mushrooms, p. 275, Parsley Buttered *New Potatoes,* p. 361, Buttered Spinach, *Grapefruit* and Avocado Salad—*Banana Cake.*

Here is another delicious way of combining grapefruit and avocado pear:

Jellied Grapefruit and Avocado   *Yield:* 6 servings
Salad

1 pkg. (13½ oz.) frozen grapefruit   ¼ tsp. salt
sections, thawed   1 c. diced avocado pears
1 pkg. orange or lemon flavored   maraschino cherries (about 10)
gelatin   salad greens
1½ c. hot water   mayonnaise or salad dressing

Drain grapefruit sections, reserving juice. Dissolve gelatin in hot water and add ½ c. grapefruit juice and salt. Chill until mixture is consistency of thick raw egg white, then pour into mold. Arrange grapefruit sections, avocado and maraschino cherries in gelatin and chill until firm. Unmold on salad greens and serve with mayonnaise.

Dinner: Stuffed *Pork Chops,* p. 241, *French-Fried Potatoes,* Scalloped *Lima Beans,* p. 336, Jellied *Grapefruit* and Avocado Salad—*Brownies.*

As a salad or a dessert, this adds fine flavor:

Jellied Grapefruit, Tangerine and Dates

Yield: 4–6 servings

1 pkg. (13½ oz.) frozen grapefruit sections, thawed

1½ c. tangerine sections and juice (orange sections may be used instead)

¼ c. chopped dates

1½ tbsp. (1½ envelopes) unflavored gelatin

⅓ c. cold water

reconstituted frozen orange juice

¼ c. frozen lemon juice

Drain grapefruit and tangerine sections, reserving juice. Combine grapefruit and tangerine sections and add dates. Soak gelatin in cold water for 5 min. To juice drained from the fruits add enough orange juice to give 1¼ c. liquid. Heat the liquid and dissolve gelatin in it, then add lemon juice.

Chill the gelatin mixture until syrupy, and pour a small amount of it in mold. Arrange some of the fruit in it, chill until firm and add remaining gelatin and fruit in layers. Chill until set and unmold. Serve on salad greens or as a dessert, topping with whipped dessert topping or custard sauce.

Dinner: *King Crab Imperial, French-Fried Potatoes,* Parmesan *Broccoli,* p. 342, Jellied *Grapefruit,* Tangerines and Dates in Lettuce Cups with Dressing—*Strawberry* Shortcake, p. 420.

The light, sweet-sour taste makes this unusual:

Grapefruit and Pineapple Salad

Yield: 6 servings

1 pkg. (13½ oz.) frozen grapefruit sections, thawed

1 pkg. (13½ oz.) frozen pineapple chunks, thawed

1 pkg. (3 oz.) cream cheese

crisp salad greens

French dressing

1 pimiento, sliced thin

Drain grapefruit sections and pineapple chunks. Cut cream cheese into small cubes. Toss fruit pieces and cheese cubes lightly together, with French dressing. Arrange on salad greens and garnish with pimiento strips.

Dinner: *Lobster Newburg,* Baked Potato, *Spinach* in Onion Sauce, p. 369, *Grapefruit* and *Pineapple* Salad—*Ice Cream* with Praline Sauce, p. 434.

OTHER GRAPEFRUIT SECTION RECIPES

Artichoke Hearts and Grapefruit Salad. *See p. 327.*

Blackberry Grapefruit and Orange Compote. *See p. 376.*

Pineapple and Grapefruit Ginger Cocktail. *See p. 402.*

Shrimp and Grapefruit Salad. *See p. 290.*

Grapefruit and Crabmeat Cocktail. *See p. 272.*

LEMON JUICE AND LEMONADE

Everyone's favorite, and with no lemons to squeeze:

Lemon Meringue Pie *Yield:* 9-inch pie

5 tbsp. frozen lemon juice, thawed	3 egg yolks
5 tbsp. cornstarch	2 tbsp. butter or margarine
1 c. sugar	9-inch baked pie shell, cooled
¼ tsp. salt	3 egg whites
½ c. cold water	6 tbsp. sugar
1½ c. boiling water	⅛ tsp. salt

Combine cornstarch, 1 c. sugar and ¼ tsp. salt thoroughly, then add cold water and make smooth paste. Add boiling water slowly and cook until thickened, stirring constantly. Beat egg yolks slightly, add hot mixture to them, return to kettle and cook slowly about 2 min. longer, stirring constantly. Blend in butter and lemon juice and cool to lukewarm. Turn into 9-inch baked pie shell.

Prepare meringue from egg whites, 6 tbsp. sugar and ⅛ tsp. salt (see directions, p. 199). Place meringue over filling in swirls and bake in slow oven, 325°F., for 15–20 min. or until golden color.

> **Dinner:** Roast *Chicken* with Oyster Stuffing and Gravy, p. 302, *Candied Yams,* Panned *Spinach,* p. 369, *Peas* and Cheese Salad, p. 360—*Lemon* Meringue Pie.

So light and so delicate . . . really ethereal:

Lemon Chiffon Pie *Yield:* 9-inch pie

½ c. frozen lemon juice, thawed	1½ c. sugar
1 tbsp. (1 envelope) unflavored gelatin	4 egg whites
	9-inch pie shell, baked and cooled
¼ c. water	1 c. dessert topping, or heavy cream, whipped
4 egg yolks	

Soak gelatin in water for 5 min. Meanwhile, beat egg yolks well and add 1 c. sugar, salt and lemon juice to them. Cook egg yolk mixture in top of double boiler over hot water, until consistency of custard, stirring constantly. Add soaked gelatin to hot custard mixture, stirring to dissolve gelatin. Chill, and when mixture is consistency of raw egg white, beat vigorously with rotary or electric beater until very fluffy. Beat egg whites until foamy, and add remaining ½ c. sugar gradually, continuing to beat until stiff and glossy, then fold them into fluffy gelatin mixture. Pour into baked pie shell. If gelatin mixture is not stiff enough to stand up well in center of pie, chill the last third of it before adding it to pie. Chill several hours or overnight, until firm. Just before serving, whip dessert topping or cream and top pie with it.

Dinner: Broiled *Lamb Chops, Potatoes au Gratin, Peas and Carrots,* Tossed Green Salad—*Lemon* Chiffon Pie.

Somewhat like bisque tortoni, but with the zest of lemon:

Frozen Lemon Dessert　　　　*Yield:* 6 servings

2½ tbsp. frozen lemon juice,　　1½ tbsp. sugar
　thawed　　　　　　　　　　½ c. thoroughly chilled evaporated
1 egg yolk　　　　　　　　　　milk or cream
¼ c. sugar　　　　　　　　　　butter or margarine
1 egg white　　　　　　　　　½ c. crushed vanilla wafers

Beat egg yolk well in top of double boiler, add ¼ c. sugar and lemon juice, and cook over hot water, stirring, until thickened, about 2 min.

Beat egg white until foamy, add 1½ tbsp. sugar gradually and beat until stiff. Fold beaten egg white into lemon mixture. Whip evaporated milk or cream and fold into lemon mixture. Rub sides and bottom of ice cube tray or other mold with butter and spread half the crushed wafers in the bottom of it. Add lemon mixture and sprinkle remaining crushed wafers on top. Place in freezer until firm.

Luncheon or Supper: Tomato Stuffed with *Turkey* Salad, p. 316, Cole Slaw, Potato Chips, *Rolls,* Jelly—Frozen *Lemon* Dessert.

Here is a cake and a sauce, all in one:

Lemon Custard Pudding   *Yield:* 6 servings

¼ c. frozen lemon juice, thawed   2 tsp. grated lemon rind or ½ tsp.
½ c. sifted flour   lemon extract
1½ c. sugar   2 tbsp. melted butter or margarine
½ tsp. baking powder   1½ c. milk
¼ tsp. salt   3 egg whites
3 egg yolks

Sift flour, 1 c. sugar, baking powder and salt together. Beat egg yolks until light, add lemon rind (or extract), lemon juice, butter and milk, and beat thoroughly. Stir in dry ingredients and beat until smooth.

Beat egg whites until frothy, then add remaining ½ c. sugar gradually, beating after each addition and finally until they hold good peaks. Fold egg white mixture into egg yolk mixture. Pour into 2-qt. greased casserole, set in pan of hot water and bake in moderate oven, 350°F., about 45 min. or until golden brown. Chill at least an hour before serving.

The upper part of the pudding is cake-like and the lower part is a soft custard which serves as a sauce for the pudding.

> **Dinner:** *Snapper Soup*—Braised *Duck,* p. 319, *Candied Yams,* Hot *Artichoke Hearts* Vinaigrette, p. 326, Tossed Salad—*Lemon* Custard Pudding.

Light as a feather, and . . . so tasty:

Lemon Soufflé   *Yield:* 4–5 servings

3 tbsp. frozen lemon juice, thawed   ⅔ c. sugar
4 egg yolks   1 tsp. grated lemon rind, or ¼ tsp.
4 egg whites   lemon extract

Beat egg yolks until thick and lemon colored, then beat in sugar gradually. Add lemon juice and lemon rind (or extract), and beat well. Beat egg whites until stiff but not dry and fold them into the egg yolk mixture. Turn into 2-qt. greased casserole and set in pan of hot water. Bake in moderate oven, 350°F., for 45–60 min. or until knife inserted into center comes out clean.

> **Dinner:** Baked *Haddock* with Cheese Sauce, p. 256, Mashed Potatoes, *Asparagus Spears,* Chef's Salad—*Lemon* Soufflé.

A sauce with many uses . . . with cottage pudding, steamed pudding,
fruit pudding, and on pound cake cut in thin slices:

Lemon Sauce   *Yield:* 1 cup
2 tbsp. frozen lemon juice, thawed   1 c. boiling water
½ c. sugar   2 tbsp. butter or margarine
1 tbsp. cornstarch $1/_{16}$ tsp. salt

Mix cornstarch and sugar thoroughly, add boiling water gradually
and mix until smooth. Boil about 5 min., or until thickened, stirring
constantly. Add butter, lemon juice and salt.

The most refreshing of all summer drinks:

Lemonade   *Yield:* 4 tall glasses
$2/_3$ c. frozen lemon juice, thawed $3^1/_3$ c. cold water
½ c. finely granulated sugar   ice cubes

Mix sugar and cold water in pitcher until sugar is dissolved. Add
lemon juice and mix well. Just before serving, add ice cubes.

Fun to make . . . and still more fun to eat:

Crisp Lemon Cookies   *Yield:* about 4 doz. cookies
$1/_3$ c. plus 1 tbsp. frozen lemonade   2 c. flour
   (not diluted), thawed   1 tsp. baking powder
½ c. softened butter or margarine   ¼ tsp. salt
¾ c. sugar

Cream butter, gradually adding sugar and creaming until mixture
is consistency of hard sauce. Sift flour, baking powder and salt together. Add dry ingredients and lemonade alternately to creamed
mixture, beating well after each addition. Form dough into ball,
cover, and place in refrigerator several hours to chill.

Shape pieces of dough into ¾-inch balls and place on cooky sheet
about 2 inches apart. Dip the bottom of a glass tumbler into flour,
and press the tumbler evenly on each ball of dough to form thin
rounds with slightly ruffled edges. Bake in moderate oven, 325°F.,
for 18–20 min. depending on thickness.

Some like it before dinner, others prefer it afterwards:

Whisky Sour   *Yield:* 4 servings
1 can (6 oz.) frozen lemonade,   crushed ice
  thawed   maraschino cherries
½ c. (4 oz.) bourbon whisky   orange slices
¼ c. water

Place lemonade (undiluted) in cocktail shaker, add bourbon and water and shake well. Add crushed ice and shake again. Pour into cocktail glasses, and garnish with maraschino cherry or orange slice, if desired.

Rosy as a sunset, cooling and welcome to the taste:

Claret Lemonade   *Yield:* 1 serving
¼ c. (2 oz.) frozen lemon juice,   ice cubes
  thawed   maraschino cherries
1–2 tbsp. sugar   orange slices
½ c. (4 oz.) claret wine

Add sugar to lemon juice and claret wine, and mix until sugar is dissolved. Pour into serving glass and fill with ice cubes. Decorate with maraschino cherry and orange slice, if desired.

Of all the long, cool drinks, the most popular:

Tom Collins   *Yield:* 1 serving
2 tbsp. frozen lemon juice, thawed   chilled, carbonated water
3 tbsp. (1½ oz.) gin   2 or 3 mint leaves, and maraschino
1 tbsp. finely granulated sugar   cherry, if desired
2 or 3 ice cubes

Put lemon juice, gin and sugar into 10-oz. glass and stir well. Add ice cubes and fill glass with carbonated water. Decorate with mint leaves and maraschino cherries, if desired.

Cuba Libre

Substitute light rum for gin, and cola for carbonated beverage in the recipe for Tom Collins, above. Omit sugar.

Rum Collins

Substitute light rum for gin, in recipe for Tom Collins, above.

Chilled to the bone?   Gather 'round a log fire and sip:

Hot Toddy   *Yield:* 1 serving
2 tbsp. frozen lemon juice, thawed   1 tsp. sugar
¼ c. (2 oz.) whisky   hot water

Place lemon juice, whisky and sugar in 10-oz. glass and mix well.
Fill glass with hot water, and stir well.

Looks as innocent as pink lemonade, but don't be deceived:

Sloe Gin Fizz   *Yield:* 1 serving
2 tbsp. frozen lemon juice, thawed   3 ice cubes
¼ c. (2 oz.) sloe gin   chilled, carbonated water

Place ice cubes in 10-oz. glass and pour lemon juice and sloe gin
over them.   Fill glass with carbonated water.

OTHER LEMON JUICE RECIPES

Citrus Banana Sherbet. *See p. 396.*
Raspberry Sherbet. *See p. 407.*
Raspberry Grape Punch. *See p. 407.*
Strawberry Punch. *See p. 414.*

MIXED FRUITS

This is definitely the best frozen fruit salad ever:

Frozen Fruit Salad   *Yield:* 3–4 servings
1 pkg. (12 oz.) frozen mixed fruit,   2 tbsp. chopped maraschino
  thawed   cherries
½ pkg. (scant ¼ c.) lemon-flavored   ¼ c. heavy cream or dessert
  gelatin   topping, whipped
¼ c. water   crisp lettuce
speck salt   watercress, if desired
3 tbsp. mayonnaise

Drain fruit, reserving juice. Add water to juice and heat (not to boiling). Add gelatin to hot liquid and stir until it is dissolved, adding salt and mayonnaise and blending well. Chill until the mixture is the consistency of raw egg white, then fold in fruit and maraschino cherries, cutting any large pieces like peaches into bite-sizes. Whip dessert topping or heavy cream and fold it into gelatin mixture.

Turn into mold and chill until firm, then unmold on crisp lettuce and garnish with watercress, if desired.

If not to be used soon, this salad may be stored in the freezer. Remove from freezer long enough before serving for fruits to be not hard-frozen. The salad may be used in small servings as an accompaniment to the main course, or in larger servings as a dessert salad.

Dinner: *Cream of Potato Soup*—Scalloped *Oysters,* p. 277, *Broccoli* with Onion Sauce, p. 341—Frozen *Fruit* Salad, *Brownies.*

Luscious fruit, marshmallows and pecans . . . what a surprise:

Fruit Surprise Dessert

Yield: 3–4 servings

1 pkg. (12 oz.) frozen mixed fruit, thawed
½ pkg. (scant ¼ c.) strawberry-flavored gelatin
½ c. water

$^1/_3$ c. halved pecans
about 30 miniature marshmallows
1 tbsp. sugar
½ c. dessert topping or heavy cream

Drain mixed fruit, reserving juice. Add water to juice and heat, but not to boiling. Add gelatin to hot liquid and stir until dissolved. Chill until the consistency of raw egg white, then fold in fruit, pecans and marshmallows. Add sugar to dessert topping or heavy cream and whip, then fold into gelatin mixture. Pour into individual molds, or large party mold and chill until firm. To unmold, set mold in hot water an instant and invert onto serving dish.

Dinner: *Beef-Vegetable Soup*—*Turkey* Casserole, p. 315, *Candied Yams,* Tossed Green Salad—*Fruit* Surprise Dessert, *Cookies.*

ANOTHER MIXED FRUITS RECIPE

Fruit Melange. *See p. 447.*

ORANGE JUICE

An unusual dessert, delicate texture and flavor:

Orange Cake Pudding

Yield: 4–6 servings

½ c. reconstituted, frozen orange juice
2 tbsp. frozen lemon juice, thawed
½ c. sugar
2 tbsp. flour
⅛ tsp. salt
2 tbsp. melted butter or margarine

1 tsp. grated lemon rind, or ¼ tsp. lemon extract
1 c. milk
2 egg yolks, well beaten
2 egg whites, beaten stiff

Combine sugar, flour and salt well. Then combine butter, lemon juice, orange juice and lemon rind (or extract) and add to sugar-flour mixture. Mix well. Combine egg yolks with milk, and add to mixture, then finally fold in beaten egg whites. (The mixture should be thin, like uncooked custard.)

Pour mixture into greased individual baking dishes or baking pan about 6 x 10 in. and place in pan of hot water. Bake in moderate oven, 350°F., about 30 min. or until custard is set.

Luncheon or Supper: *Escalloped Chicken and Noodles, Asparagus* Aspic Salad, p. 328—*Orange* Cake Pudding.

As easy as 1-2-3, and delicious served as a sundae with thawed fruit or berries:

Frozen Orange Cream

Yield: about 1½ qt.

1 c. reconstituted frozen orange juice
2 tbsp. frozen lemon juice, thawed
1 tsp. grated lemon rind, or ¼ tsp. lemon extract

1 can (14½ oz.) evaporated milk, thoroughly chilled
¾ c. sugar

Whip evaporated milk and gradually add sugar, continuing to beat until stiff. Fold in the orange juice, lemon juice and rind or extract. Place in ice cube tray or other mold and put in freezer to freeze. Do not stir during freezing.

Dinner: Tomato Juice—Swiss *Steak,* p. 220, *French-Fried Potatoes,* Parmesan *Broccoli,* p. 342, *Rolls*—Frozen *Orange* Cream with *Raspberries.*

Orange, lemon and banana flavors are superb together:

Citrus Banana Sherbet   *Yield:* 6–8 servings

½ c. reconstituted frozen orange   ½ c. sugar
   juice   ¼ tsp. salt
3 tbsp. frozen lemon juice, thawed   1 medium banana
1 c. milk   1 egg white

Dissolve sugar and salt in milk. Mash banana (there should be about ½ c. mashed). Add banana, orange and lemon juice to milk and turn into ice cube tray or other freezing mold. Place in freezer until slightly mushy. Then beat egg white until stiff and fold it into freezing mixture. Put mixture back in mold and freeze until consistency of a firm mush. Meanwhile, put bowl and beater in refrigerator or freezer to chill. Beat freezing mixture in cold bowl with cold beater (rotary or electric) very quickly until it is smooth, but not allowing it to melt. Quickly return it to the mold and to the freezer and freeze until firm. For a still smoother mixture, beat again during freezing, if desired.

> **Luncheon or Supper:** Browned *Oysters* on Toast, p. 280, *Asparagus* with Egg Sauce, p. 330, Tossed Green Salad—*Citrus* Banana Sherbet, Cookies.

Make the sponge cake ahead, and then this is easy:

Orange Charlotte Russe   *Yield:* 10–12 servings

1 c. reconstituted frozen orange   4 egg yolks, beaten
   juice   4 egg whites
1 tbsp. (1 envelope) unflavored   1 tbsp. lemon juice
   gelatin   1 tsp. grated lemon rind, or ¼ tsp.
3 tbsp. water   lemon extract
1 c. milk   1 sponge cake (see directions,
½ c. sugar   p. 194) or about 1 doz. lady
1 tbsp. cornstarch   fingers
⅛ tsp. salt

Soak gelatin in water for about 5 min.   Scald ¾ c. milk in top of double boiler.   Combine sugar, cornstarch and salt and add slowly to milk, stirring, then cook in top of double boiler until thickened, stirring constantly.

Combine remaining ¼ c. cold milk with beaten egg yolks.   Add hot milk mixture to egg yolk mixture, return to double boiler and cook about 5 min. longer, stirring.   Add softened gelatin and stir until gelatin is dissolved.

Beat egg whites until stiff but not dry and fold them into the hot mixture.   Fold in orange juice, lemon juice and rind (or extract). Chill the mixture until partially set, but not firm.

Cut through center of sponge cake, making two layers.   Cut both layers of cake into 1-inch fingers and arrange fingers in bottom of spring mold or casserole (lined with waxed paper), allowing ½-inch space between them.   (If lady fingers are used, split them crosswise, and arrange as for sponge cake fingers.)

Pour orange mixture gently over fingers and place rest of fingers on top of filling, fitting them closely together.   Chill thoroughly (preferably overnight).   Unmold on serving dish.

Dinner: *Fish* au Gratin, p. 260, Baked Potato, Piquant *Peas* p. 359, Assorted Relishes—*Orange* Charlotte Russe with *Strawberries.*

A sauce of fluffy deliciousness:

Fluffy Orange Sauce

Yield: 1½–2 c. sauce

½ c. reconstituted frozen orange juice

2 tsp. frozen lemon juice, thawed

1 tsp. grated lemon rind, or ¼ tsp. lemon extract

5 tbsp. sugar

2 egg yolks, beaten

2 egg whites

⅛ tsp. salt

1 tsp. vanilla

Combine orange juice, lemon juice and rind (or extract), sugar and beaten egg yolks in small saucepan and stir constantly over low heat until thick.   Remove from heat and cool slightly.   Add salt to egg whites and beat until stiff, then fold them lightly into sauce, folding in vanilla toward the end.   Serve warm, or after chilling.

A sauce with many uses, especially to serve with cake:

Hot Orange Sauce   *Yield:* about 1 c. sauce

¼ c. reconstituted frozen orange   speck cinnamon
  juice   ¾ c. boiling water
½ c. sugar   1 tbsp. lemon juice
1 tbsp. cornstarch   ¼ tsp. orange extract
speck salt   2 tbsp. butter or margarine

Combine sugar, cornstarch, salt and cinnamon thoroughly in sauce-pan, gradually add boiling water and stir until smooth. Bring to boil and cook until thickened, stirring constantly. Add orange juice, lemon juice, orange extract and butter. Heat to serving temperature.

The children will relish this, and it is festive for a party, too:

Orange Milk Punch   *Yield:* 4 tall glasses

1 c. reconstituted frozen orange   3 c. milk
  juice   4 tsp. sugar

Combine all ingredients and shake vigorously or beat well. Serve icy cold.

A sparkling, flavorful punch or first course:

Orange Grape Cocktail or Punch   *Yield:* 8 cocktail or 12 punch
                                servings
½ c. reconstituted frozen orange   ½ c. reconstituted frozen grape
  juice   1 qt. chilled ginger ale

Combine fruit juices, add ginger ale and serve.

One of the few frostings that taste even better the day after being made:

Creamy Orange Frosting   *Yield:* enough for an angle food
                                cake, or a two-layer cake
¼ c. reconstituted frozen orange   2 c. confectioners (**XXXX**) sugar,
  juice   sifted
¼ c. softened cream cheese   ¼ tsp. salt
2 tbsp. softened butter or
  margarine

Cream the cheese with butter until fluffy, gradually add sugar, salt and orange juice and beat until very smooth and creamy.

Orange Soufflé
Prepare as for Lemon Soufflé, p. 390 using orange juice in place of lemon juice, and orange rind or extract.

OTHER ORANGE JUICE RECIPES

Citrus Banana Sherbet.   *See p. 390.*
Raspberry Sherbet.   *See p. 407.*
Raspberry Grape Punch.   *See p. 407.*
Orange Marashino Sauce.   *See p. 404.*
Strawberry Punch.   *See p. 414.*

PEACHES

So little trouble, and such a delicious dessert:

Peach Refrigerator Pie   *Yield:* 6 servings

1 pkg. (12 oz.) frozen peaches, thawed
evaporated milk
1 pkg. lemon-flavored gelatin

1 egg
speck salt
$1^1/_3$ c. crushed vanilla wafers
¼ c. softened butter or margarine

Drain peaches, reserving juice, and cut peaches into small pieces. To the peach juice add enough evaporated milk to make 1¾ c. liquid, and heat liquid almost to boiling. Add liquid to gelatin, stirring until gelatin is dissolved, then allow to cool slightly. Add salt to egg and beat well, and fold egg into gelatin mixture. Chill until consistency of raw egg white.

Meanwhile, blend crushed wafers and softened butter thoroughly together in pie plate, and press the mixture firmly over the bottom and sides of the plate.

When gelatin mixture is chilled until syrupy, whip with rotary or electric beater until fluffy, then fold in peaches and pour over wafers in pie plate. Chill until firm.

Dinner: Southern *Beef* Roll with Cheese Paprika Sauce, p. 229, Buttered Onions, *French-Cut Green Beans,* Head Lettuce with French Dressing—*Peach* Refrigerator Pie.

Peaches and coconut make a delightful twosome:

Coconut Peach Pie　　　　　　*Yield:* 9-inch pie

1 pkg. (12 oz.) frozen peaches,　　¼ c. sugar
　thawed　　　　　　　　　　　1 pkg. coconut cream pie filling
1⅓ c. fine graham cracker crumbs　2 c. milk
¼ c. softened butter or margarine　dessert topping or heavy cream

Blend 1 c. cracker crumbs, soft butter, and sugar thoroughly in 9-inch pie plate, and press the mixture firmly over bottom and sides of pan. Chill well

Cook pie filling with milk, as directed on package. Add drained peaches and let mixture cool to room temperature. Pour into pie shell and place in refrigerator to chill. Top with remaining cracker crumbs and whipped dessert topping or whipped cream.

　　Luncheon or Supper: *Alaska King Crab, Lima Bean* Casserole. p. 337, *Asparagus* Aspic Salad, p. 328—Coconut *Peach* Pie.

Apple Brown Betty? . . . No, peaches . . . and they are dandy:

Peach Brown Betty　　　　　　*Yield:* 5 servings

1 pkg. (12 oz.) frozen peaches,　　1 tsp. cinnamon
　thawed　　　　　　　　　　　¼ tsp. nutmeg
1½ c. dry bread crumbs or graham　¼ tsp. ground cloves
　cracker crumbs　　　　　　　　½ tsp. salt
¼ c. melted butter or margarine　　¼ c. currants or seedless raisins,
1 tbsp. lemon juice　　　　　　　　if desired
2 tbsp. sugar

Sift sugar and seasonings together, combining thoroughly. Drain peaches. Combine butter with crumbs and line bottom of 1-qt. casserole with about one-third of these. Cover with half the drained peaches, sprinkle with half the lemon juice and peach juice combined. Cover with remaining crumbs, peaches and juices in alternating layers, adding currants or raisins if desired, and top with crumbs. Bake in moderate oven, 350°F., about 40 min. covering the casserole the first 15 min. so crumbs will not brown too quickly.

　　Dinner: Roast *Loin of Pork* with Onion Stuffing, p. 240, Gravy, Mashed Potatoes, Savory Creamed *Spinach,* p. 368, Tomato and Cucumber Salad—*Peach* Brown Betty.

Peaches and cream, in a luscious, rich dessert:

Peach Mousse

1 pkg. (12 oz.) frozen peaches, thawed
$1/_3$ c. sugar

Yield: 6 servings

$1/_8$ tsp. salt
2 tsp. lemon juice
1 c. heavy cream

Crush the peaches in their juice, add sugar, salt and lemon juice and stir until sugar is dissolved. Whip cream and fold peach mixture into it. Pour into freezing mold and place in freezer until firm. Do not stir during freezing.

> **Dinner:** Broiled *Steak* with Mushrooms, p. 215, Mashed Potatoes, *Brussels Sprouts* in Tomato, p. 347, *Rolls—Peach* Mousse.

Nowadays, peaches and strawberries can come together:

Peach Strawberry Compote

1 pkg. (12 oz.) frozen peaches, thawed
1 pkg. (10 oz.) frozen strawberries, thawed

Yield: 8 servings

2 tbsp. lemon juice
coconut, if desired

Combine peaches and strawberries, adding lemon juice. If convenient, chill the compote an hour or so before serving, to permit the fruit flavors to blend. When serving, top with coconut, if desired.

> **Dinner:** *Swiss Steak with Sauce, French-Fried Potatoes,* Buttered *Carrots, Green Bean* and *Cauliflower* Salad, p. 335—*Peach Strawberry* Compote.

OTHER PEACH RECIPES

Roast Loin of Pork with Peaches. *See p. 239.*
Pork Chops with Peach Stuffing. *See p. 243.*
Mock Peach Cobbler. *See p. 447.*
Peach Upside Down Cake. *See p. 415.*
Peach Cream Roll. *See p. 416.*
Peach Meringue Glacé. *See p. 416.*
Peach Chiffon Pie. *See p. 417.*
Peach Puff Pudding. *See p. 418.*
Peach Shortcake. *See p. 420.*
Peach Devonshire Tarts. *See p. 420.*
Cooked Peach Jam. *See p. 421.*

PINEAPPLE CHUNKS

As a cocktail or a dessert, this is a tasty serving:

Pineapple Grapefruit Ginger Cocktail   *Yield:* 6 servings

1 pkg. (13½ oz.) frozen grapefruit sections, thawed
1 pkg. (13½ oz.) frozen pineapple chunks, thawed
1 tbsp. finely diced, preserved ginger

1 tbsp. ginger syrup
3 tbsp. sugar
maraschino cherries

Combine grapefruit sections, pineapple chunks and their juices. Add remaining ingredients and place in serving dishes. Garnish with maraschino cherries.

Another fine possibility, for either cocktail or dessert:

Pineapple Orange Mint Cocktail   *Yield:* 6 servings

1 pkg. (13½ oz.) frozen pineapple chunks, thawed
4 navel oranges

¼ lb. after-dinner mints, crushed
sprays of fresh mint, if desired

Section oranges, removing all membranes. Combine pineapple chunks, orange sections and juices, add crushed mints and combine lightly. Place in serving dishes, and garnish with mint sprays if desired.

A spicy change, for an appetizer or a salad:

Spiced Pineapple Salad   *Yield:* 3 servings

1 pkg. (13½ oz.) frozen pineapple chunks, thawed
¼ c. vinegar
2 tbsp. sugar
¼ tsp. salt

3 whole cloves
1 stick cinnamon
crisp lettuce
mayonnaise

Drain pineapple. To juice, add vinegar, sugar and seasonings and simmer about 10 min. Add pineapple chunks and bring to boil. Keep in refrigerator until serving time, preferably several hours.

Then drain (removing cloves and cinnamon), and serve on crisp lettuce with mayonnaise.

Dinner: *Roast Beef Hash,* Mustard *Cauliflower* and *Peas,* p. 350, Spiced *Pineapple* Salad—*Chocolate Cake.*

A spicy, sweet-sour gelatin salad:

Pineapple Orange Gelatin Salad   *Yield:* 4–6 servings

1 pkg. (13½ oz.) frozen pineapple chunks, thawed	¼ tsp. allspice
¼ c. vinegar	1 pkg. orange-flavored gelatin
1 stick cinnamon	crisp lettuce
5 whole cloves	mayonnaise

Drain pineapple, measure juice and add enough water to make 1½ c. liquid. Place pineapple and liquid in saucepan and boil 2 min. (If pineapple is not thoroughly heated, gelatin will not set.) Remove pineapple chunks and place them in refrigerator. To hot liquid in saucepan, add vinegar and spices and simmer about 10 min., covered. Strain to remove spices. Again measure liquid and add boiling water to make 2 c. liquid. Pour hot liquid over orange gelatin and stir until gelatin is dissolved. Pour into 1-qt. mold or individual molds. Chill until a thick syrup, then add chilled pineapple chunks, and chill until firm. Unmold on crisp lettuce and serve with mayonnaise.

Dinner: *Pork Chop* Dinner, p. 241, Buttered *Brussels Sprouts,* *Pineapple* Orange Gelatin Salad—*Ice Cream* with Caramel Sauce, p. 434.

An especially good partner for pineapple is cream cheese:

Pineapple and Cheese Salad   *Yield:* 4 servings

1 pkg. (13½ oz.) frozen pineapple chunks, thawed	French dressing
	crisp lettuce
1 pkg. (3 oz.) cream cheese, chilled	pimiento strips, or paprika

Drain pineapple. Cut cream cheese into small cubes. Combine pineapple chunks and cream cheese cubes by tossing lightly with a fork, adding French dressing.

Arrange on crisp lettuce and garnish with pimiento strips or sprinkle with paprika.

Luncheon or Supper: Fried *Smelts* with Tarter Sauce, p. 257, Buttered *Mixed Vegetables, Pineapple* and Cheese Salad—*Lemon Cream Pie.*

This should be presented in full color, such a fine picture:

Pineapple Upside Down Cake   *Yield:* 8 servings

1 pkg. (13½ oz.) frozen pineapple chunks, thawed
3 tbsp. butter or margarine
½ c. sugar, preferably brown
halved maraschino cherries
½ c. chopped nuts
quick mix plain cake batter (see p. 193)
orange pineapple sauce (see below)

Drain pineapple chunks, reserving juice for sauce. Melt butter in cake pan 8 x 8 x 2 in. and sprinkle sugar over bottom of pan. Arrange pineapple chunks over sugar in pan. Place halved maraschino cherries between pineapple chunks, allowing at least one-half cherry per serving. Sprinkle nuts over pineapple. Then place cake batter over fruit. Bake in moderate oven, 350°F., for 40 min. or until done. While still hot, turn out, upside down, on serving plate. Serve with orange pineapple sauce.

Orange Pineapple Sauce   *Yield:* 1²/₃ c.

¾ c. sugar
3 tbsp. cornstarch
½ tsp. salt
⅛ tsp. cinnamon
²/₃ c. pineapple juice (drained from chunks)
3 tbsp. butter or margarine
2 tsp. lemon juice
¾ c. reconstituted frozen orange juice

Mix sugar, cornstarch, salt and cinnamon together in small saucepan. Add pineapple juice gradually and bring to a boil, stirring constantly. Boil gently until thickened, stirring constantly, then remove from heat. Add butter, lemon juice and orange juice and blend well. Bring just to boil again and serve hot.

Dinner: *Pork* Chop Suey on Rice, p. 243, *Egg Rolls,* Tossed Green Salad—*Pineapple* Upside Down Cake with *Orange* Pineapple Sauce.

OTHER PINEAPPLE CHUNK RECIPES

Squash Baked with Pineapple. *See p. 371.*
Grapefruit and Pineapple Salad. *See p. 387.*
Lobster and Pineapple Salad. *See p. 275.*
Lamb Chops with Minted Pineapple. *See p. 442.*
Hawaiian Carrots. *See p. 349.*

RED RASPBERRIES

Another quick and easy one, and delicious:

Raspberry Tapioca Pudding

1 pkg. (10 oz.) frozen raspberries, packed in sugar or syrup, thawed
2½ tbsp. quick-cooking tapioca
½ c. sugar

Yield: 4 servings

⅛ tsp. salt
1 tbsp. lemon juice
dessert topping, whipped, or additional thawed raspberries

Drain raspberries. Measure juice and add enough water to make 1¼ c. liquid. Combine tapioca, sugar and salt and add this mixture to liquid, stirring to keep smooth. Cook mixture over low heat, stirring constantly, until tapioca is clear. Remove from heat and add lemon juice and raspberries. Chill thoroughly. Serve with whipped dessert topping, or with additional raspberries.

> **Luncheon or Supper:** Scotch Pancakes (*Veal*) with Tomato Sauce, p. 249, Tossed Vegetable Salad—*Raspberry* Tapioca Pudding.

Creamy, delicate pudding, topped with red raspberries:

Raspberry Cream Pudding

1 pkg. (10 oz.) frozen red raspberries, packed in sugar or syrup, thawed
2 c. milk
½ c. sugar
¼ c. flour

Yield: 6 servings

¼ tsp. salt
2 egg yolks, beaten
1 tsp. vanilla
1 tbsp. butter or margarine
2 egg whites

Scald milk in top of double boiler. Combine sugar, flour and salt and add slowly to hot milk, stirring. Cook until thickened, stirring constantly. Add some of this hot mixture to beaten egg yolks and combine well, then return to top of double boiler and continue to cook 3–5 min., stirring constantly. Remove from heat, add vanilla and butter and cool slightly. Beat egg whites until stiff and fold them into the mixture. Chill in serving dish. When serving, top with raspberries which are barely thawed.

> **Luncheon or Supper:** *Chicken* Pie with Curry Biscuits, p. 306, Buttered *Broccoli Spears,* Tossed Salad—*Raspberry* Cream Pudding.

And top it with a generous scoop of vanilla ice cream:

Raspberry Pie

Yield: 8-inch pie

1 pkg. (10 oz.) frozen red raspberries, thawed
½ c. sugar
2 tbsp. cornstarch
⅛ tsp. salt

pastry for two-crust, 8-inch pie (see directions, p. 196)
1 tbsp. lemon juice
1 tbsp. butter or margarine

Combine sugar, cornstarch and salt thoroughly, and add to mixture of lemon juice and raspberries. Line bottom of pie plate with lower crust and add raspberry mixture. Dot filling with butter and cover with top crust. Make seal between upper and lower crusts around the edge and cut gashes in top crust to allow steam to escape.

Bake in hot oven, 450°F., 15 min.; then reduce heat to moderate, 350°F., and bake about 20–25 min. longer.

> **Dinner:** Broiled *Ocean Perch Fillets* with Mustard Sauce, p. 263, *French-Fried Potatoes,* Buttered *Asparagus*—*Raspberry* Pie à la mode.

Red raspberries in raspberry gelatin, doubly delicious:

Jellied Raspberries

Yield: 6–8 servings

1 pkg. (10 oz.) frozen red raspberries, thawed
2 tbsp. frozen lemon juice, thawed

1 pkg. raspberry-flavored gelatin
1 c. dessert topping or heavy cream, whipped, if desired

Drain raspberries, reserving juice. Pour lemon juice over raspberries and combine lightly. To the raspberry juice add enough water to make 1½ c. liquid. Heat the liquid (not to boiling) and add raspberry gelatin, stirring until dissolved. Chill until gelatin mixture is syrupy, then fold in raspberries without mashing them.

If desired, fold in whipped dessert topping or whipped cream. Turn into individual molds or ring mold and chill until set. Unmold and serve.

Dinner: *Lamb* Stew, p. 235, Mashed Potatoes, Head Lettuce with French Dressing—Jellied *Raspberries, Brownies.*

Another doubly delicious raspberry dessert:

Raspberry Sherbet   *Yield:* 8 servings

2 pkg. (10 oz. each) frozen red rasp-   ¼ c. reconstituted frozen orange
  berries, thawed   juice
1 c. sugar   ¼ c. frozen lemon juice, thawed
2 c. water
1 pkg. raspberry-flavored gelatin

Combine sugar and water, boil 5 min. and remove from heat. Add gelatin and stir until dissolved. Place in refrigerator until slightly thickened. Meanwhile, put raspberries through coarse sieve and add these with orange juice and lemon juice to gelatin mixture. Turn into ice cube tray or other mold and place in freezer until the consistency of a firm mush. Meanwhile, put bowl and beater in refrigerator or freezer to chill. Beat freezing mixture in cold bowl with cold rotary or electric beater very quickly until it is smooth, but not allowing it to melt. Quickly return to the mold and the freezer and freeze until firm. For a still smoother mixture, beat again during freezing, if desired.

Lunch or Supper: Scalloped *Oysters* and *Corn,* p. 280, Buttered *Broccoli,* Tomato, Cucumber and Onion Ring Salad—*Raspberry* Sherbet.

This is a deliciously fruity punch:

Raspberry Grape Punch   *Yield:* 12 servings

2 pkg. (10 oz. each) frozen red rasp-   ½ c. frozen lemon juice, thawed
  berries, thawed   1 c. reconstituted frozen pineapple
3 c. reconstituted frozen grape   juice
  juice
1 c. reconstituted frozen orange
  juice

Press raspberries through sieve or cheesecloth to remove seeds, extracting all the juice. Add remaining ingredients and serve very cold, stirring just before serving.

A jam which stays fresh-flavored and colorful:

Uncooked Raspberry Jam   *Yield:* 10 jelly glasses
4 pkg. (10 oz. each) frozen rasp-   ¾ c. water
  berries (4½ c.), thawed   1 pkg. powdered pectin
5 c. sugar

Mash or chop the berries in their juice, stir in sugar and let stand until sugar is dissolved (20–30 min.), stirring occasionally. Before using, taste to be sure no sugar remains undissolved.

Then boil pectin and water together 1 min., stirring constantly. Remove from heat, add raspberries and stir 2 min. Pour into clean jelly glasses, cover loosely and let stand until set (overnight or 24 hrs.). Seal with paraffin or cover tightly. Since the fruit in this jam has not been sterilized, it must be stored in the freezer if not used within a couple of weeks.

Note: To make this jam in smaller amounts, use the above proportions, assuming that 1 pkg. powdered pectin contains 5 tbsp.

OTHER RED RASPBERRY RECIPES

Raspberry Cream Roll. *See p. 416.*
Raspberry Meringue Glacé. *See p. 416.*
Raspberry Chiffon Pie. *See p. 417.*
Raspberry Pinwheels. *See p. 419.*
Raspberry Whip. *See p. 419.*
Raspberry Shortcake. *See p. 420.*
Raspberry Devonshire Tarts. *See p. 420.*
Raspberry Puff Pudding. *See p. 418.*
Raspberry Sauce. *See p. 430.*
Cooked Raspberry Jam. *See p. 421.*

RHUBARB

Rhubarb and loganberry flavors, together in a sauce:

Rhubarb Loganberry Sauce   *Yield:* 6–8 servings

1 pkg. (16 oz.) frozen rhubarb,   ½ c. sugar (more if preferred)
  thawed   2 tbsp. cornstarch
1 pkg. (10 oz.) frozen loganberries, ¼ tsp. salt
  thawed

Cook rhubarb until almost tender and add loganberries. Combine sugar, cornstarch and salt thoroughly and add slowly to hot fruits, stirring. Cook gently until thickened and clear, stirring constantly. Chill if desired.

Serve this with the main course, or as a dessert salad:

Rhubarb Salad Ring   *Yield:* 8 servings

1 pkg. (16 oz.) frozen rhubarb   ½ c. chopped nuts
1 pkg. strawberry or raspberry or   crisp lettuce
  cherry-flavored gelatin   mayonnaise
½ c. chopped apples

Cook rhubarb until tender, then dissolve gelatin in it. Chill until syrupy. Pour into mold and fold apples and nuts into gelatin mixture, distributing them well. Chill until firm. Unmold on crisp lettuce and serve with mayonnaise.

Dinner: Old Fashioned *Beef* Stew, p. 223, *Rhubarb* Salad Ring, *Rolls—Butter Pecan Ice Cream* with Butterscotch Sauce, p. 432.

Rhubarb and orange, baked together, are a special:

Rhubarb Special   *Yield:* 4 servings

1 pkg. (16 oz.) frozen rhubarb,   ¼ tsp. grated orange rind
  partially thawed   ½ c. sugar
slices from 1 medium navel orange

Remove all membranes from orange slices, and place them in bottom of greased 1-qt. casserole. Combine sugar with grated orange rind and sprinkle over orange slices. Add rhubarb and combine well. Bake uncovered in hot oven, 400°F., about 30 min. or until rhubarb is tender. Serve hot, or if preferred, chill and serve cold.

Dinner: *Minestrone*—Italian Spaghetti with *Meat* Balls, p. 225, Tossed Salad with Italian Dressing—*Rhubarb* Special, *Cookies.*

Have you tried it warm, topped with fruit ice cream?

Rhubarb Pie   *Yield:* 7-inch pie

1 pkg. (16 oz.) frozen rhubarb   speck salt
²/₃ c. sugar   pastry for two-crust, 7-inch pie,
1½ tbsp. cornstarch   see p. 196
2 tsp. lemon juice   1 tbsp. butter or margarine

Place rhubarb in saucepan and heat until about ½ c. juice can be drained off. Drain. Combine sugar and cornstarch well, and stir into rhubarb juice. Add lemon juice and salt, then add rhubarb. Roll out pastry and line bottom of 7-inch pie plate with it. Add rhubarb mixture and dot with butter. Place upper crust over it, seal edges of upper and lower crusts together and cut gashes in upper crust to allow steam to escape. Bake in hot oven, 450°F., for 15 min.; then reduce heat to moderate, 350°F., and bake about 25 min. longer or until done.

Luncheon or Supper: *Ground Beef* in Barbecue Sauce, p. 225, on Split Rolls, Buttered *Lima Beans,* Endive Salad with French Dressing —Warm *Rhubarb* Pie with *Peach Ice Cream.*

An especially delicious rhubarb pie:

Rhubarb Meringue Pie   *Yield:* 8-inch pie

1 pkg. (16 oz.) frozen rhubarb   grated rind of 1 orange, or ¼ tsp.
1 c. sugar   orange extract
1½ tbsp. cornstarch   8-inch pie shell, baked and cooled
2 egg yolks, slightly beaten   (see p. 198)
1 tbsp. butter or margarine   2 egg whites
¹/₃ c. reconstituted frozen orange   ¼ c. sugar
  juice   speck salt

Place rhubarb in saucepan and bring slowly to boiling point. Blend well 1 c. sugar with cornstarch, slowly stir into hot rhubarb, and cook until thickened, stirring constantly. Add small amount of hot mixture to egg yolks and combine, then return to saucepan and cook slowly about 1 min. longer, stirring. Add butter, orange juice and rind (or extract). Cool mixture.

Pour rhubarb mixture into pie shell and cover with meringue. To prepare meringue, beat egg whites until foamy, gradually add ¼ c. sugar and continue to beat until stiff enough to hold good peaks, and is glossy. Place meringue on pie in swirls. Bake pie in slow oven, 325°F., 15–20 min. or until meringue is delicately browned.

Dinner: *Chicken* Cacciatore, p. 303, with Spaghetti, Tossed Green Salad with French Dressing, *Garlic Bread—Rhubarb* Meringue Pie.

OTHER RHUBARB RECIPES

Strawberry Rhubarb Sherbet. *See p. 411.*

Rhubarb Puff Pudding. *See p. 418.*

SLICED STRAWBERRIES

A favorite combination, always:

Strawberry and Rhubarb Sherbet *Yield:* 6–8 servings

1 pkg. (10 oz.) frozen sliced strawberries, thawed	1 tbsp. (1 envelope) unflavored gelatin
1 pkg. (16 oz.) frozen rhubarb	speck salt
¾ c. sugar	2 tbsp. lemon juice
6 tbsp. water	1 egg white

Crush strawberries, add ¼ c. sugar and combine until it is dissolved. Cook rhubarb, ¼ c. water and ½ c. sugar until rhubarb is tender, then drain. Soak gelatin in 2 tbsp. cold water for 5 min., then dissolve it in hot rhubarb juice. Cool gelatin mixture, then add strawberries, rhubarb, salt and lemon juice and pour into ice cube tray or other mold and put in freezer. When mixture is slightly mushy, beat egg white until stiff, fold it into the freezing mixture and return to freezer. Meanwhile, put bowl and beater in refrigerator or freezer to chill. When mixture is consistency of firm mush, beat in cold bowl with cold beater (rotary or electric) very quickly until it is smooth but not allowing it to melt. Quickly return it to the mold and the freezer and freeze until firm. For a still smoother product, beat again during freezing, if desired.

Luncheon or Supper: *Turkey* Salad, Tomato Stuffed with Cottage Cheese, Cole Slaw—*Strawberry* and *Rhubarb* Sherbet, *Chocolate Cake.*

A velvety-smooth, strawberry cream dessert:

Strawberry Mousse   *Yield:* 8 servings
1 pkg. (10 oz.) frozen sliced straw-   2 egg whites
   berries, thawed   1½ c. heavy cream
1 tsp. lemon juice   ½ c. sugar
¼ tsp. salt

Press strawberries through coarse sieve, add lemon juice and salt.
Beat egg whites until foamy, then add ¼ c. sugar gradually, continuing to beat until they hold good peaks.   Fold the whites into berries.
Add remaining ¼ c. sugar to cream and whip.   Fold whipped cream
into berry mixture, carefully.

Pour into ice cube tray or other mold and freeze until just firm,
stirring once when the mixture is almost frozen.

> **Dinner:** Roast *Beef* with Yorkshire Pudding, p. 214, Gravy, Mashed
> Potatoes, Buttered *Broccoli,* Creamed Onions—*Strawberry* Mousse.

Wonderful as a dessert, or for evening refreshments:

Baked Strawberry Alaska   *Yield:* 6–8 servings
2 pkg. (10 oz. each) frozen sliced   4 egg whites
   strawberries, thawed   ⅛ tsp. cream of tartar
1 qt. vanilla or strawberry ice   ½ c. sugar
   cream, brick   sheet or sponge cake, ½-inch thick

Well in advance of making the Alaska, scoop out enough ice cream
from the top of the brick to hold the strawberries, leaving an inch rim
around all edges.   Put ice cream back in freezer to get very hard.
Cut cake to be ½ inch larger than ice cream brick on all sides.

Put several thicknesses of paper on a small board which fits into
the oven, and place cake on board.

Add cream of tartar to egg whites, beat until foamy, then add sugar,
one tablespoon at a time, beating after each addition until the
meringue holds good peaks and is glossy.

Place ice cream brick on cake, leaving ½-inch of cake uncovered
on all sides.   Put strawberries into top of ice cream brick, then cover
ice cream and strawberries with meringue in swirls, covering all the
cake and ice cream with meringue.   Bake at 450°–500°F. until

One of the favorites of American desserts...strawberry shortcake. Baked as one large cake, it is especially elegant

delicately browned, about 5 min. With large spatula or pancake turner, transfer to serving platter and serve at once.

Note: For suggestions for preparing the Alaska ahead of time, see Baked Alaska, p. 423.

Dinner: *Steak* in Red Wine, Baked Potato, *Broccoli* Hollandaise, p. 329, Tossed Green Salad—Baked *Strawberry* Alaska.

Perfect for any festivity with punch in the menu:

Strawberry Punch   *Yield:* 3 doz. punch servings

2 pkg. (10 oz. each) frozen sliced   2 c. reconstituted frozen orange
   strawberries, thawed   juice
½ c. sugar (less if preferred)   1½ qt. ice water
1½ c. frozen lemon juice, thawed

Crush the strawberries from one package, add sugar and let stand about 30 min. Then add lemon juice, orange juice and ice water. Just before serving, add the other package of strawberries, without crushing them.

Here is a strawberry jam which stays fresh-flavored and colorful:

Uncooked Strawberry Jam   *Yield:* 12–14 jelly glasses

3 pkg. (16 oz. each) frozen   7 c. sugar
   strawberries, packed in syrup,   1½ c. water
   thawed   2 pkg. powdered pectin

Mash or chop the strawberries in their juice, stir in sugar and let stand until sugar is dissolved (20–30 min.), stirring occasionally. Before using, taste to be sure no sugar remains undissolved.

Then boil pectin and water together 1 min., stirring constantly. Remove from heat, add strawberries and stir 2 min. Pour into clean jelly glasses, cover loosely and let stand until set (overnight or 24 hrs.). Seal with paraffin or cover tightly.

Since the fruit in this jam is not sterilized by cooking, it must be stored in the freezer unless it is to be used soon.

Note: To make in smaller amounts, use the proportions as above, assuming that 1 pkg. powdered pectin contains 5 tbsp.

OTHER STRAWBERRY RECIPES

Peach Strawberry Compote. *See p. 401.*

Sherried Strawberries. *See p. 447.*

Strawberry Cream Roll. *See p. 416.*

Strawberry Meringue Glacé. *See p. 416.*

Strawberry Chiffon Pie. *See p. 417.*

Strawberry Puff Pudding. *See p. 418.*

Strawberry Pinwheels. *See p. 419.*

Strawberry Whip. *See p. 419.*

Strawberry shortcake. *See p. 420.*

Strawberry Devonshire Tarts. *See p. 420.*

Strawberry Sauce. *See p. 430.*

Cooked Strawberry Jam. *See p. 421.*

VERSATILE RECIPES FOR FRUITS

Served warm or after cooling, this calls for encores:

Fruit Upside Down Cake

1 pkg. (12–16 oz.) frozen fruit,[1] thawed
1 tbsp. butter or margarine
1/4 c. sugar (preferably brown)
1 or more blanched almonds, or other nuts, per serving

Yield: 8 servings

maraschino cherries cut in halves, if desired
quick-mix cake batter (see directions, p. 193

Drain fruit thoroughly. Melt butter in 8-inch square pan and sprinkle sugar over pan. Arrange fruit and nuts over sugar, and maraschino cherries if desired. Drop cake batter over fruit and bake in moderate oven, 350°F., about 40 min. or until cake is done. While still hot, turn out on serving plate, fruit side up, and serve. (May be cooled before serving, if preferred.)

> **Dinner:** *Steak* in Red Wine, p. 216, *French-Fried Potatoes, Green Beans* with Mushrooms, p. 332, *Artichoke* Salad with Vinaigrette Dressing, p. 326—*Peach* Upside Down Cake.

[1] Peaches or red sour pitted cherries.

This is an excellent use for cake roll, for any party:

Fruit Cream Roll   *Yield:* 10 servings

1 pkg. (9–12 oz.) frozen fruit[2] or   1 c. dessert topping, or heavy
  berries,[2] thawed   cream
cake roll (see directions, p. 193)   ¼ c. sugar
                                            ½ tsp. vanilla

Prepare cake, roll in waxed paper as directed, and allow to cool. Unroll cake. Whip dessert topping or heavy cream with sugar added, and spread whipped mixture on cake. Roll up again, wrapping in waxed paper, and hold in refrigerator until serving time. Immediately before serving, cut roll crosswise into serving pieces and top each slice generously with barely thawed fruit or berries.

Note: If preferred, spread cake with softened ice cream instead of whipped dessert topping.

> **Dinner:** Roast *Leg of Lamb* with Mint Sauce, Parsley Buttered *New Potatoes,* p. 361, *Asparagus* with Lemon Butter—*Strawberry* Cream Roll.

This will make you feel you are a pastry chef, but it is really not difficult to make:

Fruit Meringue Glacé   *Yield:* 12 servings

1 pkg. (9–12 oz.) frozen fruit[2]   1 c. finely granulated sugar
  or berries,[2] barely thawed   ½ tsp. vanilla
4 egg whites   1 c. dessert topping or heavy cream
¼ tsp. salt   (or use ice cream)

Take eggs from refrigerator at least an hour before making the meringues so they will be at room temperature (to give larger volume on beating). Cover 2 baking sheets with heavy waxed paper.

To egg whites in large bowl, add salt and beat until they are foamy. Then begin adding sugar in tablespoon portions, beating after each addition. Beat until very thick and glossy, adding vanilla

---

[2] Peaches, blackberries, blueberries, boysenberries, loganberries, raspberries, strawberries.

toward the end of beating. The whites should be stiffer than for pie meringues.

Drop mixture on baking sheet from pastry bag or by heaping tablespoonfuls, making about 12 portions, 2 inches apart. By swirling with a spoon, shape each portion into a 3-inch mound about ¾-inch thick. Have sides smooth and tops irregular.

Bake in very slow oven, 250°F., about 50 min. Meringues should be slightly crisp and delicately browned.

Cool thoroughly, then remove from paper with broad spatula. Cut away a circle about 1½ inches from top of each meringue. Whip dessert topping or heavy cream and fill centers of meringues with it, or if preferred, fill with ice cream. Add thawed fruit, replace tops on meringues and garnish with additional fruit.

Dinner: *Crabmeat* Newburg, p. 273, on Rice, Buttered *Artichoke Hearts,* Tossed Green Salad with French Dressing——*Raspberry* Meringue Glacé.

Handsome is as handsome does . . . and this does handsomely:

Fruit Chiffon Pie

Yield: 9-inch pie

1 pkg. (9–12 oz.) frozen fruit[3] or berries,[3] thawed
3 egg yolks
1 pkg. lemon or orange-flavored gelatin

3 egg whites
speck salt
¼ c. sugar
9-inch pie shell, baked and cooled, see p. 198

Drain fruit or berries, reserving juice. Place egg yolks in top of double boiler. Put fruit or berry juice in measuring cup and add enough boiling water to make 1 c. liquid. Add this hot liquid slowly to egg yolks and cook over hot water until slightly thickened, about 3 min., stirring. Remove from heat, add gelatin, stirring until gelatin is dissolved. Chill until syrupy, then add drained fruit or berries.

Add salt to egg whites and beat until foamy. Then gradually add sugar, continuing to beat until whites are stiff and glossy. Fold egg whites into gelatin mixture. Turn into baked pie shell. If mixture

[3] Peaches, raspberries, strawberries.

is not stiff enough to pile well in center of pie, chill the last third of the filling before adding it.   Chill until firm.

> **Dinner:**   Tomato Juice—*Turkey Tetrazzini, French-Cut Green Beans,* Head Lettuce with Russian Dressing—*Strawberry* Chiffon Pie.

This fluffy fruit pudding may be varied in many ways:

Fruit Puff Pudding

Yield: 4 servings

1 pkg. (9–16 oz.) frozen fruit[4] or
  berries,[4] thawed
$^1/_3$ c. sugar (omit if fruit is packed
  in syrup)
1 tbsp. flour

2 tsp. lemon juice
1 tbsp. butter or margarine
sponge topping (see below)

Place fruit or berries in saucepan.   Blend flour well with sugar, or if sugar is omitted (because fruit is packed in syrup), blend flour with lemon juice.   Add flour (with sugar or lemon juice) slowly to fruit, stirring, and bring mixture slowly to boil, stirring constantly.   Add butter (and lemon juice if not already added) and pour into 1-qt. casserole.   Cover with sponge topping and bake in slow oven, 325°F., about 40 min.

Sponge Topping

1 egg
⅛ tsp. salt
⅛ tsp. cream of tartar
¼ tsp. grated lemon rind, or few
  drops lemon extract

3 tbsp. sugar
¼ c. flour
¼ tsp. vanilla

Combine egg, salt, cream of tartar and grated lemon rind (or extract) and beat until foamy.   Add sugar, one tablespoon at a time, continuing to beat.   Sift flour in tablespoon portions over top of mixture, folding flour in carefully after each addition.   Toward the end, fold in vanilla.

> **Dinner:** *Chicken* à la King, p. 304, Parsley Buttered *New Potatoes,* p. 361, Buttered *Broccoli, Grapefruit* and Avocado Salad, p. 386— *Rhubarb* Puff Pudding.

[4] Peaches, rhubarb, blackberries, blueberries, boysenberries, loganberries, raspberries, strawberries.

Biscuit pinwheels . . . berries and a pool of luscious berry sauce:

Berry Pinwheels   *Yield:* 6 servings

1 pkg. (9–12 oz.) frozen berries,[5]   ¾ tsp. salt
    partially thawed   3 tbsp. sugar
1 c. water   ¼ c. shortening
2 tsp. lemon juice   ½–²/₃ c. milk
2 tbsp. flour   melted butter or margarine
¼ c. sugar   2 tbsp. sugar
1½ c. flour   ½ tsp. cinnamon
2¼ tsp. baking powder   cream, if desired

To about two-thirds of the berries, add water and lemon juice and bring to boil. Combine 2 tbsp. flour and ¼ c. sugar and add to hot berries, stirring, and cook until thickened, stirring constantly. Pour into baking pan about 8 inches square.

Prepare shortcake dough from 1½ c. flour, baking powder, salt, 3 tbsp. sugar shortening and milk (see directions p. 197), and roll dough to rectangle about ½-inch thick. Brush top of dough with melted butter and sprinkle with 2 tbsp. sugar combined with cinnamon. Spread dough with remaining berries and roll up dough from narrow end. Cut crosswise into 8 pieces (pinwheels).

Place pinwheels with cut side down, over berries in baking pan. Bake in hot oven, 425°F., about 30 min. Serve hot, with cream if desired.

Dinner: *Porterhouse Steak,* Mashed Potatoes, *Green Beans* with Mushrooms, p. 332, Tomato Salad—*Blueberry* Pinwheels with Cream.

So light and fluffy, a perfect ending for a hearty dinner:

Berry Whip   *Yield:* 6 servings

1 pkg. (9–12 oz.) frozen berries,[5]   3 tbsp. water
    thawed   2 egg whites
¼ c. sugar   ⅛ tsp. salt
1 tbsp. (1 envelope) unflavored   custard sauce, p. 201
    gelatin

[5] Blackberries, blueberries, boysenberries, loganberries, raspberries, strawberries.

Drain berries and add enough water to juice to make 1 c. liquid. Add sugar to liquid, and heat.   Soak gelatin in cold water 5 min., then add this to hot berry juice and stir until gelatin is dissolved. Chill this mixture until it is the consistency of raw egg white, then beat with rotary or electric beater until very light and fluffy.   Add salt to egg whites and beat until stiff.   Fold egg whites into gelatin mixture and pour part of this into mold.   Add berries in layers alternately with remaining whip.   Chill until set.   Unmold and serve with custard sauce.

Dinner: *Stuffed Pork Chops,* p. 241, Baked Sweet Potatoes, Deviled *Brussels Sprouts,* p. 344, Chef's Salad—*Raspberry* Whip with Custard Sauce.

Everybody's favorite, any time of year:

Fruit Shortcake   *Yield:*   6 servings
1 pkg. (9–16 oz.) frozen fruit[6] or   dessert topping or heavy cream
   berries,[6] thawed
shortcake dough from 2 c. flour
   (see directions, p. 197)

Roll out biscuit dough and cut into individual biscuits, or into two large " cakes," and bake as directed.   When baked, spread fruit or berries between layers of biscuit and on top of them.   Top with whipped dessert topping or whipped cream.

Dinner: *Fried Smelts,* p. 257, *Potatoes Hashed in Cream, Peas* with Tiny Onions, p. 359, Cabbage Slaw—*Loganberry* Shortcake.

Probably the very kind the "knave of hearts" stole from the queen:

Devonshire Tarts   *Yield:* 4–8 tarts, dessert size
1 pkg. (9–16 oz.) frozen fruit[6] or   4–8 tart shells (dessert size) baked
   berries,[6] thawed   and cooled
1 pkg. (3 oz.) cream cheese   sugar
$1/_3$ c. cream   currant or crabapple jelly, if desired

⁶ Peaches, blackberries, blueberries, boysenberries, loganberries, raspberries, strawberries.

Drain fruit or berries thoroughly (strawberries are especially fine for these tarts). Combine cream cheese with cream, beating until smooth, then spread a layer in each tart shell. Put a layer of drained fruit on top, sprinkle lightly with sugar and let stand until sugar is dissolved. If desired, glaze the surface by pouring melted currant, crabapple or other tart, colorful jelly over the top.

The proportion of cream cheese to fruit may be varied as desired. Large tarts may be served as dessert, tiny ones for teas.

A quick and easy, and tasty, jam from any frozen fruit:

Cooked Jam

Yield: 5 jelly glasses, 6 oz. each

3 c. frozen fruit[7] or berries,[7] thawed

2½ c. sugar

$1/3$ c. water

2 tsp. lemon juice

1 pkg. dry pectin

Combine dry pectin thoroughly with ½ c. sugar. Then mix with thawed fruit, water and lemon juice in large saucepan, stirring well. Bring quickly to a fast boil over high heat. Add remaining sugar and bring to a full, rolling boil. Boil hard 1 min., stirring constantly. Remove from heat and skim off any foam. Let stand about 5 min., alternately skimming and stirring. Ladle quickly into sterilized jelly glasses. Cover with hot paraffin, ⅛-inch thick, immediately or within 12 hours of preparation.

[7] Peaches, blackberries, blueberries, boysenberries, loganberries, raspberries, strawberries.

CHAPTER 18

Many Ways to Use Ice Creams

INTRODUCTION

An assortment of ice creams in your freezer . . .never a dull dessert!

Ice cream is a fine climax for any luncheon or dinner menu, especially if the flavor is unusual—peppermint stick, spumoni, Burgundy cherry or ripple ice creams, to mention only a few. There is no need to make the ice cream, unless you particularly want to do so. But several quarts of your favorite flavors always come in handy, and in the summer when ice cream is most popular you may want it in gallon lots, especially if there are children to enjoy it.

Combine ice cream with sauces, fruits and nuts, and the variety of home-made sundaes you can achieve will rival the best of ice cream parlors. With syrups, fruit and carbonated beverages, ice cream sodas, milk shakes and "refreshers" can be made to order right at home.

Refreshments demanded at odd hours are no trouble with ice cream on hand, so another hostess problem is solved to the satisfaction of everyone.

Remove the ice cream from the freezer about 15 min. before it is to be served so it will soften enough to respond to the spoon or scoop. Then use it as you wish.

DESSERTS À LA MODE

Probably there is no more popular way of using ice cream than in desserts à la mode. Almost any kind of pie is more hearty and more festive served à la mode, especially fruit pies, pumpkin pie and mincemeat pie. Brownies à la mode make a splendid dessert. Crepe suzettes à la mode served with fruit sauce are superb. Hot waffles à la mode with hot maple syrup are a cold-weather dessert not to be surpassed. And there are plenty more which are welcome for family or party menus.

ICE CREAM AND CAKE DESSERTS

Ice Cream Sandwiches

Place a slice of cake on the serving plate and top with a layer of ice cream (the ice cream may need to be softened slightly, to make it spread). Place another layer of cake on the ice cream and serve with any of the sauces which are described later in this chapter. Garnish with whipped dessert topping or whipped cream or in any way desired.

Angel food, sponge cake, loaf cake or fruit cake that is not too rich may be used for this dessert. You can make "sandwiches" by placing a layer of ice cream between two large cookies, too, and the children will enjoy these.

Ice Cream Roll

Prepare Cake Roll, p. 193, and spread with softened ice cream. Roll up as usual, then roll in waxed paper to hold it in place, and put in the freezer until serving time. When ready to serve, remove waxed paper and cut crosswise into slices 1–1½ inches thick. Serve it plain, or with whipped dessert topping, whipped cream or any sauce. Chocolate flavored cake and peppermint stick ice cream are a popular combination. Or use strawberry ice cream on plain cake, with thawed, frozen strawberries, topped with whipped cream.

Ice Cream Cup Cakes

Cut a thin slice from the top of each cup cake. Hollow out the center of the cakes and fill the hollows with ice cream. Replace the tops and serve with sauce and garnish if desired.

Spice cakes are delicious with butterscotch, coffee or burnt almond ice cream, and the combination of chocolate cake and peppermint stick ice cream is also popular. A variation of this may be prepared by baking cake in ring molds (individual or large), and filling the center of the ring with ice cream.

Baked Alaska

Use about 1 quart of ice cream, preferably purchased as a brick. If not in brick form, thaw it only enough so it can be molded into a brick, then return it to the freezer to harden well.

Prepare a Cake Roll, p. 193. Select a board which will fit into your oven, cover it with heavy paper and then with waxed paper. Place the cake on the waxed paper. Then put the ice cream brick on the cake, and cut the cake so it extends only about 1 inch beyond the ice cream on all sides. Prepare meringue from 3 egg whites, 6 tbsp. sugar and ½ tsp. vanilla (see directions, p. 199); cover the top and sides of the ice cream brick thickly with meringue, making attractive swirls.

Place the board in oven and brown meringue quickly at 450°–500°F. Slip dessert from paper with large spatula or pancake turner on to a platter and serve at once. Cut crosswise in slices 1–1½ inches thick.

Since a meringue baked as above will collapse soon after it is baked, it should usually be served immediately after taking it from the oven. But this is not always convenient, and there are several alternatives. You can prepare the Baked Alaska the day before, baking as usual, and put it immediately into the freezer, to serve it the following day. The quality of the meringue will be somewhat different—somewhat like marshmallow—but is very satisfactory. Or you can arrange the dessert without the meringue and keep it in the freezer until the last minute, then prepare the meringue and bake it, and serve at once.

Ice Cream Ball on Cake

Cut a slice of cake (angel food, sponge or loaf cake) about 1–1½ inches thick and place on serving plate. Shape a scoop of ice cream into a ball, roll it in chopped nuts of any kind, or toasted coconut or other coating, and place on the slice of cake. Serve with your choice of sauce and garnish.

If preferred, omit rolling ice cream ball in coating, place ball on slice of cake and serve with barely thawed fruit of your choice, or fruit sauce or any of the sauces described in the following pages. With vanilla or peach ice cream on plain cake, Orange Maraschino Sauce, p. 433, is particularly attractive because of its unusual flavor and bright color.

Bombes

For bombes, ice cream is molded into rather deep molds (melon type preferred), with the center of the ice cream hollowed out. The

Split your éclairs, cream puffs or hard meringues, and place ice cream between the layers, then serve with your favorite sauce or with thawed, frozen fruit. This makes a deluxe dessert

center is then filled with a different kind of ice cream, or mousse or sherbet or any other kind of frozen mixture. A 1- or 2-quart mold may be used, and the two kinds of frozen mixtures may be selected to give the colors and flavors you prefer.

Thaw the ice cream barely enough to be able to mold it, and place it in the mold. With the back of a spoon, press the ice cream against the bottom and sides of the mold, leaving the center hollow. Then fill the center with the other frozen mixture and put into the freezer at once.

Ice Cream Pies

For these, the "crust" is one kind of ice cream, and the "filling" is another kind, selecting the flavors and colors appropriate for your menu.

Line a pie plate with ice cream which has been thawed barely enough to mold it, and press it firmly against the bottom and sides of the pan, to make the "crust." Do not bring the edge of the "crust" quite out to the edge of the outer rim of the pie plate, and leave a good hollow for the "filling." Put this in the freezer until the ice cream is hard. Then add the other ice cream for the "filling," thawed just enough to mold it, and again put the pie in the freezer.

For a "meringue," the pie may be topped with sweetened, whipped cream (see directions, p. 151). For a pie combining chocolate and mint flavors, fold into the whipped cream, 6 medium chocolate-peppermint patties which have been chilled and cut in pieces. The pie should be taken from the freezer about 15 min. before serving time.

Ice Cream Clowns or Witches

Scoop out a ball of ice cream for the head, and place it on a large, round cooky. Attach colored coconut for the hair and make eyes, nose and mouth from licorice or cut raisins. Give the witch or clown an ice cream cone for a hat, topped with a gum drop if you wish. These are fine for children's parties.

Cream Puffs or Éclairs with Ice Cream

Split cream puffs or éclairs to remove the tops, and fill the center with ice cream. Replace the top and serve with any of the sauces listed on pages 431–435.

Baked Alaska Tarts

Prepare individual tart shells and allow to cool. Into each shell put a scoop of ice cream and cover very quickly with meringue well out to the edge of tart shell and thoroughly covering the ice cream. Place in a hot oven, 450°–500°F., until the meringue is delicately browned (about 5 min.). Serve at once. The novelty-flavored ice creams are especially appropriate for this dessert.

Meringues Glacé

Prepare meringues, p. 416, and as soon as removed from the oven, carefully slice off the upper third of each meringue. Just before serving, place a scoop of ice cream in each meringue, replace tops and serve with sauce or icy-cold thawed, frozen fruit.

Peach Melba

Place a square of cake on each serving dish and top with a generous scoop of vanilla ice cream and icy-cold, thawed, frozen peaches. Serve with grenadine syrup or raspberry sauce, p. 430. Or if pre-

A delectable parfait with frozen blueberries and sliced peaches

ferred, omit cake, serving ice cream topped with peaches and grenadine syrup or raspberry sauce in dessert dish.

PARFAITS

Well chosen indeed is the name "parfaits" (French for "perfect") for these desserts. In tall, slender glasses, arrange alternate layers of ice cream and rich, colorful syrups or fruits, then garnish attractively. You could not ask for a more stunning climax for a dinner party.

Chocolate Marshmallow Parfait

Alternating layers of chocolate sauce, ice cream (vanilla, mint or peppermint flavor) and marshmallow sauce, p. 432, make a delicious parfait. Top with marshmallow sauce and garnish with chopped nuts and/or a maraschino cherry.

Butterscotch Marshmallow Parfait

This is similar to chocolate marshmallow parfait above, using butterscotch sauce in place of chocolate sauce. It is especially good with Butterscotch Almond Sauce, p. 432.

Brandied Peach Parfait

Arrange alternate layers of brandied peaches and vanilla or peach ice cream in parfait glasses. Top the parfait with whipped cream and garnish with finely chopped pecans.

Prepare brandied peaches as follows:

1 pkg. (12 oz.) frozen peaches, thawed	1/3 c. brandy
1/2 c. sugar	

Cook peaches gently in their syrup, with sugar, until very tender. Remove peaches and continue to cook syrup until it is rather thick (230°F.), about 5 min. of gentle boiling. Place fruit and syrup in jar, add brandy, cover tightly and store in cool place.

Tutti-Frutti Parfait

Prepare this exactly as Brandied Peach Parfait above, but using the following tutti-frutti sauce in place of brandied peaches.

1/4 c. brandy	1/2 c. seedless raisins, halved
1/2 c. sliced peaches	1/2 c. dates, cut in pieces
1/2 c. raspberries or strawberries	2 c. sugar
1/2 c. pineapple chunks	

Pour brandy into a jar which holds at least a quart. Add mixed fruits to brandy, in alternating layers with sugar. Cover tightly and store in cool place.

Crème de Menthe or Crème de Cocoa Parfait

In parfait glasses, arrange alternating layers of crème de menthe or crème de cocoa and vanilla or chocolate ice cream, or some of both flavors. Top the parfait with dessert topping, whipped, or whipped cream.

Ambrosia Parfait

Truly "food for the gods" is this parfait:

10 pitted dates	½ c. salted almonds
½ c. boiling water	½ c. water
½ c. maraschino cherries	½ c. sugar
½ c. figs (canned in heavy syrup)	2–4 tbsp. rum

Let dates stand in boiling water 3 min., drain and cut them in small pieces. Cut maraschino cherries in quarters, cut figs in eighths and cut almonds in strips. Put ½ c. water in saucepan, add sugar, bring to boil and boil gently about 3 min. (to 230°F.). Add fruits and nuts to cooked syrup and allow to cool. Add rum (judge amount according to its strength and desired flavor). If sauce is too thick, add maraschino cherry juice or fig juice to give desired consistency.

Arrange alternate layers of fruit mixture and vanilla ice cream in parfait glasses. Top with whipped dessert topping or whipped cream.

FROSTED FRUIT SUNDAES

With an assortment of ice creams and frozen fruits in your freezer, you are always ready to make a delicious ice cream sundae. There are endless numbers of ice cream flavors and fruits to make the combinations of your choice. For a party, with serving-portions of sweetened, whipped cream in your freezer, you have a fine topping for the sundaes.

Another quick and easy sundae is made by pouring a frozen juice concentrate, thawed but not diluted, over the ice cream. Any of the juices, ades or punches are wonderful used this way.

A few of the frozen fruits need sugar added to make them suitable for ice cream toppings, and some are better if the syrup is thickened with a little cornstarch. Following are a couple of recipes for these.

Berry Sauce   *Yield:* ¾ c. sauce
1 c. frozen berries, thawed   ¼ c. sugar

Combine berries with sugar and cook over low heat until mixture is a rather heavy syrup.

Red Cherry Sauce   *Yield:* 1½ c. sauce
1 pkg. (10 oz.) red sour pitted   speck salt
    cherries, thawed   2 tbsp. butter or margarine
½ c. sugar
1 tbsp. cornstarch

Drain cherries, reserving juice. Combine sugar thoroughly with cornstarch and salt and gradually stir in ¾ c. cherry juice (add water to make ¾ c., if necessary). Bring to boil, stirring, and boil gently about 2 min., stirring constantly. Remove from heat and add butter and cherries. This sauce is particularly good with plain cake and vanilla ice cream.

OTHER SAUCES AND GARNISHES FOR SUNDAES

There are literally countless numbers of ice cream sundaes you can make, using different flavors of ice cream, different sauces and different garnishes. All you need is some imagination in selecting the ones to be combined for various occasions. Vanilla ice cream is always a good basic flavor, so is peach ice cream. But use others for variety. The more elaborate sundaes such as "Banana Split" can be made at home, too, with your own combination of fruits, sauces and garnishes.

Garnishes

Here are some garnishes to keep on hand for frequent use:

Toasted Coconut	Maraschino Cherries
Chopped Preserved Ginger	Marshmallow Whip
Crumbled Maple Sugar	Dessert Topping
Ground Peanut Brittle	Jams, Jellies, Marmalade
Crushed Candy	Diced Marshmallows
Chopped Caramel Popcorn	Colored Shot or Sugar
Coarsely Shaved Sweet Chocolate	Nuts—Whole or Chopped
Chocolate Shot or Chips	Chopped Candied Fruits in Syrup

Chocolate Peppermint Sauce   *Yield:* ¾ c. sauce
½ lb. chocolate peppermint patties   3 tbsp. cream

Melt chocolate peppermint patties in top of double boiler, add cream and stir well. Serve hot or cold. If served cold, additional cream may be necessary to give desired consistency.

Maple Syrup Sauce
Boil maple syrup until it is a thick syrup, and serve hot or cold. If it becomes too thick or "sugary" on cooling, add a small amount of water.

Maple Cream Sauce   *Yield:* about 1 c. sauce

1 c. maple syrup or maple sugar   1 tsp. vanilla
½ c. top milk or light cream

Boil syrup and cream to soft-ball stage (about 232°F.). Beat 1 min. and add vanilla. Add more cream when serving, if necessary to give desired consistency.

Chocolate Sauce   *Yield:* 2¾ c. sauce
1¾ c. water   ½ tsp. salt
5 oz. unsweetened chocolate $1/_3$ c. light corn syrup
2 c. sugar   2 tbsp. butter or margarine

Place water and chocolate in saucepan and boil together gently about 4 min., stirring. Add sugar, salt and corn syrup and boil gently 4 min. longer, stirring. Add butter and beat vigorously until well blended. Serve hot or cold.

Chocolate Peanut-Butter Sauce   *Yield:* ¾ c. sauce
½ c. chocolate sauce (see above)   ¼ c. evaporated milk
3 tbsp. peanut butter

Combine chocolate sauce and peanut butter thoroughly, add evaporated milk in tablespoon portions, blending thoroughly.

Mocha Sauce   *Yield:* 1 $^2/_3$ c. sauce
2 oz. unsweetened chocolate   ¼ c. light corn syrup
¾ c. strong (double strength) speck salt
   coffee
1½ c. sugar

Melt chocolate in top of double boiler, add coffee gradually, blending well. Add sugar, corn syrup and salt, put over direct heat and bring to a boil. Boil gently over medium heat for about 20 min., or until it reaches the soft-ball stage (about 232°F.). Serve hot or cold.

Butterscotch Sauce

Yield: 1 ²/₃ c. sauce

1½ c. light brown sugar
¼ c. butter or margarine

½ c. cream

Combine all ingredients in top of double boiler and cook, uncovered, over boiling water for about 30 min. Serve hot or cold. For a darker, richer sauce, use dark brown sugar.

Butterscotch Almond Sauce

To Butterscotch Sauce (see above), add ¹/₃–½ c. slivered, toasted almonds.

Marshmallow Sauce

Yield: 3¾ c. sauce

1½ tsp. unflavored gelatin
1¼ c. cold water
2 c. sugar
½ tsp. cream of tartar

1 egg white
1½ tsp. vanilla
¼ tsp. salt

Soak gelatin in ¼ c. cold water about 5 min. Combine 1 c. cold water, sugar and cream of tartar and boil gently about 20 min., or until it spins a thread when dropped from a spoon (236°F.). Remove from heat, add soaked gelatin, stirring until gelatin is dissolved. Allow to cool to about lukewarm temperature.

Add egg white, vanilla and salt to gelatin mixture and beat very vigorously with rotary or electric beater until sauce is white and stiff. Store in tightly covered jar in cool place (not as cold as refrigerator).

If necessary, rewhip before serving, and if desired add small amount of lemon, vanilla, orange, almond or other extract.

Ginger Marshmallow Sauce

Yield: about 1¼ c. sauce

1 c. marshmallow sauce (see above)

3 tbsp. finely chopped ginger (crystallized or preserved)

Rewhip marshmallow sauce, if necessary. Add ginger and blend well.

Pineapple Marshmallow Sauce   *Yield:* 1½ c. sauce

1 c. marshmallow sauce (see p. 432)   ½ c. well drained, crushed, canned pineapple

Rewhip marshmallow sauce, add crushed pineapple and blend well.

Candied Fruit Marshmallow Sauce   *Yield:* about 1½ c. sauce

¼ c. finely chopped, candied mixed fruit

4 maraschino cherries, finely chopped

$^1/_3$ c. water

¼ c. sugar

1 c. marshmallow sauce (see p. 432)

Combine candied fruits, maraschino cherries, water and sugar in saucepan, and boil gently until syrup is thick (8–10 min.). Remove from heat and chill. Rewhip marshmallow sauce, if necessary, and add to cooled fruit mixture.

The fruit mixture prepared from the first four ingredients is delicious used as a garnish on delicately flavored ice cream sundaes.

Ginger Pear Sauce   *Yield:* 2 c. sauce

1 lb. firm pears (Seckel variety preferred)

1 lemon

$^1/_3$ c. chopped, preserved ginger

1½ c. sugar

Pare, core and quarter the pears. Chip rind thinly from lemon, then pare the entire white from the lemon, and cut the pulp in thin slices, removing seeds. Add lemon rind and pulp to pears.

Add ginger and sugar to pear and lemon mixture, combine carefully with a fork, cover tightly and let stand overnight. The following day, boil the mixture gently, stirring occasionally, until pears are clear and syrup is somewhat thickened and light amber in color (about 30 min. boiling, or to 220°F.). Allow sauce to cool, then store in tightly covered jar in cool place.

Orange Maraschino Sauce   *Yield:* 2 c. sauce

1½ tbsp. cornstarch

¼ c. sugar

¼ c. cold water

1½ c. reconstituted frozen orange juice

2 tbsp. chopped maraschino cherries

2 tbsp. maraschino cherry juice

$^1/_3$ c. slivered salted almonds

speck salt

Combine cornstarch with sugar, add cold water and blend. Add orange juice, bring slowly to boil, stirring, and boil gently about 5 min. Remove from heat and chill. Add remaining ingredients and mix well.

This sauce is particularly fine for serving with delicately flavored cake and vanilla ice cream.

Honey Peanut-Butter Sauce *Yield:* 1½ c. sauce
1 c. strained honey 1 tbsp. grated orange rind
½ c. peanut butter crunch

Blend ingredients well and heat slowly, stirring constantly. Remove from heat as soon as mixture comes to boil.

Peppermint-Stick Sauce *Yield:* 1½ c. sauce
1 c. sugar ¾ c. finely crushed
¼ c. water peppermint-stick candy
½ c. light corn syrup ½ c. evaporated milk

Place sugar, water and corn syrup in small saucepan and heat, stirring until mixture boils, then boil gently until mixture reaches soft-ball stage (236°F.). Add ½ c. peppermint-stick candy and stir over low heat until candy is almost dissolved. Add evaporated milk and blend. Cool mixture, then add remaining peppermint-stick candy.

The peppermint-stick candy added after mixture is cool provides bits of candy in the sauce.

Caramel Sauce *Yield:* ¾ c. sauce
1 c. sugar ½ tsp. vanilla
¾ c. boiling water speck salt

Place sugar in heavy saucepan and liquefy it over moderate heat, stirring constantly to liquefy sugar evenly, crushing any sugar lumps. Heat until sugar is amber in color. Remove from heat and add boiling water *very* slowly, stirring constantly until sugar is all dissolved. Cook until slightly thickened. Add vanilla and salt.

Praline Sauce

Prepare as for caramel sauce above, and when cool add ¼ c. chopped pecans.

Coffee Caramel Sauce

1 c. sugar
½ c. strong (double strength) coffee
2 tbsp. cornstarch

Yield: 1½ c. sauce
3 tbsp. water
2 tbsp. butter or margarine
⅛ tsp. salt

Caramelize sugar in heavy saucepan, as for preparing caramel sauce p. 434). When sugar is liquefied and amber color, remove from heat. Add coffee *very* slowly, stirring constantly, until sugar is all dissolved. Blend cornstarch with water to make smooth paste and add this slowly to sugar mixture. Cook gently until mixture boils and thickens. Add butter and salt. Serve hot or cold.

Raisin and Nut Sauce

2½ c. sugar
1¼ c. water
2 tbsp. light corn syrup
1 c. seedless raisins, halved

Yield: 3 c. sauce
3 tbsp. lemon juice
1 tsp. grated lemon rind
½ c. chopped walnuts
speck salt

Place sugar, water and corn syrup in saucepan, cook over medium heat until mixture boils, then cover and boil gently 2 min. Remove cover and cook about 3 min., or until slightly thickened (220°F.). Add remaining ingredients. Serve hot or cold.

ICE CREAM SODAS

For summer refreshments, there is nothing more welcome than ice cream sodas. Just keep some carbonated beverages on hand, then with your assortment of ice creams in the freezer, you are always ready to make a delicious beverage. Here are just a few of the many combinations you can prepare.

Raspberry or Strawberry Ice Cream Soda

2 tbsp. (rounded) frozen raspberries or strawberries, thawed
2 tbsp. sugar
1 tbsp. cream

Yield: 1 serving
1 c. carbonated water
1 large scoop vanilla ice cream

Crush the berries to a pulp, put into serving glasses, add sugar and cream and combine well. Add half the carbonated water and stir, add the ice cream and finally add the remaining carbonated water and stir well. Serve at once.

Chocolate Ice Cream Soda　　　　*Yield:* 1 serving

2 tbsp. chocolate sauce, p. 431　　1 large scoop vanilla or chocolate
2 tbsp. cream　　　　　　　　　　　ice cream
1 c. carbonated water

Pour chocolate sauce and cream into serving glass and mix, then add half the carbonated water and combine well. Add ice cream and remaining carbonated water, stir well and serve at once.

Mocha Ice Cream Soda　　　　*Yield:* 1 serving

1½ tbsp. chocolate sauce, p. 431　　1 c. carbonated water
1½ tbsp. strong (double strength)　　1 large scoop vanilla, chocolate
　coffee　　　　　　　　　　　　　　or coffee ice cream
1 tbsp. cream

Combine chocolate sauce, coffee and cream in beverage glass. Add half the carbonated water and stir well, then add the remaining carbonated water and ice cream. Stir well and serve at once.

Root Beer Ice Cream Soda　　　　*Yield:* 1 serving

1 tbsp. cream　　　　　　　　　　1 large scoop vanilla or coffee ice
1 c. root beer　　　　　　　　　　　cream

Combine half the root beer with cream in serving glass, add ice cream and remaining root beer, stir well and serve at once.

Lemon-Lime Ice Cream Soda　　　*Yield:* 1 serving

1 tbsp. cream　　　　　　　　　　1 c. lemon-lime soda
1 large scoop vanilla ice cream, or
　lemon or lime sherbet

Combine half the lemon-lime soda with cream in beverage glass. Add ice cream or sherbet and remaining soda, mix well and serve at once.

FROSTED DRINKS AND MILK FLOATS

Cool and healthful drinks made from milk and ice cream are wonderful for teen-agers and for adults who need not worry about calories.

Chocolate Frosted　　　　*Yield:* 1 serving

1 c. milk　　　　　　　　　　　　1 large scoop vanilla or chocolate
2–3 tbsp. chocolate sauce, p. 431　　ice cream

Combine ingredients in jar, cover tightly and shake until mixture is frothy and ice cream is almost melted. Serve at once, in tall glasses.

Chocolate Malt Frosted   *Yield:* 1 serving

Prepare as for Chocolate Frosted (p. 436) but add 2 tbsp. malted milk powder.

Strawberry Frosted   *Yield:* 1 serving

2 tbsp. (rounded) frozen   1 c. milk
   strawberries, thawed   1 large scoop vanilla or strawberry
1 tbsp. sugar   Ice Cream

Crush berries to a pulp, add sugar and combine well. Place in jar with milk and ice cream, cover jar tightly and shake until mixture is frothy and ice cream is almost melted. Serve at once, in tall glasses.

Mocha Frosted   *Yield:* 1 serving

½ c. milk   1 large scoop chocolate ice cream
½ c. strong (double strength) coffee

Combine ingredients in jar, cover tightly and shake until mixture is frothy and ice cream is almost melted. Serve at once, in tall glasses.

Coffee Frosted   *Yield:* 1 serving

½ c. milk   1 large scoop vanilla or coffee ice
½ c. strong (double strength) coffee   cream

Combine ingredients in jar, cover tightly and shake until mixture is frothy and ice cream is almost melted. Serve at once, in tall glasses.

Three-Flavor Float   *Yield:* 3 servings

1 can (6 oz.) frozen pineapple-   2 c. milk
   orange juice concentrate, thawed   3 large scoops vanilla or peach
1 medium banana   ice cream

Mash banana with a fork, add undiluted fruit juice and milk, and beat with rotary or electric beater until smooth. (If preferred, put these ingredients in electric blender and blend well.) Pour into tall serving glasses and to each glass add a scoop of ice cream.

CHAPTER 19

Frozen Foods for Thirty-Minute Meals

QUICK MEALS . . . PLANNED, OR FOR EMERGENCIES

In keeping with the pace of our modern way of life, it is often necessary to prepare a meal in a hurry. With a well-stocked freezer, these meals need not be quick snacks, but instead can be delicious dinners, luncheons or suppers.

In families where the homemaker is employed outside the home, such quick meals may be the rule rather than the exception. It is advisable to plan menus for these meals well ahead, so that the necessary foods will be on hand, and so that frozen foods needing to be thawed can be placed in the refrigerator before leaving for work in the morning. This is the way to plan, too, for any occasions when the homemaker needs to be away the hour or two before dinner, when she would normally expect to prepare the meal.

Then there are always emergencies in any family, when it becomes necessary to prepare a good lunch or dinner on short notice. If the man-of-the-house calls on short notice to say he would like to bring an office colleague home for dinner, it is so much more pleasant if the welcome can be a genuine one, rather than a "bring him if you must." The homemaker who is familiar with the frozen foods on the market, or has plenty of her own home-frozen ones, can keep the latchstrings always out to guests.

In Chapter 1 are lists of frozen foods available on the market, including prepared and cooked ones. There is an abundance of these from which to select, for each course. Instructions for preparing these for serving are given on the packages, so you can plan the time needed for having them ready.

There are plenty of frozen foods for first courses which can be used for quick meals. Fruit juices, punches or ades may be your choice. Or any of the many frozen soups need only a few minutes to reheat.

For the main course, there are countless frozen entrées suitable for quick meals, and, of course, almost any kind of frozen vegetable is fine for a quick meal, whether you choose a raw one or one already prepared and frozen in a sauce. Fruits which are to be used in salads for serving with the main course need to be thawed ahead of time.

For desserts, frozen baked cakes of many kinds may be purchased, pies which need only partial thawing, or other pies to be baked and served hot for a quick meal. And there are a great many fine, specialty desserts which only need to be thawed.

Or the homemaker who does a good deal of her own freezing may well have in the freezer a good assortment of prepared and cooked foods which are splendid for quick meals. For directions for freezing these and preparing them for the table, see Chapters 9 and 10.

In the pages that follow are suggestions for Thirty-Minute Meals. These are meals for which the main course can be ready within 30 min. of the time you enter the kitchen. The desserts can be ready 20–30 min. later, or when the main course is completed. Some desserts may be thawing, others baking, while everyone is enjoying the main course.

RECIPES FOR QUICK MEALS

For the convenience of the reader, the following lists of recipes in this book have been compiled, for use in preparing quick meals.

Meat, Poultry, Fish and Shellfish Recipes for Quick Meals

Following are recipes for meat, poultry, fish and shellfish dishes which can be prepared within 30 min:

Vegetable Recipes for Quick Meals

Following are recipes for vegetable dishes which can be prepared within 30 min:

Desserts for Quick Meals

Many frozen fruits are delicious served "as is," as soon as thawed, and for quick meals they can be thawed in cold water. They may be served with cookies, brownies or cake.

With novelty-flavored ice creams in the freezer, a good dessert is always ready with no preparation whatever. Ice cream sundaes, parfaits and other ice cream desserts are also quickly prepared when frozen fruits, sauces or other ice cream accompaniments are on hand. For suggestions for these, see Chapter 18.

The following are fruit recipes which can be prepared within 45–60 min., so they will be ready by the time the first course is completed. Those which require cooking will be served hot.

ADDITIONAL RECIPES FOR QUICK MEALS

For the Main Course

The following are additional recipes for main-course dishes which can be prepared within 30 min. Some of the methods used are unusual, and are only recommended for emergencies.

Meat and Poultry Recipes

Lamb Chops with Currant Sauce.—Pan-fry 4 *lamb chops* (thawed before cooking or not, as convenient). Toward the end of cooking, add ¼ c. currant jelly, pinch of dry mustard, dash of Worcestershire sauce and 2 tbsp. lemon juice.

Lamb Chops with Minted Pineapple.—Pan-Fry 4 *lamb chops* (thawed before cooking or not, as convenient). Meanwhile, remove pineapple from 1 pkg. (13½ oz.) *pineapple chunks* and thaw in saucepan over very low heat. Add ¼ c. mint jelly to pineapple and continue to heat slowly, stirring occasionally so pineapple becomes uniformly green. Serve chops with hot, minted pineapple.

Broiled Lamb Chops with Peach Slices.—Broil 4 *lamb chops* (for chops more than 1 inch thick to be cooked within 30 min., thaw before cooking). Meanwhile, thaw 1 pkg. (12 oz.) *peaches* in cold water. If peaches are not quite thawed when chops are done, remove from package and place in saucepan over very low heat until pieces can be separated. When chops are done, place several peach slices over each chop and broil until peaches are delicately browned.

Barbecued Beef Patties.—Pan-fry 4–6 *ground beef patties* (thawed or not before cooking, as convenient). Meanwhile, reheat 1 pkg. *barbecue sauce.* Serve sauce over patties. *French-fried potatoes* and any desired *vegetable* go well with these patties.

Steak Sandwiches.—Pan-fry *thin steaks* (sandwich type) without thawing, and slip them between toasted buns or buttered toast slices. Serve with chili sauce or ketchup.

Hamburgers with Welsh Rarebit.—Pan-fry 4 *ground beef patties* (thawed or not before cooking, as convenient). Meanwhile, reheat 1 pkg. *Welsh rarebit* in top of double boiler. Serve Welsh rarebit over beef patties in toasted sandwich buns.

Quick Beef Stew.—Cube cooked meat and brown it in hot fat in skillet, adding chopped green pepper and sliced onions. Meanwhile, cook 1 pkg. (10 oz.) *peas and carrots* or *mixed vegetables.* Prepare gravy by thickening stock (if on hand), or by dissolving bouillon cube in hot water and thickening it. Serve with hot *baking powder biscuits.*

Deviled Pork Chops and Vegetables.—Without thawing, brown 4 *pork chops* (½ inch thick) slowly in pressure saucepan, sprinkling with salt and pepper. Add 2 tbsp. water and 2 tsp. garlic wine vinegar (cider vinegar can be used, if preferred). Spread chops with 1 tbsp. prepared mustard. Arrange 2 large potatoes, quartered, around and over the chops, 3 carrots cut in strips and 1 medium onion, sliced. Cook 10 or 11 min. at 15 lbs. pressure. Reduce heat at once.

Chili Dinner.—Reheat 1 pkg. *chili con carne* in top of double boiler. Meanwhile, cook quick-cooking rice, spaghetti or noodles. To serve, pour chili con carne over cereal.

Fried Chicken with Cranberry-Orange Relish.—Sprinkle thawed, *cut-up frying chicken* with salt and pepper and cook in pressure saucepan with ½ c. water for 18 min. at 10 lbs. pressure (or cook according to pressure saucepan directions). When chicken is done, reduce heat at once and arrange chicken on broiler pan. Brush pieces well with melted butter or margarine and brown under broiler. Thicken stock for gravy and pour over chicken. Serve with thawed *cranberry-orange relish.*

Fish and Shellfish Recipes

Jiffy Fish Fillets.—Cut *fish fillets* crosswise into serving pieces, without thawing. Place in pressure saucepan, add ¼ c. water, sprinkle with salt and pepper and top with ½ c. chopped onions and ¼ c. cornflakes. Cook at 10 lbs. pressure for 7 min. if fillets are about 1 inch thick, or 8 min. if 2 inches thick. Reduce heat at once.

Fish Poached in Milk.—Thaw 1 lb. *fish fillets* in cold water, just enough to separate pieces. Arrange fillets in skillet which fish will almost fill. Sprinkle with salt and pepper and add enough milk to almost cover the fish. Cover closely and cook over low heat until fish flakes well, 10–20 min.

Easy Shrimp and Peas.—Prepare medium cream sauce, using 1½ c. milk (see directions, p. 200). Or use 1 can condensed cream of mushroom or celery soup and add $^{1}/_{3}$–½ c. milk. Place in top of double boiler and add 1 pkg. (12 oz.) *precooked shrimp* (thawed or not, as convenient). Meanwhile, cook 1 pkg. (10 oz.) *green peas* and drain. Just before serving, add peas and if desired add 2 tbsp. sherry wine. Serve on hot *waffles*.

Creamed Shrimp and Lobster.—Place 1 can *condensed cream of shrimp soup* (without thawing) in top of double boiler over rapidly boiling water. Add 1 pkg. (6 oz.) *lobster meat* or about 1 c. Lobster meat may be thawed or not, as convenient. Keep water boiling vigorously, stirring occasionally to thaw evenly and to combine shrimp and lobster meat without crushing them. Reheating time is 25–30 min. if lobster meat was not previously thawed. Meanwhile, prepare quick-cooking rice. Serve creamed shrimp and lobster over rice and garnish with parsley.

Scallops Hurry Curry.—Place 1 pkg. (10 oz.) *scallops* in cold water to thaw for 20 min. Then add scallops to boiling water, bring water back to boiling, reduce heat and simmer until tender, 3–4 min., depending on size of scallops. Meanwhile, prepare medium cream sauce, using 1½ c. milk (see directions, p. 200). Or use 1 can condensed cream of mushroom or celery soup and add $^{1}/_{3}$–½ c. milk. To the sauce, add 2 tsp. curry powder and 2 tsp. lemon juice. Add scallops to sauce and serve over spaghetti, noodles or rice.

Crabmeat Rarebit.—Place 1 pkg. *Welsh rarebit* in top of double boiler and add 1 pkg. (6 oz.) *cooked crabmeat,* thawed or not, as convenient. Keep water in lower part of double boiler boiling vigorously and stir occasionally to thaw and heat evenly and to distribute crabmeat through the rarebit. Reheating time, 25–30 min. if crabmeat was not previously thawed. Serve on toast points, noodles or rice.

Broiled Cheese 'n Crabmeat Boats.—Thaw 1 pkg. (6 oz.) *cooked crabmeat,* in unopened package, in cold water 20 min. Flake crabmeat apart and combine with ¼ c. mayonnaise, 1 diced dill pickle and 1 tsp. Worcestershire sauce. Split 4 hamburger buns and spoon crabmeat mixture into them. Top each bun with slice of American cheese and broil 5 inches from source of heat, until cheese melts. Top with other half of bun and serve.

Oysters aux Champignons.—Place 1 can condensed cream of mushroom soup, undiluted, in top of double boiler and add 1 pkg. (12 oz.) *oysters,* thawed or not, as convenient. Meanwhile, cook 1 pkg. (10 oz.) *asparagus* or *broccoli cuts* or *cut corn,* or *green beans,* and drain. Make a smooth paste of 1½ tbsp. flour and 3 tbsp. water and add slowly to mixture in top of double boiler, stirring until thickened. Add drained vegetable and serve on toast points. Garnish with parsley.

Vegetable Recipes

Welsh Rarebit Lima.—Reheat 1 pkg. *Welsh rarebit* in top of double boiler. Meanwhile, cook 1 pkg. (10 oz.) *lima beans* and drain. Add lima beans to Welsh rarebit and serve on toast points.

Vegetable Dinner.—*Asparagus spears, baby whole carrots, spinach soufflé* and *French-fried potatoes* make a colorful combination, and there are many others.

Squash Mallow.—Thaw *cooked squash* slowly in skillet (see p. 325), and season well with salt and pepper. Transfer to shallow, greased casserole or individual ramekins and cover top with marshmallows. Place in hot oven, 425°F., until marshmallows are puffed and golden brown, about 15 min.

Succotash in Tomato Cream.—Cook 1 pkg. (12 oz.) *succotash,* adding 1 c. diced celery toward end of cooking, and drain. Add 1 c. crisp, cooked bacon and 1 can condensed tomato soup, undiluted, heated. Serve on toasted English muffins, hot corn bread or toast squares.

Scrambled Maize.—Cook 1 pkg. (10 oz.) *cut corn,* and drain. Prepare 4 or 5 eggs as for scrambling, and add corn. Pour into skillet and scramble. Serve, garnishing with paprika.

Vegetable Omelet.—Cook 1 pkg. (10 oz.) *mixed vegetables* and drain. Prepare a 4-egg omelet according to any favorite recipe. Meanwhile, heat 1 can condensed tomato soup without diluting. Add drained vegetables to hot soup. When omelet is done, turn onto platter, pouring some vegetable mixture over it before folding, and the rest on top.

Minted Peas and Carrots.—Cook 1 pkg. (10 oz.) *peas and carrots* and drain. Add 1 heaping tablespoon mint jelly and 2 tbsp. butter or margarine and reheat.

Cauliflower with Cheese Sauce.—Prepare medium cream sauce using 1½ c. milk (see directions, p. 200), or use 1 can condensed cream of celery or mushroom soup and add ⅓–½ c. milk. Cook and drain 1 pkg. (10 oz.) *cauliflower.* Just before serving, stir ¾ c. grated, sharp Cheddar cheese into hot sauce and heat only until cheese is melted. Serve cheese sauce over cauliflower and sprinkle with paprika.

Corn and Mushroom Soup.—Cook 1 pkg. (10 oz.) *cut corn* and drain. Add 1 can condensed cream of mushroom soup (undiluted) and blend. Add 4 c. scalded milk and heat in top of double boiler. Meanwhile, brown 1 small onion, sliced, in 1 tbsp. hot fat, adding ½ tsp. salt and speck pepper. Add onion to soup and simmer 5–10 min. longer.

Green Beans Creole.—Cook 1 pkg. (9 oz.) *green beans (French style* or *cut).* Meanwhile, brown 1 tbsp. chopped onion in 2 tbsp. butter or margarine and add ⅓ c. chili sauce. Drain beans and combine with sauce.

Poached Eggs on Spinach.—Cook 1 pkg. (10 oz.) *spinach.* Meanwhile, poach eggs, allowing 1 or more per serving. When spinach is tender, drain and arrange in nests on serving plates. In each nest, place 1 or more poached eggs. Sprinkle eggs with paprika.

Creamed Carrots with Bacon.—Cook 1½ c. *diced carrots.* Meanwhile, prepare medium cream sauce, using 1½ c. milk, or use 1 can condensed cream of celery or cream of mushroom soup and add ⅓–½ c. milk. Fry bacon slices until crisp. Combine carrots and cream sauce and top with bacon slices. Garnish with parsley.

Golden Brussels Sprouts.—Cook 1 pkg. (10 oz.) *Brussels sprouts.* Meanwhile, melt ¼ lb. processed cheese in top of double boiler with 2 tbsp. milk. Drain Brussels sprouts thoroughly. Pour cheese sauce over sprouts and sprinkle with paprika.

For Dessert

The above dishes for the main course are planned to be ready within 30 min. of the beginning of preparation. The following desserts are ones which will be ready within 20–30 min. later, so will be ready when the main course is completed.

Sherried Strawberries.—Thaw 1 pkg. (10 oz.) *sliced strawberries* in cold water. Meanwhile, dissolve 3 tbsp. confectioner's sugar in ¼ c. sherry wine. Pour sweetened wine over strawberries. Serve on plain cake or lady fingers, if desired.

Fruit Shortcake.— Thaw *fruit* or *berries* in cold water. Meanwhile, prepare piping hot baking powder biscuits. Prepare your own dough (see instructions, p. 197), or use biscuit mix, or use frozen *baking powder biscuits.* Whip *dessert topping* or heavy cream. Put shortcake together just before serving.

Apple, Blueberry, Cherry or Mince Pie à la Mode.—Bake your choice of *pie* while preparing and serving main course. Serve hot with *vanilla* or *fruit ice cream.*

Mock Peach Cobbler.—Thaw 1 pkg. (12 oz.) *peaches* in cold water about 20 min. Place peaches with their juice and ¾ c. water in saucepan and heat, but not to boiling. Combine 2 tbsp. cornstarch, ¼ c. sugar and ¼ tsp. nutmeg and add to hot juice. Simmer until mixture thickens and pour into dessert dishes lined with lady fingers or pieces of sponge cake. Serve with a small scoop of *vanilla* or *peach ice cream,* or a mound of whipped cream.

Fruit Melange.—Thaw 1 pkg. (12 oz.) *mixed fruit* in cold water. Remove fruit from package and add chopped maraschino cherries and nuts. Top with whipped cream and toasted coconut.

Fruit and Cookies.—Thaw *peaches, raspberries* or other *berries* or *mixed fruit* in cold water. Meanwhile, bake frozen *refrigerator-type cookies* according to directions. Serve cookies with fruit.

Fruit Dessert Salad.—Thaw 2 or 3 kinds of shapely fruits (grapefruit sections, blueberries, raspberries, pineapple chunks, etc.), in cold water. Drain fruit or berries and arrange attractively on crisp lettuce or other greens. Serve with Fruit Salad Dressing (p. 204), or with cream mayonnaise (half mayonnaise and half cream).

Mint Jelly Parfait.—In parfait glasses, place spoonful of green mint jelly, and add spoonful of *vanilla ice cream*. Repeat layers until glasses are almost filled. Top with whipped cream or whipped *dessert topping* and coconut or chopped nutmeats.

MENUS FOR THIRTY-MINUTE MEALS

Dinners

Shrimp in Casserole, p. 289
Piquant *Peas,* p. 359   Buttered *Baby Whole Carrots*
Grapefruit and Avocado Salad, p. 386
Sesame Seed Rolls
Chocolate Ice-Cream with Mocha Sauce, p. 431

Vegetable Soup
Lobster Newburg on Toast Points
Buttered *Cauliflower*   *French Cut Green Beans*
Head Lettuce with Thousand Island Dressing
Hot *Apple Pie* with *Ice Cream*

Steak with Mushroom Sauce, p. 219
French-Fried Potatoes   *Broccoli* with Horseradish Sauce, p. 343
Pineapple and Cheese Salad, p. 403
Lemon Cream Pie

Cream of Potato Soup
Chicken à la King, p. 304, in *Patty Shells*
Buttered *Peas and Carrots*
Assorted Relishes
Peach Strawberry Compote, p. 401

Broiled *Lamb Chops*
Potato Puffs   *Artichoke Hearts* with Curry Mayonnaise, p. 326
Waldorf Salad
Cloverleaf Rolls
Vanilla Ice Cream with *Sliced Strawberries*

Scallops and Mushrooms, p. 282
Crinkle-Cut Potatoes   Buttered *Asparagus Spears*
Sliced Cucumbers in Sour Cream Dressing
Raspberries and Cream

Luncheons or Suppers

Open-Faced Hamburgers *(Beef)*, p. 224
Grilled Tomatoes   *Squash Mallow*, p. 445
Chocolate Cake

Creamed *Pork* and Celery, p. 244, on *Cornmeal Muffins*
Buttered *Brussels Sprouts*   *Apple Sauce*
Head Lettuce with Russian Dressing
Caramel Pecan Cookies

Pineapple-Grapefruit Juice
Crabmeat Rarebit, p. 444, on Rice
Buttered *Peas*
Blueberry Crumb Pudding, p. 377

Lamb Chops with Minted *Pineapple*, p. 442
Hot *Potato* Salad, p. 362   Sliced Tomatoes
Fruit Melange, p. 447

Welsh Rarebit Lime on Toast Points, p. 445
Buttered *Cauliflower*
Tossed Vegetable Salad
Mock *Peach* Cobbler, p. 447

Cream of Potato Soup
Pork, Apple and Celery Salad, p. 246
Assorted Relishes
Honey Nut Muffins
Strawberry Shortcake, p. 447

CHAPTER 20

Frozen Foods for Parties and Other Occasions

PARTIES

Extending hospitality to our friends is one of the nicest uses we can make of our own home. However, when the hostess has had too much work to do just before the party, she is tired and excited, and the guests sense her confusion. But with a freezer and good plans for using it, so much can be prepared ahead of time, that the day itself is relaxed and enjoyable for both hostess and guests.

A glance at the assortment of frozen foods in the display cabinets in the larger stores will give you plenty of ideas for party foods which may be purchased to help plan party menus. In the menus that follow, many of these are included. Also included are some of the dishes for which recipes are provided in this book.

Then, too, there are just endless kinds of foods which can be prepared days ahead, frozen and ready for reheating or simple, final preparations. Sherbets in the freezer give a tasty decoration for your first-course fruit juice or fruit cup. Practically any kind of soup, and a great many main-course dishes suited to parties can be frozen. For suggestions for all of these, see Chapter 9, Freezing Prepared and Cooked Main Course Foods and Soups.

Cooked shrimp should not be stored in the freezer more than a few weeks. If you need cooked shrimp for a rather large group, it is convenient to buy raw shrimp, cook and freeze them. Then they are all ready for using as you wish.

For dessert, almost any kind of pie or cake can be frozen; so can many kinds of desserts. For suggestions about these, see Chapter 10, Freezing Baked Goods and Desserts. Don't forget that even cream puffs, éclairs, petits fours and hard meringues can be baked and kept in the freezer. Frozen fruit salads are also wonderful for parties. And for suggestions for ways in which ice creams in your freezer will provide gala desserts, see Chapter 18.

451

If you are going to need a lot of canapés, by freezing them, you can prepare a kind or two each day for a few days, and in this way collect a wider variety than if they all had to be made at one time.

You can prepare "dips" for cocktail parties a week or two ahead and freeze them; also don't forget you can freeze serving-portion mounds of sweetened, whipped cream, all ready to top your party dessert.

Your freezer is just the place for putting a sweet, frosty rim on your party beverages glasses. Into one saucer, pour lemon juice about ¼-inch deep, and into another one finely granulated or confectioner's sugar to about the same depth. Dip the rims of the glasses first in the lemon juice, then in the sugar, and put them into the freezer at once.

Eggnog can be frozen, too, and here is a fine recipe for one:

Eggnog Bowl   *Yield:* 15 punch-cup servings

6 egg whites   2 c. milk
6 egg yolks   2 c. bourbon
¾ c. sugar   2 tbsp. rum
2 c. whipped cream or whipped   grated nutmeg
    dessert topping

Beat egg whites until they hold good peaks, gradually adding ¼ c. sugar during beating. In separate bowl, beat egg yolks, adding remaining sugar (½ c.) during beating. The egg yolk mixture when beaten should be very stiff. Fold beaten egg whites into beaten egg yolks and combine well, by folding. Add whipped dessert topping or whipped cream, milk, bourbon and rum. Stir thoroughly and chill. Turn into punch bowl and serve in punch cups, sprinkling each cup with grated nutmeg.

Punch Bowl Ring

A colorful and tasty ring for your punch bowl will give it a festive air, and here are directions for making one.

ginger ale   frozen mixed fruits or melon balls,
frozen, concentrated fruit juice,   orange, lemon or lime slices, and
    punch or ade   maraschino cherries

Place a thin layer of ginger ale in a ring mold and place in freezer to freeze. Then add a layer of frozen fruit juice, punch or ade, adding only about half as much water as the can directs, add more ginger ale, and fruit pieces. Freeze again. Then add a final layer of these, filling the mold almost to the top and freeze again.

To unmold, dip the mold in hot water only a few seconds, and invert the mold until the ring drops out. Put the ring back in the freezer until serving time. Slip the ring into punch in the punch bowl.

Select the flavor and color of the fruit juice, punch or ade according to the flavor and color of the punch, and select the amounts according to the size of the ring mold and amount of punch.

Ice Bowl

You can make your own bowl of ice in which to serve any salad, punch or servings of ice cream. For a buffet or refeshment table, this lends an unusual touch of sophistication.

Start this preparation about 24 hrs. before you need the ice bowl. You need two bowls, one of them about 2 inches narrower and 2 inches shallower than the other. Fill the large bowl about one-half to two-thirds full of water and place it in the sink or on a tray to catch the overflow of water. Place the smaller bowl inside the large one, weighting it down so it sinks to an inch from the bottom of the large bowl. If necessary, add water so it comes to about an inch from the top of the bowls.

You need to keep the small bowl centered within the large one during freezing. To do this, attach one end of cellulose tape to the rim of the small bowl and the other end to the rim of the large bowl, and repeat this at intervals around the top, keeping the small bowl centered.

Put this arrangement on a level place in the freezer until the water is hard-frozen. Then remove from the freezer, take off the tape and let stand at room temperature until the small bowl can be removed from the ice bowl and the ice bowl can be removed from the large bowl. At room temperature of about 70°F., this takes 20–30 min. Do not thaw in water, since this may cause the ice bowl to crack. Return the ice bowl to the freezer until ready to use it.

When serving, place the ice bowl with its contents on a large tray, surrounded with dishes containing various sauces, fruits, relishes, nuts or other accompaniments for the course.

The ice bowl does not melt quickly, but if desired, place a base of foil under it to catch any drippings.

Tinted Ice Cubes for the Punch Bowl

These, as they float in the punch, give it an added air of festivity. Add food coloring to the water in the ice cube tray, choosing a color to contrast with the color of the punch. To each cube, add a maraschino cherry, or any other tasty colorful bit, if you like. Add the ice cubes to the punch just as you are ready to serve.

Party and Holiday Menus

The following are some menus to help you in planning your parties and holiday occasions. Many of the frozen foods included are available in the supermarket or frozen food store. And some of the recipes you can prepare ahead yourself, and have ready in the freezer, so that the festive day will be an unhurried one.

Dinner Parties.—There is no more pleasant way to entertain a group of congenial friends than to enjoy fine food together, at an attractive table, in a relaxed atmosphere. The menus below are designed for serving at the dinner table.

Vichyssoise
Steak in Red Wine, p. 216
Mashed Potatoes   *Peas* with Tiny Onions, p. 359
Artichokes in Curry Mayonnaise, p. 326
Tossed Green Salad with Roquefort Dressing
Rolls
Strawberry Baked Alaska, p. 412
Demi-Tasse

Mixed Fruit Cocktail
Shrimp Casserole, p. 289
Buttered *Brussels Sprouts*   *Green Beans* with Mushrooms, p. 332
Grapefruit and *Pineapple* Salad, p. 387
Toasted *Cherry* Chiffon Pie, p. 382
Coffee   Tea

Grapefruit and *Crabmeat* Cocktail, p. 272
Leg of Lamb Burgundy, p. 233
Parsley Buttered *New Potatoes,* p. 361   *Asparagus Spears*
Cauliflower with Almond Butter, p. 351
Frozen Fruit Salad *(Mixed Fruit)*, p. 393
Créme de Menthe Parfait, p, 429
Demi-Tasse

By freezing many of the preparations ahead of time, the work for an elaborate buffet dinner like this one is far simpler

Buffet Dinners.—A buffet dinner provides a hostess with a delightful and gracious way in which to entertain a number of guests. When planning the menu for a buffet dinner, try to avoid foods that might spill easily, and perhaps, too, avoid those which would necessitate the use of a knife. You will want to provide plenty of small tables or perhaps trays for your guests, so they may arrange themselves in small groups to enjoy their dinner and a social hour. And you may want to arrange some facilities in the living room for serving dessert and beverage.

Pineapple, Grapefruit and Orange Juice
Lobster Newburg on Toast Points, p. 276
Buttered *Baby Carrots*   *Broccoli* Parmesan, p. 342
Asparagus Aspic Salad, p. 328
French Vanilla Ice Cream with Coffee Caramel Sauce, p. 435
Coffee   Tea

Tomato Juice Cocktail
Chicken Salad de Luxe, p. 308
Creamed *Peas* and Mushrooms in Toast Baskets, p. 358
Spiced *Pineapple* Salad, p. 402
Assorted Relishes   Rolls
Peach Melba, p. 426
Coffee   Tea

Oyster Cocktail, p. 278
Curried *Turkey* in Rice Ring, p. 316
Piquant *Peas*, p. 359   *Corn* Fritters, p. 355
Cucumber and Tomatoes in Sour Cream Dressing
Layer Cake with Creamy *Orange* Frosting, p. 398
Coffee   Tea

Bridge Luncheons.—Everyone enjoys a tasty luncheon, but a group of women anticipating an afternoon of bridge together are in an especially fitting mood for one.   Here are two menus which will help set the stage for these gatherings.

Shrimp and *Grapefruit* Salad, p. 290
Hot *Baking Powder Biscuits*   *Raspberry* Jam, p. 408
Assorted Relishes
Crème de Cocoa Parfait, p. 429
Coffee   Nuts   Mints

Ramekins of Baked *Lobster* and Mushrooms, p. 275
Grapefruit and Avocado Salad, p. 386
Hot *Garlic Bread*
Pecan Pie with Whipped Cream
Coffee   Tea

"Brunches."—Any sports week-end, Sunday or holiday provides a perfect time for a "brunch."   An attractive table, plenty of hot coffee and the menus such as suggested below should provide wonderful times for your guests.

Mixed Fruit
Chicken *Livers* in Scrambled Eggs, p. 313
Broiled Tomatoes
Doughnuts   *Danish Pecan Twist*
Preserves   Marmalade
Coffee

Peach Strawberry Compote, p. 401
Pork Sausage Patties   *Waffles* with Syrup
Coffee   *Strawberry* Jam, p. 414
Coffee

Formal Teas.—In the United States nowadays, the "Formal Tea" is more likely to turn out to be a "Formal Tea and Coffee," as custom bows to the favorite American beverage. But whether you serve tea or coffee or both, this is one of the most gracious ways in which to honor a house guest or a visiting celebrity. The menu includes an assortment of varied dainties, and the nicest of our table appointments are put to good use. Special friends of the hostess, or honored guests, are asked to pour.

Crabmeat Party Sandwiches
Rolled Watercress Sandwiches   *Asparagus* Rolls, p. 331
Nut Bread with Cream Cheese
Tea *Cookies*   Petits Fours
Nuts   Mints
Tea   Coffee

Curried *Crabmeat* Fantasies, p. 274
Chicken Salad, and *Lobster* Salad Party Sandwiches
Cream Cheese and Chive Pinwheels
Devonsire Tarts *(Fruit),* p. 420   Dainty *Brownies*
Tea   Coffee

Cocktail Parties.—While these are "Cocktail Parties," the thoughtful hostess always provides a non-alcoholic beverage for guests who may prefer one. You might try serving a light dessert toward the close of the party, and you may be surprised to find how well it will be received.

Cocktails
Fruit Punch with Punch Bowl Ring, p. 452
Crabmeat Celery Curls, p. 272   Savory *Shrimp,* p. 286
Chicken Liver Canapés   Cheese Curls
Potato Chips with Dips   Olives
Banana Cake
Coffee

Cocktails
Orange-Grape Cocktail, p. 398
Hot *French-Fried Fantail Shrimp* with Tartar Sauce
Herring Fillets in Sour Cream on Crackers
Assorted Raw Vegetable Snacks
Brownies
Coffee

Easter Sunday Dinners.—Church services, the Easter parade—then home to a delicious dinner, based on the traditional baked ham. Here are a couple of menus for these spring days.

Beef-Vegetable Soup
Baked Glazed Ham
Candied Yams   *Broccoli* with Curry Mayonnaise, p. 326
Orange *Pineapple* Gelatin Salad, p. 403
Assorted Relishes
Rolls
Chocolate Ice Cream with Peppermint Stick Sauce, p. 434
Coffee

Mixed Fruit with *Lemon Sherbet*
Baked *Ham Slices*
Potatoes au Gratin   *Squash* Mallow, p. 445
Buttered *Baby Lima Beans*
Grapefruit and *Pineapple* Salad, p. 387
Assorted Relishes
Rolls
Peach Mousse, p. 401
Coffee

Thanksgiving Dinners.—The holiday dear to the hearts of all Americans—a time for reunions and rejoicing. You may wish to serve the traditional fare, roast turkey, or to break the convention and have duckling, as in the second menu.

Oyster Cocktail, p. 278
Roast *Turkey* with Sausage Stuffing, p. 314
Giblet Gravy
Candied Yams   Glazed Onions
Green Beans with Mushrooms, p. 332
Cranberry-Orange Relish
Hot *Rolls*
Pumpkin Chiffon Pie, p. 364
Coffee

Mock Turtle Soup
Roast *Duckling* with Browned Rice Stuffing and *Orange* Sauce, p. 317
Broccoli with Garlic Butter, p. 342   *Squash* New Orleans, p. 370
Celery Hearts   *Cranberry-Orange Relish*   Ripe Olives
Hot *Rolls*
Mince Pie with *Ice Cream*
Coffee

Christmas Holiday Open House.—Christmas is a wonderful time to get together with neighbors and friends, old and new. Open your home to them, and warm their spirits with a menu like this one.

Eggnog Bowl, p. 452
Fruit Punch Bowl with Tinted Ice Cubes, p. 454
Assorted (*Turkey* or *Shrimp* Salad) Party Sandwiches
Potato Chips and Dips
Christmas Cookies   Christmas Cake
Christmas Candies
Coffee

Courtesy of Aluminum Company of America

With eggnog and other "goodies" in the freezer, you are all ready for a Christmas carol party

Teen-Age Parties.—The following menus are created in an attempt to satisfy the amazing appetites of this delightful section of our population. The first menu is for a buffet dinner. The second is designed to give the young ladies an opportunity to display their culinary prowess by preparing the sandwiches and sundaes for their "dates."

Buffet Dinner

Ground *Beef* in Barbecue Sauce, p. 225 on Split Buns
Potato Salad, p. 362   Baked Beans
Cabbage Slaw   Assorted Relishes
Tossed *Fruit* Salad   Potato Chips
Strawberry Frosted, p. 437   *Brownies*
Coffee

Summer Chef Party
"Do-It-Yourself" Sandwiches[1]
"Mixed-Up" Salad   Potato Chips and Dips
Cool Party Punch with Punch Bowl Ring, p. 452
"Chef's Choice" *Ice Cream* Sundaes[2]

OUTDOOR COOKERY

Whether on a grill or rotisserie, on our own premises or on picnic grounds, outdoor cookery has become very popular. The informality of the out-of-doors coupled with hearty appetites make these occasions enjoyable for family groups or larger ones. Many kinds of frozen foods help you to plan cook-outs so that they require the minimum amount of effort; they should include many of the prepared and cooked foods on the market.

Frozen vegetables are handy for outdoor cookery. Frozen corn on the cob is especially fine. Thaw the corn fully, brush each cob generously with butter and sprinkle with salt, then wrap the individual ears snugly in aluminum foil. Grill over hot coals, allowing about 20 min. The ears are really roasted in this way.

Other vegetables may be cooked in aluminum foil. Thaw the vegetables enough to separate the pieces and place them on a large sheet of freezer foil or on a double thickness of household foil. Dot with butter and sprinkle with salt. Place another layer of foil over the vegetables, and fold the edges of foil together tightly all around the edge, leaving plenty of space in the package for steam to cook the vegetables. Place this package several inches from the heat, and turn once during cooking. The time required for cooking is longer than for boiling, but not as long as for oven-baking. It is difficult to estimate the exact time needed, and you can't open the package to test the vegetables. For this reason, it is somewhat easier to boil the vegetables over the grill; use large coffee or shortening cans to save your saucepans.

Many meat, fish and poultry dishes which are ordinarily cooked on top of the range, under the broiler, or in the oven may well be

[1] For these, have on hand such as: rolls, bread, butter, sliced tomatoes, cheese, ham, cold chicken, cold turkey, salami, crisp bacon, lettuce, mayonnaise, prepared mustard and Russian dressing.

[2] For these, have on hand scoops of assorted ice creams, and bowls of assorted ice cream sauces (see Chapter 18), nuts, maraschino cherries, whipped dessert topping.

Many kinds of frozen foods are splendid for cooking on a grill on your patio

cooked on an outdoor grill, using a skillet on the grill or not, according to your preference and the recipe. The following are some of the meat and poultry recipes in this book which lend themselves particularly well to outdoor cookery.

Frying-pan Barbecue, p. 227   Hamburgers en Brochette, p. 226
Lamb Kabob, p. 236   Mexican Rolls, p. 223
Barbecued Rump Roast, p. 217   Deviled Pork Chops, p. 242
Saybrook Kabobs, p. 216   Broiled Stuffed Hamburgers, p. 226

Menus for Outdoor Cookery

The following are some menu suggestions for meals to be prepared out-of-doors. The first set of menus is for picnics away from home, and the second is for serving on your own patio.

Picnics

Hamburgers en Brochette (*Ground Beef*), p. 226
Buttered *French-Cut Green Beans*   Potato Salad, p. 362
Cabbage Slaw   Sliced Tomatoes   Assorted Relishes
Fruit Salad   *Brownies*
Hawaiian Punch   Coffee

Broiled Stuffed Hamburgers (*Ground Beef*), p. 226
Baked Beans   Cole Slaw
Green Bean and Carrot Salad, p. 334
Hot *Rolls*
Cherry Pie
Coffee

Patio Parties

Charcoal Broiled *Sirloin Steaks*
French-Fried Potatoes   Deviled *Brussels Sprouts*, p. 344
Tomato and Onion Ring Salad
Assorted Relishes
Blueberry Muffins
Apple Pie   Cheddar Cheese
Coffee

Barbecued *Rump Roast,* p. 217, on Hard Rolls
Green Beans and Mushrooms, p. 332   *Corn on the Cob*
Tossed Vegetable Salad with French Dressing
Toasted *Cherry* Chiffon Pie, p. 382
Iced Coffee   *Lemonade*

Lamb Kabobs, p. 236
Hot *Potato* Salad, p. 362   *Peas* with Tiny Onions, p. 359
Celery Hearts   Carrot Sticks   Olives
Hot *Rolls*
Lemon Meringue Pie, p. 388
Iced Tea   *Pineapple-Orange Juice*

LUNCH AND PICNIC BOXES

For day-to-day lunch boxes, when sandwiches are frozen in advance, there is no longer the early morning rush to get them ready in time. For directions for freezing sandwiches, see Chapter 11. Lettuce and other salad greens cannot be included in the sandwich before it is frozen, but they can be wrapped separately in the lunch box, and if desired, they can be slipped into the sandwich at lunch. The cold sandwich helps to keep them fresh.

Apple sauce or any fruit sauce may be frozen in half-pint containers, and if placed in the lunch box it will be thawed by noon. Baked apples frozen individually are good treats for the lunch box, too.

Or for dessert, cake may be wrapped and frozen in individual portions for the lunch box, and pies may be frozen in single-serving wedges. If the wedges are frozen in individual plastic containers, seal the top of the container on with freezer tape. Tarts which are not runny when thawed may be frozen for the lunch box, too. And cookies from the freezer are a welcome addition to the lunch box menu.

All these are good possibilities for picnic boxes, too. With some sandwiches in the freezer, an impromptu picnic is always possible on short notice.

SOME SPECIAL DIETS

Weight Control

If you need to lose weight and your doctor has recommended a low-calorie diet as part of your reducing program, you will be interested in knowing some ways in which frozen foods can help plan attractive, varied menus. You will still need to abide by the rules of the *Daily Food Guide* (see p. 15), placing an emphasis on the selection of foods which provide adequate protein, minerals and vitamins, but with fewer total calories daily than you have been accustomed to having.

Low-calorie diets usually include plenty of vegetables which are low in starch and protein and therefore low in calories. The fact that so many of these are available frozen makes it easy to plan interesting, tasty menus. The following vegetables, available frozen, provide, as a rule, between 20 and 50 calories per serving, and so are appropriate for this purpose: artichoke hearts, asparagus, green and wax beans, broccoli, Brussels sprouts, carrots, cauliflower, okra, spinach, other greens, and summer and winter squash.

Green peas provide somewhat more calories than the above vegetables per serving, and corn, lima beans, black-eyed peas and pumpkin provide considerably more, so are not among the low-calorie vegetables.

There are numerous other frozen foods which can help provide variety in reducing diets, and one that not everyone thinks of is fish and shellfish. Many of these are lower in fat content (and so lower in calorie value) than any kind of meat or poultry. This is true of all lean (non-fatty) fish (for a list of these, see p. 253). Of the commonly used frozen fish, cod, haddock, sole and whiting are especially low in fat. On the other hand, lake trout, mackerel, salmon, smelts, tuna fish and whitefish are fatty fish, and these provide about as many calories per serving as do most lean meats and poultry.

There are several frozen preparations on the market, manufactured by reliable companies specifically for use in reducing programs. You may find that one of these suits your purpose well.

For those needing high-calorie foods to help gain weight, there is an abundance of these available frozen, so this is a matter of preference and judgment in selecting those which are appropriate for the individual.

Low-Sodium Diets

If your doctor has prescribed a low-sodium diet for you or for someone in your family, you will be interested to know which of the commercially frozen fruits and vegetables may be considered low in sodium. All the commercially frozen fruits except apples belong in this category. And the following commercially frozen vegetables belong in this category, too: asparagus, green beans, wax beans, cut corn, corn on the cob, okra, French-fried potatoes and squash (yellow crookneck and winter). During the processing for freezing, apples, black-eyed and green peas, and lima beans are usually treated with salt solutions, and this increases their salt content. Mixed vegetables containing any of these may have been treated in the same way.

If any treatment used in processing a frozen fruit or vegetable has made its salt content higher than that of the original fresh product, the package will indicate this fact, since this is a government requirement for labeling.

Sugar-Restricted Diets

A homemaker with a member of the family who is diabetic is often anxious to know whether fruits may be frozen with little or no sugar. Some fruits are regularly frozen without the addition of sugar or syrup, but most of them keep far longer in the freezer if they are sweetened. Some of them can be frozen unsweetened if they are not stored too long. See the instructions for freezing the kind of fruit in which you are interested.

Freezing Special-Diet Recipes

Occasionally there is a member of the family for whom the doctor has prescribed a diet which necessitates special recipes. With a freezer, you can prepare the usual recipe for 4–6 servings, and the portion not needed at once can be frozen in single-portion servings for later use. To learn whether the recipes in which you are interested will freeze satisfactorily, see the directions for freezing prepared and cooked foods, Chapters 9 and 10.

Index

469